CONSTRUCTING NATIONALITIES IN EAST CENTRAL EUROPE

AUSTRIAN HISTORY, CULTURE, AND SOCIETY
General Editor: Gary B. Cohen, Center for Austrian Studies,
University of Minnesota

Volume 1
Austrian Women in the Nineteenth and Twentieth Centuries:
Cross-Disciplinary Perspectives
Edited by David F. Good, Margarete Grandner, and Mary Jo Maynes

Volume 2
From World War to Waldheim: Culture and Politics in Austria and
the United States
Edited by David F. Good and Ruth Wodak

Volume 3
Rethinking Vienna 1900
Edited by Steven Beller

Volume 4
The Great Tradition and Its Legacy: The Evolution of Dramatic and Musical
Theater in Austria and Central Europe
Edited by Michael Cherlin, Halina Filipowicz, and Richard L. Rudolph

Volume 5
Creating the "Other": Ethnic Conflict and Nationalism in Habsburg
Central Europe
Edited by Nancy M. Wingfield

Volume 6
Constructing Nationalities in East Central Europe
Edited by Pieter M. Judson and Marsha L. Rozenblit

CONSTRUCTING NATIONALITIES IN EAST CENTRAL EUROPE

Edited by

Pieter M. Judson

and

Marsha L. Rozenblit

Berghahn Books

NEW YORK • OXFORD

Published in 2005 by
Berghahn Books

www.berghahnbooks.com

First paperback edition published in 2005, Reprinted in 2009
Hardback reprinted in 2006

Library of Congress Cataloging-in-Publication Data

Constructing Nationalities in East Central Europe / Pieter M. Judson and Marsha L.
Rozenblit, editors.
  p. cm. — (Austrian and Habsburg studies ; 6)
  ISBN 978-1-57181-175-2 (alk. paper : hbk) -- 978-1-57181-176-9 (alk. paper : pbk)
  1. Nationalism—Europe, Central—History. 2. Europe, Central—Politics and
government—19th century. 3. Europe, Central—Politics and government—20th
century. I. Judson, Pieter M. II. Rozenblit, Marsha L., 1950– III. Series.

DAW1048.C66 2004
943'.0009'034—dc22

                                                    2004056045

British Library Cataloguing in Publication Data

A catalogue record for this book is available from
the British Library.

For our Teacher

ISTVÁN DEÁK

ACKNOWLEDGEMENTS

The editors would like to take this opportunity to thank the many people who made this volume possible. First of all we express our appreciation to the authors for their insightful articles. Their efforts have resulted in a volume of essays that makes a significant contribution to understanding how nationalities constructed themselves in East Central Europe in the nineteenth and twentieth centuries. We thank Jason Kneas and Julia Skory of the University of Maryland Geography Department for the excellent quality maps they produced for this volume, and we thank Theresa Brown of the Swarthmore College Department of History for her help with the editing.

We would also like to express our gratitude to Professor Gary Cohen, Director of the Center for Austrian Studies at the University of Minnesota, for his scholarly work on these issues, work that called into question the nature of national identity in Central Europe long before it became fashionable; for his insightful comments, suggestions, and help to all of us over the years; and for his willingness to include this volume in this series in Austrian History sponsored by the CAS with Berghahn Books. We would also like to thank all the people at Berghahn Books who made this book a reality: to Marion Berghahn, who warmly supported this project, and to Maria Reyes who saw the volume through production.

Finally we want to thank our teacher, István Deák. The breadth of his scholarly interests, the high standards that his scholarly inquiry set for historians in the field, his concern for good and clear writing, and his generous intellectual support makes him the model academic historian. In great admiration, we dedicate this book to him.

P.M.J. and M.L.R.
April 2004

CONTENTS

LIST OF MAPS

LIST OF ILLUSTRATIONS

PREFACE

Gary B. Cohen

The essays in this volume originated in papers delivered at a symposium of extraordinary interest held at Columbia University in March 2000, entitled "Dilemmas of East Central Europe: Nationalism, Dictatorship, and the Search for Identity." The Harriman Institute and The Department of History of Columbia University together with the Center for Austrian Studies at the University of Minnesota sponsored this conference, which brought together a gifted group of scholars who are opening new vistas of modern Central and East-Central European history. Pieter M. Judson and Marsha L. Rozenblit organized the symposium, and they made the subsequent selection of papers for this volume, offering suggestions for revisions, and editing the final versions that appear here.

The high quality and interest of the Columbia University symposium in March 2000 was a tribute to the Seth Low Professor of History at Columbia, István Deák, who taught all the presenters of papers, either as undergraduate or graduate students. The range and originality of their work testifies not only to the quality of the students drawn to Central and East Central European studies at Columbia in the last several decades but also to the stimulus, inspiration, and scholarly discipline which Professor Deák has provided during his long career in seminars, lecture courses, and direction of individual research. Professor Deák has been an extraordinary model and guide both to his students at Columbia and to many scholars elsewhere.

All the essays here, in various ways, address the development of popular nationalist loyalties, identities, and politics in Central and East-Central Europe since the eighteenth century. They bear witness to the great changes in historical research on nationalism and popular identities that have taken place in the last two or three decades. Previously, historians tended to study European national identities as the natural and inevitable outgrowth of longstanding popular cultural factors, largely accepting at face value nationalists' claims about the origins of their group identities. In recent years, though, scholars have come to study national loyalties as fundamentally dynamic phenomena that individuals and groups construct under specific historical circumstances, loyalties that can be transformed or exchanged or may be held in ambiguous relationships together with other allegiances. The essays in this volume demonstrate richly the imagination and creativity which historians have brought to bear in developing these new studies of the development of modern nationalist loyalties and solidarities.

Much the same imagination and creativity, combined with a healthy skepticism for much of the traditional conventional wisdom in Central and East Central European historiography, has characterized the scholarly work as well as the teaching of István Deák. His interests have ranged widely during the course of his long career as an historian. His first book, based on his doctoral dissertation, was *Weimar Germany's Left-Wing Intellectuals: A Political History of the Weltbühne and Its Circle* (Berkeley and Los Angeles, 1968). Most recently, he has written on war crimes trials and processes in the twentieth century. Research and teaching on Habsburg Central Europe, however, has occupied most of Professor Deák's career. Perhaps the most salient quality of his work in this field has been the independence of his perspective—a profoundly thoughtful and informed skepticism that has given him the ability to raise critically important questions which widely held master narratives have excluded. This skepticism has endowed his writings with a distinctive freshness of outlook.

Prof. Deák's independence of view and healthy skepticism were apparent as early as 1967 at the famous conference on the Austro-Hungarian Compromise and its consequences held in Bloomington, Indiana. At that meeting, Deák presented a comment for a panel on the dominant nationalities of the Monarchy as integrating and disintegrating factors in the polity. He essentially threw the standard conceptualization of the critical nationality conflicts in the political history of the Monarchy back in the faces of the panelists, suggesting that,

> ... the subject of this debate is neither justified nor valid.... I would argue that there were no dominant nationalities in the Austro-Hungarian monarchy. There were only dominant classes, estates, institutions, interest groups, and professions.

Conventional historiography was certainly sensitive to social differences and conflicts in the lands of the old Monarchy, but most older historians essentialized ethnic and national differences and let them cover over other factors.

In István Deák's writings on nineteenth century Austria and Hungary which have followed since 1967, he has typically presented fresh, probing perspectives, which have broken through conventional wisdom and long-held nationalist mythologies. This was clearly apparent in his book *The Lawful Revolution: Louis Kossuth and the Hungarians, 1848–1849* (New York, 1979), still one of the very finest accounts in any language of the political career of Louis Kossuth and the revolution and warfare of 1848–49 in Hungary.

Professor Deák's other great book on Austro-Hungarian history, *Beyond Nationalism: A Social and Political History of the Habsburg Officer Corps, 1848–1918* (New York and Oxford, 1990), was a bold foray in social and administrative history. In this study, he took an unfashionable path in studying one of the major institutions of the Habsburg state. In the army officer corps, he examined one of the most important institutions that worked for a broader unity and engendered some real Habsburg state loyalty and identity. In the process, he also helped remind us that there were important state institutions and administrative structures during the last decades of the Monarchy that continued to function better than many observers would allow and that left important legacies to the successor states. That so many of Prof. Deák's students, as represented in this volume, are doing similarly pathbreaking work represents perhaps the strongest evidence of his inspiration and continuing legacy. I am deeply grateful to the editors, Pieter M. Judson and Marsha L. Rozenblit, and to Marion Berghahn and her colleagues at Berghahn Books for bringing this volume to publication.

CONTRIBUTORS

Peter Black worked as staff historian and chief historian at the Office of Special Investigations in the U.S. Department of Justice from 1978 to 1997, and has been the Senior Historian at the United States Holocaust Memorial Museum since 1997. He has also taught twentieth-century European history at George Mason University, American University, and Catholic University. He is the author of *Ernst Kaltenbrunner: Ideological Soldier of the Third Reich* (Princeton University Press, 1984).

David Frey is an Assistant Professor of History at the U.S. Military Academy at West Point. He received his Ph.D. from Columbia in 2003.

Benjamin Frommer is an Assistant Professor of History at Northwestern University. His first book, *National Cleansing: Retribution Against Nazi Collaborators in Postwar Czechoslovakia,* is forthcoming from Cambridge University Press.

Eagle Glassheim is an Assistant Professor of History at Princeton University, where he teaches East Central Europe and the history of ethnic cleansing and genocide. He is working on a book on the nobility in Czechoslovakia from 1918 to 1948. In addition, he is working on a comparative study of resettlement of ethnically cleansed regions of Poland and Czechoslovakia after the Second World War.

Paul Hanebrink is an Assistant Professor of History at Rutgers University–New Brunswick, where he has taught since 2001. He is currently completing a book manuscript entitled "In Defense of Christian Hungary. Religion, Nationalism, and Antisemitism in Hungary, 1890–1944."

Pieter M. Judson is Professor and Chair of the History Department at Swarthmore College. His 1996 book, *Exclusive Revolutionaries. Liberal Politics, Social Experience and National Identity in the Austrian Empire, 1848–1914,* won the Herbert Baxter Adams prize of the American Historical Association in 1997 and the Austrian Cultural Institute's book prize for 1998. He is also the author of *Wien Brennt! Die Revolution von 1848 und ihr liberales Erbe* (1998), a study of 1848 in Austria.

Daniel A. McMillan was an Assistant Professor of German History at Eastern Illinois University. He now lives in New York City, and is attending the Fordham University School of Law.

Robert Nemes is Assistant Professor of History at Colgate University. He is currently completing a book on the emergence of civil society and nationalism in nineteenth-century Budapest.

Claire E. Nolte is Professor of History at Manhattan College in New York City. She is the author of *The Sokol in the Czech Lands to 1914: Training for the Nation* (Palgrave-Macmillan, 2002).

Cynthia Paces is Associate Professor of History at The College of New Jersey. The author of numerous articles on national memory, religion, and gender in Bohemia, she is currently completing a book manuscript on Prague in the twentieth century.

Alon Rachamimov teaches modern European history at Tel Aviv University. His book, *POWs and the Great War: Captivity on the Eastern Front*, was published in 2002 by Berg Publishers.

Marsha L. Rozenblit is the Harvey M. Meyerhoff Professor of Jewish History at the University of Maryland, College Park, where she has been on the faculty since 1978. She is the author of *The Jews of Vienna, 1867–1914: Assimilation and Identity* (State University of New York Press, 1983) and *Reconstructing a National Identity: The Jews of Habsburg Austria during World War I* (Oxford University Press, 2001).

Michael K. Silber is currently the Chair of the Department of Jewish History at the Hebrew University, Jerusalem and the Director of its Rosenfeld Center for the History of the Jews in Hungary and the Habsburg Empire. In addition to many articles on the Jews of Hungary, he has edited *Jews in the Hungarian Economy, 1760–1945* (Jerusalem, 1992) and an autobiography by Ávráhám Munk. He is currently working on a book on the 1848/49 Revolution in Hungary and the Jews and a monograph on "A Portuguese Baron at the Viennese Court: Life and Legend of Diego d'Aguilar, an Eighteenth-Century Jewish Nobleman."

Daniel Unowsky is Assistant Professor of Central European History at the University of Memphis. He is currently completing a book manuscript on Habsburg imperial celebrations during the reign of Franz Joseph.

Patricia von Papen-Bodek is a historian of Nazi Germany, whose research focuses on anti-Semitic research institutes both in Germany and in Nazi-occupied Europe. Her articles include a study of the career of the historian Wilhem Grau, one of the key figures of National Socialist *Judenforschung*.

Nancy M. Wingfield is Associate Professor of History at Northern Illinois University. She is the author of *Minority Politics in a Multinational State: The German Social Democrats of Czechoslovakia, 1918–1938* (East European Monographs, 1989) and co-author, with Joseph Rothschild, of *Return to Diversity: A Political History of East Central Europe since World War II*, 3rd ed. (Oxford University Press, 2000). In addition, she has edited *Creating the Other: Ethnic Conflict and Nationalism in Habsburg Central Europe* (Berghahn Books, 2003), and, with Maria Bacur, *Staging the Past: The Politics of Commemoration in Habsburg Central Europe, 1848 to the Present* (Purdue University Press, 2001).

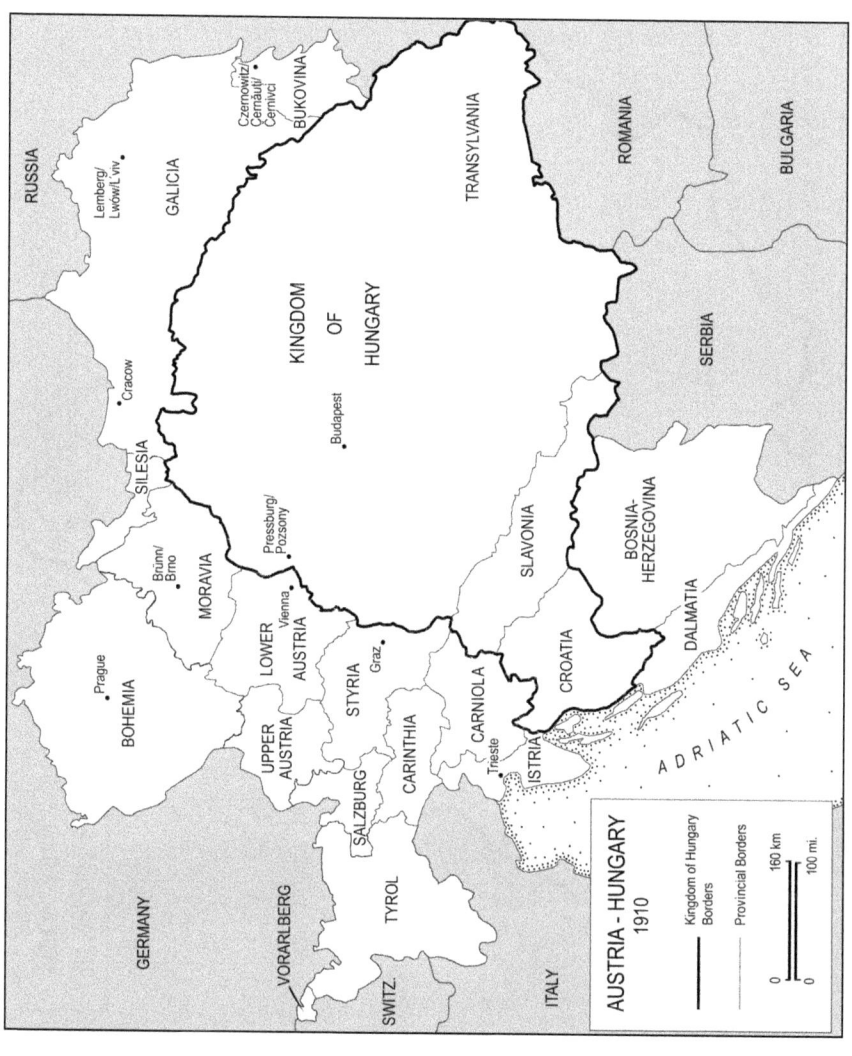

AUSTRIA - HUNGARY
1910

——— Kingdom of Hungary Borders

---------- Provincial Borders

0   160 km

0   100 mi.

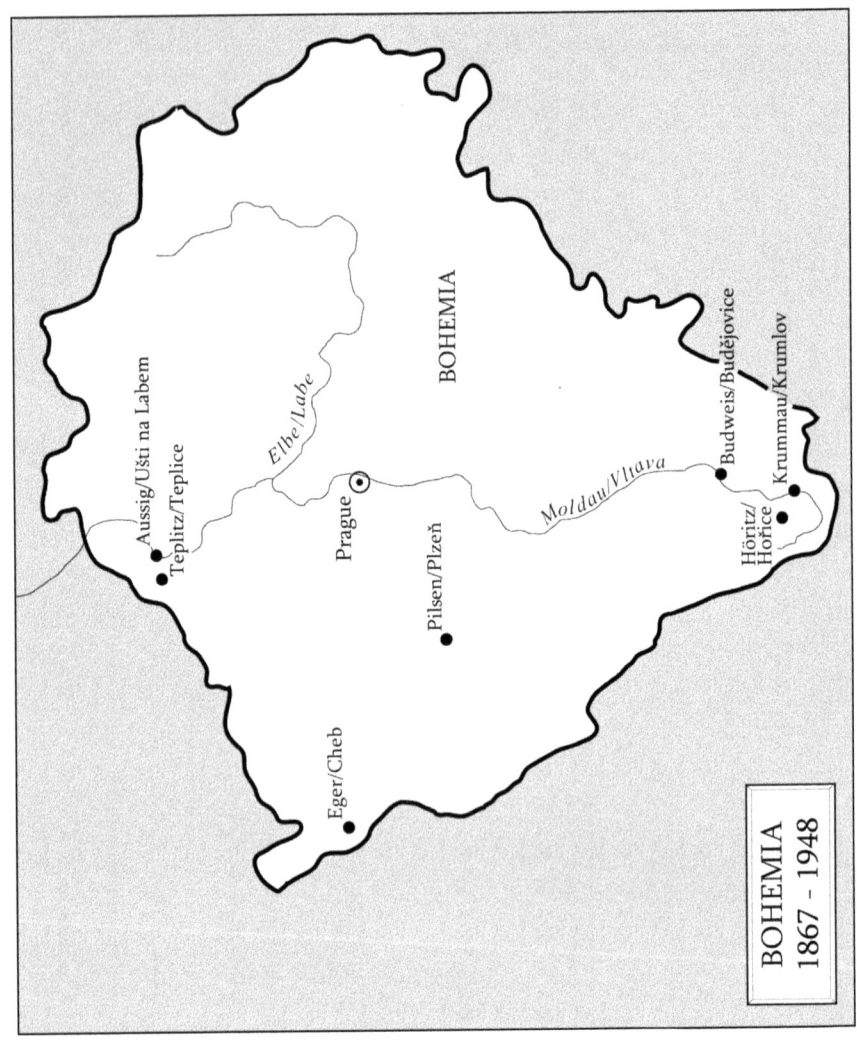

EAST CENTRAL EUROPE
BETWEEN THE WARS

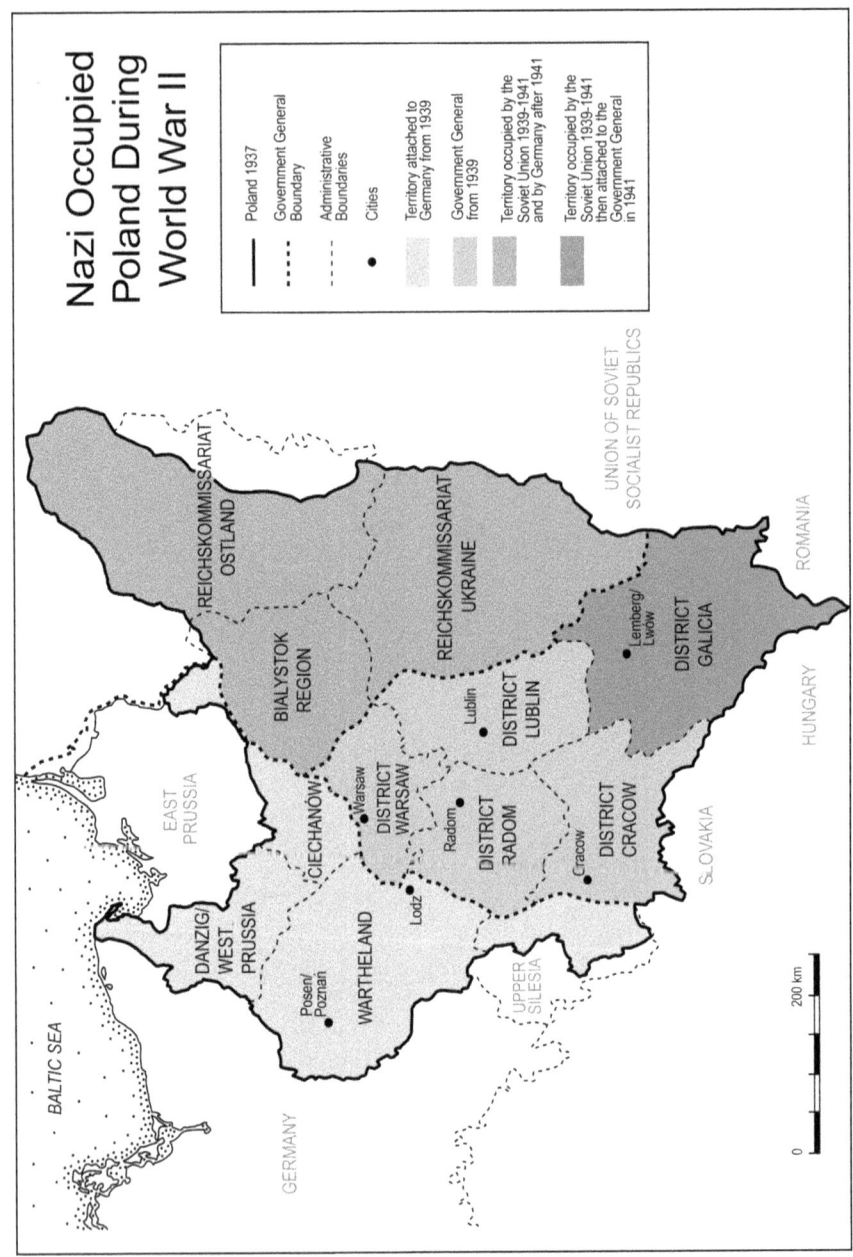

Nazi Occupied
Poland During
World War II

Poland 1937

Government General
Boundary

Administrative
Boundaries

Cities

Territory attached to
Germany from 1939

Government General
from 1939

Territory occupied by the
Soviet Union 1939-1941
and by Germany after 1941

Territory occupied by the
Soviet Union 1939-1941
then attached to the
Government General
in 1941

BALTIC SEA

GERMANY

EAST
PRUSSIA

DANZIG/
WEST
PRUSSIA

WARTHELAND

Posen/
Poznan

Lodz

CIECHANOW

Warsaw

DISTRICT
WARSAW

Radom

DISTRICT
RADOM

Cracow

DISTRICT
CRACOW

UPPER
SILESIA

SLOVAKIA

REICHSKOMMISSARIAT
OSTLAND

BIALYSTOK
REGION

Lublin

DISTRICT
LUBLIN

REICHSKOMMISSARIAT
UKRAINE

Lemberg/
Lwow

DISTRICT
GALICIA

UNION OF SOVIET
SOCIALIST REPUBLICS

ROMANIA

HUNGARY

0

200 km

CONSTRUCTING NATIONALITIES IN EAST CENTRAL EUROPE

Introduction

Pieter M. Judson

Only a century separates us from the largely nonnational world that was Habsburg Central Europe, yet today it is almost impossible to imagine that world. So completely has the idea of nation come to dominate our ways of understanding modern society that it requires a superhuman effort on the part of scholars, politicians, activists, or informed observers to imagine a world not shaped by the overpowering categories of the nation-state and its global system. Despite—or perhaps because of—decades of scholarship, nationalism's origins are almost always debated in terms that naturalize the prior existence of nationalism's own object—the nation. The current popularity of constructivist explanations that acknowledge the importance of historical contingency and that gesture toward the "invention" of nations has not diminished the power of nationalist teleologies to shape histories of nationalism. The persistence of the nation as the prime mover in the telling of its own history is hardly surprising, and the historian of nationalism faces the ongoing challenge of writing critically about a phenomenon whose imagined origins only confirm the apparent naturalness of its being.[1]

The contributors to this volume have taken up the challenge to write about nationalism without accepting the historical necessity either of nations or of the nation-state. Their essays recapture the contours of a nonnationalized world, as they examine why and how this world produced nationalist ideologies and movements. The authors emphasize both the contingency and diversity of specific forms of national identity in order to avoid relying on ahistorical presumptions of eternal identities. More importantly, they explore the ways in which those new beliefs about nation coexisted with other traditional forms of self-identification, forms whose social power was often far more compelling than that of nationalism.

The setting for these essays is Habsburg Central Europe; that is, those territories in Central Europe that until 1918 formed a part of, or had been influenced by their proximity to, the Habsburg dynastic holdings. This region offers the unique opportunity to investigate the rise of nationalism in territories and among populations that for the most part were not claimed by self-styled nation states until after 1918, much later than in much of the rest of Europe. Although several groups within the Empire in the nineteenth century claimed to have formed "nations" in both a traditional and modern sense of the term, the Habsburg state did not itself attempt a nationalization of its peoples in the ways that the self-proclaimed French, Italian, or German nation states had. At least until 1867 the Habsburg state functioned as a collectivity where patriotism or loyalty to the dynasty rather than an ideology of shared *nation-ness* bound subjects and later citizens to the greater polity. After 1867 this tradition lived on in the Austrian half of the Monarchy, known as Cisleithania, while the Kingdom of Hungary, or Transleithania, adopted the kind of aggressive nationalizing policies that characterized most other European states.

In the past decades, social scientists have increasingly interrogated the claims for fundamental *nation-ness* made for their citizens by the governments of France, Italy, or the German Empire. Eugen Weber's classic *Peasants into Frenchmen* famously theorized the nineteenth-century French state's need to create a French nation out of diverse peoples characterized by different languages, customs, and traditions who happened to live within the borders of France. Schools, increased transportation and trade, as well as military service all helped to create a larger sense of common French identity among these regional populations. Similarly, recent work on the notion of *Heimat* and on regionalism in the German Empire reveals that to a large degree, nationalism served as a critical instrument for establishing state hegemony over local society after the official unification of 1871. And what historian of nationalism is unfamiliar with the oft-quoted words of Massimo d'Azeglio, who admonished his colleagues in the first Italian Parliament: "Gentlemen, we have made Italy: now we must make Italians"? In each of these examples, historians tended to elide the work of *nation* building with the particular requirements of modern *state* building. The French state needed an educated citizenry, and a loyal army; the German and Italian states sought to forge a centrally unified society from a politically, economically, and socially fragmented Central Europe.[2]

The Cisleithanian half of the Habsburg Monarchy presents us with a powerful example of modern state building not linked to nation building. In the 1860s Austrian governments legislated a system of secular education that mandated eight years of schooling for Austria's children. They built thousands of new schools, founding institutions to train the teachers who staffed them, men and women who themselves often brought their modernizing and their nationalist convictions to every corner of rural Austria. At the same time, the Cisleithanian state created a new system of administration that included a strong dose of communal self-rule for rural and urban communities of all sizes.[3] An explosion of new roadways, canals, railway lines, and communications networks brought several traditionally more isolated regions into contact with the commercial and political centers of the Monarchy. Service in the military, as Michael Silber so aptly shows, had become itself an important mark of modern citizenship in Austria well before the French Revolution.[4] It is less clear whether the dynastic state and its ideologists worked to any significant degree to popularize forms of patriotic self-identification. This question gained retrospective relevance, after the rise of a mass politics organized around competing nationalist demands appeared to have taken over the workings of the Imperial Parliament in Vienna and many of the provincial diets in the 1880s. Recently, scholars including Daniel Unowsky have studied several less obvious ways in which the Habsburg state engaged in precisely this kind of ideological work, either by offering a patriotic alternative to nationalism, or by attempting to fold nationalist loyalties into a larger imperial one.[5]

Clearly, what made Cisleithania different is that any impetus towards the nationalization of society there was produced by social forces that rarely harmonized with the demands of this modernizing, centralizing state. Constitutional guarantees of the rights of language use in education, administration, and provincial government became the basis for politicians of all kinds to demand reform, and build interested local constituencies. In an era of growing mass politics that culminated in universal manhood suffrage for the Imperial Parliament in 1907, nationalist politicians attempted to mobilize ever-greater numbers into their movements. And by the 1890s, thanks to political agitation and to several key decisions of Austria's Supreme and Chief Administrative courts, language use in every aspect of public life had indeed become a fertile ground for reform politics.[6] It was nationalist movements "from below" that created nationalized populations, both by mobilizing people into politics dominated by nation, and by forcing unwilling governments to recognize nations as real corporate entities. While the state tried to avoid giving rights specifically to "nations," preferring to recognize the rights of "language groups," nationalist activists made sure that in public debate over issues such as the Imperial census results, linguistic issues were understood as national ones.

In order to contain the emerging politicization of largely linguistic differences within society, the state became increasingly multinational in character, as opposed simply to being dynastic in character. This is most apparent in the provincial and local compromise agreements fostered by the state in Bukovina, Galicia, Moravia, and the city of Budweis, which were meant to diffuse the political explosiveness of nationalist conflict. The best known of these, the Moravian Compromise of 1905, tried to divide up the political institutions, the school system, and local administration according to nationality. Under the new laws, for example, Czechs would elect their own candidates to a special Czech curia in the diet. Their candidates would no longer run against German candidates. Yet such agreements produced several unintended consequences that increased the pace of nationalization rather than slowing it. By compelling people to register themselves as either Czech or German, the Compromise law demanded that the Moravians become national, even if their own self-identification was organized around non-national principles such as "Moravian," "Habsburg," "Iglauer," or "Catholic." As Jeremy King has compellingly argued, by 1914, "'Nations' started becoming constituent members of Cisleithania, recognized by the law and proportionally equal before it in the exercise of significant political rights." Crucially, it was the nationalist movements themselves that had forced an unwilling Cisleithanian state to nationalize many of its administrative and institutional structures. "In a trend with few European parallels," writes King, "the state began to become multinational."[7]

Clearly several elements of modernity had helped to produce the nationalist movements, including the rise of literacy, constitutional rule, infrastructural improvements, and mass politics. Nevertheless, of the many elements this nineteenth-century state might have required to help it carry out an ambitious policy of centralist modernization, nationalism among its citizens was certainly not one of them. At most, the Habsburg state depended on a modern version of the kind of dynastic patriotism that had traditionally cemented the relationship between ruler and ruled.

The century between the revolutions of 1848 and the population transfers (or "national cleansing") of the mid-twentieth century saw the nationalization of culturally complex, multilingual societies throughout Europe. Cultural diversity and multilingualism did not necessarily disappear from the scene during this period, as we know from nationalists' own frequent complaints about their tenacity. Nevertheless, public representations of those phenomena almost certainly vanished from the public eye. How had this happened? How did nationalist discourses, tropes, identities, visions, come to occupy the available ideological space in the public sphere? The "fact" of nationalization has variously been explained in terms of theories of modernization, state building, and nation building, each of which treats the process of nationalization as something inexorable, a necessary component to a society's "achievement" of modernity. Social scientists agree that several kinds of contingent factors may shape these larger developments, yet their overall structural approaches have made them far less attentive to the "hard work" (ideological, political, and social) that nationalism required of its local proponents in order to succeed. Ultimately, only the combined efforts of particular individuals and groups working at every level of society could define and produce so-called national communities in Habsburg Central Europe.

Analyzing the hard work of the nationalists requires paying serious attention to the different local and regional contexts in which nationalist movements developed, something also missing in broader structural approaches. After all, activists shaped their strategies to make opportunistic use of every available local political and cultural space in which they might make their arguments. Too often, social scientists have treated categories such as language use or ethnicity as broad, unchanging, ahistoric facts, without seeing that the very processes of nationalization, combined with the opportunities offered by specific local political structures, actually created those "facts." Czech activists, for example, might not have defined their nation so fully around the issue of language use and focused their efforts so entirely on achieving linguistic rights, had not the constitutional guarantees in the 1867 constitution created a political opportunity for them. German nationalists in the Tyrol, for example, defined their particularly German identity in terms of their Catholic faith, their loyalty to the Empire, and the myth of Andreas Hofer's opposition to foreign (French) invasion during the Napoleonic Wars. This understanding of what it meant to be German diverged sharply from that of Styrian German nationalists who celebrated their local identity in terms of their independence from the Catholic clergy. Similarly, Slovene-speaking liberals in the 1860s saw their best hope in an alliance with German Liberalism and German culture, while Slovene conservatives attacked the anti-clericalism of this progressive conceptualization of nation.[8] In each of these cases the idea of "nation" gained some resonance only thanks to its articulation with particular concerns and values that characterized regional social life.

If we move away from the public realm of politics to examine the behavior of peasants or workers who lived in linguistically mixed regions, what evidence we have often points to the irrelevance of language use in constituting social identities. We rarely hear the voices of those who lived easily between so-called nations, yet their experience was hardly rare. Nationalists might demand education in the national language, often complaining about the denationalization of children sent to a school of a language other than their own. Parents in some rural communities of Bohemia and Moravia, however, felt differently. They regularly sent their children to neighboring villages (the so-called *Kindertausch*) as a way to ensure that they would learn a second language, a useful skill in a multilingual community! Slovene-speaking parents in Southern Styria often demanded German classes for their children, much to the dismay of Slovene nationalists, while German-speakers in the region intermarried and socialized easily with their Slovene neighbors, despite the hysterical warnings of German nationalists. Even after 1900, Czech nationalists in Prague found it necessary to threaten Czech-speaking parents with boycott by the larger community if they continued to send their children to the few remaining German-language schools. In Moravia after 1905, nationalists gained the right to reclaim children from the "wrong" school if they could prove that such children were not fluent in the language of instruction. Census results in several rural regions of the Monarchy demonstrate that national "side switching" took place regularly. None of these issues would have come before the courts, none of them would have exercised nationalist activists had the public truly been nationalized.[9]

Although nationalists in Cisleithania may have often challenged the constituted authorities, they made excellent use of the legal, ideological, and institutional tools that those self-same and unwitting authorities made available to them in order to pursue the nationalization of local populations. Their use of such legal strategies forced them to downplay and later to reject the very existence of those "in-between" people who might use more than one language, or who chose not to align themselves with one nation or another. Their purpose was, of course, to coerce unwilling neighbors into the national community, and this too would produce devastating effects in the twentieth century.

The essays in this volume make us aware just how complex, multidimensional, contradictory, and often unsuccessful, the nationalization process in Habsburg Central Europe could be. The authors document attempts and failures by nationalist politicians, organizations, and activists to teach Central Europeans a sense of national self-identification. At the same time, the authors in this volume demonstrate some limits to the effects of nationalist activism. Movements, activists, and politicians by themselves could never realize the kind of full nationalization of society they envisioned, for several reasons. As many of these essays suggest, competing constructions of the nation within movements and larger societies made it impossible to achieve broad consensus on just what the nation was, who constituted it, and what characterized it. In the century following 1848, nationalist activists within the same nation often promoted competing visions, posing many compelling alternative outcomes that were highly conceivable at the time, but were foreclosed by later accidents of history. Behind their repeated calls for national unity, rival factions *within* Czech, German, Italian, Polish, Slovene, Italian, and Ukrainian movements in Cisleithania continuously raised the stakes against each other, just as radical political commitment in Hungary was understood increasingly in terms of nationalist radicalism. The Young Czechs, for example, defeated the old Czechs decisively in the parliamentary elections of 1891 by making a virtue of their greater nationalist vigor. By the first decade of the twentieth century, however, they found themselves outflanked on this very issue by the even more nationally radical Czech National Socialists.[10] In Hungary, meanwhile, nationalist radicalism often stood in for a socially oriented populism, and politicians seeking to dethrone the liberal Hungarian political elite depicted themselves as more strongly committed to the nation.

Equally problematic to nationalists was their apparent inability to reach every part of the nation with their message. To remedy the apparent apathy among those who somehow remained impervious to their message, nationalists increasingly demanded that individuals make the nation the basis for decisions about all kinds of matters heretofore considered private—marriage, child rearing, and consumption habits. The nation was no longer simply a matter of politics and public life. Or rather, public life was now understood to extend into the family—what nineteenth-century liberal theorists had formerly considered to be a private sphere.[11] On balance, however, society could only disappoint those revolutionary radicals who dreamed of a nationalist paradise devoid of social relations that enabled groups to mix with each other, and characterized forever by the absence of the intrusive "Other." The essays here remind us that despite the considerable influence nationalist movements exercised over the press or legislative debate, the realization of their most extreme fantasies of national purity could only be attempted using the dictatorial state powers characteristic of twentieth-century authoritarian regimes.

This volume focuses in particular on the nexus between political activism and ideological nationalization. The spaces that political structures made available to activists often defined the particular parameters of their activism, but activists' creative uses of such spaces were often truly breathtaking in their scope and ambition, to the point that even the a-national Cisleithanian state came to accept several of the nationalists' assumptions. The volume opens with Michael Silber's examination of an eighteenth-century debate over the relationship between particular cultural forms of self-identification, in this case Jewish identity, and the questions of state citizenship. Silber's essay on Jewish soldiers and the new requirements of citizenship imposed by Joseph II demonstrates the lengths to which the modernizing Austrian state would go to impose a new concept of equal citizenship on its diverse peoples, well before the revolutionary French Republic's *levée en masse*. Silber illustrates the ways in which a citizenship of equivalence swiftly became normalized in the 1780s, at least in the eyes of the state. Once the Emperor had determined he would extend military service to his Jewish subjects, he and his advisers quickly found themselves forced to remove other barriers to "interchangeability," barriers that no longer could be justified. If Jews were to serve in the military, then they must also be eligible for advancement. If Christians were to serve under Jewish officers in some cases, then the legalized privilege of the Christian in civil society must be ended. Without the acceptance of such notions of the fundamental interchangeability of citizens, the idea of nations can not take root. Silber suggests, however, that the modernizing regime's desire to forge a citizenship of "interchangeable individuals," such as that posited by Ernest Gellner for example, does not necessarily have to produce the modern idea of nationality, nor even the modern link between language or culture and nation. It might just as easily produce a state-based patriotism.[12]

Robert Nemes's piece examines the creation of early public political and national cultures in Central Europe, using the example of Hungary in 1848. Unlike their French counterparts, Central Europeans had little experience of mass political participation or activism before the mid-nineteenth century. During those first glorious March days in Buda-Pest, and indeed throughout the Empire, activists forged new institutions where they debated and hoped ultimately to influence public policy. Their preferred instrument for debating and spreading the new alternative forms of politics and self-identification, even in the era predating mass politics, was the traditional voluntary association. To this important location for a new kind of politics in 1848, Nemes adds another instrument of the emerging political culture, namely, the newly, more politically aggressive newspaper. Nemes analyzes the many ways that everyday practice contributed to the formation of new political cultures, from choice of dress, to forms of address, to physical gesture, to styles of rhetoric.

The greater availability of many of these forms of expression to a larger mass of people beyond the traditional political classes in Hungary also made these symbols into important popular elements of nationalist activism. In his analysis of the German Gymnastics Associations before 1871, Daniel McMillan too demonstrates how in the absence of a political nation, German nationalists attempted to infuse all spheres of social life with their particular patriotic, nationalist, and political meanings. In both cases, the association became the preferred space within which the nation might be created, as well as the preferred instrument for its promotion and realization in society at large. Within the confines of the local club with its face-to-face relationships, the more abstract concept of nation could more easily be understood in terms of social commonalities. Here too, enlightenment concepts of the administrative equivalence of citizens were appropriated by civil society in the form of nationalism, and were promoted broadly from below. Whether club members engaged in gymnastics, debate, singing, or charity, they understood themselves to be equals when it came to their national commitment and activism. This is clear, for example, from the ideological differences that developed within the larger gymnastics movement analyzed by McMillan. He draws a distinction between those who understood the importance of gymnastics to the nation in biological terms, and those who conceived of its benefits in experiential and political terms. Speculating that the eventual victory of the former helped transform German nationalism by accomplishing its realignment with a politically conservative elite after 1871, McMillan nevertheless demonstrates that certain liberal beliefs about the relationship of the individual to authority were translated into the language of those who promoted a biological view. Liberal concepts about society and activism were thus not as far removed from a nationally conservative consensus as many historians may have believed.

McMillan's analysis of early debates about the character of national belonging (biological or experiential) alerts us to several important themes raised by the authors of the next essays. These reveal the fundamental diversity within nationalist activism in the late nineteenth century, as early associational efforts produced larger and more influential political and social movements. While the nation, as subject of debate or object of political activism, was by this point a recognizable presence in educated society, it clearly remained the property of social minorities who attempted, with varying degrees of success, to make it universal by nationalizing their compatriots. Many of these efforts were made possible only with the institutional reforms in the Habsburg Monarchy that began in 1848–49 and were taken up again in 1861. Nationalist movements made increasing use of the constitutional and legal tools the reformed system afforded them, despite [or because of!] the fact that the system's creators displayed very little interest in nations or nationalism. The very laws that created communal autonomy and those that legislated the equality of language use on a local and regional basis in schools and public services opened up potential spaces for popular political activism.[13] Czech nationalist activists in Cisleithania developed these opportunities immediately, followed later by Polish, German, Slovene, Italian, Croatian, and Ukrainian nationalist activists. Yet, as the essays here remind us, none of these movements in fact constituted an ideologically unified, coherent phenomenon, and none followed a clear developmental trajectory. None could agree internally on the precise definition of the nation, and none could easily mediate between promoting a broad nationalist agenda and integrating newly enfranchised groups into its ranks.

Controversies around self-definition were themselves rooted in the social conflicts created by a new mass politics, as increasingly varied social groups gained access to the political system. As several of the contributors show, nationalist organizations tried to contain the growing potential for disagreement within the nation, but often at a cost to their own political effectiveness. While several of the authors here document the numerical successes of nationalist movements, they also suggest the utter inability of nationalists to achieve the kind of universal relevance for their particular views. Nationalist movements often spent as much time fighting internal battles as they did fighting each other. Groups as varied as the nobility, the gentry, the Imperial bureaucracy, the urban middle classes, and the urban and rural *Mittelstand* jostled each other to assert particular formulations of the national interest, and thus to universalize their particular needs. As nationalism became the currency for most political debate in both Cisleithania and Transleithania, it served as an effective tool for anyone interested in scoring political points. Nationalism not only polarized political society, it also divided the very groups it claimed were united nations.

In his essay on the Bohemian nobility, Eagle Glassheim analyzes the ways that this traditionally influential social group reinvented itself—not without some difficulty—in order to maintain its privileged role in Bohemian, Cisleithanian, and later Czechoslovakian politics. Progressive reform of the electoral system and the rise of mass politics threatened to marginalize the nobility's formidable political influence at several levels of government. Glassheim charts the ways that the nobles, both individually and as a group, aligned themselves loosely with one nationalist party or another in Bohemia. The nobility fought to promote a particular kind of nationalist vision that would help it to maintain its independent privileged position in society, by securing it influence within the broad Czech and German nationalist coalitions. Ideally, this independent role would allow the nobility to maintain its traditionally close relationship to the Imperial dynasty by exercising a moderating influence on the occasionally radical excesses of Czech and German nationalists. At the same time, this vision attempted to justify the nobility's key independent position in Bohemian affairs in more modern ideological terms, rather than in terms of traditional feudal privilege. This noble activism created considerable potential for conflict within both the Czech and German nationalist movements, exacerbating tension between moderates and radicals. The latter elements asserted a vision of the nation far too socially egalitarian for the nobility, while the moderates in the nationalist movements increasingly came to value the nobility as a key ally.

The malleable nature of nationalist ideology and its potential service to very different kinds of political goals also informed the way local communities understood new symbols, cults, rituals, and celebrations organized around the idea of the nation. Pieter M. Judson examines the nationalist movements' discovery of leisure-time activities such as tourism around 1900, and their increasing sponsorship of local festivals, as potential instruments for promoting nationalist causes. As nationalist activists sought new and more effective strategies for nationalizing populations, they turned increasingly to the notionally private realm of consumption as a way of reaching more potential converts to nationalism. This form of activism went well beyond economic boycotts that demanded people do their shopping or their hiring among one nation or another. One German nationalist guide to the Trentino, for example, even demanded that nationally conscious tourists patronize German-owned establishments only, listing those hoteliers and restaurateurs whose German commitment was deemed acceptable.[14] Yet beyond the rhetoric, Czech or German nationalists who fostered tourism to the so-called language frontier at the turn of the century could not control the ways in which individual tourists actually experienced those regions. Nationalist pride was one thing, but German-speaking travelers to the South Tyrol (in the tradition of Goethe) often sought precisely to experience the exoticism of an Italian milieu. Similarly, Czech- or German-speaking travelers to the Bohemian Woods often came more for the fresh air and beautiful views than to contribute to the nationalist conflict in the region. Nor could nationalists control the ways in which local villagers themselves ultimately understood the significance of their own cultural performances for tourists. Nationalists might promote a nationalist tourism, but did it help to nationalize the locals, or did it simply earn them more money?

Nationalists found it just as difficult to control the meanings they hoped to attach to historically important individuals such as Jan Hus or Joseph II. In their essay, Cynthia Paces and Nancy M. Wingfield explore the multiple meanings attached to these figures by the Czech and German nationalist movements in the nineteenth century. In particular, the choice of Hus as national symbol caused considerable discord among Czech nationalists, between secular and more religiously Catholic Czechs. Such conflict could in turn create considerable division within a supposedly unified national society. After 1918, the more secular Czech nationalists who ruled the new Czechoslovakia tended to equate all public symbols of Catholicism with the old Empire, with its dynasty, and also with the concept of an alien German rule. They promoted a cult of Jan Hus precisely because of his historic challenges to the religious authority of Rome. For many devout Catholic Czechs (not to mention Slovaks), however, religious icons such as the Marian column in Prague or local statues of St. John Nepomuk held an important religious significance that bore no political connection to the old Empire or to German nationalism. In addition, Catholics tended to view Hus as a heretic. This conflict produced concerted battles among different groups of Czech nationalists over the use of public space both in Prague and in cities and towns throughout Bohemia.

This was particularly problematic, as Paces and Wingfield point out, after 1918 when the new self-styled Czechoslovak nation state determined to rid its public spaces of all symbols of what it considered to be an imperial or German past. It also set up severe clashes with its own German-speaking minority. This latter group, while being technically citizens of the new state, was implicitly defined by such actions (toppling of statues) as an alien nation. The ongoing clashes over the symbolic uses of public space analyzed by Paces and Wingfield also suggest the degree of anxiety about their own identity that plagued the nationalist rulers of the successor states. They might present their new states to the world as modern and united nation-states, yet their use of force to nationalize public space reflects their continued use of discourses of national victimization long after the fall of the Empire. In the case of Czechoslovakia, such discourses would eventually help to produce the brutal policy that required the expulsion of as many national "Others" as possible after the Second World War.

Claire E. Nolte analyzes the difficulty of forging a real social political unity around as slippery a concept as national identity, or in her case, "Slav identity," on an interregional, indeed on an international level. Her essay traces the attempts by Czech nationalists to use the growing *Sokol* gymnastic movement as a vehicle to revive Slav cooperation within the Monarchy and in Europe after 1900. Conflicts between Czech nationalists and Polish nationalists over Russian or Ukrainian participation, for example, all but doomed attempts to project the *Sokol* as a mass movement of united Slavdom. They failed despite the superficial but aesthetically impressive images of mass unity projected at the Prague *Slet* of 1912. Nolte's essay conveys the significant triumphs of a movement that mobilized thousands of Czech speakers into its ranks, but also hints at the degree of dilution of ideological commitment inherent in such a remarkable expansion.

Daniel Unowsky reminds the reader that the nationalists were certainly not the only activists in Cisleithania to deploy political symbols, create festivals, or stage manage aesthetically impressive images of mass unity in order to encourage a sense of political community. His analysis of the Imperial Jubilee celebrations of 1898 traces the ways in which the Habsburg court asserted several patriotic and a-nationalist visions for Cisleithania, visions that made dynastic loyalty the cornerstone of a vigorous Austrian patriotism. While the symbolic role assigned to Emperor-King Franz Joseph changed from 1848 until 1916, the court produced Jubilee events in 1898 and 1908 in which a range of cultural, religious, social, political, and nationalist groups throughout the Monarchy vied to participate. Some historians (writing from the vantage point of a nationalized world) have faulted the Monarchy for not developing a more compelling ideology of its own to serve as a form of self-identification for its citizens. Seen in the context of a not-yet-nationalized world, the court's efforts elaborated by Unowsky appear compelling. They are not necessarily the functional equivalent of nationalist rituals and symbols, but their collective effects may actually have been more far-reaching than those of the nationalists' efforts. Recent work on the Tyrol, for example, suggests that these efforts to promote patriotism bore fruit in their ability to shape local understandings of nation. The German nation in Tyrol came to be defined by its very loyalty to dynasty and Church, and this produced a distinctive form of German nationalism that actually reinforced the very patriotism Unowsky's Court officials sought to produce.[15]

The next two essays examine complex issues of identification—of both the self and those ascribed externally—in a wartime context that juxtaposes an a-national state with an increasingly nationalized society. Both Alon Rachamimov and Marsha Rozenblit document the degree to which those who worked to nationalize Habsburg society had achieved an uneven degree of success by 1918. The authors remind the reader of the multiplicity of loyalties—class, religion, locality, family, state, and even nation—that often coexisted uneasily within the same individual. Each uses the particular stresses caused by the war as a lens to examine questions of self-identification and loyalty among populations particularly hard-hit: for Rachamimov, Austro-Hungarian POWs in Russia; for Rozenblit, Jews in Cisleithania. Both also demonstrate from very different perspectives that the classic notion of a collapsing Monarchy, brought down by long-term nationalist rebellion, is misleading at best. In the case of the POWs, Rachamimov finds that the state itself, repeating the truisms of some nationalist activists, was all too eager to find sedition among certain linguistic groups—Czechs and Slovenes—more readily than among German-, Magyar-, or Polish-speaking POWs. This despite the evidence produced by Rachamimov that demonstrates that members of those groups in fact displayed a far greater sense of loyalty to the state than the government recognized. Thanks largely to the superior system of censorship developed by Austro-Hungarian officials—one envied and eventually copied by the Germans—Rachamimov is able to trace the ways in which comparable utterances by POWs of different language were evaluated for their loyalty. In many cases, these evaluations rested far more on prior assumptions of a group's relative degree of loyalty or disloyalty to the state than on some objective reading of the letters themselves.

Rozenblit analyzes Austrian Jewish experiences of identity that included loyalty to a Habsburg state that protected them from anti-Semitism, loyalties to particular national cultures, as well as loyalty to their own Jewish sense of identity. The war brought very different Jewish worlds together, as refugees fled Galicia and Bukovina to cities like Vienna or Prague. The encounter highlighted cultural differences at the same time as it underscored common Jewish interests in the perpetuation of the Monarchy. At the same time, the end of the war and the demise of the Imperial state brought catastrophe for many Jews who suddenly found themselves trapped in the new self-styled nation states that defined citizenship on the basis of national belonging. As the quintessential a-nationals, Jews often found themselves lost in a newly nationalized world where the civil rights of the individual that underlay constitutional rulings in Cisleithania gave way to a more organically defined citizenship that defined rights on the basis of ascribed group identities. Jews responded to this catastrophe by turning to Zionism or Jewish nationalism or by hoping that the new states would somehow find a place for them despite the frightening growth of exclusionary anti-Semitism.

Rozenblit points directly to the kinds of social and cultural upheaval engendered by the disappearance of the a-national imperial state structure at the end of the First World War. The narratives promoted in the interwar period by all national groups focused on either the triumphs or the tragedies experienced by different nations, and ignored the more individual tragedies of those who found themselves without state identities in 1918. The First World War and especially its aftermath created situations of severe social dislocation for many individuals and social groups in the former Empire, particularly Jews. Nor could most minority individuals or groups hope for much aid from the constitutional guarantees that the allies extracted from the new nation-states. Czechs, Poles, and Romanians in their own nation-state continued often to behave as if they were still the victimized minorities of their former oppressors, Germans or Hungarians, and they demanded that their governments find ways to disenfranchise or at least weaken the influence of minorities considerably.[16]

The interwar years, characterized by the hopeless efforts of the new nation-states (better characterized as *nationalizing states*) to create the national societies, on which they claimed they were in fact based, saw a severe narrowing in the definitions of nation and identity in Habsburg Central Europe. Paul Hanebrink documents the ways in which nationalist self-identification in interwar Hungary became increasingly defined in terms of Christianity. Unlike the Czechoslovakian case, where religion created division within nationalist circles (Paces/Wingfield), in interwar Hungary, Christianity became understood as a larger, universal category of identity that defined Jews out of national society, while associating them with qualities that were not considered Hungarian. Given traditional Magyar concepts of nation and assimilation, this narrower understanding of Hungarism suggests the novelty of the post-1918 nation-state, as well as the new implications that anti-Semitism conveyed. From a set of attitudes or even movements within an Imperial state (that had itself disavowed anti-Semitism), anti-Semitism became a key element of nationalist identity construction. David Frey examines the ways in which interwar Hungary's film industry attempted to promote certain quite specific visions of the nation. The Hungarian political elite hoped to create a didactic film industry that would convey typically heroic Hungarian qualities, almost as a means to teach the nation how to become itself. The attempts to nationalize the film industry foundered repeatedly, however, on the continued popularity of more international-style films and the lack of available film talent when Jews were defined out of the nation. The hard work of the nationalists to produce popular films that might project a particularly Hungarian national identity came up against popular tastes that simply preferred consumerist images of cosmopolitan Budapest. Each of these essays on the interwar period demonstrates that nationalist ideology remained a highly unstable field, yet one that gave most social and political conflict its particular language. If nationalists had gained the nation-state, it was not at all clear from these ideological obsessions that their populations had yet been successfully nationalized.

The final three essays in the volume focus on the period during and directly after the Second World War, a period during which arguably the more extreme fantasies of turn-of-the-century nationalists were finally realized using technologies of the mid-twentieth century. Early nationalist activists in Habsburg Central Europe had worked hard to nationalize societies within a multicultural Empire. Yet they had done so always as a means to pursue their particular political ends within a state that itself functioned over and above individual nationalist concerns, as something of an umpire. We should not forget the importance of the Empire as an institutional context for understanding how nationalist politics had become so radical in the first place. The state always constituted a higher power to which all nations might appeal, and to which the vast majority of nationalists at least professed a fundamental loyalty. National politics had a far different significance in the imperial context than it did in the later context of the self-styled nation states. Before 1914, radical threats of national cleansing, for example, remained an empty rhetoric that at best conveyed the speaker's strong nationalist commitment. No one before 1914 seriously imagined such a threat becoming policy. Without the institutional framework of the multicultural Empire, this kind of nationalist rhetoric took on a new and more sinister relevance after 1918. By the period of the Second World War and its immediate aftermath, such talk could easily become policy, backed up by new technologies and radical authoritarian rule. These factors made it conceivable, even possible, to implement the most radical fantasies of nineteenth-century nationalists, often with the crusader's passion.

These visionary policies, however, required much more than a capable bureaucratic infrastructure for their successful implementation. They rested on the critical ideological work of nationalist experts to determine the authentic boundaries of the nation: who belonged, who did not, and on what basis. In her essay on the Hungarian Institute for Research into the Jewish Question, Patricia von Papen-Bodek explores the personnel and ideological links between that institution and Alfred Rosenberg's Institute in Frankfurt, as well as the relationship of both institutes to the German Foreign Office and the Reich Main Office for Security (RSHA) in the 1930s and 1940s. Other recent historians have demonstrated the ways that a new emphasis on *Ostforschung* in the 1920s gradually replaced the interest scholars had formerly devoted, for example, to Germany's African colonial holdings under the *Kaiserreich*. *Ostforschung* focused popular attention in Germany on the imagined German heritage in Eastern Europe, as well as on the other peoples of the region and what their ideal relationship to Germans ought to be.[17] Von Papen-Bodek's example illustrates the ways that this new *Ostforschung* could produce intellectual justifications for all kinds of nationalist arguments, in particular justifying persecution of the Jews. She demonstrates that Nazi Germany's involvement with research institutions in Eastern Europe such as the Hungarian Institute did not simply create Eastern scholarship that parroted its German counterpart. Rather, the German institutions helped to reinforce existing schools of thought in the East that created the borders of the nation and excluded some from membership. *Ostforschung* did not simply involve the application of Western ideas to institutions in the East, as many scholars assume, but the so-called *Judenforschung* of these Institutes had catastrophic results during World War II.

An examination of the implementation of radical nationalist population policies in formerly Habsburg Central Europe in the 1940s does suggest, however, that dictatorial and often foreign-imposed state forms were necessary to carry them out. The ambitious policies of national or ethnic cleansing that it was imagined would *finally* produce national societies required several levels of perpetrators. The brutality of their efforts sometimes masks the point that the perpetrators themselves were rarely clear about where to draw the boundaries between national and nonnational. Peter Black's essay on the recruitment and activities of the *Sonderdienst* in Nazi-occupied Poland, in the Government General, indicates that the determination of just who counted as *Volksdeutsche* usually depended on local, pragmatic, and situational factors. The Nazis themselves could not be consistent on this matter when it came to local policing institutions like the *Sonderdienst*. Yet those people categorized as *Volksdeutsche* for the sake of their mobilization into such Nazi institutions often had to be remade into Germans. And while these so-called *Volksdeutsche* assumed the hoped-for privileges that a German ethnic identity gave them in local society during the War, they often felt themselves to be different from the Reich Germans who had mobilized them. Certainly they were treated as lesser beings when removed from the context of local Polish society and sent to Germany.

The nationalization of societies, of academic disciplines, of the professions, and of bureaucracies, along with brutal policies of mass murder and population transfer, enabled regimes at mid-century to accomplish what had hitherto been only imagined on a local scale. They accomplished the overwhelming task of nationalizing their societies. Benjamin Frommer's essay on postwar Czechoslovakia analyzes a governmental system of retribution for so-called minor offenses against national honor, the so-called Small Decree. The Decree was meant to clarify the hitherto permeable boundaries between the Czech and German nations during the expulsions of the Sudeten Germans, at a time when several people had recently claimed a serial allegiance to both nations. The object of the decree, as Frommer points out, was to suggest that the citizen owed a particular kind of allegiance to the nation that superseded any allegiance to the state. According to this logic, Czechs who had fraternized or collaborated in small ways with Germans might not have directly betrayed their state, but they had certainly betrayed their nation, and could legally be punished.

The application of the decree also demonstrates the degree to which local contingencies continued to determine the question of who belonged to what nation, and on what basis an individual might find himself accused of wartime collaboration. Collaboration, like national identity, turned out to be a highly slippery concept, given the radical regime changes citizens had been subjected to between 1938 and 1948. Whether one was considered a German or a Czech, a collaborator or a resister, depended both on the vagaries of how different regimes had defined these terms, and on the basis of often-accidental choices individuals had made in order to survive war and occupation. The Beneš decrees regarding the expulsion of the Germans from postwar Czechoslovakia might appear clear in their intent, but in fact they had continuously to be refined in their application. As late as 1945, the terms "Czech" and "German" meant little in terms of many people's experience, particularly in cases of so-called mixed marriage, or where their bilingualism had enabled individuals at different times to claim allegiance to both sides. The new regime ascribed nationality on the basis of external objective features, in order to determine who was to be expelled and who might remain. In doing so, Czechoslovakia's new rulers fulfilled the demands of nationalist radicals and departed from traditional practice under the Empire that had allowed individuals to decide their own nationality (and to change it).

Whether or not these policies succeeded in their object, the fact remains that social scientists for the most part now accept the fiction of nations and ethnicities as real and legitimate categories of human experience. By excavating the histories of those who did the hard ideological work involved in translating such categories into reality, we hope to contribute to new ways of thinking about nationalism. The world may experience an overabundance of nationalism in the early 21st century, but that is no reason for social scientists to accept a framework imposed by the idea of the nation or its state.

A Word on Place Names

Many places in Habsburg Central Europe had several names. In addition to the official government names that might be German (in Cisleithania) or Hungarian (in Transleithania), local peoples referred to places in their own languages. Since the demise of the Habsburg Monarchy, the nationalizing states that replaced it privileged the names given to places by the dominant nationalities of those states. We have chosen to use English place names where they exist (Vienna, Prague, Cracow). In all other cases, despite the obvious awkwardness involved, we have chosen to use all the names of a given place. Thus we refer to Lemberg/Lwów/L'viv or Budweis/České Budějovice, and often reverse the order of the names to suit the particular context.

Notes

1. Rogers Brubaker makes this point forcefully in *Nationalism Reframed. Nationhood and the National Question in the New Europe* (New York, 1996), esp. 13–17. For an example of this problematic kind of focus on the real origins of nations, see Anthony D. Smith, "The Origins of Nations," in *Ethnic and Racial Studies* (July 1989): 340–367.
2. Eugen Weber, *Peasants into Frenchmen. The Modernization of Rural France, 1870–1914* (Stanford, 1976); E.J. Hobsbawm, *Nations and Nationalism Since 1780. Programme, Myth, Reality* (Cambridge and New York, 1990), 44; Celia Applegate, *A Nation of Provincials: The German Idea of Heimat* (Berkeley, CA, 1990); Alon Confino, *The Nation as Local Metaphor: Württemberg, Imperial Germany, and National Memory, 1871–1918* (Chapel Hill, NC, 1997). Although nationalists in the Habsburg Monarchy frequently aligned themselves

with visions of economic and social progress, not all movements supported the aggregation of power by the central state, often, as in the case of Czech or Polish nationalists, preferring to empower regional diets at the expense of Vienna.

3. On the system of communal autonomy instituted by the liberal government, see Jiří Klabouch, *Die Gemeindeselbstverwaltung in Österreich, 1848–1918* (Vienna, 1968); Karl Ucakar and Manfred Welan, "Kommunale Selbstverwaltung und konstitutioneller Rechtsstaat," in *Wien in der liberalen Ära,* Felix Czeike, ed. (Vienna, 1978), 5–30.

4. For the best work on the military as a supranationalist institution fostering a state-based patriotism, see István Deák, *Beyond Nationalism: A Social History of the Habsburg Officer Corps 1848–1918* (New York, 1990).

5. For an account that emphasizes the inability of the Habsburg state to orchestrate a popular form of state patriotism, see Oscar Jászi, *The Dissolution of the Habsburg Monarchy,* 3rd edition (Chicago, 1964).

6. On the nationalization of various branches of provincial and state bureaucracy, see *Das Nationalitätenrecht des alten Österreichs,* Karl Gottfried Hugelmann, ed. (Vienna and Leipzig, 1934), esp. part 3, 289–738.

7. Jeremy King, *Budweisers into Czechs and Germans. A Local History of Bohemian Politics, 1848–1948* (Princeton, 2002), 114.

8. On the character and development of Czech nationalist ideologies, see Peter Bugge, "Czech Nation-Building, National-Perception and Politics 1780–1914," (Ph.D. Diss., University of Aarhus, Denmark, 1994); on the particular character of German nationalism in the Tyrol, see Laurence Cole, *"Für Gott, Kaiser und Vaterland." Nationale Identität der deutschsprachigen Bevölkerung Tirols 1860–1914* (Frankfurt am Main, 2000); on the early character of Slovene nationalism, see Arnold Suppan, "Im österreichischen Nationalitätenstaat," in *Deutsche Geschichte im Osten Europas. Zwischen Adria und Karawanken,* Arnold Suppan, ed. (Berlin, 1998), esp. 317–325; Peter Vodopivec, "Liberalismus in der Provinz? Das Beispiel des Triestiner Hinterlandes," in *"Durch Arbeit, Besitz, Wissen und Gerechtigkeit," Bürgertum in der Habsburgermonarchie II,* Hannes Stekl, Peter Urbanitsch, Ernst Bruckmüller, and Hans Heiss, eds. (Vienna, 1992).

9. For examples of national "side switching" in the Bohemian census results from a German nationalist perspective, see J. Zemmrich, *Sprachgrenze in Böhmen* (Braunschweig, 1902), 7–10. In 1906 the Czech National Council (Narodní Rada Česká) sent threatening letters to parents whose children attended German language schools and whose Czech names suggested they were actually of Czech nationality. "With great regret we have discovered that you send your child to a German school. We are only fulfilling our duty … when we amicably inform you of the consequences of your perverted, nonsensical behavior.… If you want to be called a Czech, send your child to a Czech school! And if you don't, we will consider you a German and there will be no place for you in Czech society." Template of undated letter sent to Czech parents filed in a folder of material from 1906, Státní ústřední archiv (Central State Archive) Prague, NRČ, carton 509. The literature on *Kindertausch/handl* is remarkably limited, despite its frequent mention in contemporary memoirs, including those of Karl Renner, president of both the First and Second Austrian Republics. Karl Renner, *An der Wende zweier Zeiten. Lebenserinnerungen* (Vienna, 1946), 7, 45, 76. For other examples, see oral histories collected by Ingrid Kaiser-Kaplaner, *Tschechen und Deutschen in Böhmen und Mähren, 1920–1946* (Klagenfurt, 2002); Helmut Fiehauer, "'Kinder-Wechsel' und 'Böhmisch-Lernen': Sitte, Wirtschaft, und Kulturvermittlung im früheren niederösterreichischen-tschechischen Grenzbereich," in *Österreichische Zeitschrift für Volkskunde* 81 (Neue Serie 32). On school reclamations in Moravia after 1905, see Tara Zahra, "Reclaiming Children for the Nation: Germanization, National Ascription, and Democracy in the Bohemian Lands, 1900–1945," *Central European History* 37/4 (forthcoming 2004); Hannelore Burger, *Sprachenrecht und Sprachengerechtigkeit im österreichischen Unterrichtswesen 1867–1918* (Vienna, 1995), 193–196.

10. For radicalization within the Czech nationalist movement, see T. Mills Kelly, "Taking it to the Streets: Czech National Socialists in 1908," *Austrian History Yearbook* 24 part 1 (1998): 93–112. On radicalization among the German nationalists, see Judson, "'Not another square foot!' German Liberalism and the Rhetoric of National Ownership in Nineteenth-Century Austria," *Austrian History Yearbook* 26 (1995): 83–97; Lothar Höbelt, "Die Linke und die Wahlen von 1891," *Mitteilungen des österreichischen Staatsarchivs* 40 (1987).

11. On earlier constructions, see Isabel Hull, *Sexuality, State, and Civil Society in Germany, 1700–1815* (Ithaca, NY and London, 1996). On the collapse of public/private dichotomies in the face of nationalist claims on children, see Zahra, "Reclaiming Children."

12. Ernest Gellner, *Nations and Nationalism* (Ithaca, NY, 1983); Benedict Anderson, *Imagined Communities: Reflections on the Origin and Spread of Nationalism* (London, 1983).

13. One of the best accounts of the ways in which nationalist movements in Austria made use of existing laws and institutions to open even greater potential fields for activism is Gerald Stourzh, *Die Gleichberechtigung der Nationalitäten in der Verfassung und Verwaltung Österreichs 1848–1918* (Vienna, 1985). Several studies document this opportunist constitutional activism from the point of view of the individual movements including Bruce Garver, *The Young Czech Party 1874–1901 and the Emergence of a Multiparty System* (New Haven, 1978); Lothar Höbelt, *Kornblume und Kaiseradler. Die Deutschfreiheitlichen Parteien Altösterreichs 1882–1918* (Vienna, 1993); Pieter M. Judson, *Exclusive Revolutionaries. Liberal Politics, Social Experience, and National Identity in the Austrian Empire, 1848–1914* (Ann Arbor, MI, 1996); King, *Budweisers into Czechs and Germans;* Keeley Stauter-Halsted, *The Nation in the Village. The Genesis of Peasant National Identity in Austrian Poland, 1848–1914* (Ithaca, NY, 2000). For an excellent analysis of nationalist opportunist use of the census, see Emil Brix, *Die Umgangssprachen in Altösterreich zwischen Agitation und Assimilation. Die Sprachenstatistik in den Zisleithanischen Volkszählungen 1880 bis 1910* (Vienna, 1982).

14. Wilhelm Rohmeder, "Gasthäuser in den sprachlichen Grenzgebieten Südtirols, welche deutschen Reisenden zu empfehlen sind," in *Alldeutschen Blätter,* Sonder-Abdruck 25 (1904), 1–12.

15. Cole, *"Für Gott, Kaiser und Vaterland."*

16. In general, see Hannah Arendt, *The Origins of Totalitarianism* (Cleveland, 1958), chapter 9. On Romania, see Irina Livezeanu's exemplary analysis in *Cultural Politics in Greater Romania. Regionalism, Nation Building, and Ethnic Struggle, 1918–1930* (Ithaca, NY and London, 1995). On Poland, see Antony Polansky, *Politics in Independent Poland* (Oxford, 1972) and Timothy Snyder, *The Reconstruction of Nations. Poland, Ukraine, Lithuania, Belarus, 1569–1999* (New Haven, 2002). On Yugoslavia, see the essays in *Zgodovina Nemcev na Območu Današnje Slovenije/Geschichte der Deutschen im Bereich des heutigen Slowenien,* Helmut Rumpler and Arnold Suppan, eds. (Vienna and Munich, 1988).

17. For an excellent example of this literature in the interwar period, see Erwin Barta and Karl Bell, *Geschichte der Schutzarbeit am deutschen Volkstum* (Dresden, 1930). Lora Wildenthal analyzes the shift from activism directed toward Germany's African colonies to activism directed toward German-speaking communities in Eastern Europe in *German Women for Empire, 1884–1945* (Durham, NC, 2001), esp. 172–200. See also the important work of Vejas Liulevicius, *War Land on the Eastern Front. Culture, National Identity and German Occupation in World War I* (Cambridge, 2000); Elizabeth Harvey, *Women and the Nazi East: Agents and Witnesses of Germanization* (New Haven, 2003); and Paul Weindling, *Epidemics and Genocide in Eastern Europe 1890–1945* (Oxford and New York, 2000).

Chapter 1

FROM TOLERATED ALIENS
TO CITIZEN-SOLDIERS

Jewish Military Service in the Era of Joseph II

Michael K. Silber

The history of Jewish military service is intimately attuned to the rhythms of emancipation, a sensitive register of its advances and setbacks. With the rise of modern nationalism, Jewish participation in wars of national liberation became symbolic capital in the struggle to earn a rightful place in the nation. Whether it was the valiant defense of Warsaw by the doomed Jewish Corps in 1794 under the command of the legendary Berek Joselewicz or the enthusiasm of the Jewish volunteers who flocked to the banner during the German Wars of Liberation in the struggle against Napoleon; the loyal service of Jewish National Guardsmen and soldiers (purportedly "20,000" in number) to the Magyar cause in 1848 and 1849 (explicitly acknowledged in the prefatory remarks to the law emancipating Jews during the waning days of Kossuth's revolution); or the Jewish insurgents who joined Garibaldi's red-shirts in 1860, the valor and often the disproportionate participation of Jewish men at arms were to be repeatedly invoked to demonstrate that Jews were no stepsons of the nation, but deserved to be emancipated and regarded as genuine Poles and Germans, Hungarians and Italians.[1] As a corollary, the military also accurately mirrored the retreat from emancipation in the twentieth century. The recurring accusations of shirking and cowardice during World War I; the notorious *Judenzählung* (Jewish count) in Germany (and in some other countries as well) that sought to ascertain the percentage of Jews in combat units; the dismissal and exclusion of Jews from the officer corps during the interwar period in a number of countries; and the relegation of Jews to mock military labor battalions in World War II Hungary, all signaled attempts to reverse Jewish emancipation and expel Jews as a body foreign to the nation.[2]

The link between Jewish military service and Jewish integration, however, predates the rise of modern nationalism, albeit by a scant few years. Not national membership, but rather the capacity for patriotism and the aptitude for fulfilling the obligations of citizenship were the terms of the initial emancipatory debate. Inclusion in the state rather than in the nation was then at issue. Moreover, the debate over Jewish military service did not begin in the more familiar context of budding nationalism engendered by the French Revolution, but rather arose a decade earlier in the framework of the enlightened absolutist state and the measures initiated by the Emperor Joseph II (1780–1790) in the Habsburg lands. His reform policies vis-à-vis his Jewish subjects set in motion a many-sided discourse that came to encompass Habsburg bureaucrats; men of the enlightenment, German for the most part, but in time French as well; *maskilim,* that is, adherents of a Jewish version of the enlightenment, the *Haskala;* and finally, representatives of traditional Jewish society. Constrained by considerations of space, what follows can only touch upon some of the themes of a longer study.[3] It will be my contention here that the debate over Jewish military service as it evolved over the decade of the 1780s illustrates well the shift away from the time-honored notion (cherished by Jew and non-Jew alike) that Jews were merely tolerated aliens, to a perception that Jews were equal citizens with rights and obligations.[4] Moreover, I argue that the dynamics of this historical process can only be fully grasped if one recognizes that it was driven by the interaction between the state and the public sphere in its enlightened, *maskilic,* and traditional variations. And since the public discourse on Jewish military service most often transcended borders, the strategy of this analysis, while focusing on the policies of the Habsburg state, has been to adjust its scale of inquiry to transnational parameters.

"The most serious reason for asserting that Jews cannot obtain equal rights with the rest of the citizens," wrote the Prussian *Aufklärer* and bureaucrat Christian Wilhelm Dohm in his *Ueber die bürgerliche Verbesserung der Juden,* the seminal treatise that inaugurated the debate over Jewish integration in 1781, "is the belief that Jews are prohibited by their religion from serving in the army.... [T]hey should not ask for equal rights in a society which they decline to defend in need."[5] In the decades to come, the demand to compromise religious practices for the sake of fulfilling obligations to the state was to create a severe challenge for observant Jews. But military service also posed a cluster of problems that went beyond the question of religious compatibility with patriotic duty. In effect, it came to epitomize the general demand for "the physical, moral, and political regeneration of the Jews" (the title of a key treatise to which we will return), a process that even the most sympathetic advocates of the Jewish cause felt was a necessary prerequisite to successful integration.[6] The Jewish soldier, as we shall see, came to represent the very embodiment of the problematic of emancipation.

The history of Jewish military conscription during Joseph II's reign can be conveniently divided into three stages: during the first two years of intensive debate over Jewish integration sparked off by Dohm's pamphlet and Joseph's Edict of Toleration—from the summer of 1781 until 1783—almost every major statement for or against Jewish integration raised the question of the possibility and desirability of Jewish army service. Characteristic of this period was that neither the state nor traditional Jewish society played any part in the theoretical discussions that ranged over the psychological, physiological, and historical aspects of Jewish military service, as well as whether such service was permitted by Jewish law, the *halakha*. The debates were conducted by publicists in Austria and Germany—enlightened Gentiles for the most part, although some *maskilim* (followers of the *Haskala*, the Jewish variant of the *Aufklärung*), notably the famous philosopher Moses Mendelssohn, also participated. The second phase, from the summer of 1787 to the summer of 1788, involved deliberations within the Habsburg state and military bureaucracy over the feasibility of army service for the Jews.[7] Many of the issues that had been raised five or six years earlier were now hammered out between the Emperor, the Chancellery, and the War Council, this time with very practical results. First the Jews of Galicia, then of other Habsburg lands were called upon to provide Jewish recruits for the army. The third period, from the summer of 1788 extending into Leopold II's reign until the end of 1790, was more complicated: the traditional Jewish sector declared its opposition to military service through circulars to other Jewish communities, and petitions to the emperor. For the first time there were *maskilim* who openly clashed with the traditional leadership over this issue, while enlightened Gentile public opinion quickly closed ranks and stood squarely behind the measure. Surprisingly, however, some *maskilim* expressed sharp reservations on the desirability and fairness of Jewish army service. The first decade of the controversy surrounding the military conscription of the Jews revealed a complex interplay between enlightened absolutism, the public sphere, the *Haskala*, and traditional Jewish society.

In the autumn of 1781, Joseph II issued a number of far-reaching decrees, among them the emancipation of the serfs and several Edicts of Toleration for his non-Catholic subjects, Christians and Jews alike. Each of the provinces where major Jewish populations were to be found received its own version of a Jewish *Toleranzpatent* suited to local conditions. Altogether, eight such edicts were decreed during Joseph's reign.[8] In general, the *Toleranzpatent* removed many of the restrictions on Jewish economic activities, allowing Jews to engage in all branches of commerce and the handicrafts, and encouraged Jews to obtain secular, German education. Although initially Jewish military service received only passing mention in the internal deliberations of the Habsburg state bureaucracy,[9] clearly it was the news of Joseph's legislation that sparked off controversy over the issue both in the Habsburg lands and in the German states. Preceded by several pamphlets in Vienna and Prague,[10] it was, nevertheless, the threefold exchange between Christian Wilhelm Dohm, Johann David Michaelis, and Moses Mendelssohn that provided the most interesting statements. That Dohm was serving at the time as a bureaucrat on the Prussian War Council and Michaelis was a famous Göttingen theologian and orientalist who had specialized in the history of biblical law made for an unusually informed debate.

Could Jews be expected to discharge the duties incumbent upon them as citizens? Did their religion necessarily conflict with service in the army? Could Judaism be made to accommodate the demands of the state? These were the questions raised by Dohm in 1781 in his famous treatise on the civic improvement of the Jews. Improvement was the key concept, with a double-edged message. The state should ameliorate the political and legal position of the Jews by eliminating the discriminatory legislation of centuries. The newly created economic and cultural opportunities would in time transform and regenerate the Jews, for in their present state they were a corrupted and twisted people much in need of cultural, moral, and spiritual improvement. In general, Dohm came close to advocating civic, even political equality for the Jews. But in the closing pages of his pamphlet he conceded that if the Jewish religion placed insurmountable obstacles in the path of military service, then withholding legal equality would be perfectly understandable and justified. Two years later, in the second volume of his work, Dohm devoted an entire chapter to this question, and went even further: if their religion prevented Jews from military service, then the state should either impose a quota restricting the size of the Jewish population or expel the Jews from the country altogether.[11] "Everything depends on whether or not the following is correct," wrote Dohm, "that service by Jews in the army is prohibited by their religion."[12]

The primary obstacle was not that Judaism preached pacifism, as did some Christian sects, but rather the violation of the sanctity of the Sabbath by fighting on that day. Both Mosaic law and the evidence of ancient history, he argued, demonstrated that whether in possession of their own kingdom or after the loss of their sovereignty, Jews acquitted themselves honorably on the battlefield even on the Sabbath and "fulfilled their duty as citizens." Jewish religious law was no obstacle to military service, Dohm argued. On the contrary, "a great Jewish scholar" had assured him that military service was as permissible in the present as it had been in ancient times. Dohm's proof text was the Code of Maimonides, *The Laws of the Shabbat*, 2:23–25, which emphasized the duty to participate in defense of a besieged city on the Sabbath even if only one life was threatened. Later, Dohm would point to two oft-cited contemporary instances that buttressed his case: participation of Jews in the militia in Surinam, and the "dispensation" of the rabbi of Amsterdam in 1781 that permitted Jews to fight on the Sabbath in the battle between the Dutch and English fleets.[13]

However, all this was in theory. In practice, Dohm was compelled to concede that for the moment, German Jews were physically and morally ill-prepared to serve in the military. It would take several generations of improved treatment by the state before Jews would eventually emerge regenerated and then, returning to the "nobler and freer spirit" of the ancient Mosaic religion, "reform their religious laws and regulations according to the demands of society." And although until that time Jews could not possibly enjoy full political equality, there was no reason why the state could not treat them as useful members of society, much the same as the Quakers and other pacifist sects. Their military obligations could be fulfilled by hired substitutes, for which Jews would have to pay quite justly a special tax. While it was true that military service since ancient times had been the touchstone of true citizenship and patriotism, the nature of *modern* armies and warfare, Dohm argued, had changed all that. "In our times wars are not conducted by armies of patriotic citizens fighting for freedom and country, but by hired mercenaries in whom skilled performance, strict subordination and a slowly developing feeling of professional honor take the place of patriotic zeal.... So it is for our governments in most cases a matter of indifference whether the subject serves in the army in person or pays a sum of money, for which in many cases stronger and better skilled fighters than they can be hired."[14]

How striking that these views on the nature of modern soldiering—expressed by a Prussian war councilor, no less!—were to prove obsolete almost overnight. Not only were they contradicted by the appearance of citizen armies in revolutionary France a decade later, but even earlier, they were challenged by measures taken by Joseph II, and precisely, as we shall see, in the context of Jewish military service.

Michaelis, a prominent professor of biblical and oriental studies at Göttingen, agreed that military service was indeed the decisive issue that should determine whether Jews deserved equality, but he did not share Dohm's lukewarm optimism. "Jews will not contribute soldiers to the state as long as they do not change their religious views." For the present, he felt that the obstacles posed by the Jewish religion were insurmountable. In consequence of their belief in the messianic restoration of Israel to their land, Jews would always consider themselves a transient alien nation, and therefore were incapable of possessing patriotic sentiment. As to the Jewish legal proof of "the great Jewish scholar," Michaelis scornfully dismissed it: Maimonides had permitted Jews to wage only a defensive war. In any other category of warfare, he noted, "Jews will not fight on the Sabbath, for they are forbidden to do so if not attacked." Not only observance of the Sabbath and the innumerable holidays and fast days, but also their special diet would pose problems. "As long as they observe the laws about kosher and non-kosher food it will be almost impossible to integrate them into our ranks." And even if this could be solved by creating separate Jewish units, yet another problem would pose an insurmountable obstacle: "the oath of the Jews is one of the most complicated matters in the world." In any case, he concluded maliciously, Jews as a race were much too short to meet the criteria of modern European armies![15]

Moses Mendelssohn—no doubt Dohm's "great Jewish scholar" and perhaps the butt of Michaelis's jab on short Jews—did not address himself to the concrete *halakhic* (Jewish legal) issues, but offered instead a coldly dispassionate and rather cynical observation on the pragmatic nature of men in general. "When personal convictions conflict with the laws it is up to the individual to resolve this problem on his own. If then the fatherland is to be defended, everybody who is called upon to do so must comply. In such cases, men usually know how to modify their convictions and to adjust them to their civic duty. One merely has to avoid excessively emphasizing the conflict between the two." Of the three *Aufklärer,* Mendelssohn alone remained unperturbed by the religious problems arising out of Jewish military service, yet it is worth noting that he envisaged such a possibility only in the distant future. "In a few centuries, the problem will disappear or be forgotten." Like Dohm, he anticipated that in practice it would take a long time before Jewish society would learn to adjust to the new realities, but he did not doubt that time would gradually erode religious objections. "In this way," he concluded wrily, "Christians have neglected the doctrines of their founders and have become conquerors, oppressors and slave-traders, and in this way, Jews too could be made fit for military service. But it is obvious that they will have to be of the proper height, as Herr Michaelis wisely reminds us, unless," he added mischievously, "they are merely to be used against hostile pygmies and fellow Jews."[16]

The leisurely evolution envisaged by Mendelssohn and Dohm was not to be. Not centuries, but a scant few years were to pass before Mendelssohn's prediction was put to test. In August 1787, the governor of Galicia, Count Brigido, presented a proposal for comprehensive legislation that would determine the status of the Jews under his authority. This Edict of Toleration for the Jews of Galicia was to be much more far-reaching than any of Joseph's previous reforms. Among the many paragraphs of Brigido's proposal was one suggesting the conscription of Jews into the transport corps. On February 18, 1788, the Emperor ordered the Jews of Galicia to be recruited as drivers in the service corps and the artillery. (Jews had long served as army suppliers, and the cart driver was a familiar Jewish profession.) They were to begin serving immediately in the war that had just broken out with the Turks.[17]

The War Council was taken aback. Not only had it not been consulted on this decision, but already three years earlier it had expressed its negative views on Jewish military service. When in 1785 the Chancellery had proposed that Jews be inducted into the transport corps, the War Council had declined on the grounds that the newly created corps was a regular part of the army since 1782, and thus had no place for Jews. The Council, however, had no objection to hiring Jewish civilians on a contractual basis.[18] Now in 1788, Field Marshal Hadik, the president of the War Council, pointed to the needless difficulties that Sabbath observance and Jewish dietary laws would pose to both the army and the Jews. The Court Chancellery, however, remained unconvinced. The problems of religious observance could be solved by setting up small groups of separate Jewish *Kameradschaften* where Jews would be able to cook and worship together, as well as by encouraging commanders to exercise sensitivity and discretion when assigning Jews to do work on the Sabbath. Jewish religion and army life need not clash: as ancient history illustrated, it was precisely in the era when Jews were most true to their laws that they gained renown as a martial and often victorious people.

Undaunted, the War Council once again marshaled its arguments against conscripting the Jews. Ancient history was not relevant to present-day realities. Besides, conscripting Jews would run counter to the emperor's policy of religious toleration, for in the army they would unavoidably be coerced into violating their Sabbath and their dietary laws. In any case, Hadik concluded, there was no shortage of manpower; there were more than enough recruits available for transport. Perhaps it would be better to reconsider and suspend Jewish conscription for the duration of the war and once peace returned, to think of creating a separate Jewish corps.[19]

The emperor was not moved. There could be no question that Jews would have to serve in the army. In order to satisfy their religious needs, however, they were to be assigned exclusively to the transport corps and be allowed to set up separate *Kameradschaften* for cooking. As for work on the Sabbath, Joseph was adamant. They were to be treated exactly like Christians. Jews would not be exempt on Saturdays from carrying out those duties that Christians were obligated to perform on Sundays. On June 4, 1788, Joseph issued a court decree extending military conscription of Jews to all of his provinces.[20]

It is clear from this exchange that in his insistence that Jews be obligated to serve in the army, Joseph was not prompted by utilitarian calculations, a charge that is often leveled at the emperor by Jewish historians. It was precisely pragmatic considerations that had led the military establishment to argue that the gain in Jewish manpower would be more than offset by the logistic headaches bound to be caused by Jewish religious observance. The contrast between Joseph's uncompromising views and that of the more pliant and pragmatic War Council (or for that matter another war councilor, the Prussian Dohm) was further highlighted in the coming days. On July 10, Galician Jewry submitted a petition to the emperor requesting that Jews be exempt from military obligation altogether in light of the hardships army life would pose to religious observance. Invoking the emperor's stated policy of religious toleration, they further suggested that Jews, if not exempt from the obligation altogether, be at least able to provide substitutes or a redemption fee. Experienced mercenaries could be hired instead.[21] Joseph sharply rejected the War Council's rather self-congratulatory recommendation that the petition be granted and this despite the fact that it ran counter to the Council's overall recruiting policy. Joseph would have none of this. He stood firm and closed the matter in his resolution on September 3, 1788, dashing all hopes of exemption or substitution. In a passage that was to recur in several pieces of subsequent legislation, he stated: "Without any further considerations, the Jew as a man and as a fellow-citizen [*Mitbürger*] will perform the same service that everyone else is obligated to do. His religion will not suffer thereby. He will be free to eat what he will and will be required to work only on that which is necessary during the Sabbath, much the same as Christians are obligated to perform on Sundays."[22] Whereas Dohm, we may recall, saw no real obstacle to Jews fulfilling their obligations to the state by providing mercenary substitutes, Joseph insisted that despite their questionable utility, "the Jew as a man and a fellow-citizen" had duties that could not be palmed off, duties that he was obligated to perform in person.

Again in contrast to the War Council, Joseph and apparently the more enlightened elements of his Chancellery did not seem overly concerned over the potential clash between the Jew's religion and his obligation to the state. Entirely absent from the discussion was the *halakhic* problem that had so troubled Michaelis and Dohm, whether it was permissible to wage an offensive war on the Sabbath. The problem posed by army life to religious Jews was one not so much of principle, as of inhospitable social and cultural environment, and here Joseph was clearly impatient with the overly cautious attitude of the War Council. Jewish objections were not to be indulged; in time, as they would become more enlightened and free of their ancient prejudices, their attitudes to military service would also change. In practice, the Josephinian state was remarkably sensitive to the specific needs of the Jewish recruit. In 1788, for instance, the army provided Jewish soldiers separate uniforms free of *shatnez,* that is, the mix of fibers prohibited by Jewish law. But Josephinian sensitivity had its limits. The War Council's suggestion that Jews be concentrated in separate Jewish regiments was rejected, and even maintaining the separate *Kameradschaften* was often impossible in wartime. Jewish soldiers would usually purchase kosher food from nearby Jewish communities, but this was impracticable when Jews were stationed in locations far from Jewish settlements.[23]

In response to the objections of Galician Jewry to personal military service, Joseph and the Chancellery adopted a measure that was truly pioneering, and marked an important advance toward Jewish integration. In their petition to the emperor, the Galician deputation had argued that the Jewish soldier was denied a fair deal, because in the army no matter how dedicated or distinguished the service, there would be as little opportunity for advancement as in the civil sector.[24] Indeed, Marshal Hadik had expressly argued earlier in April that the army's esprit de corps and honor would be damaged if Jews, who were excluded in civilian life from certain advancements, would be promoted to positions of command over Christian soldiers.[25] However, in his recommendation to the emperor a few months later, Chancellor Kollowrat rejected Galician Jewry's objections as unfounded. "Since Your Majesty has graciously granted that Jews like Christians can be qualified for every public office, it therefore follows that in the military profession as well, they can look forward to all promotions which men of other faith can claim to merit."[26] Here the chancellor seemed to echo what Joseph had already decreed for non-Catholics in the 1781 Edict of Toleration: "The sole criteria in all choices or appointments to official posts are—as has long been the case in Our army, without the least difficulty and with great benefit—to be the candidate's integrity and competence, and also his Christian and moral way of life; difference of religion is to be disregarded."[27] Thus it was the discussions over Jewish military service and promotion to positions of authority over Christians that led to questions of citizenship and to notions of some sort of equality. Were Jews commissioned as officers during Joseph's reign? Perhaps, if we are to believe a newspaper correspondent from Frankfurt am Main who reported that already in

Figure 1.1 Scenes from the conscription of Jews into military service, attributed to the Viennese artist Hieronymus Löschenkohl (1753–1807) who produced several such broadsides in 1788. Reproduced in Edvard Fuchs, *Die Juden in der Karikatur: Ein Beitrag zur Kulturgeschichte* (Munich, 1921) betw. pp. 48 and 49.

1788 Prince von Hohenlohe had promoted a Jew in his Szekler Hussars to *Wachtmeister*, sergeant. "Two others who had already served as noncommissioned officers [*Unteroffiziere*], were promoted to lieutenants in the Bukassowich Freikorps."[28]

During the initial years of Joseph's reign, Jewish military service was most heatedly debated in the public sphere while the matter was noticeably absent from legislation and bureaucratic deliberations. But by the later part of the decade, it was the measures adopted by Joseph and the more enlightened of his bureaucrats that decided the issue once and for all. If before the Galician conscription, segments of enlightened opinion could still hesitate about the possibility of Jewish army service or view it as a distant prospect, after the spring of 1788 the debate moved on to a different plane. A good illustration of the widespread effect of the Habsburg legislation is the way it influenced the views of two participants in the famous essay contest sponsored by the Academy of Metz in France in 1787.[29] Zalkind Hourwitz, a member of the more radical *Haskala*, weighed the possibility of military service, but then dismissed it because the numerous Talmudic prohibitions on working, traveling, riding, etc. on the Sabbath, along with other severities "rendered the Jews absolutely incapable of military service in the field." He added, however, that they might participate in the militia for the internal defense of the kingdom. On Saturdays, Christians would take their place, while Jews would mount guard on Sundays as was the practice in Surinam and other Dutch colonies.[30] Interestingly, although Hourwitz was familiar with the Dohm-Michaelis-Mendelssohn exchange, he tended toward the cautious and skeptical assessment of Dohm. It is inconceivable, however, that Hourwitz would have taken this tack after the Galician draft had become a fait accompli. Another participant of the Metz contest, the Abbé Grégoire, also recalled some of Michaelis and Dohm's arguments for and against conscription. Unlike Hourwitz, however, he was already acquainted with the measures taken by Joseph II; moreover he knew that "the Jewish journalists of Berlin" had of late allayed the fears of their brethren concerning violations of the Sabbath.[31] As a result of Joseph's legislation, theory was now put into practice and many of the points that had previously occasioned fierce debate now no longer seemed to pose problems, and were laid to rest. Other issues, however, now loomed large.

The general Jewish public greeted news of the draft with general consternation. "There was a great mourning among the Jews," wrote representatives of Galician Jewry to Mantua, "public fasting, weeping and wailing.... Many of our people fled to the uninhabited wilderness."[32] In 1788 and in the following years, many young Jews took to hiding in the forests and other desolate areas. Others crossed the border to still independent parts of Poland, or after 1790, to Hungary, where Jews managed to regain their exemption. Flight in the Stanislau district was so massive that it prompted one hostile official to express the guarded hope that Galicia would soon be rid of its Jews.[33] "In every city of the empire where Jews live, they resist the imperial decree," wrote the German *maskil* Saul Ascher not entirely without sympathy.[34] In one celebrated instance the resistance took a violent turn as Jews armed with clubs confronted a press gang in Brody. It took armed troops hastily rushed from Lemberg/Lwów to put down this spontaneous insurrection.[35]

"There is no denying that this decree has instilled in the people an extraordinary dread and despair," wrote the enlightened anonymous "rabbi of Gradiska." The army was undeniably a disagreeable place. Military life was fraught with hardship, long years of service, unpleasant conditions, all in the company of the "lowest masses" of Gentile society. Unfortunately, the "rabbi" lamented, Jews could expect only crass prejudice from their fellow recruits, and worse, the petty tyranny of the NCOs who handled Jews with "inhuman religious hate."[36]

It was, however, the overriding fear that army life was inimical to religious observance that formed the primary objection of traditional Jews. "You must be well aware that those Jews who will be called on to serve in the army will in time forget God's Torah," despaired the circular of Galician Jewish deputies. "For who will feed them kosher food? They will have to desecrate the Sabbath, neglect prayers and God's Torah and other commandments. They will mix with the Gentiles and learn their ways, one Jew among a thousand Gentiles. This concerns the uprooting of our faith and God forbid apostasy!"[37] The circular, which was sent in the summer of 1788 to the Italian Jewish communities (and presumably others elsewhere as well) to mobilize their support at court, also seemed to hint that Jews could legitimately claim exemption from the army, at least from their own strictly *halakhic* viewpoint. "God made us faint of heart!" wailed the deputies, possibly an oblique invocation of a category that was indeed spared military service by Jewish law—cowards.

It was clear that the fears of the traditional leadership focused not on any *halakhic* violation of fighting an offensive war on the Sabbath, but rather on the sociology of religious life in the army. As those *maskilim* who were in favor of the army service pointed out, the *halakha* provided a broad leeway so that even the violation of the Sabbath and kashrut laws could be permitted under mitigating circumstances.[38] Indeed, the deputies of Galician Jewry, both in their petition to the emperor and in their circular to the Jewish communities silently conceded these points and avoided emphasizing the strictly legal issues.

Although *halakhically* permissible, it was nevertheless, clearly undesirable to have a large number of impressionable young men lead a life of religious deviance over an extended period in spite of the religious sanction—or perhaps because of it. The fears of the traditional leadership focused on the lack of time and resources to fulfill basic religious requirements; the imposed uniformity and hierarchy of the military; the pressure of peers so typical of army life; the exposure and close contact with non-Jews—at times their friendship, more often their antagonism and ridicule. All this could wear down the resolution of the most dedicated pious recruit. Indeed, as news of the first draft spread, it became clear that many young soldiers were confused when for the first time in their lives they were exposed to a nonobservant lifestyle. In his chronicle of these years, Abraham Trebitsch was to recall the contingent of young recruits from upper Moravia who passed through his hometown, Nikolsburg/Mikulov, in the summer of 1788. "Among them were those who ate non-kosher food.... They ate leavened food on Passover and drank Gentile wine. They do not observe the Sabbath...." Later, at the beginning of 1789, conscription began in his community as well, and the young, impressionable soldiers were told to take this principle to heart: "If one is coerced into sin, God forgives, but this should provide no excuse for willful transgression."[39] Many feared that the experience of these young men would not be confined to the army, that upon returning home, they and perhaps others would be unable to retain the *halakhic* distinction of army versus civilian life.

The *maskilim* who favored the emperor's move found ready answers to allay these fears. For the first time, during the summer of 1788, the idea was mooted to convene an assembly of lay and rabbinic leaders who would decide authoritatively how to reconcile Jewish religion with the demands of the state. This, the *maskilim* argued, would give firm guidelines to Jews both in the army and in civilian life, as well as reassure the state that Judaism posed no conflict to a citizen's duties.[40]

There were, however, *maskilim* who felt uneasy with Joseph's conscription of the Jews. Elia Morpurgo, Saul Ascher, and Mendel Lefin all expressed reservations about the measure, whether because of the severity and brutality with which recruitment was carried out, or because of the humiliation that service in the transport corps implied, or simply because as long as Jews remained discriminated against and were not equal citizens, there was no justice in obligating them to fulfill a citizen's duties.[41]

The Galician *Judenpatent* of 1789, however, changed all this. Jews were now granted "equality." They could participate in elections, and even be elected to public office.[42] Now that they were permitted to volunteer for combat units and apparently could be promoted to officer rank, whatever objections the *Haskala* camp may have had all but disappeared. Indeed, the lines were clearly drawn in Prague when the government contemplated extending the Galician decree to Bohemia. The conservative faction was willing to forego the promise of equality and, after Joseph II's death, petitioned Emperor Leopold to revoke military conscription and reinstate traditional communal autonomy and the rabbinical courts.[43] The *maskilim,* on the other hand, urged the state to ignore the conservative petition and presented a long brief arguing the permissibility, even the obligation of Jews to serve in the army.[44] This clash in the Habsburg realm paralleled similar debates taking place between conservatives and progressives in France during those very months on the desirability of citizenship with its new rights and obligations versus a return to the traditional communal autonomy and corporative privileges enjoyed by tolerated aliens.[45] In the Habsburg Monarchy, it was military service as a civic obligation that gave rise to a complex discourse on Jewish equality and the price of citizenship, one that came to envisage the transformation of the alien "Jewish nation" into citizen-soldiers even before the outbreak of the French Revolution.

Military conscription affected a higher percentage of Jews in the Habsburg Empire during this period than in Russia during the notorious reign of Nicholas I. Warfare interrupted intermittently by a few years of uneasy peace marked the period between 1788 and 1815. Apart from France, and Prussia toward the very end of the war, only the Habsburg Monarchy conscripted Jews during these decades. As early as 1803, one Galician bureaucrat estimated that more than 15,000 Jews had served under the Austrian flag during the French Wars. In the first decade of the nineteenth century, about 1,400 Jews were being recruited annually in peacetime, and considerably more when war was waged. Of the half-million men recruited in 1814, we can place the number of Jews at somewhere between 15,000 and 19,000. Indeed, this was close to the figure of 17,000 Jewish soldiers that an Austrian publicist had calculated was serving in 1809 alone. Thus, the claim made in 1821 by Viennese Jewry that altogether 35,000 Jewish soldiers had served in the quarter of a century of warfare with the French does not seem exaggerated.[46]

After years of service, many returned to their communities alienated from religious practice. Soldiers rapidly acquired unsavory reputations. Later rabbinic literature is replete with negative assessments of their dubious moral and religious character. In anticipation, the leaders of the Jewish community often tried to select the recruits from the more marginal elements of the community. Nevertheless, it should be noted that the Habsburg conscription did not bring about a crisis in Jewish leadership that the cantonist edicts in Russia were to generate two generations later.[47] To a large extent this can be attributed to the fact that men under eighteen were seldom drafted, and if they were, the practice ran counter to army regulations. Moreover, this was a period of constant warfare when a considerable part of the Christian population was called to arms. Despite the fact that in the popular Jewish mind military conscription was perceived as a *gezerah*—a cruel decree—the harshness of the measure was perhaps mitigated by the tacit acknowledgement that Jews were not being singled out for discrimination. Basically they were treated justly, placed on a footing as equal as one could attain in a society that still preserved class and estate distinctions.

A new sense of patriotism swept the Jewish communities in the last third of the eighteenth century, a growing identification with the monarch, the state, and the inhabitants of the land. A certain shift in political culture was discernable even in the traditional establishment.[48] While not all aspects of Joseph II's reforms were universally appreciated, nevertheless, the logic of citizenship with its rights and obligations became increasingly internalized. During the reigns of his successors there was a retreat from the ambitious vision of Joseph II. His nephew Francis, who ascended to the throne in 1793, eventually decreed a much-truncated version of the Galician *Judenpatent* for his Bohemian lands in 1797, a piece of legislation that well illustrates the contradictions between leftover liberal rhetoric and increasingly reactionary measures that became the hallmark of Habsburg policy toward the Jews in the early nineteenth century.[49] Nowhere were these inconsistencies felt more than in the demand that Jews fulfill their duties as citizen-soldiers while continuing to suffer old disabilities. In 1810, the leaders of Hungarian Jewry presented a petition requesting that the Toleration Tax be abolished. "In the past, the Toleration Tax meant exemption from military service. From this exemption one concluded that the Jew, therefore, was not regarded as a native because he did not defend the country and was excluded from the rights of a citizen [*Bürger*].... For almost twenty years now this nation [*Nazion*] is no longer exempt from this obligation; the Jew must now spill his blood as well as the Christian in the defense of the fatherland. In most European states the consequence that one draws from this circumstance is that once Jews fulfill the obligations of a citizen, they should be invested with the rights of the citizen."[50] The petitioners pleaded to no avail. Well over a generation was to pass until the Toleration Tax was abolished in 1846, on the eve of the 1848/1849 revolutions. Then, a renewed attempt was made to realize the unfulfilled promise of integration in return for military service, but under much changed circumstances. This time what was at stake was not citizenship under the enlightened absolutism of Joseph II, but rather membership in the awakening nation.

Notes

1. Majer Bałaban, ed., *Album pamiątkowy ku czci Berka Joselewicza, pułkownika wojsk polskich w 125-letnią rocznicę jego bohaterskiej śmierci 1809–1934* (Warsaw, 1934); Moritz Stern, *Aus der Zeit der deutschen Befreiungskriege 1813–1815*, 5 vols. (Berlin, 1918–1938); Béla Bernstein, *Az 1848/1849-iki magyar szabadságharcz és a zsidók* (Budapest, 1898); Gina Formiggini, *Stella d'Italia, stella di David: gli ebrei dal Risorgimento alla Resistenza* (Milan, 1998).

2. Werner T. Angress, "Prussia's Army and the Jewish Reserve Officer Controversy Before World War I," *Leo Baeck Institute Yearbook [LBIYB]*, vol. 17 (1972):19–42; idem, "The German Army's 'Judenzählung' of 1916," *LBIYB*, vol. 23 (1978):117–137; Jacob Rosenthal, "'The Counting of the Jews' by the German Army in the First World War" (Hebrew) (Ph.D. Diss., Hebrew University, 2002); Randolph L. Braham, ed., *The Wartime System of Labor Service in Hungary: Varieties of Experiences* (New York, 1995).

3. I plan to publish some of the key documents relating to the initial conscription of Jews in Galicia in 1788 with English translations in a forthcoming annual of *Gal-Ed: On the History of the Jews in Poland*. A companion piece, exploring the efforts of the intercessor (*shtadlan*) Koppel Theben to exempt Hungarian Jews from army service, will appear in the *Simon Dubnow Institute Yearbook*.

4. This assertion must be hedged by two caveats: equality was to be realized within what was still a quasi-feudal society that persisted in maintaining legally differentiated orders; and citizenship was within the context of an enlightened absolutist empire, rather than the modern nation-state.

5. Christian Wilhelm Dohm, *Ueber die bürgerliche Verbesserung der Juden* (Berlin, 1781). I use the English translation of Helen Lederer, "Concerning the Amelioration of the Civil Status of the Jews" (typescript ms., Hebrew Union College, Cincinnati, 1957), 75.

6. The reference is to Abbé [Henri-Baptiste] Grégoire, *Essai sur la régénération physique, morale et politique des juifs: ouvrage couronné par la Société Royale des Sciences et des Arts de Metz, le 23 août 1788* (Metz, 1789).

7. Three important studies based on archival materials are Gerson Wolf, "Wie wurden die Juden in Oesterreich militärpflichtig?" *Wiener Jahrbuch für Israeliten 5628* (Vienna, 1868), 34–66; Wenzel Zácek, "Zu den Anfängen der Militärpflichtigkeit der Juden in Böhmen," *Jahrbuch der Gesellschaft für Geschichte der Juden in der ČSR [=JGGJČ]*, vol. 7 (1935): 265–303; and especially Erwin A. Schmidl, *Juden in der k. (u.) k. Armee, 1788–1918—Jews in the Habsburg Armed Forces [=Studia Judaica Austriaca XI]* (Eisenstadt, 1989), 96–103. I owe much to this fine study. A superb overview is István Deák, *Jewish Soldiers in Austro-Hungarian Society*, Leo Baeck Memorial Lecture 34 (New York, 1990). I, too, dealt with this subject earlier in my master's thesis (submitted to István Deák), "Absolutism, Hungary and the Jews: A Comparative Study of Military Conscription of the Jews in the Habsburg Lands: 1788–1815" (Columbia University, 1977), which however, was based only on published sources.

8. This is the sequence: Bohemia (10 October 1781); Silesia (15 December 1781); the Italian lands (rather a reiteration of existing privileges at the end of 1781); Vienna and Lower Austria (the most familiar, 2 January 1782); Moravia (13 February 1782); Hungary (31 March 1783); and Galicia (27 May 1785 and 7 May 1789). The 1789 Galician *Judenpatent* was meant to be applied uniformly throughout each of the provinces of the empire, and the measure was prevented only by Joseph's premature death in 1790. The texts of the edicts are conveniently assembled in Joseph Karniel, *Die Toleranzpolitik Kaiser Josephs II.* (Stuttgart, 1986), 547–585. Some of the key pieces of Joseph's legislation can be found in English translation in C.A. Macartney, ed., *The Habsburg and Hohenzollern Dynasties in the Seventeenth and Eighteenth Centuries* (New York, 1970).

9. One such remark was made by Staatsrat Kressl in the summer of 1781, see A.F. Pribram, ed., *Urkunden und Akten zur Geschichte der Juden in Wien, 1526–1847 (1849)*, 2 vols. (Vienna and Leipzig, 1918), vol. I, 443; another by the Hungarian Chancellery in the fall of 1782, cited by Henrik Marczali, "A magyarországi zsidók II. József korában" [Hungarian Jews in the Era of Joseph II], *Magyar Zsidó Szemle [MZsSz]* I (1884): 358–359.

10. *Die Juden so wie sie sind, und wie sie seyn sollen. Zweyte Auflage* (Vienna, 1781), 34–38. The booklet was written after Joseph's intentions became known in the summer (see 45), but before any of the Edicts of Toleration were issued in the fall. The illustration on the title page depicts a number of Jews, one of whom is shouldering a rifle with a bayonet. More in-

fluential was [Ignatz Klinger], *Über die Unnütz- und Schädlichkeit der Juden im Königreiche Böheim und Mähren. Zweyte Auflage* (Prague, 1782). This pamphlet attacked the liberal position taken by L.A. Hoffmann, *Über die Duldung der Juden* (1781) written already in 1780, while Maria Theresa was still alive. Klinger notes in the second edition the popularity of the first run, which had sold 700 copies in two days (75). It played an influential role in the discussions among government circles in the fall of 1781, especially in Bohemia. Many concurred with Klinger, though their tone was more restrained. The pamphlet was already discussed on 8 October 1781 by the censor commission. See Ludwig Singer, "Zur Geschichte der Juden in Böhmen in den letzten Jahren Josefs II. und unter Leopold II.," *JGGJČ*, vol. 6 (1934): 245–248. On 20 October 1781, Joseph II himself approved the manuscript. Sebastian Brunner, *Mysterien der Aufklärung* (Mainz, 1869), 390. The Viennese edition of this work was further discussed in 1782 in the *Staatsrat* (1807/1782); see Oskar Sashegyi, *Zensur und Geistesfreiheit unter Joseph II. Beitrag zur Kulturgeschichte der Habsburgischen Länder* [=*Studia Historica* 16] (Budapest, 1958), 55.

11. Christian Wilhelm Dohm, "Fortgesetzte Beantwortung des Einwurfs, dass die Juden nicht zu Kriegsdiensten fähig seyn würden," in his *Ueber die bürgerlichen Verbesserung der Juden,* 2 vols. (Berlin and Stettin, 1783), vol. II, 242.

12. Dohm, "Concerning the Amelioration of the Civil Status of the Jews," 75.

13. See his letter to Mendelssohn, 23 October 1781, in Alexander Altmann, "Letters from Dohm to Mendelssohn," *Salo Wittmayer Baron Jubilee Volume* (Jerusalem, 1975), vol. I (English section), 46; the appendix to the French translation of Dohm's pamphlet first published in April 1782, *De la réforme politique des Juifs* traduire par Jean Bernoulli, Préface et Notes de Dominique Bourel (Paris, 1984), 111–112; and Dohm's reply to his critic, "33. Ueber die *Juden Toleranz,* Antwort auf oben Heft LVIII, S. 250 Berlin, 5 April 1782," in August Ludwig Schlözer, *Briefwechsel, meist historischen und politischen Inhalts,* Theil X, vols. LV–LX (Göttingen, 1782), 279–283.

14. Dohm, "Concerning the Amelioration of the Civil Status of the Jews," 80–83.

15. Johann David Michaelis, "Hr. Ritter Michaelis Beurtheilung: Ueber die bürgerliche Verbesserung der Juden von Christian Wilhelm Dohm," in Dohm, *Ueber die bürgerlichen Verbesserung der Juden,* vol. II, 44–64. The translations are from *The Jew in the Modern World: A Documentary History,* edited by Paul R. Mendes-Flohr and Jehuda Reinharz (New York, 1980), 38.

16. Moses Mendelssohn, "Anmerkung über diese Beurtheilung [Michaelis] von Hrn. Moses Mendelssohn," in Dohm, *Ueber die bürgerlichen Verbesserung der Juden,* vol. II, translation in *The Jew in the Modern World,* 43.

17. Wolf, "Wie wurden die Juden in Oesterreich militärpflichtig?" 60–61.

18. Kriegsarchiv, Hofkriegsarchiv, Vienna [from herein KA HKR] 1785-16-887; Schmidl, *Jews in the Habsburg Armed Forces,* 100–102.

19. "… würden die Juden sich selbst über ihr Gesetz aber wegsetzen, so würde dadurch ein Euer Majestät Gesinnungen und Anordnungen grad entgegengesetztes Kennzeichen von dem Toleranzsystem sich veroffenbaren, dass derlei Juden eigentlich gar keine Religion haben." 8 April 1788, Hadik to the Chancellery, KA HKR 1788-47-326.

20. Joseph issued two very similar imperial resolutions at the end of April and on 20 June 1788, the latter as §52 of a draft of the new Galician *Judenpatent.* See Singer, "Zur Geschichte der Juden in Böhmen," 205–206 for the text.

21. Petition of the Galician deputies, H. Bernstein, Chaim Margoles, and Juda Lebel Meyerhoffer, Vienna, 10 July 1788, KA, HKR 1788-47-563, Beiläge.

22. "Ohne weitere Modalitäten soll der Jud als Mensch, als Mitbürger zu allem denjenigen verwendet werden, was jedem anderen obliegt, seine Religion wird dadurch nicht gekränkt, weil ihm freigelassen werden muß das zu essen, was er will und zu er nichts anderem am Sabbath verhalten werden muß, als was die Noth fordert und was auch der Krist am Sontag zu thun schuldig ist." Singer, "Zur Geschichte der Juden in Böhmen," 239. Among

other pieces of legislation incorporating the passage is the reply of the Hungarian *Statthal-terei* on 1 September 1788 to Hungarian Jewry's petition in *MZsSz* XV (1898): 91–92.

23. Schmidl, *Jews in the Habsburg Armed Forces,* 107–111.

24. "*Siebentens* hätte der jüdische Konskriptionsstand wenn auch dessen zum Militär abgebende Individuen sich auf die vortrefflichste Art in Allerhöchsten Herrendiensten, und ihrer Konduite auszeichneten, so wenig Aussichten zu einem Avancement, als sie im Zivil-staate ..." Petition of Galician deputies, 10 July 1788, KA, HKR 1788-47-563, Beiläge.

25. Hadik to Chancellery, 8 April 1788, KA, HKR 1788-47-326.

26. "Das Besorgniss, dass sie keine Beförderungsaussicht haben. Nachdem Euer Majestät den Juden, die Fähigkeit zu allen Aemtern, wie Kristen zu gelangen gnädigst ertheilen haben, so versteht sich von selbst, dass ihnen auch in dem Militarfach alle jene Behohnungen bevorstehen, auf welche das Verdienst anderer Glaubensgenossen Anspruch hat." Kollowrat to Joseph, 18 August 1788, Magyar Országos Levéltár. A 39 Magyar Kancellária. Acta Gen-eralia 14,918/1788. Apparently, Kollowrat was referring to Joseph's decision in June to per-mit Jews to serve as county doctors. See below.

27. "The Toleration Patent," in Macartney, *Habsburg and Hohenzollern Dynasties,* 157.

28. *Vossische Zeitung,* 13 June 1789, quoted in Ludwig Geiger, "Vor hundert Jahre," *Zeitschrift für die Geschichte der Juden in Deutschland,* vol. 3 (1889): 187. It is not clear just how reli-able this report may be. Erwin Schmidl found only one specific instance in the archives where a Jew had applied for a commission in 1789; however, he was turned down. Moyses Zier from Prague had served previously as an ensign in the East Indies. See Schmidl, *Jews in the Habsburg Armed Forces,* 114.

29. The question posed was: are there means to render Jews more happy and useful in France? The chairman of the academy, Pierre Louis Roederer, specifically instructed the contestants to examine "what have been the effects of the recent laws in their favor by neighboring countries and what can one infer from them." See Abraham Cahen, "L'émancipation des Juifs devant la société royale des sciences et des arts de Metz en 1787 et M. Roederer," *Re-vue des études juives,* vol. 1 (1880): 99. The translation is from Frances Malino, "Attitudes toward Jewish Communal Autonomy in Prerevolutionary France," in Frances Malino and Phyllis Cohen Albert, eds., *Essays in Modern Jewish History: A Tribute to Ben Halpern* (Madi-son, WI, 1982), 101.

30. Zalkind Hourwitz, *Apologie des Juifs en réponse à la question: est-il des moyens de rendre les Juifs plus hereux et plus utiles en France?* (Paris, 1788), 36–39.

31. He was undoubtedly referring to the letter of Trieste Jewry published in the Berlin Hebrew journal *ha-Measef.* Grégoire urged that Jews be dispersed among the various units so that "necessity, example, and harmless ridicule" would have in time a corrosive effect on their prejudices. Abbé Grégoire devoted all of chapter 18 of his *Essai sur la régénération physique, morale et politique des Juifs* to this question.

32. Letter of the Galician deputies, Hirsh Bernstein of Brody and Chaim Margolis of Lem-berg/Lwów, to the Mantuan Jewish community, 17 June 1788, Central Archives for the History of the Jewish People (CAHJP), Jerusalem, microfilm HM 5193, JCA Filza 216, doc. 1. To my knowledge this is the only version of the Galician document that has been located, and was first referred to by Shlomo Simonsohn, *History of the Jews in the Duchy of Mantua* (Jerusalem, 1977), 475, n. 501. I wish to thank Lois Dubin for generously bring-ing this important reference to my attention. Presumably, the better known published re-sponse of the Jews of Trieste was to a variant of this letter. A sympathetic Galician bureaucrat was to write a generation later, "Emigration, general fasts, repentance and dep-utations to Vienna were the immediate reactions." See Michael Stöger, *Darstellung der gesetz-lichen Verfassung der galizischen Judenschaft,* 2 vols. (Lemberg, Przemysl, Stanislawow, and Tarnow, 1833), vol. 2, 65.

33. A. Wojtowski, *Die Politik der preussischen Regierung gegenüber den polnischen Juden,* 18, cited by F. Friedman, *Die galizischen Juden im Kampfe um ihre Gleichberechtigung (1848–*

1868) (Frankfurt am Main, 1929), 130, n. 2. In the Tarnopol and Rzeszów districts, only two recruits were found to fill the 100-man quota, and these were Jewish vagabonds from Poland. Majer Bałaban, *Dzieje Żydów w Galicyi i w Rzeczypospolitej krakowskie, 1772–1868* (Lwów, 1916), 37. "In Bohemia one encounters several young men of well-to-do parents who have emigrated to various places," wrote Saul Ascher. See his anonymous *Bemerkungen über die bürgerliche Verbesserung der Juden veranlasst bei der Frage: Soll der Jude Soldat werden?* (Frankfurt am Oder, 1788), 35, e. One such instance was described in the memoirs of the lapsed Frankist, Moses Porges (Leopold Porges von Portheim), who was smuggled out of Prague to Saxony in 1798, at the age of 17. "The general recruiting of 1798, when the young men were dragged out of bed in the middle of the night, was the cause of my going into hiding at friends (Salom. Brandeis); a few weeks later it was decided that in order to evade the danger I should emigrate to Germany." C. Seligmann, "Eine Wallfahrt nach Offenbach: Zur Geschichte der Jakob Frankschen Bewegung," *Frankfurter israelitisches Gemeindeblatt,* vol. 10 (1932), 121. (Note that despite Frankist enthusiasm for things military, the Porges family did not react differently than other Jews.) In his memoirs, Ascher Lehmann (b. 1769) also wrote a vivid description of conscription in Prague. See Monika Richarz, ed., *Jewish Life in Germany* (Bloomington, IN, 1991), 57.

34. [Ascher], *Bemerkungen über die bürgerliche Verbesserung der Juden,* 35, note e.

35. The Brody incident was described in (Carl Feyerabend), *Cosmopolitische Wanderungen durch Preussen, … Gallizien und Schlesien in den Jahren 1795 bis 1798* (Germanien [Danzig], 1803), vol. IV/2, 55. The passage is quoted in full by Wolfgang Häusler, *Das galizische Judentum in der Habsburgermonarchie im Lichte der zeitgenössischen Publizistik und Reiseliteratur von 1772–1848* (Munich, 1979), 64–65 and referred to by Stanisław Schnür-Pepłowski, *Cudzoziemcy w Galicyi, 1787* (Cracow, 1898), 112 and A.Y. Brawer, *Galicia and its Jews* (Hebrew) (Jerusalem, 1956), 183–184.

36. *Schreiben eines Rabbi aus Gradiska zur Entscheidung, dass die jüdische Religion dem Kriegsdienste nicht im mindesten widerspreche. Aus dem Hebräischen treu übersezt…* (Vienna, 1788), 6–7, 17.

37. Letter of the Galician deputies to the Mantuan Jewish community, 17 June 1788, CAHJP, HM 5193, JCA Filza 216, doc. 1.

38. The most important statements of *maskilim* in favor of military conscription include the letter of an anonymous *maskil* to Galician Jewry in *ha-Measef,* vol. 5 (1787/1788), 331–334; the letter of the "rabbis" of the Trieste community, 30 June 1788 (signed actually by the lay leaders Moshe Levi, Abraham b. Yosef Morpurgo, and Elia b. Moshe Luzzatto in the name of the rabbi) in *Ha-Maessef,* vol. 4 (1787/1788), 386–388 (the date, which is missing, is from a copy of the letter in the Mantuan Jewish community archives); the pamphlet of the "rabbi of Gradiska" (almost certainly Eliah Morpurgo), signed 14 July 1788, *Schreiben eines Rabbi aus Gradiska;* a letter of Morpurgo's in an entirely different vein written on 3 September 1788 in Y.Ch. Jare, "Letter to my People from Elia Morpurgo" (Hebrew) *Ha-'Olam,* vol. 1 (1907), 37–38; O.E. King, *Soll der Jude Soldat werden? Unparteiisch beantwortet. Sammt einer authentischen Beylage von der Triester Judengemeinde* (Vienna, 1788), which appends the letter of Trieste in German translation; and the petition to Leopold II of the Prague *maskilim,* Raphael Joel Basch, Moses Fischer, Joachim Lucka Lederer, and Samuel Levi (Gerson Wolf in *Ben Chananja,* vol. 5 [1861], 62 adds Baruch Jeitteles), dated 26 November 1790, in Singer, "Zur Geschichte der Juden in Böhmen," 219 ff.

39. Abraham Trebitsch, *Qorot ha-'Itim* (A Chronicle of the Times) (Brünn, 1801), paragraph 59.

40. Jare, "Letter to my People from Elia Morpurgo."

41. Jare, "Letter to my People from Elia Morpurgo"; [Saul Ascher], *Bemerkungen über die bürgerliche Verbesserung der Juden;* N.M. Gelber, "Mendel Lefin-Satanower and his Proposals to Improve the Jews of Poland at the Great Sejm" (in Hebrew), in *Abraham Weiss Jubilee Volume* (New York, 1964), 287, article 3.

42. "... den Unterschied, den die Gesetzgebung bisher zwischen christlichen und jüdischen Untertanen beobachtet hat, aufzugeben und den in Galizien wohnenden Juden all Begünstigungen und Rechte zu gewähren, deren sich unsere übrigen Untertanen zu erfreuen haben. In allgemeinen also soll die galizische Judenschaft von nun an in Rechten sowohl als Pflichten volkommen wie andere Untertanen angesehen." Preamble of the Galician *Judenpatent,* 7 May 1789. For active and passive franchise in local communal affairs, see §16; for volunteers to combat units §49. Josef Karniel, "Das Toleranzpatent Kaiser Josephs II. für die Juden Galiziens und Lodomeriens," *Tel Aviver Jahrbuch für deutsche Geschichte,* vol. 11 (1982): 75, 78, 87.

43. There were several petitions, all dating from the same month. The most detailed was submitted by Samuel Landau, Marcus Karpeles, and Seligmann Kalmus on 21 May 1790; Singer, "Zur Geschichte der Juden in Böhmen," 215–216.

44. See the 2 June and 26 November 1790 petitions in ibid., 217–218, 229–232.

45. The debate in France began in August 1789 and continued until April 1790. Eliahu Tscherikower, *Yehudim be-'Itot Mahapekha* (Tel Aviv, 1957), 78–85, 91–97 and Arthur Hertzberg, *The French Enlightenment and the Jews* (New York, 1968), 344–348. Conservatives and *maskilim* clashed also in the Batavian Republic in 1796 over communal autonomy and emancipation. See Herbert Bloom, "Felix Libertate and the Emancipation of Dutch Jewry," in *Essays on Jewish Life and Thought, Presented in Honor of Salo Wittmayer Baron* (New York, 1959); Menachem Eljakiem Bolle, *De opheffing van de autonomie der kehilloth (joodse gemeenten) in Nederland, 1796* (Amsterdam, 1960), and S.E. Bloemgarten, "De Amsterdamse Joden gedurende de eerte jaren van de Bataafse Republiek (1795–98)," *Studia Rosenthaliana,* vol. 1 (1967): 49–60.

46. Franz Josef Jekel, *Pohlens Staatsveraenderungen und letzte Verfassung,* 3 vols. (Vienna, 1803), vol. 2, 58; *Der Jude,* vol. 1 (1832): 208 and the petition of Viennese Jewry, 31 December 1821 in Sigmund Husserl, *Gründungsgeschichte des Stadt-Tempels der israel. Kultusgemeinde Wien* (Vienna-Leipzig, 1906), 51. For a more extended discussion of these figures, see my Ph.D. dissertation "Roots of the Schism in Hungarian Jewry: Cultural and Social Change from the Reign of Joseph II until the Eve of the 1848 Revolution" (Hebrew), (Hebrew University, 1985), 105–108.

47. Michael Stanislawski, *Tsar Nicholas I and the Jews: The Transformation of Jewish Society in Russia, 1825–1855* (Philadelphia, 1983), 13–34.

48. Marc Saperstein, "War and Patriotism in Sermons to Central European Jews: 1756–1815," *LBIYB,* vol. 38 (1993): 3–14.

49. For the so-called *Systemalpatent* for Bohemian Jewry, see Simon Adler, "Das Judenpatent von 1797," *JGGJČ,* vol. 5 (1933): 199–229. For a comparison with the 1789 Galician *Judenpatent,* see Singer, "Zur Geschichte der Juden in Bohmen," 273–277.

50. I. Reich, "Rosenthal Eliah," *Beth-El* (Pest, 1867), vol. 2, pt. 1, 87.

Chapter 2

THE REVOLUTION IN SYMBOLS

Hungary in 1848–1849

Robert Nemes

The great figures of the Convention floated before his eyes. A magnificent new dawn was surely breaking. Rome, Vienna and Berlin were in revolt; the Austrians had been kicked out of Venice; the whole of Europe was in ferment. It was time to hurl oneself into the fray and perhaps help events along; he [Frédéric] was also greatly attracted by the clothes which, it was said, the Deputies would be having. He could already see himself wearing a tricolor sash and a waistcoat with lapels.

—Gustave Flaubert, *A Sentimental Education*[1]

The 1848 revolutions were long described in terms of what they did not accomplish, rather than what they actually achieved. Like Flaubert's Frédéric Moreau, more interested in clothes than constitutions, the actors in 1848 seemed a pale reflection of the generation of 1789. From this perspective, the mid-nineteenth-century revolutions stood out for their conspicuous lack of success, a judgment neatly contained in A.J.P. Taylor's famous description of the revolution in the German lands as a turning point that failed to turn.[2] Starting with the publication of Peter Stearns's *1848: The Revolutionary Tide in Europe* (1974), however, English-language scholarship in the last three decades has emphasized the diversity of revolutionary experiences and has largely overturned this verdict.[3] Once viewed as an ignominious failure, the revolutions are now seen as a "pioneering venture in mass political mobilization" and as a watershed in the development of modern nationalism.[4] Recent writing on collective memory has further underlined the lasting importance of 1848 for a wide range of social groups and political regimes.

The reevaluation of the 1848 revolutions rests upon two distinct historiographical trajectories. The first is the rediscovery that the 1848 revolutions were a transnational, even transatlantic phenomenon. Arguably, no other revolution, before or since, affected so many European states; the revolutionary tremors reached even Britain and left only Russia untouched. "Europe appears to us as a huge volcano," intoned Richard Wagner in 1849. "Yes, we notice that the old world falls into pieces and a new one emerges, because the sublime Goddess of revolution rages on the wings of the storms."[5] But the transnational dimensions of the revolutions were often lost or minimized by nationalist historians in the late nineteenth and early twentieth centuries. Only in the decades after the Second World War, in an era of increased European integration, did scholars begin to look again at the European character of the 1848 revolutions.[6] In part, this required paying more attention to events in often overlooked parts of Europe—in Scandinavia, the Netherlands, and Romania, for example. István Deák's *The Lawful Revolution* (1979) perhaps did more than any other work to introduce the Hungarian case to Western audiences.[7] The mid-nineteenth-century revolutions, in short, came to be seen as part of a Europe-wide eruption, in which interaction, mutual influence, and imitation shaped events across the continent.

At the same time, recent developments in social and cultural history have encouraged scholars to think more broadly about the possibilities for political participation.[8] This has involved more studies of the revolutions' impact on the countryside, on small towns, and on a wide range of social groups, such as women, Jews, and artisans. In these studies, emphasis often shifts away from the formal political sphere of ministers and parliaments to the public sphere of newspapers, voluntary associations, demonstrations, symbols, and everyday practices. It is now clear that the revolutionary upheaval signaled the arrival of a new political culture in Europe, one marked by mass participation in elections, public meetings, and political clubs, as well as by a wide repertoire of political and patriotic symbols. This literature has shown the value of examining the revolutions in their local contexts and of emphasizing the role of religion, gender, class, and national loyalties.

Drawing upon these two interpretive frameworks, this essay looks at the upsurge of public activity in Buda-Pest in 1848.[9] The focus is on revolutionary symbols: national colors, coats of arms, forms of address, and even the clothes so admired by Flaubert's Frédéric. Scholars have argued that particularly in moments of crisis, such symbols can both act as a bridge between political elites and their followers and at the same time help define the boundaries of political and national communities.[10] Taking this as its starting point, this chapter looks anew at the revolutionary enthusiasm of early 1848, the subsequent militarization of public life, and the dynamic of repression and resistance that characterized 1849. The aim is to uncover the ways in which revolutionary politics and Hungarian patriotism were negotiated on the ground by ordinary men and women. This is, of course, only one piece of the complex story of the revolution in Hungary: the emphasis here is on Buda-Pest rather than the countryside, on Hungarian political actors rather than on their Serb, Slovak, or Croat counterparts, on the middle and upper classes rather than priests, peasants, or workers, and on patterns of extra-parliamentary activity rather than on the sweeping political narrative of 1848–1849.

"On the Altar of the Homeland"

As students of the French Revolution and heirs to the Romantic Era, the participants in 1848 attached great importance to the symbolic dimension of their struggles. There was a wave of iconoclasm in the first days of each revolution, as people tore down royal coats of arms and cast aside their top hats, frock coats, and wigs, which were seen as symbols of the old order. Outside of France, however, the revolutions stopped at "the foot of the throne," and violent attacks on the royals themselves were unthinkable. Most revolutionaries were content to rename streets and squares, to insist that national anthems be played, and to plaster everything with the national colors. Some symbols were explicitly political: the mania for constitutions, for example, produced constitutional "hats, ties, umbrellas, biscuits and even a constitutional polka."[11] Other symbols had more patriotic resonances. National dress took on a new importance, particularly in Central Europe. In Prague, the *Čamara,* a buttoned jacket, came into vogue in 1848 and remained a symbol of Czech nationalism. The prevalence and meaning of such displays often changed over the course of the revolution, yet this explosion of symbolic activity undoubtedly allowed a wide range of people to demonstrate their political allegiances and national loyalties.

There was relatively little destruction or desecration of symbols of imperial-royal authority in Hungary. The Habsburgs themselves remained popular, and newspapers reacted hostilely to Sándor Petőfi's republican poem "To the Kings," which contained the provocative line: "No matter what shameless flatterers say, there is no longer a *beloved* king!"[12] Most Hungarians would have supported Louis Kossuth's proposal that Emperor-King Ferdinand rule not from Vienna but from Buda. This quixotic but popular suggestion had no chance of realization, yet it reflected the Hungarians' belief that theirs was a lawful revolution directed only against Metternich and the evil "Camarilla" surrounding the king, and that Buda-Pest, not Vienna, should be the center of the Monarchy. It is also further evidence of how fully Hungary's political leaders understood the importance of symbolic gestures. Kossuth's arrival in Vienna in the first days of the revolution, for example, had been memorable not just because it demonstrated the waning of imperial authority and the waxing of Hungarian influence, but also because the Hungarian delegation had been "resplendent in their gala national dress, girt with their richly studded swords, and bearing egret feathers in their caps."[13]

In Buda-Pest, revolutionaries insisted on the public display of Hungarian symbols. The response was at first confused, since officials in Buda ordered that imperial colors (black-yellow) and insignia (the double-headed eagle) be removed from public buildings and be replaced by the Hungarian tricolor and coat of arms, whereas officials in Vienna conceded only that Hungarian symbols could now appear alongside (and preferably below) the imperial ones.[14] The matter was finally resolved in Law XXI in April, which read:

§ 1. The national colors and coat of arms shall be restored to their ancient rights.
§ 2. With the tricolor cockade having been adopted as a civil symbol (*polgári jelkép*), it is also established that the national flag and coat of arms shall be used on every public building and public institution, in all public celebrations, and on every Hungarian ship.[15]

If the first paragraph, with its language of restoration rather than of revolution, provides a justification for the law, the second shows clearly the determination of the Hungarian leadership to use symbols to demonstrate the new balance of power.

Ordinary people were no less ostentatious. Drawing on a rich repertoire of national symbols, most of them created or popularized in the 1830s and '40s, men and women danced national dances, sang patriotic songs, recited patriotic poems, donned national costumes, and extolled the virtues of the Hungarian language. Consumers could purchase engravings of revolutionary leaders, which began to appear soon after March 15. The engraver Joseph Tyroler (who would later print Hungary's banknotes) advertised portraits of Batthyány and Kossuth "in memory of the glorious achievements of our times, as well as of the immortal service of both worthy men in the rebirth of the dear fatherland."[16] Those with deeper pockets could show their support for the revolution through public donations, which became increasingly common after the decision to establish a Hungarian army in late May. The Pest Jewish community loaned the government 50,000 florins without interest, and at the same time offered 100 florins to 100 volunteers who completed three years of service. The well-heeled National Casino likewise placed 20,000 florins and all its silverware "on the altar of the homeland" (a commonly repeated phrase), while a wealthy merchant donated two chests of gold and silver wares, which were displayed in front of the National Museum.[17] Smaller donations, often as little as one florin, also poured in from the countryside, and in scenes worthy of nineteenth-century opera, women handed over their jewelry to the Hungarian government.

Names were also changed to reflect the new conditions. Predictably, streets were renamed in honor of Batthyány and Kossuth. In mid-April, the Opposition Circle, long a gathering place for Pest liberals, officially changed its name to the Radical Circle and adopted a new set of bylaws. "The Radical Circle," they read, "is a social club for those who desire to strengthen and give voice to the development of our constitution on the basis of the democratic spirit, liberty, equality, and fraternity."[18] Newspapers hurriedly followed suit: the liberal *Életképek*

(Sketches of Life) appended *Népszava* (Voice of the People) to its title, while the conservative *Honderű* (Serene Homeland) was reincarnated first as the radical *Reform* (Reform) and later as the short-lived *Nép-elem* (People's Element).[19] Other revolutionary titles included *Kossuth Hirlapja* (Kossuth's Paper), *Munkások Újsága* (The Workers' Newspaper), *Köztársasági Lapok* (Republican Pages), and *Die Patriot* (The Patriot). To emphasize its break with the old regime, the liberal *Pesti Hirlap* (Pest News), which had been in circulation since 1841, after March 15, 1848 began numbering its issues from one again. This was a minor (and inexpensive) alteration, but like the others described here, it suggested that a new era had dawned.

One of the singular aspects of the Hungarian revolution was the extent to which it encouraged individuals to adopt new names. There were precedents for this: in the 1790s some Frenchmen had exchanged their Christian names for those of the Roman Republic, and thus Jean had become Gracchus or Brutus.[20] In Hungary in 1848, many people with German or Slavic surnames showed their patriotism by voluntarily adopting Hungarian-sounding names. This change involved more than a few drinks and a burst of patriotic enthusiasm, since those wishing to change their names had to petition the Interior Minister and pay a three-florin fee. In this way the writer and translator Karl Benkert cleverly reversed the syllables of his surname and became Kertbeny. While some people with German names translated them directly into Hungarian (hence the draftsman Nikolaus Liebe—in English, Nicholas Love—became Miklós Szerelmey), others were more inventive in their choice of Hungarian surnames. Thus the fisherman Jakob Schroeder became Jakab Varsai—the rough equivalent in English of going from Jacob Taylor to Jacob Weir or, more loosely, to Jacob the Fish-Catcher.[21] Revolution or no, people also had a fondness for aristocratic names. For example, the journalist Karl Lesigan became Károly Andorffy, a name worthy of a count.[22] A number of women—likely widows—also appear in the sources, such as Eleanora Pellett, who changed her surname to Szivesy.[23]

Many of those who adopted new names were Jews. Mihály Táncsics, who organized young Jews into their own militia unit, gave each recruit a new, Hungarian-sounding name.[24] Other individuals made the decision on their own. A ministerial announcement from June 1849, for example, approved the request of the medical student Móric Eisler to change his surname to Vasfi—literally, "man of iron."[25] But becoming "Hungarian" had never been simple for Jews: it was not enough simply to speak Hungarian and to take a Hungarian name. Non-Jewish writers had long insisted that Jews abandon religious and cultural practices that set them apart from the mainstream community (and these were the writers who viewed Jews with relative tolerance, the ones who did not fantasize about either expelling or converting the Jews en masse). Within the Jewish community, the 1848 revolution gave a strong impetus to reformers. In early May, for example, the Jewish Magyarization Society circulated a petition calling on "Hungarians of the Mosaic faith" to introduce "changes required by our age" and to abandon all traditions—such as distinctive dress, dietary laws, and the Sabbath—that could give rise to charges of separatism.[26] In July 1848, the newly-formed Hungarian Central Reform Association began to raise money to purchase church organs for Jewish synagogues and to translate German Jewish prayer books into Hungarian. In this environment, it is perhaps not surprising that a number of leading Jews converted to Christianity. The converts included several prominent Pest merchants, such as Jónás Kunewalder, who until then had been the head of the Pest Jewish community.[27] Any number of factors—expediency, perceived pressure, revolutionary enthusiasm, Hungarian national loyalty—may have been at work here, but this was undoubtedly a highly symbolic demonstration of revolutionary solidarity.

Among political radicals, the revolution sparked debates on language and social hierarchy. Invoking the principle of equality, a handful of writers called for the abandonment of titles of nobility, a provocative suggestion in Hungary, where nobles made up more than 5% of the population and dominated social and political life. To set an example, the writer Mór Jókay dropped the noble suffix -y from his surname and began writing Jókai.[28] Others called for more egalitarian forms of address, and thus some radicals, obviously inspired by the French Revolution, urged people to address one another simply as "citizen" (*polgártárs*). This practice seems to have taken root in 1848, at least in Pest. "Titles came to an end; the whole world was citizen and citizeness," recalled one revolutionary.[29] Such was not the case with Mihály Táncsics's suggestion that Hungarians address one another as *"kend,"* a form of address used exclusively by Hungarian peasants, akin to requiring all Americans to call one another "pardner."[30] There were obvious limits to what the wider population would accept—more evidence of the gap between the Pest radicals and most of the political public—yet these efforts suggest the extent to which some enthusiasts hoped to carry the revolutionary struggle into all areas of life.

The emphasis on patriotic and political symbols contributed to debates surrounding the role of women in public life. Across Europe, a small number of female activists used the 1848 revolutions to challenge the traditional exclusion of women from the political public. "When they say the people," wrote Louise Otto, editor of the Saxony-based *Frauen Zeitung* (Women's Newspaper), "women do not count."[31] In Hungary, the revolution offered new roles to women, and in its first months women sewed banners, wore the national colors, and took part in street demonstrations. In late April, a new group called the Radical Hungarian Women published a twenty-four-point petition, which asserted that women should "actively take part in public affairs as much as possible," a demand with little precedent in Hungary.[32] The petition was conventional in that it highlighted the role women could play as patriotic wives and mothers, and reminded women not to forget "about the woman's realm and responsibilities." But it also encouraged women to take up their pens in service of "freedom, the homeland, and women" and to form a network of associations across the country. Underscoring the significance of symbolic acts, the petition called on women to speak the Hungarian language, purchase domestic goods, wear national costumes, and dance national dances, such as the *csárdás,* a whirling dance with roots in the countryside. The experience of women during the Hungarian revolution was ultimately a mixed one—like men, women held views across the political spectrum and few substantive gains for them would come out of 1848. Yet the revolutionary experience was important in that it mobilized women and laid the groundwork for their seeing themselves as a discrete group of citizens.[33]

But what of those who did not rush to don the national costume, dance the *csárdás,* or address their friends as "citizen"? The forging of national communities often involves attacks on perceived domestic or foreign "enemies," and in Buda-Pest in 1848, revolutionaries often used symbolic criteria to distinguish friend from foe. The boundaries of the national community, ill-defined in the 1840s, were becoming more distinct. To refuse to embrace all things "Hungarian" was to invite suspicion. This could be and was taken to extremes: "those Hungarian women who avoid the national literature and arts and deem only foreign ones worthy of attention," warned the Radical Hungarian Women, "women who, for example, subscribe to German or French papers and read only foreign books are forever despised, and we will expel these traitorous, degenerate girls from our circles."[34] The patriotic frenzy affected even Catholic priests, not a group one might expect to embrace revolution. Father János Szerenespataki, for instance, called on his fellow priests to demonstrate their patriotism by wearing the *atilla*—a Hungarian jacket, part of the national costume—in public and by growing beards, since, with few exceptions, the Hungarian political leadership was bearded.[35] There is an almost comical air to these suggestions, but the priest's concern is obvious: he does not want priests to lag in their outward displays of Hungarian national loyalty.

What is striking about Buda-Pest in 1848 is how rapidly and enthusiastically ordinary men and women adopted the revolution's symbols. In this they were often behaving like their fellows across Europe. The language, colors, and costumes were Hungarian, but the basic symbolic repertoire—flags, slogans, and anthems—was largely the same. Ostensibly national symbols, in other words, were deeply influenced by transnational patterns. France in particular was the model to be emulated, as was clear from the formation in Buda-Pest of a committee of public safety, the ubiquitous cockades, and the performance of the French anthem at public events.[36] But the Hungarians must also have been watching events elsewhere in the Habsburg Monarchy, where Viennese radicals paraded in black, red, and gold to show their German alignment, and Croat activists demanded wider use of their language, colors, clothing, and dances. If the Hungarian case was different, then, it was only in the breadth and endurance of the political consensus behind the Hungarian language and other national symbols. It was not enough to support the revolutionary cause; one had to do so in the Hungarian language. This was not just the view of radical hotheads: the Hungarian parliament turned away a German-speaking MP who did not know Hungarian, telling him that he had two months to learn the language.[37] Indeed, for some Hungarian nationalists, language was only the starting point, and they were ready to exclude from the national community anyone who did not look, act, or pray like a "Hungarian."

"To Fight for the Homeland is a Beautiful Thing"

By fall 1848, revolution had turned into war in Hungary. The success of the revolutionary Hungarian armies was unique in 1848–1849, but in the end they too succumbed to overwhelming Austrian and Russian forces. There are many reasons why the collapse did not come earlier—Kossuth's charisma and tireless energy played a major role, as did the unexpected skill of several generals. But this resistance would not have been possible without the remarkable support of the wider population, and it is estimated that one in two Hungarian (that is, Hungarian-speaking) families contributed to the military struggle in one way or another.[38] In Buda, men and women volunteered to work on the fortifications on Castle Hill, and in Pest, military conflict tamed the radicals, who threw themselves behind the war effort. Petőfi and Vasvári had already enlisted in the army by the end of September, and many other Pest youth followed their example. Those who did not were open to criticism: "To fight for the homeland is a beautiful thing," said one parliamentary deputy, "but to parade around with a red ribbon and cockade is not."[39] Public gatherings in Pest for the remainder of 1848 accordingly had a strong military flavor. Audiences in the National Theater, for example, included large numbers of men in uniform. Similarly, when the Radical Circle held a banquet in honor of visiting Polish revolutionaries in November, the mood, music, and guests were all serious, and toasts were somberly drunk to the army and to Kossuth.[40]

The Hungarian armies experienced initial success, but the fighting did not go well in late 1848. At the end of December, with enemy armies rapidly approaching and its own forces nowhere in sight, the Hungarian government, with its banknote press, armaments industry, and parliament in tow, retreated from Buda-Pest to Debrecen in the eastern part of the country. Austrian troops under Field Marshal Windisch-Graetz thus occupied both Buda and Pest in early January without firing a shot. A few residents openly welcomed the imperial forces, but much of the population was more cautious, knowing that occupation meant continued hardships and the quartering of soldiers. For their part, the Austrian authorities rapidly moved to assert control over public life: they forbade assemblies, meetings, and balls; closed down clubs, casinos, and cultural associations; and banned some newspapers while replacing the editors of others. With great ceremony, they disinterred and reburied General Ferenc Lamberg, the royal commissioner and commander-in-chief murdered by a mob in late September 1848.[41] The authorities also removed Hungarian coats of arms from public buildings and painted the National Museum, the site of so many mass meetings in 1848, Habsburg yellow. Finally, in a move that had both symbolic and financial overtones, the occupying authorities declared that all "Kossuth notes" (banknotes issued by the Hungarian government) were now worthless.

If the occupying authorities understood the significance of symbolic gestures, so too did the population of Buda-Pest. The son of a Pest guild master was arrested for refusing to sit at the table with army officers quartered in his house.[42] The librarian Gábor Mátray, who kept a detailed diary during the occupation, recorded that someone had shouted "Long live Kossuth" in the National Theater and escaped, while an apprentice had shouted in Hungarian "Jellačić is a scoundrel" to a passing imperial officer and had escaped only because the officer thought he had said "Hurrah for Jellačić!"[43] In sum, there is anecdotal evidence that a large part of the population was waiting for the return of the Hungarian army. "We celebrated March 15," wrote one Pest citizen about the one-year anniversary of the revolution. "True, just secretly. We looked at one another, we clicked glasses, and everyone knew whom we were toasting. Our lips were silent, but our hearts were filled with patriotic thoughts."[44] Such displays were not a threat to the occupying forces, but they serve as a reminder of the breadth of support for the revolutionary cause in Buda-Pest, as well as a demonstration of the many ways that it could manifest itself.

The Hungarian leaders repaid this loyalty in full. In the spring of 1849, the main Hungarian army, which had vanished into the northern mountains in January, suddenly reappeared and won an impressive series of battles under the command of General Arthur Görgey. After months of retreats and evasions, the Hungarians found themselves on the offensive. Instead of carrying the war into Austria, Görgey's forces instead decided to assault the fortress of Buda, which was guarded by four thousand determined Austrians. Strategically, the move was a disaster, since it allowed the reeling Habsburg forces to regroup and tied up Hungarian forces for weeks. But the siege and capture of Buda had immense political symbolism, and at the time were viewed as Hungary's greatest triumph. "Will there be someone," mused Pál Hunfalvy in his diary, "who has seen the siege of Buda, has watched the people of Pest, and has lived there through worries and battles, who will describe these eighteen days as Thucydides would have?"[45] The days following the fall of Buda were filled with a victory parade, a massive celebration in the city park, and a burial procession for fallen Hungarian soldiers, in contrast to the treatment of the Austrian commander, who was thrown in a trench.[46] On June 5, Kossuth reentered Pest in a gilded carriage and was greeted by large, enthusiastic crowds. The Hungarian government and parliament also returned to the city, and on June 24, in a highly symbolic act, the Minister of the Interior officially created "Budapest" from the municipalities of Buda and Pest and Óbuda. The decree read in part: "the splendor, strength, power and greatness of the national capital is dependent on its unity, of which our country, attacked in an unjust war, now stands in most particular need."[47] Revolutionary Hungary now had its capital.

To the dispassionate observer, this newly-minted national capital must have looked like an oversized Potemkin village. People again were in the streets, Hungarian national symbols decorated the walls, and associations had reopened their doors. In early July, however, the Hungarian government was forced to abandon

Budapest and move to Szeged in southern Hungary. Austrian and Russian forces occupied the city later that month, making the unification of Budapest a dead letter. The Hungarian revolution would soon end, and Buda, Pest, and Óbuda would not be united again until 1872–1873.

The victorious Austrians attempted to remove all traces of the revolutionary "contagion" from Hungarian public life. They closed political clubs, shut down journals and newspapers, and arrested and imprisoned revolutionary leaders. German replaced Hungarian as the language of administration, public meetings were permitted only with the prior approval of the authorities, and the wearing of Hungarian colors or costumes was strictly forbidden. The famous Café Pilvax was renamed Café Herrengasse. Other shopkeepers were given forty-eight hours to add German to their shop signs and to remove all traces of red, white, and green lettering.[48] Individuals who had changed their surnames fared no better, and in September 1849, the Austrian authorities nullified all name changes that had been registered since March 1848.[49] Even the wearing of beards became suspect.

The revolutionary experience, however, could not be erased so simply. In part, this was because the Habsburgs themselves accepted some of the changes of the revolution, including, most notably, the abolition of serfdom. The principles of constitutional and parliamentary government, full equality for Jews, linguistic rights for all national groups, and expanded civil liberties had also taken firm root in 1848–1849, and would form the basis of liberal political demands in coming decades. Other gains were less tangible but no less significant: the revolution had broken down barriers to participation in public life, allowing a large number of ordinary men and women to demonstrate their political and patriotic convictions in the streets, in associations, and in symbolic displays. Such activities could be divisive, but it seems possible to argue that many residents of Buda-Pest came to see themselves, at least for short periods, as part of a Hungarian national community.[50] In this light, the 1848 revolutions are significant for contributing to the halting emergence of national political cultures in the second half of the nineteenth century.

The national framework would also influence the memory of the 1848 revolutions. As recent scholarship has shown, this "nationalization of memory" often elided the pan-European dimension of the revolutions.[51] Similar elisions occurred within Hungary, yet as Alice Freifeld has recently pointed out, perhaps "no country has so successfully exploited revolutionary failure for political gain."[52] The memory of 1848 has proven to be as elastic as it is durable, and every political regime in Hungary from 1867 to the present has sought to appropriate 1848 to bolster its own legitimacy. The revolution has stood for national independence, for radical social change, and for liberal reforms. It will be interesting to see, as Hungary becomes increasingly enmeshed in wider administrative, military, and economic structures, if the European dimensions of the revolution will also begin to reemerge.

Notes

1. Gustav Flaubert, *A Sentimental Education*, trans. Douglas Parmé (Oxford, 1989), 340.
2. A.J.P. Taylor, *The Course of German History: A Survey of the Development of Germany Since 1815* (New York, 1946), 68.
3. Peter Stearns, *1848: The Revolutionary Tide in Europe* (New York, 1974).
4. Jonathan Sperber, *The European Revolutions, 1848–1851* (Cambridge, 1984), 163. Also see Alex Körner, ed., *1848—A European Revolution? International Ideas and National Memories of 1848* (Houndshills, Eng., 2000); R.J.W. Evans and Harmut Pogge von Strandmann, eds., *The Revolutions in Europe 1848–1849* (Oxford, 2000); and Dieter Dowe et al., eds., *Europe in 1848: Revolution and Reform*, trans. David Higgins (New York, 2001).
5. As cited in Axel Körner, "The European Dimension in the Ideas of 1848 and the Nationalization of Its Memories," in Körner, *A European Revolution*, 15.
6. François Fejtö, ed., *The Opening of an Era: 1848* (New York, 1948) was an innovative work in this regard, but one that seems to have found little immediate resonance.
7. István Deák, *The Lawful Revolution: Louis Kossuth and the Hungarians 1848–1849* (New York, 1979). Interestingly, at the same time that Western scholars were learning about Hungary, Hungarian scholars were beginning to look beyond their own borders. As Deák has noted, "Every generation has judged the events of 1848–49 according to its own *Weltanschauung*, and only in recent years have some Hungarian historians come up with a more balanced judgment. They now see the Hungarian events of 1848–49 as part and parcel of a great ecumenical European upheaval, which put an end to one of the longest periods of relative European peace." See Deák, "The Revolution and the War of Independence," in *A History of Hungary*, ed. Peter F. Sugar (Bloomington and Indianapolis, 1990), 210.
8. Two influential works indicative of this trend are Lynn Hunt, *Politics, Culture, and Class in the French Revolution* (Berkeley, 1984) and Jonathan Sperber, *Rhineland Radicals: The Democratic Movement and the Revolution of 1848–1849* (Princeton, 1991).
9. The hyphen in "Buda-Pest" is a reminder that the cities of Buda and Pest were juridically separate until their union, briefly in 1849, and then permanently in 1872–1873. Many contemporaries used "Buda-Pest," and it appeared in works by Stephen Széchenyi, John Paget, Rudolf Alt, and others.
10. See Árpád von Klimó, "Die Bedeutung von 1848/49 für die politische Kultur Ungarns," in *1848 im europäische Kontext*, ed. Helgard Fröhlich, Margarete Grandner, and Michael Weinzierl (Vienna, 1999), 204–222; and Rudolf Jaworski, ed., *1848/49 Revolutionen in Ostmitteleuropa* (Munich, 1996).
11. Jiří Kořalka, "Revolutions in the Habsburg Monarchy," in Dowe, *Europe in 1848*, 153, 162. Not to be outdone, the Hungarians had their own constitutional *csárdás*, the Hungarian national dance.
12. László Deme, *The Radical Left in the Hungarian Revolution of 1848* (Boulder, CO, 1976), 47–48.
13. Deák, *Lawful Revolution*, 74.
14. Erzsébet F. Kiss, *Az 1848–1849-es magyar minisztériumok* (Budapest, 1987), 51–52.
15. Dezső Márkus, ed., *Magyar Törvénytár. 1836–1868 évi törvényczikkek* (Budapest, 1896), 244.
16. *Der Ungar*, 11 April 1848, 688, cited in Jenő Zsoldos, *1848–1849 a magyar zsidóság életében* (Budapest, 1998), 96.
17. "Nemzeti áldozatkészség," *Pesti Hirlap*, 25 May 1848, cited in Ferenc Bay, ed., *1848 napisajtója* (Budapest, 1948), 60–61.
18. Magyar Országos Levéltár R 151 *Az Ellenzéki Kör jegyzőkönyve*, Minutes of 16 April 1848 assembly.

19. Domokos Kosáry, *The Press During the Hungarian Revolution of 1848–1849* (Boulder, CO, 1986). Kosáry notes (p. 45) that the number of periodicals in Hungary rose from 65 in 1847 to 152 during the revolution.

20. R.R. Palmer, *Twelve Who Ruled* (Princeton, 1969), 147.

21. On name changes, see [Márton Szentivány], *Századunk névváltoztatásai* (Budapest, 1895), 15–22; and György Spira, *Vad tűzzel* (Budapest, 2000), 83–84. "Tailor," it should be noted, is a common translation of "Schroeder," if not the only possible one. Naturally, it had always been both easier and more common for people to switch between different first names (e.g., for "John" to call himself either Johann or János).

22. Hungarian orthography does not use double consonants, so the second "f" in Andorffy was a superfluous but aristocratic flourish, since there were a number of old noble families in Hungary with similar names (e.g., the Counts Dessewffy).

23. Changing one's name of course was nothing new to women, who did so when they married. On Pellett / Szivesy, see Budapest Főváros Levéltára IV. 1106/a. 99–1848.

24. Mihály Táncsics, *Életpályám* (Budapest, 1949), 245. Non-Jewish members of the March Youth also joined Táncsics's unit.

25. *Közlöny,* 26 June 1849, 526, in Zsoldos, *1848–1849,* 230–231.

26. "A pesti és aradi zsidók reformtervei," *Pesti Hirlap,* 3 May 1848, 393, in Zsoldos, *1848–1849,* 115–116 (quotation 115); "A Magyar Középponti Reformegylet felhívása," *Kossuth Hirlapja,* 10 August 1848, 159, in Zsoldos, *1848–1849,* 192–194.

27. *Hetilap,* 11 April 1848, 459.

28. Mór Jókai, "Congrev-Rakéták. Pillanatnyi fényül némelly sötétebb helyekre," *Életképek,* 21 May 1848, 657–660.

29. [Mária Csapó] Mrs. Sándor Vachott, *Emlékiratok (Szemelvények)* (Budapest, n.d.), 72.

30. Táncsics, *Életpályám,* 242. Táncsics had changed his name in 1848 from the more Slavic-sounding Stancsics.

31. Cited in Gabriella Hauch, "Did Women Have a Revolution? Gender Battles in the European Revolution of 1848/49," in Körner, *A European Revolution,* 65.

32. "A Radikál Magyar Hölgyek Kivánatai," *Életképek népszava,* 30 April 1848, 521–523. See also Robert Nemes, "Women in the 1848–1849 Hungarian Revolution," *Journal of Women's History* 13, no. 3 (2001): 193–207.

33. See Susan Zimmermann, *Die bessere Hälfte. Frauenbewegungen und Frauenbestrebungen im Ungarn der Habsburgermonarchie, 1848 bis 1918* (Vienna, 1999).

34. "A Radikál Magyar Hölgyek Kivánatai," 523.

35. János Szerenespataki, "Fölszólitás a magyar papsághoz," *Nemzeti Ujság,* 6 April 1848, 1089.

36. See Deme, *Radical Left,* 9–13.

37. Kořalka, "Revolutions in the Habsburg Monarchy," in Dowe, *Europe in 1848,* 153.

38. R.J.W. Evans, "1848–1849 in the Habsburg Monarchy," in Evans and von Strandmann, *Revolutions in Europe,* 202.

39. Pál Hunfalvy, *Napló 1848–1849* (Budapest, 1986), 159. Wearing red alone instead of the tricolor had been a mark of political radicalism since the beginning of the revolution.

40. On the theater, see Gábor Kerényi, ed., *Magyar színháztörténet* (Budapest, 1990), 355; on the Radical Circle, see Gyula Kéry, ed., *A magyar szabadságharcz története napi-krónikákban* (Budapest, 1899), 650–651.

41. Gábor Mátray, *Töredék jegyezmények Magyarország történetéből 1848/49-ben* (Budapest, 1989), 59, 86–87, 120–123.

42. Spira, *Vad tűzzel,* 92.

43. Mátray, *Töredék jegyezmények,* 72, 99.

44. György Gracza, *Az 1848-49-iki magyar szabadságharcz története* (Budapest, n.d.), 4:202–203, cited in Alice Freifeld, *Nationalism and the Crowd in Liberal Hungary, 1848–1914* (Washington, D.C., 2000), 84.

45. Hunfalvy, *Napló,* 272.

46. Freifeld, *Nationalism and the Crowd,* 85.

47. Ágnes Ságvári, *Budapest: The History of a Capital* (Budapest, 1973), 89–90.

48. Mátray, *Töredék jegyzemények,* 269.

49. Szentiványi, *Századunk névváltoztatásai,* 13–15.

50. The extent to which 1848 may also have encouraged Hungarians to see themselves as Europeans is a subject that needs further research.

51. See Körner, *A European Revolution;* and Charlotte Tacke, ed., *1848: Memory and Oblivion in Europe* (Brussels and New York, 2000).

52. Freifeld, *Nationalism and the Crowd,* 2. See also Martha Lampland, "The Politics of History: Historical Consciousness and the Hungarian Revolutions of 1848/49," *Hungarian Studies* 6, no. 2 (1990): 185–194; and John Mason, "Hungary's Battle for Memory," *History Today* 50, no. 3 (2000): 28–34.

Chapter 3

NOTHING WRONG WITH MY BODILY FLUIDS

Gymnastics, Biology, and Nationalism
in the Germanies before 1871

Daniel A. McMillan

As liberal-democratic revolutions swept across Central Europe in March of 1848, many liberals and democrats confronted a question whose importance seemed obvious: what should the gymnasts do? An early answer came from Ernst Steglich, a moderate Dresden liberal who edited a weekly journal titled *The Gymnast: Journal against Physical and Mental Crippling*. Published since 1846, this had become the newspaper of record for the burgeoning movement of gymnastics clubs.

"How should the gymnasts behave in these politically agitated times?" Steglich asked. "Like German men," he answered, "precisely because many men are no longer German and many Germans are no longer men." Declaring that "loyalty" and "truth" defined the German character, he concluded that no gymnast could support the moribund German Confederation, which had clearly ignored truth. Loyalty, on the other hand, did mean loyalty to the various German princes. "In a hundred battles [the German man] has sung: 'the Fatherland is my bride.' In a hundred battles the German nation has shown that it joyfully squirts [*verspritzt*] its blood for its princes." Further signaling his moderate liberal convictions, Steglich insisted that "no gymnast can be found at the side of those who, out of blind passion, low conceit, and filthy egoism, hate everything established and want to tear it down, and therefore mutinously stir up the masses."[1]

Before, but especially during and after the revolutionary years 1848–1849, Steglich and many other leading gymnasts insisted that gymnastics clubs should not discuss politics in their meetings, and not support any specific party or policy. At the same time, he and other liberal notables in the movement clearly signaled their own political goals: constitutional monarchy rather than democratic republic, and leadership by notables, to whom others should defer, rather than autonomous action by the masses. Such notables praised gymnastics mainly for its effect on the *body*: it would moderate physical appetites (and thus dampen political passions), and it would fend off the creeping effeminacy and physical degeneration that seemed to threaten everywhere. The reigning metaphor of this biologized discourse was that of the bodily humors: well-trained, obedient young gymnasts would abstain from alcohol or tobacco, moderate other appetites, refrain from masturbation, and strengthen their bodies. Thus they would retain enough "sap" or blood that they could "joyfully squirt" it at the proper time and place, i.e., in defense of a benevolent monarchy against a foreign enemy, preferably the French.

In contrast, gymnasts who wanted to mobilize their clubs for political action—or at least for political education and discussion—tended to praise the *experience* of being a gymnast. Egalitarian sociability and self-government within the clubs would enhance each member's self-respect and desire to participate in politics. Intimidating exercises would strengthen the will and build the confidence needed for active citizenship.

Thus, within the gymnastics movement after 1848—and frequently even before that—the more a gymnast wanted to restrain the movement's political activism, the more likely he would deploy a biologized language. By the 1860s, this biologized discourse and the political quiescence it heralded had gained a tenuous hegemony within the gymnastics movement, which had mobilized much of German liberalism's mass following. This biologized language may also have eased the transition between the emancipatory nationalism of the left and the increasingly racialist nationalism of the right, which took place on the territory of the German Empire from the 1870s to the 1890s.

Before developing this argument further, it is necessary to survey the history of the gymnastics movement, and its connection to liberal and democratic politics in nineteenth-century Germany.[2] Founded in 1811 to promote national renewal and rebellion against French occupation, the gymnastics clubs were the first political mass organization in modern German history.[3] Most German states banned gymnastics as a revolutionary threat in 1820, and repression decimated the movement after the democratic insurrections of 1849. Nevertheless, gymnastics clubs revived again and again, each time in greater numbers: 150 local groups and about 12,000 members in 1818; roughly 300 clubs in 1847, growing to perhaps 500 in the revolutionary years 1848–1849; and nearly 2,000 clubs and about 170,000 members in 1864.[4]

The gymnastics movement developed out of the same social milieu as German liberalism: the urban middle classes, especially but hardly exclusively in Protestant regions. Like liberalism, gymnastics took hold first among the elite "bourgeoisie of education" [*Bildungsbürgertum*], then among a progressively wider range of the middle strata, including by the 1860s such "petty bourgeois" groups as artisans and primary schoolteachers, as well as a part of the emerging working class. Gymnastics clubs gave liberal political activism its first organized venue, and they were always seen—by friend and foe alike—as bulwarks of "progressive" or "liberal" sentiment and values. Such values and sentiments included a longing for German unity, praise for active citizenship (practiced within the clubs), and a quasi-religious faith in progress through education, whereby exercise completed the individual's harmonious *Bildung*, developing body and character in tandem with the intellect.[5]

Liberal notables led many gymnastics clubs, if not most, while the rank-and-file members constituted a large part of liberalism's broader petit bourgeois constituency. Alone among nineteenth-century Germany's nationalist associations, the gymnastics movement maintained a continuity of organizational forms, personnel, and agitational practices across the three greatest eras of liberal and nationalist popular mobilization before the German Empire was created: the 1810s, the 1840s, and the 1860s. When militant democrats seceded from the liberal camp in 1848, they took a large part of the gymnastics movement with them; so too did the emerging labor movement in the 1860s and the socialist party in the 1890s use gymnastics for political ends.

This link between gymnastics and politics had emerged in two steps, framed in two separate discourses, within two distinct sets of circumstances. The pedagogical theory of the late German Enlightenment emphasized chiefly physiological arguments for exercise: civilization had allegedly weakened the naturally healthy human body with rich food, warm clothing, and insufficient exercise. Among other evils, this luxury produced an excess of the bodily humors, which in adolescence would seek an outlet in masturbation, in turn draining young men of their vitality and aging them prematurely. These physical weaknesses in turn corrupted morality and character: permanently weak and sickly, accustomed to satisfying every appetite and avoiding every discomfort, men of the late eighteenth century supposedly lacked loyalty, determination, willpower, and physical and moral courage.[6]

In these early texts, the link to politics appeared only faintly, in vague references to the need for moral courage in citizenship. The more direct instrumentalization of exercise for politics came after Napoleon defeated and occupied Prussia in 1806. When Friedrich Ludwig Jahn responded to this national emergency by founding the gymnastics movement, he seldom spoke of physiology, and instead praised the experience of exercise. Jahn believed that joyful play in the open air would cement bonds of affection between his young gymnasts, which they could then generalize to an attachment to the German nation. Social equality at the place of exercise would further enhance and symbolize the patriotic bond. Undertaking intimidating exercises on the high bar or climbing rope, they would overcome their fear, strengthen their will, and enhance their confidence. Thus improved and ennobled, they would rally to the defense of the Fatherland.[7]

During the movement's first decade, both discourses freely mingled, and advocates gladly used whatever arguments they could to win others to the gymnastic cause. Some of the most vivid imagery of health, fertility, and the ample supply of bodily fluids came from the radically democratic gymnasts led by Karl Follen, whose brother Adolf Ludwig edited an 1819 collection of gymnasts' songs.[8]

After the movement was crushed in 1819–1820, however, a process of differentiation set in. Gymnastics in voluntary associations was politically suspect, and so gymnastic exercise was first revived in private schools, and in government-controlled facilities in Munich and Stuttgart. The first general calls to reestablish gymnastics and rehabilitate it politically came from medical doctors and educators who warned of pervasive physical degeneration, especially among students at elite secondary schools: heavy mental exertion supposedly enervated the body, unless balanced by physical exercise.[9] A German parliament first discussed a plan for gymnastics in schools in March of 1837. Addressing the upper house of the Saxon *Landtag,* a Dr. Grossmann warned that "our era inclines … from strength to weakness, from the courage to live to weariness of life." Ill health threatened not only the overtaxed students, but also the children who worked in Saxony's textile mills, where they "get used up so early [in life] that they must physically wither."[10] Reporting on Grossmann's initial petition, a deputation of the upper house likewise warned of advancing physical decline, especially among elite students, who faced inevitably increasing mental exertion as the sum of knowledge expanded.[11]

Probably alluding to masturbation, Grossmann promised that "many sins, which lurk in the darkness, are rooted out" by gymnastics, as "famous pedagogues" had long recognized. Repeatedly assuring the state's ministers that gymnastics posed no political danger, Grossmann nonetheless saw two political benefits. Shared exercise during the youthful years would forge bonds of affection between boys who would later become either citizens or civil servants, and thus would mitigate antagonisms between state and society. More generally, Grossman declared that a "physically hearty younger generation, not raised like [fragile] hothouse plants, is the state's most precious treasure." Grossmann also argued that gymnastically trained boys would need only a short time for military training and thus would fear conscription less. In all of these debates, no one argued that exercise produced more active, independent citizens.[12]

During the relatively depoliticized 1830s, gymnastics for girls also got its start, notably through the private lessons offered in Dresden by J.A.L. Werner, who also helped inspire the 1837 *Landtag* debate. Then and later, the men who taught girls' gymnastics never argued that it promoted patriotism or otherwise prepared anyone for citizenship. Instead they promised that it would improve girls' health and ward off creeping degeneracy. Writing in 1844, a Dr. Stucke warned that women in poor health passed on their weaknesses to future generations, accelerating the degeneration (*Entartung*) visible in every European city. Exercise for girls would reverse this decline, making future generations "healthier, stronger, more agile, more cheerful, prettier, and better."[13]

When the gymnastics movement of men's voluntary associations revived in the 1840s, and began to grow in political militance, a sharper disjunction emerged between the politically safe language of physical health, and the more provocative idea that exercise emboldened citizens to act politically. Already in 1846, the liberal notables who led so many clubs worked to dampen the clubs' political enthusiasm. Gymnastics, they argued, had nothing to do with politics, and gymnasts should never discuss politics in their meetings.[14] Writing in 1846, the aforementioned Ernst Steglich declared that the purpose of all gymnastics was *"the freedom of the gymnast."* He explained that "freedom" meant the ability to use all of one's physical and mental powers, and the freedom from physical and moral weakness. His contemporaries had suffered a general decline in health because they had neglected their bodies; lack of movement let their bodily "juices" or "humors" (*Saefte*) stagnate, producing hypochondria and a range of other ills. Gymnastic exercise would get these "juices" moving again, enlivening the whole body. He also argued that gymnastics strengthened the will, whereby "will" meant control over one's passions and appetites, and control meant "freedom." Indirectly attacking the more politically active gymnasts, Steglich complained that not enough gymnastics teachers understood this truth about freedom. If they did, then more gymnasts would gain their own freedom, instead of "preaching to others" about it. Only when a people had "moral freedom," Steglich admonished, would they have political freedom, "for only prejudice and passion" block the path to freedom.[15]

Moral freedom might well remain a distant goal, but the March revolutions of 1848 soon brought complete freedom of association, assembly, and press in most German states. Many gymnastics clubs quickly became party clubs, debating the burning political issues of the day. When the democratic party took shape in opposition to moderate liberalism, dozens of gymnastics clubs promptly advertised their democratic allegiance: only a democratic republic, they declared, could be an acceptable form of government for a united Germany.[16]

With the new political openness and activism came more frequent utterances of the discourse praising gymnastics as a school of citizenship. Dedicating the new *Turnplatz* (gymnastics facility) in the Saxon town of Bautzen, on 18 June 1848, a club officer named Schaarschmidt called it

> a *school of energy, of order, and of civic-mindedeness,* so that there should be as little lack of courage and energy to repel any attempt at oppression—whether from a foreign ruler or our own—as a lack of virtue and civic spirit upon the great *Turnplatz* of public life.

The reference to "our own" ruler must have seemed rather pointed to the civil and military officials who attended the Bautzen festival.[17]

During the revolutionary years, most of the senior leaders of the movement advised their fellow gymnasts to separate politics from gymnastics: join political party clubs if you must, so they said, but limit yourselves to exercise and sociability when participating in a gymnastics club. The movement's newspaper hewed to this line with determination.[18] Even before the failed democratic insurrections of 1849, the editors expressed sympathy for any German government that would shut down gymnastics clubs that had behaved as political clubs.[19]

After the 1849 insurrections, many German states did in fact selectively repress the gymnastics movement, shutting down clubs that had displayed excessive political militance, while sparing those that had stuck mainly to exercise, song, and less controversial affirmations of national sentiment. In Saxony, the government signaled its views in September 1849 by planting an unsigned essay in the *Leipziger Zeitung*.[20] Gymnastics, it declared, had become "indisputably the most pernicious instrument" of revolutionary democrats; in the Dresden insurrection barely five months earlier, the gymnasts had been the "*only* capable fighters" for the "party of insurrection," while not a single one had joined the defenders of "law and order." The article further compared the gymnasts and their sponsors among pedagogical theorists to "termites," which had been quietly gnawing, unseen, for decades. Contemporary youth had been badly misled, "as if ... by a new pied piper of Hamelin."

Denouncing gymnastics as "a weed," or as "seed" sown by "evildoers," this article nonetheless affirmed that youth badly needed exercise. The population had been in physical decline since the Middle Ages, and now suffered from a wide range of ills, especially in the cities and in manufacturing regions. Hedonism had become general, and youths prematurely aged. Therefore, it concluded, the state must promote gymnastic exercise in the public schools, but only to strengthen the body. School officials should also strictly supervise the gymnastics clubs of adults, in order to keep them from engaging in any political activity.

During the 1850s, vigorous police work reduced the movement to about 100 clubs, or roughly one-fifth of its size in early 1849. Politically militant gymnasts— if they had not already been imprisoned or shot—often fled to the United States, where many later fought on the Union side in the Civil War. Those gymnasts who remained in Germany, and those clubs that survived, generally took the German state governments at their word: those gymnasts suppressed political activism within the clubs, asked governments to introduce gymnastics in the schools, and redefined their own contribution to national unity and the public welfare. After the early 1850s, gymnasts seldom argued that exercise and club sociability produced active citizens. They emphasized instead that exercise made young men fit for military service, the better to defend the nation against attack, presumably from France. They spoke of widespread moral and physical decline, and offered gymnastics as a cure. They formed volunteer fire departments, the better to use their agility and strength in the service of the common good.[21]

All of these purposes or functions for gymnastics helped the movement's leaders focus on physiological, or otherwise biological (or crypto-biological) arguments in favor of gymnastics. The ascendancy of this biologized discourse, and the political quietism it heralded, found expression at the first national festival of German gymnasts, held at Coburg in June of 1860. The movement had begun its spectacular revival about one year earlier, as state governments applied the law of association more liberally, while the war of 1859 seemed to herald new dangers and opportunities in foreign affairs: Piedmont, in alliance with Louis Napoleon's France, defeated the Habsburgs and set in motion the unification of Italy. Not only did Piedmont's triumph set an inspiring example for German nationalists, but it also served as a powerful warning that revolutionary nationalism was on the march in France again, and that Germans needed their own nation-state if they did not want to repeat their painful experience of the first Napoleonic wars.

Roughly 1,000 delegates from clubs in all the German lands gathered in Coburg for three days of celebration and discussion. Most of the leaders present strove—through their speeches and through their mastery of parliamentary procedure—to suppress any overt political activism. In particular, they thwarted a move to establish a national umbrella organization linking all gymnastics clubs. When one delegate called for a toast honoring those gymnasts who had become political refugees during the 1850s, the meeting's chair distracted the delegates from the ensuing conflict by getting everyone to sing a patriotic song from the Wars of Liberation.[22]

Instead, the movement's leaders emphasized that exercise prepared gymnasts for military service, implied that a war would soon bring about German unity, and cloaked their appeals in biologized language. After calling for all clubs to begin military training, especially bayonet practice, a club leader from Herborn (in Nassau) issued a closing exhortation to the delegates:

> Thus I wish that [just] as the human heart drives the blood through all parts of the human body to nourish, strengthen, and enliven [it], this gymnasts' assembly in the heart of the German Fatherland also pumps an enlivening energy [*belebende Kraft*] through all German regions, that the German people rejuvenates itself, and especially that youth will become manly, because only a people with energy and will can [long] survive in the flow of time.[23]

The gymnasts' shifting discourses concerning the meaning of exercise and its relationship to politics have at least two broader implications for the study of German history. First, as nationalism on the territory of the German Empire moved from the political left to the political right, the nation became defined more often in racialist terms, and nationalists increasingly concerned themselves with public health and the emerging "science" of eugenics.[24] The association of biological language and ideas with political quietism in the gymnastics movement may well have paved the way for this change in German nationalism, and may also provide clues to its underlying logic.

A second point is less obvious, but perhaps of greater import. Both discourses produced by the gymnasts—politically subdued and heavily biologized, on the one hand, and politically assertive and experiential, on the other—reflected a broader tendency in German liberalism to see individual character and energy as the fundamental prerequisites of good citizenship, and the sheet anchors of a free and stable political order. This author has elsewhere argued[25] that an unusually heavy political emphasis on individual character may have distinguished Germany from other Western and Central European polities during the nineteenth and twentieth centuries. If this argument evokes the memory of the moribund *Sonderweg* thesis, so be it.[26]

This peculiarity of German history—if peculiarity it be—had roots as varied as they were deep, but three possible sources merit special attention. One was the distinctively German ideal of *Bildung*, which is usually translated as "education," but which means a great deal more: the autonomous development of an individual's many potentialities into a unique and harmonious whole. The gymnasts proclaimed themselves champions of *Bildung*, matching the body's development to that which the schools provided for the mind.

The politicization of individual character may also have drawn strength from the narrow limits placed on public discourse and political activity in the German states during the formative years before 1848. Constrained in their ability to write and talk about the actual levers of power—which in all states remained firmly in monarchical hands—German liberals found it easier and more natural to think of politics in psychologized terms, to speak of character rather than of explicit political programs. One should of course not take this argument too far. Saxony and the southern and southwestern states did acquire elected parliaments with limited powers, some in 1818 and others in the period 1830–1832, following the Paris revolution of 1830. Even in the constitutional states, however, press censorship usually remained strict, and no explicitly political voluntary associations were tolerated.

A third point at which the political emphasis on character took root was in German liberals' pervasive and stubborn faith in consensus, and their corresponding belief that political conflict was illegitimate. These beliefs have long been regarded as an unfortunate peculiarity of German political development,[27] although their origins, and some of their implications, remain poorly understood.

The postulate that character determines politics fits naturally with the faith in consensus, indeed it is a central assumption underpinning that faith, because only a citizenry of rational and virtuous men could be expected to subordinate their disparate inclinations to the achievement of an idealized common good. Unfortunately, the obverse of consensus is intolerance, and if good character would naturally lead to support for liberalism (and thus consensus), opponents of liberalism would have to be very bad men indeed. Karl von Rotteck, for example, divided opponents of the "party of progress" into six categories: those who did not recognize that natural law must dictate positive law; men gripped by an irrational fear of revolution; aristocrats and others who clung to their traditional privileges; people "whose God is merely the most immediate material interest"; "deplorable weathervanes" who changed their opinions from day to day, influenced or intimidated by others; and men who supported progress but were overly timid.[28]

This personalization of politics—and demonization of opponents—fueled the bitter fratricidal conflict between the liberal movement and its democratic twin during the revolutionary years 1848–49. So too did it inspire liberal persecution of political Catholicism during the *Kulturkampf* of the 1870s, and liberal support for the suppression of Social Democracy thereafter. The Social Democrats, themselves the offspring of liberalism in so many ways, constructed a hermetically sealed alternative culture,[29] prizing ideological conformity above practical political goals, longing for a revolutionary utopia, and repaying their own political ostracism with contempt for the other parties.

Hopelessly divided by antagonisms between the separate parties, the imperial German parliament was in no position to wrest greater power from the crown. Unlike the nations of Western Europe, Germany did not make the transition to parliamentary government until war and revolution destroyed the old order in 1918. Divisions between the parties undermined the Weimar Republic, and ended only when Hitler—who took most of his voters from the liberal camp—abolished all parties save one, declared consensus the order of the day, and set out to create a new, yet familiar, kind of German citizen: healthy and vigorous in body, self-sacrificing in character, and triumphant—so to speak—in will.

Notes

1. Ernst Steglich, "Wie haben sich die Turner in der jetzigen politisch bewegten Zeit zu verhalten?" *Der Turner. Zeitschrift gegen geistige und leibliche Verkrüppelung* 3 (1848): 89–90.
2. This survey of the movement's history is based on the author's Ph.D. thesis: "Germany Incarnate: Politics, Gender, and Sociability in the Gymnastics Movement, 1811–1871" (Columbia University, 1997).
3. Writing about the period 1815–1820, E.R. Huber characterized the importance of the gymnastics movement in this way: "Unter den organisierten Kräften, die sich der Sache der deutschen Einheit und Freiheit verschrieben, nahm das von *Friedrich Ludwig Jahn* (1778–1852) gestiftete Turnwesen bald den ersten Platz ein." In Huber, *Deutsche Verfassungsgeschichte seit 1789,* 4 vols. (Stuttgart, 1957–1961), vol. 1, 704. Similarly, Hans-Ulrich Wehler characterized the gymnasts as the "bedeutendste 'organisatorische Erscheinungsform' des frühen deutschen Nationalismus," in his *Deutsche Gesellschaftsgeschichte,* vol. 2 (Munich, 1987), 402. Thomas Nipperdey described the gymnasts as "an early form [or precursor] of political party," attributing to them far-reaching political goals, saying that they profoundly influenced an entire generation of schoolboys and university students: "Ihr Geist hat, auch unmittelbar nach 1815, eine ganze Generation von Schülern und Studenten ergriffen, sie waren - über alle deutsche Staatsgrenzen hinweg - eine Bewegung, ja - man sprach vom 'Turnstaat' - ein Staat im Staat." Nipperdey, *Deutsche Geschichte 1800–1866. Bürgerwelt und starker Staat* (Munich, 1983), 279.
4. Dieter Düding, *Organisierter gesellschaftlicher Nationalismus in Deutschland (1808–1847): Bedeutung und Funktion der Turner- und Sängervereine für die deutsche Nationalbewegung* (Munich, 1984), 58–60, 66–99, 319; McMillan, "Germany Incarnate," ch. 3; Georg Hirth, ed., *Zweites statistisches Jahrbuch der Turnvereine Deutschlands* (Leipzig, 1865).
5. See especially good examples in the writings of the great pedagogue Adolf Diesterweg, who directed a group of gymnasts in the 1810s, and wrote often about the need for physical education in subsequent decades. See in particular his 1842 address to the *Pädagogische Gesellschaft* in Berlin, "Alaaf Preussen!," reprinted in Georg Hirth and F.R. Gasch, eds., *Das gesamte Turnwesen,* Part 1 (Vienna, 1894), 599–608.

6. See in particular J.C.F. GutsMuths, *Gymnastik für die Jugend*, unaltered edition of the 1793 first edition (Vienna, 1893).

7. Johann Jakob Wilhelm Bornemann, *Der Turnplatz in der Hasenheide* (Berlin, 1812); Edmund Neuendorff, *Geschichte der neueren deutschen Leibesübung*, 4 vols. (Dresden, 1932–1936), 2: 133–156.

8. Adolf Ludwig Follen, *Freye Stimmen Frischer Jugend* (Jena, 1819).

9. In particular, Karl Ignaz Lorinser, "Zum Schutz der Gesundheit in den Schulen," *Medicinische Zeitung* (1836), Nr. 1.

10. Kingdom of Saxony, *Mittheilungen über die Verhandlungen des Landtags* (1837): 1507.

11. Kingdom of Saxony, *Landtags-Acten* (1836–1837), Beilage zur 1sten Kammer, 1ste Sammlung, 406.

12. Saxony, *Mittheilungen* (1837): 1508.

13. Dr. Stucke, "Einige Bemerkungen über die Frage, ob das Turnen auch Mädchen und Jungfrauen zu empfehlen sei?" *Jahrbücher der Turnkunst* 2 (1844): 98–105, esp. 99–100, 105.

14. E.g., "Turnwesen und Politik," *Der Turner* 2 (1847): 249–252; August Hitzschold, "Die Turnvereine und die politische Opposition," *Der Turner* 2 (1847): 337–340.

15. Ernst Steglich, "Was ist das Ziel der Turnerei?" *Der Turner* 1 (1846): 50, 58, 66–67, emphasis in the original.

16. See the statutes of the *Demokratischer Turnerbund*, published *in Der Turner* 3 (1848): 408–409.

17. *Der Turner* 3 (1848): 219–220.

18. Ernst Steglich, "Wie haben sich die Turner in der jetzigen politisch bewegten Zeit zu verhalten?" *Der Turner* 3 (1848): 89–90; lengthy footnote, *Der Turner* 4 (1849): 59–60; Anonymous, "Noch etwas Politik!" *Der Turner* 4 (1849): 93–94; the opposing view in Anonymous, "Die Politik," *Der Turner* 4 (1849): 41–42, 49–52, 57–59.

19. Editorial of 8 March, in which the editor accused "southern German" gymnastics clubs of using gymnastics only as a pretext for political activism, and concluded: "Wir dürfen es daher auch den dortigen Regierungen nicht zu sehr verargen, wenn sie dagegen einschritten." In *Der Turner* 4 (1849): 75.

20. Anonymous, "Das Turnwesen im Königreiche Sachsen betr."; *Leipziger Zeitung*, Nr. 273, 30 September 1849, 5161–5164. A rough draft of this article, dated 18 September 1849 and marked "Für Aufnahme in die Leipziger Zeitung," is in the files of the Saxon Education Ministry, Staatsarchiv Dresden, Ministerium für Volksbildung, Nr. 13075.

21. See the report of the club in Markranstädt (Saxony), *Deutsche Turn-Zeitung* (1858): 54–55; D.G.M. Schreber, "Die Turnanstalt als Schule der Männlichkeit," *Neue Jahrbücher der Turnkunst* (1858): 169–170. By 1869, fully 49 percent of the gymnastics clubs had either a fire brigade or a rescue company, according to the movement's third statistical yearbook, as analyzed by Michael Krüger in his *Körperkultur und Nationsbildung: Die Geschichte des Turnens in der Reichsgründungsära - eine Detailstudie über die Deutschen* (Schorndorf, 1996), 69.

22. Theodor Georgii, ed., *Das erste deutsche Turn- und Jugendfest zu Coburg den 16.–19. Juni 1860. Ein Erinnerungsblatt für Deutschlands Turner* (Leipzig, 1860), 51, 81.

23. Ibid., 121–122.

24. See in particular Paul Weindling, *Health, Race and German Politics between National Unification and Nazism, 1870–1945* (New York, 1989). However, as Weindling points out, eugenicist thinking was very much not a monopoly of the nationalist right.

25. "The Politics of Energy and Character: Gymnastics and the Particularities of German Liberalism," presented at the workshop, "Liberalism and Civil Society in Modern Britain and Germany," Harvard University, 15–17 November 1996.

26. That is, the thesis that Germany followed a "special path" to modernity, although the content of Germany's putative distinctiveness (read: pathology) has varied widely in the his-

torical literature. The standard critique of the *Sonderweg* thesis is David Blackbourn and Geoff Eley, *The Peculiarities of German History. Bourgeois Society and Politics in Nineteenth-Century Germany* (New York, 1984). This author contends that although Germany's development very closely resembled that of its neighbors—making any sweeping argument about a "special path" seem exaggerated—certain very specific differences in political culture had far-reaching consequences.

27. Ralf Dahrendorf, *Society and Democracy in Germany* (New York, 1967).
28. Rotteck, "Bewegungs-Partei und Stillstands-Partei," *Staats-Lexikon* 2 (1835): 562–563.
29. Vernon L. Lidtke, *The Alternative Culture: Socialist Labour in Imperial Germany* (New York, 1985).

Chapter 4

BETWEEN EMPIRE AND NATION

The Bohemian Nobility, 1880–1918

Eagle Glassheim

In 1898 Oswald Count Thun introduced a haunting metaphor for what nationalism was doing to the Habsburg Empire. "Austria is crawling out of her skin," he wrote. "The moment is coming, with giant strides, when the national element alone will prevail—We (the nobility) will be crippled, because, duty bound, we feel ourselves to be more Imperial than the Emperor."[1]

When Thun wrote these words, he was lamenting the nationalist convulsions that had seized Bohemia after the Badeni Language Ordinances of 1897. Once again, the Czech-German national conflict had turned the Austrian parliament into a madhouse, with inkpots flying and legislative activity at a standstill. Thun and his fellow Bohemian nobles in the parliament not only shrank from the populist demagoguery of the Czech and German nationalists, but they also feared that nationalism would tear apart the Habsburg Empire. At the same time, though, the two leading noble political parties held fast to alliances with some of the very same national parties that were behind the chaos in the parliament. This irony gives some sense of the difficult balancing act, between empire and nation, that nobles maintained in the last decades of the Habsburg Monarchy's existence.

The Bohemian nobility serves as a particularly prominent and revealing indicator of the rapid, but contested, nationalization of political culture in the Austrian lands of the Monarchy. Poised to benefit substantially from economic modernization, the nobility was ambivalent towards related processes of social and political emancipation. They implicitly raised the question whether nationalism was an inevitable outgrowth of the awakening of the masses, or if alternatives to a national order were viable in a modern society. Along with Jews, army officers, and many bureaucrats, nobles had a tremendous stake in the shape of the new order.

On the one hand, most nobles realized the need to adapt to economic, social, and political changes that altered the face of Europe and the Monarchy in the nineteenth century. Their survival as a wealthy and influential class depended on it. But too much adaptation would undermine their distinction as a caste apart in Habsburg society. Citing the influential work of Pierre Bourdieu, Anthony Cardoza points out how modernization forced the Italian nobility "to change so as to conserve."[2] This article focuses on how members of the Bohemian high nobility—those of the rank of Count and above—changed in order to conserve, how they tried to save their status and wealth by adapting themselves to a changing society and eventually to nationalist politics. As the primary source of wealth in the Austrian half of the Dual Monarchy made the transition from property to industry and finance, the Bohemian nobility diversified their investments and maintained their position as an economic elite. Socially, they reversed an early nineteenth-century engagement with bourgeois patriotic circles, thereby maintaining their exclusivity and status.

Nobles faced their biggest challenge, but also some hope of salvation, in the field of politics. Though Emperor Franz Joseph introduced constitutional rule and steadily expanded suffrage after 1860, the Austrian political system retained a few distinctly undemocratic features, a fact that Bohemian nobles exploited with some success. In addition, nobles managed to maintain considerable influence at court. At the Emperor's behest, they dominated top governmental posts in both Prague and Vienna. But because nobles also had to work within a parliamentary system, they could not ignore democratic political forces entirely. By the 1880s, Czech and German national parties controlled enough seats in the *Reichsrat* to make them necessary partners for achieving a stable majority. The Monarchy thus depended on a balance of national and supranational forces, and the nobility strove to be the "weight in the balance," the key to the precarious system's survival.

The greatest threat was that the balance would tip permanently in favor of nationalism, bringing down the Empire and the nobility both. Well aware of this danger, nobles advanced their own version of Czech and German national identities, moderated by a strong imperial loyalty. Though such a national-imperial identity had many adherents—perhaps more than historians have credited—by the late nineteenth century it was increasingly beleaguered.[3] Nationalists would have little patience with so-called "amphibians," and they criticized nobles for remaining aloof from national battles. As national assertiveness increased, noble dedication to the Emperor rose proportionately. Unlike in neighboring Germany, where the Prussian Junkers found a niche in democratic politics, most of Bohemia's nobles gravitated away from their bourgeois national allies, choosing, finally, empire over nation.[4]

Changing to Stay the Same: Nobles and Modernization in the Nineteenth Century

Traditional historiography has cast doubt on the desire or ability of nobles to come to terms with the modernization of society and politics.[5] The very word "aristocracy" has a premodern ring to it, both quaint and a little menacing to the democratic ear. To Marxists, aristocracy, and the landed property that underlay it, was the bedrock of feudalism, which was the dominant economic, social, and political system up to the eighteenth century. Eric Hobsbawm and countless others have written of the birth of "modernity" in the dual French and Industrial Revolutions of the late eighteenth and early nineteenth centuries, revolutions presumed to have doomed the nobility to a rapid decline relative to the "triumphant middle class."[6]

With the 1981 publication of Arno Mayer's provocative book *The Persistence of the Old Regime in Europe,* historians have begun to rethink the thesis of aristocratic decline in the nineteenth century.[7] David Higgs has shown that French nobles retained both considerable status and class cohesiveness well into the nineteenth century.[8] For Italy, Anthony Cardozza writes of a nobility that survived modernization by both diversifying its economic interests and closing itself off to bourgeois influence.[9] Historians of the Habsburg Monarchy too have belatedly begun to examine the persistence of noble power and wealth in the last decades of the Monarchy's existence. Recent Czech and German research has demonstrated that in Bohemia, as in much of Europe, the nobility was still around throughout this period of change, still very wealthy, and still wielding substantial influence.

Nobles and Economic Modernization

Just as Habsburg and Bohemian society was changing dramatically in the nineteenth century, so too was the Bohemian nobility. Ever since its mythical origins in the thirteenth century,[10] the Bohemian nobility regularly reinvented itself. As royal/imperial power advanced and receded, nobles sought to defend their interests or press their advantages. They also responded flexibly to economic changes. As early industrialism spread in the eighteenth century, Bohemian nobles took advantage of new sources of profit, digging mines on their land and expanding into food processing and light industry.[11] In the nineteenth century, nobles were prominent investors in Austrian banks and railroads.[12] In the 1870s, noble-owned foundries produced 41 percent of Bohemia's iron;[13] in 1886 they owned 80 of the province's 120 sugar refineries.[14]

Bohemia's nobles also made the transition from seigneurialism to capitalist agriculture relatively smoothly. When Joseph II abolished serfdom in 1781, nobles turned increasingly to wage labor, and successfully maintained production. During the pre-March period (1815–1848), the Bohemian nobility tended to favor the abolition of mandatory labor services (*robot*) performed by the peasantry.[15] The final elimination of seigneurialism in 1848 left nobles with an economic windfall; they promptly invested government and peasant compensation payments in stock, industry, and improvements of their remaining property.[16] As Milan Myška writes, "Estate owners transformed themselves into great agrarian capitalists."[17]

Because the Bohemian nobility possessed a large proportion of noble-managed domanial land (as opposed to rustical land with peasant tenure), the 1848 reform left nobles with millions of hectares of farm and forest.[18] Writing in 1908, Alfred Maria Mayer called Bohemia "a land of latifundists *par excellence.*" While Bohemia's proportion of land in large holdings was close to that in East-Elbian Prussia, the number of landholders was far smaller. A mere 362 families owned 36 percent of the surface area of Bohemia in the early twentieth century.[19] The largest holdings, in the hands of the 38 landowners with over 10,000 ha (hectares), covered 18 percent of the province's area.[20] Nobles made up the overwhelming majority of the large estate owners; the top 63 personal landowners during the First World War were nobles or royalty. The Krumlov/Krumau Schwarzenbergs alone owned 176,000 ha, the so-called "Schwarzenberg Kingdom" in southern Bohemia. To put that in perspective, the Schwarzenberg estates spanned 680 square miles, or approximately 65 percent of the area of Rhode Island. The Colloredo family owned 58,000 ha, the Fürstenbergs 40,000 ha, the Liechtensteins 37,000 ha (not to mention scores of thousands more hectares in Moravia).[21] No non-noble holdings came anywhere close to these vast estates.

On both arable land and forests, nobles took advantage of the economy of scale. Families such as the Schwarzenbergs and the Waldsteins had been the first to mechanize farming in Bohemia, and their estate management tended to be efficient and progressive (though their pension funds and social insurance were decidedly paternalistic in tone).[22] Nobles also happened to own the best land in Bohemia, and among the best in Europe. With the final emancipation of the peasantry in 1848, nobles smartly held on to much of their most productive land. Efficient practices, mechanization, and good land combined to produce large-estate grain yields that were more than twice those of smaller holdings (under 200 ha).[23] Forests, which made up around two-thirds of large estate total acreage in the historic provinces, were rarely profitable at anything less than 1,000 ha. Only large estate owners could afford to hire foresters and to develop long-range harvesting plans.[24]

Nobles and Social Modernization of the Habsburg Empire

A good Marxist might ask whether a noble is still noble if he becomes a successful capitalist. If "nobility" were defined solely in terms of the relationship to production, then the answer would be no. Both in terms of law and of economic behavior, Bohemian nobles were no longer feudal after 1848.[25] But they nonetheless retained a distinct social identity as a nobility well into the twentieth century. Part of this collective identity had economic roots. Nobles owned vast estates in Bohemia and Moravia, and contemporaries often used the term "great estate owner" (*Grossgrundbesitzer/Velkostatkář*) and "noble" interchangeably in the late nineteenth century. But a constellation of other elements defined their identity as a separate and influential caste in capitalist Europe. Nobles shared actual ties of kinship (maintained through endogamy) and friendship (maintained through social exclusivity).[26] They also shared symbolic ties: preservation of a distinct honor code, veneration of family lineage, and the idealization of a manor-house lifestyle. Writing of Italian nobles in the late nineteenth century, Anthony Cardoza could just as well have been referring to the aristocracy in Bohemia and Moravia: "Social resources, when accompanied by sufficient wealth, allowed a portion of the old nobility to reinvent a collective identity for themselves, an identity that helped to preserve their cohesion and exclusivity, and to legitimate their influential role in public life."[27]

Central to this exclusivity was the preservation of the "house," meaning the family and its property. The Bohemian high nobility strictly protected its bloodlines, rarely marrying outside of a small group of high aristocrats with the titles of count and prince. Nobles were particularly aware of family histories, often paying full-time archivists and maintaining substantial historical libraries. They also held on to the family patrimony through the practice of primogeniture, which was in many cases legally protected by entail, known in German as a *Fideikommiss*. These specially granted dispensations required imperial permission to break, thus ensuring the continuity of a family's estate. In 1900, there were still 58 *Fideikommisse* in Bohemia and 24 in Moravia-Silesia.[28] Even families without an officially sanctioned entail tended to practice primogeniture, the result being a remarkably stable group at the height of the Bohemian landed elite into the twentieth century.

The "house" found its concrete expression in noble chateaux, which crowned sprawling country estates. Just as nobles had marked their ascendancy in the seventeenth century by building great Baroque palaces and mansions in Bohemia, in the nineteenth century many families used architecture to reassert the historical depth of their claims to distinction and power. Turning to historic styles, particularly neo-Gothic, they stressed the continuity of family tradition and their enduring status as a caste apart. As the Harrach family laid the foundation stone for their castle, Hradek, in 1841, they evoked this symbolic mixture of past and present. It is the master's intention, the dedication read,

> to leave behind for centuries to come—for himself and his heirs—a worthy abode in the bosom of Bohemia, not only as an ornament given in [this] highly resplendent castle, but also as a proof of his devotion and heartfelt love for his ancestral homeland … May our Lord give that this castle will shine for centuries as the seat of [our] glorious … dynasty that arose in gray antiquity.[29]

Like so many other castles in Bohemia, Hradek marked the junction of past and present, noble and subject, family and country. It was to be a renewed symbol of nobility, a new seat for an old family.

The mid-century renovation of Sychrov, a Baroque castle in Northern Bohemia, provides a splendid example of the symbolism wrapped up in nineteenth century aristocratic architecture. In 1820 the Rohans, a recent French émigré family, purchased Sychrov from the Waldsteins (the Wallensteins of Thirty Years' War fame). Soon fully integrated into the cosmopolitan Habsburg nobility, the Rohans rebuilt the castle in the neo-Gothic style popular among Bohemian nobles at mid-century. Once completed, the old-new castle was, as one art historian puts it, a *"Gesamtkunstwerk."* The interior was thoroughly modern in amenities, but neo-traditional in décor, featuring "coats of arms, history paintings and ancestral portraits." The Gothic façade incorporated hints of the original Baroque and early nineteenth-century Classical additions. Two towers crowned the garden side of the castle: the sturdy, angular "Austrian" tower representing their new homeland, and the round and tapering "Breton" tower, a fanciful evocation of the family's French heritage. As Inge Rohan's account of the reconstruction concludes, "With Sychrov [Camille Rohan] had built a monument for himself and his successors, a costly reliquary in which he reverently integrated the evocation of an ancient family tradition with the hopes for a future similar to the remote and glorious past."[30]

Nobles maintained their symbolic distance from the lower classes through a range of customs and social practices. Foremost among these was hunting for sport, to which nobles devoted countless hours and resources. Prince Karl/Karel[31] V Schwarzenberg (1886–1914) shot over 11,000 animals in his short lifetime (he himself died in the hunting grounds of the East in the Great War).[32] Nobles regularly hunted in large parties, with guests often making extended stays at their host's manor. Horse breeding and racing was also a noble obsession, so much so that Alois Prince Liechtenstein reportedly spent from three to five percent of his ample income on his stables.

The most popular noble meeting place in Vienna was the exclusive Jockey Club, "the social center of gravity of the nobility."[33] In Prague, nobles congregated at the Prague *Ressource,* another social club with an entirely noble membership. Gary Cohen notes that almost no nobles joined the German Casino in Prague, and they rarely mingled in bourgeois society.[34] A contemporary observed in 1908 that nobles in Prague rarely attended balls and public events unless "absolutely necessary."[35] Further contributing to noble exclusivity, Bohemia's aristocracy was wealthy enough that it rarely needed to marry *nouveaux riches* to remain solvent. Noble endogamy helped to ensure a largely closed social life. Interestingly, Bohemian nobles had had closer social (though not marital) ties with bourgeois patriots in the late eighteenth and early nineteenth century, but these ties receded in the wake of the 1848 revolution.[36] This retreat from "democratic sociability" served to both isolate and insulate the nobility to some extent from the increasing democratization (and nationalization) of everyday life in the late nineteenth century.

Nobles and Political Modernization in the Habsburg Empire

Though nobles lost most of their legal privileges—such as labor services and pat-rimonial courts—in 1848, in politics they retained certain legal and customary advantages up to the end of the Monarchy. Most notably, a complex curial sys-tem for elections to the *Reichsrat* and Bohemian Diet gave nobles a dispropor-tionate number of representatives in both bodies. In the *Reichsrat* in Vienna, which until 1897 had elections in four curias, large landowners received 85 deputies out of a total of 353.[37] This made them a key player in coalition build-ing, leverage that one or the other of the two major aristocratic parties consis-tently used to its advantage. Though the government of Casimir Badeni added a universal curia in 1896, bringing the total number of delegates to 425, landown-ers maintained their influential position. Only after the abolition of the curial system and adoption of universal suffrage in 1907 did the nobles lose their rep-resentation in the lower house of the *Reichsrat*. Even so, they retained a lock on the *Herrenhaus*, the upper house, until 1918.[38] The noble proportion of the Bo-hemian Diet, or provincial assembly, was even greater than it was in the *Reichs-rat*, with the landholding curia filling 70 seats out of a total of 242.[39] In Moravia, the first curia had 30 out of 100 representatives until 1905, and 30 out of 151 after that.[40] Both of the provincial assemblies retained the curial system until the end of the Monarchy, thus ensuring noble influence. In just one example of the use of this influence, large landowners took advantage of their domination of the *Herrenhaus* to block Agrarian Party legislation in 1905 that would have elimi-nated sugar refinery monopolies.[41]

Locally, after 1848 nobles lost the privilege (many would say burden) of pro-viding patrimonial courts in their districts. Even so, imperial favor kept important regional bureaucratic positions in the hands of the nobility. Since their tremen-dous land holdings usually made nobles the largest taxpayers in rural communes, they also received special positions on communal councils.[42] As Solomon Wank writes, "The whole system of provincial and local government and administra-tion in which the nobility held key posts and exercised great influence offered possibilities of political control and assured that noble interests would be benev-olently treated in conflicts with bourgeoisie and peasants."[43] Nor can one dis-count the persistence of deference to nobles on the local level. Through their patronage and leadership in churches, charities, and cultural and economic or-ganizations, nobles remained in many areas the local *"Herren."*[44]

Bohemian nobles also continued to dominate top positions in the imperial cabinet, bureaucracy, and foreign service until the end of the Empire. From the adoption of the constitution in 1867 to the end of the Monarchy, 23 of 26 prime ministers in Austria were nobles, and many of these came from the ranks of the Bohemian and Moravian aristocracy.[45] Nicholas von Preradovich reports that in 1918 nobles still held 56 percent of the highest posts in diplomacy in Austria, 57 percent in administration, and 25 percent in the army.[46] Though their proportion of leading positions in the army represented a substantial decline, William Godsey concludes that the percentage of old nobles in the Foreign Office actually increased from 44 percent to 60 percent between 1868 and the early twentieth century.[47] Above all, the high nobility retained substantial influence in the court of Emperor Franz Joseph. The always high-born Grand Chamberlain controlled access to the Monarch, usually limiting social contacts to those who could demonstrate at least sixteen quarterings (four generations) of nobility.[48] William Godsey has recently identified 474 families that were considered *hoffähig*, or presentable at court, during the Dualist period from 1867 to 1918. Of these, 161 (34 percent) had considerable land holdings in the historic provinces of Bohemia, Moravia, and Austrian Silesia.[49] Not only did *entrée* to court mark the limits of noble high society, but it also determined who would have the Emperor's ear. Given the frequent failures of Cisleithania's parliamentary system, access to Franz Joseph could be of crucial importance in swaying government policy.

There has been spirited debate in Habsburg historiography about the degree to which the Austrian half of the Monarchy democratized in the late nineteenth century.[50] On the one hand, governments ruled at the behest of the Emperor, not of parliament. If parliamentary life ended up deadlocked (and this happened frequently), the imperially appointed government could, on the basis of Article 14 of the constitution, rule without an electoral mandate. This, combined with occasional reversions to martial law in Bohemia, leads Solomon Wank to refer to the Empire as "a constitutional monarchy which still bore strong traces of a dynastic *Obrigkeitsstaat* (authoritarian state)."[51] On the other hand, by the late nineteenth century the Monarchy was remarkable for the democratic institutions it did have in place, and it was widely known as a *Rechtstaat*, where the rule of law was supreme. Historians have recently paid particular attention to the development of local governmental institutions that had a decidedly liberal stamp.[52]

In fact, governance in the Austrian lands of the Habsburg Monarchy was a function of a hybrid political system that combined elements of both bureaucratic and democratic rule. Neither elected bodies nor the Emperor's representatives felt they could rule without taking the other into account. The result was a particular and sustained reliance on the nobility to play a kind of intermediary role, active both in democratic institutions (albeit with disproportionate representation) and in imperial government and administration. As we shall see, the nobility played this role to their advantage, professing their allegiance to the crown on the one hand and to the people on the other. This cautious and calculated balancing act would ensure their remarkable survival at the heights of political power in the late nineteenth century.

Austria Crawling out of Her Skin: Nobles and Nationality Politics, 1880–1900

After the revival of constitutional political life in the Empire in 1860, Bohemian nobles divided into two factions, one centralist and one federalist.[53] The Constitutionally Loyal Large Landowners (*Verfassungstreue Grossgrundbesitzer*) supported Viennese centralism. They remained devoted to the "Austrian state idea," a territorial notion that posited a spiritual unity of Cisleithania's manifold nations under the umbrella of the Emperor.[54] These nobles tended to favor German as the universal language of the state and Vienna-centered Germandom (*Deutschtum*) as the glue holding the Empire together. Just as many Bohemian nobles had benefited from their support of the Emperor in the Thirty Years' War of the seventeenth century, these nobles now considered a close alliance with the Monarch to be in their best interests.

Members of the second faction, the Feudal Conservatives (*Feudale Konservativen*), favored Bohemian autonomy within a federalized Empire. Basing their claims on the historic rights of the Bohemian Crown (*Staatsrecht*), the Feudals hoped to increase their power by strengthening the institutions, local and provincial, in which they retained the most influence. They drew on a long tradition of Bohemian noble opposition to Habsburg centralism, including during the Thirty Years' War, the War of the Austrian Succession in the 1740s, and the centralizing reforms of Joseph II. Unlike in the first two examples, however, the Feudals did not seek the overthrow of the Habsburgs; they simply believed federalism to be the best means of securing the Empire's (and their own) future.

Two trends pushed the noble parties in the direction of national politics in the 1860s. First, the Czech National Party adopted the *Staatsrecht* program as its own in an effort to win autonomy for Bohemia, and thus self-rule for the Czechs. Though the Czech national movement had worn decidedly liberal colors in the Revolution of 1848, Palacký and other Czech leaders concluded that the Habsburgs would be more receptive to a conservative appeal for historic rights than to liberal demands invoking the natural right of self-determination.[55] Second, with the steadily expanding suffrage of the late nineteenth century, Bohemian Germans of all political stripes realized that, barring a division of Bohemia, centralism was their best protection against Czech dominance in the province. The two noble factions, therefore, allied themselves with respective centralist and federalist national parties—the Verfassungstreue with the Germans and the Feudale with the Czechs—hoping to maintain their influence in an increasingly nationalized and democratized political world.

To nobles in the late nineteenth century, there appeared to be few alternatives to their ambivalent alliances with nationalist political parties. A class-based appeal would only have worked so long as the franchise were extremely limited; instead, the ever-widening curial system gave the middle classes of all nationalities substantial representation, and bourgeois parties tended to be nationalist. Given socialist hostility to the aristocracy, a cross-class "internationalist" alliance against the national parties was also unlikely. Moreover, by the late nineteenth century, Czech social democrats were almost as nationalist as the Czech bourgeois parties, finding little common cause with their Austro-German counterparts.[56]

Like many traditionally a-national actors in the late Habsburg Empire, nobles faced a narrowing of options when it came to politics. By the late nineteenth century, nation became the most common language of aspirations and interests, the coin of political contest in the Monarchy.[57] National identity increased in salience, to a point where it became difficult for any but the most isolated individuals to avoid identification with one of the Monarchy's eleven nations. Though early stirrings of national identification were manifest in Bohemia at the beginning of the nineteenth century, a combination of factors turned nation into the preeminent political loyalty it became by 1900. First, the economic success and growing middle class of the Czechs gave them less and less reason to assimilate to Germandom as they advanced socially. As Jeremy King and other historians have pointed out, two discrete, socially diverse national communities were in place by the 1860s.[58] The Czechs had reached a critical juncture in their national development. They could achieve enough of their aspirations as Czechs to obviate the need to assimilate; yet not all their aspirations were met, and many blamed Habsburg favoritism towards Germans for inhibiting further progress.

Second, the Monarchy ironically institutionalized emerging national divisions with a number of bureaucratic innovations in the 1880s and 1890s. Starting with the 1880 census, Habsburg officials asked all Austrian citizens to declare their language of daily use (*Umgangssprache*). Though this was not technically a question about nationality, it effectively became one. Forced to choose only one language (in spite of widespread bilingualism in Bohemia and elsewhere), respondents increasingly were aware that they were making a political decision that would affect school budgets, the distribution of bureaucratic posts, and other regional funding priorities. Jeremy King aptly notes that, in an age of limited suffrage, the battle over *Umgangssprache* became the only truly democratic contest in Bohemia.[59]

Imperial governments also encouraged mixed localities to "solve" disputes over funding for Czech and German schools by creating separate school boards elected by national curias. In places where this occurred, voters had to register for one or the other curia and could only vote for a single school board. In a precedent-setting case in 1887, an imperial court ruled that binationality (i.e., registration in both curias) rendered a citizen ineligible to run for school board in either curia.[60] Gerald Stourzh demonstrates that the school board pattern repeated itself in hundreds of institutions in Bohemia and Moravia by the early 1900s. Most prominently, the Moravian compromise of 1905 divided Czechs and Germans into separate voting rolls (cadasters), which then elected a pre-set proportion of representatives to the Moravian Diet in Brünn/Brno. Overruling earlier precedents that made the choice of nationality entirely subjective, a 1907 court ruling determined that "according to the Moravian compromise law, the state's authorities were indeed both competent and obliged to settle in doubtful cases, on the basis of objective indications, the national/ethnic attribution of a person."[61] This was an ominous precedent. The government had in effect institutionalized and thus hardened the previously fluid national divisions in Bohemian and Moravian society. Perversely, Habsburg public officials now undertook to enforce these divisions.

Feudal Conservatives

In 1860, with these nationalizing institutional changes still decades away, the Czech national movement remained in the noble-friendly Palacký's genteel hands. With the advent of constitutionalism, a large faction of the Bohemian nobility joined forces with Palacký's Czech National Party in pursuit of recognition of the Bohemian *Staatsrecht*. These self-styled "Feudal Conservatives" were a diverse bunch, including ancient Czech families such as the Sternbergs or Lobkowiczs and post–White Mountain immigrants such as the Buquoys or Thuns. Some took Czech affinities much farther than others, ostentatiously speaking Czech in public and favoring Czech employees for top positions on their estates. On the other hand, many insisted on their membership in a territorially defined "Bohemian nation," and saw the alliance with the Czechs as purely tactical. Members of the Schwarzenberg clan were known for their public speeches in superb Czech; other Conservatives did not speak Czech at all. What they all shared was a dedication to Bohemian historic rights, which, in the oft-quoted words of one Schwarzenberg, "we will defend, come what comes, as long as it is within our power, sacrificing our very lives and fortunes."[62]

The Schwarzenbergs were consistently among the leaders of the Feudals, and their own diversity perhaps best illustrates the diversity of opinion within the party itself—on all issues, that is, except a basic commitment to Bohemian *Staatsrecht*. Divided into two powerful and distinct lines since the Napoleonic Wars, the Schwarzenberg primogeniture (Krumlov/Krumau branch) was the largest landowning family in Bohemia. The secundogeniture (Orlík/Worlik branch) also owned vast estates, but it was known even more for its political engagement. At mid-century, the family was typically divided, with Johann Prince Schwarzenberg (patriarch of the primogeniture) seeking Bohemian autonomy, and his younger brother Felix Schwarzenberg leading the forces of absolutist centralism. In the decades that followed, both branches would be stalwarts of the Feudal Conservatives, with the primogeniture tending towards the binational ideal of Bohemianism (sometimes called utraquism[63]) and the secundogeniture towards the Czech cause. Typical of the largest Bohemian magnates, both branches were relatively progressive in their estate management and markedly conservative and clerical in their politics.

Two Orlík Schwarzenbergs played a prominent role in the foundation of the Conservative Party in 1860. The outspoken Bedřich/Friedrich Schwarzenberg (1799–1870) was a strong proponent of federalism, which he saw as the best way to strengthen the Monarchy. Though he opposed both Czech and German nationalist tendencies, he believed the dynasty must rely in Bohemia on the majority Czechs, the Bohemian people. He also promoted closer ties of the Conservative nobility with Czech politicians. As he wrote to Vincenc Auersperg in 1862, the nobility needed national roots to ensure its long-term survival: "In my opinion, the nobility … is rooted in the people (*Volk*) itself: it can support the crown and tree top, but its roots lie in the soil of the people.… Only those nobil-

ities rooted in the people have withstood the storms of revolution." In Schwarzenberg's view, excessive centralization had caused the French Revolution of 1789,
and the disaster that followed had been the result of a nobility that had lost touch
with the people.[64]

Bedřich's nephew, Karl/Karel III Prince Schwarzenberg (1824–1904), took
his uncle's recommendation to heart. He "supported Czech literature, dedicated
several valuable gifts to the National Museum, and twice donated relatively high
sums for the construction of the [Czech] National Theater."[65] In his correspondence with members of the Czech National Party, he wrote, "When the nobility
is not faithful to history, when it no longer stands within the nation, when it
does not have roots in the nation, then it must lose its ground, like a tree with
roots undermined, with the first gust of wind."[66] Repeating his uncle's metaphor,
Schwarzenberg offered the Conservative nobility an ideology of sorts, but one
tempered by a profound distrust of popular sovereignty. "I absolutely share your
view," Schwarzenberg wrote to Auersperg, "that the nobility, if it embraces an
unadulterated national politics, is simply digging its own grave."[67] Some nobles
were willing to put roots in the soil of the nation, but few were willing to min-
gle with that soil as equal to equal.

Schwarzenberg's son, Karl/Karel IV (1859–1913), though also professedly a
friend of the Czechs, publicly condemned the populist aspects of the Czech national movement. When Czech nationalists wanted to dedicate a plaque to Jan
Hus in front of the National Museum in 1889, Karl/Karel IV Schwarzenberg
spoke out against the plan in the Bohemian Diet: "In the beginning the Hussite
movement contained many honorable characters. But unfortunately, the Hussites
quickly degenerated into a band of thieves and arsonists."[68] A staunch Catholic,
Schwarzenberg did not hide his distaste for the fifteenth-century heretic Hus and
Hus's latter-day nationalist champions, who made him out to be a crypto-Protestant
Czech national hero. He also reportedly added, referring to the radical Young
Czechs, "We Schwarzenbergs will fight against you neo-Hussites, with the same
vigor as the knights of the rose fought against the old Hussites."[69] Schwarzenberg's outburst inspired Czech nationalists to seek a much larger monument on
Old Town Square instead of a modest plaque. It also spurred the rapid rise of
the Young Czech party, which opposed the Czech National Party's (Old Czech)
alliance with what it considered to be a reactionary nobility.[70]

Karl/Karel IV's brother, however, would be instrumental in building bridges
to those very same radicals. Bedřich Schwarzenberg (1862–1936) had been known
as a supporter of the Czech cause since his election to the Bohemian Diet in
1893. In 1896 he gave a rousing speech in the Austrian *Reichsrat* calling for the
equality of the Czech and German languages within the Bohemian bureaucracy.[71] Speaking for the Feudal Conservative caucus, he declared "complete solidarity with the Czech (*böhmisch*) people" in the name of the "states rights idea."
Given the Czech majority in Bohemia, it was only fair that the Czechs receive
equal rights for their language. "The states rights program," he added, "would
advance the well-being of not only the Kingdom of Bohemia, but also the entire

Monarchy."[72] Speaking to a crowd of Czech supporters in České Budějovice/ Budweis in 1898, he went even farther, insisting "Everyone must be either Czech or German.... There is no place here for amphibians."[73] The young Bedřich Schwarzenberg may have been something of an exception with his extreme Czech sympathies; in 1897 he became one of the only nobles to be elected to the *Reichsrat* from outside of the landholding curia, winning the Budějovice district on a Czech slate.[74] Even so, his speech to the *Reichsrat* was representative of the Feudal Conservatives' caution in support of Czech interests. Like Schwarzenberg, party leaders couched their support of the Czechs in rhetoric emphasizing historic rights and loyalty to the Monarchy.

The Old Czechs and the Feudal Conservatives had adopted the *Staatsrecht* program for different reasons, the former as a palatable way to appeal to the Emperor for autonomy, the latter to emphasize their traditional rights in Bohemia. But both agreed that a legalist/legitimist argument would carry far more weight in Vienna than an appeal to natural rights.[75] In 1894, Francis Thun summarized the Conservatives' somewhat watered-down program to Emperor Franz Joseph: "(1) the unity and integrity of the country (Bohemia); (2) equal rights for both languages of the country; (3) the right to elect the king in case the Habsburg family becomes extinct; and (4) the selection of representatives from Moravia and Silesia to attend any possible coronation ceremony." Thun was emphatically not seeking independence, or, at this point, even full autonomy for Bohemia.[76]

Nor did the Czechs have any illusions that Conservative nobles had suddenly become Czech patriots. Palacký's son-in-law and successor as Old Czech political leader, František Rieger, was, according to Gordon Skilling, "well aware that the bulk of the feudal nobles had no real sympathy with the Czech national cause and 'were Bohemians [Böhmen] and nothing more,' defending state right in the interests, not of the nation, but of their class."[77] To the Czechs too, the political tie with the Conservatives was one of convenience; as Rieger put it, "The alliance with the nobility we need for the sake of the court. If the nobles did not go with us, they would suspect us there as dangerous rebels and revolutionaries."[78] For the nobles, the Czechs guarded against a slide into political irrelevance; for the Old Czechs, the nobles provided access to the highly exclusive court of Franz Joseph. From 1879 to 1891 the Czech National Party (Old Czechs), Feudal Conservatives, German Clericals, and Poles joined in support of Prime Minister Eduard Taaffe's government, the so-called Iron Ring. Though the Old Czechs found themselves sharing power with the help of the nobility, they had to support the coalition's conservative and clerical program in the hopes of gaining occasional concessions for the Czechs.[79]

This came to be too much for the Young Czechs—and indeed most Czech voters—to bear. Eduard Grégr, the leader of the Young Czechs, wrote of the Old Czechs: "The whole delegation is hitched to the government carriage; Clam [the Feudal Conservative leader] sits on the box-seat and whips them and they pull like blind men—for they do not know why—simply on the word of Clam that all will be well!"[80] Drawing on the radical nationalist critique of noble perfidy in

1848, the Young Czechs began in the late 1880s calling for an end to the alliance, "casting off the chains of foreign influences ... [inaugurating] a Czech policy, a real national policy."[81] In the elections of 1891, the Young Czechs dominated the Czech vote; in keeping with their anti-conservative, anti-noble rhetoric, they then ended the Czech alliance with the Feudal Conservatives. But five years later, the Young Czechs had lost some of their radical edge to the new mass parties on the left, and they renewed the alliance with the Conservatives.[82] In a joint manifesto of March 1897, both parties pledged their support for the state's rights program and for bilingualism in internal as well as external bureaucratic business.[83] In 1901, the much-reduced Old Czechs joined the now-moderate Young Czechs in a single Czech Club, and together they reaffirmed their alliance with the Conservative nobles.[84]

Even so, many of the Feudals were uneasy with Young Czech nationalism, and the party would increasingly distance itself from the alliance in the early 1900s. Both the raucous style and the democratic implications of nationalist politics could not but alienate the nobility. Karl/Karel III Schwarzenberg, who would later be instrumental in rebuilding the alliance with the Czechs, privately noted to Alois Aehrenthal in 1893 that "a further agreement with the Young Czechs would lead to nothing, and only the quick and energetic suppression of the democratic scum (*Brut*) of the *Národní listy* [the Young Czech newspaper] can bring the necessary clarification and pacification of [Bohemia]." Schwarzenberg concluded by indicating his preference for "an absolute regime in Bohemia and Vienna" that would clear up the mess that was Austrian politics.[85]

When Franz Joseph's Prime Minister Casimir Badeni tried to impose a linguistic compromise on Bohemian Czechs and Germans in 1897, the political mess became an outright crisis. The so-called Badeni Ordinances made Czech and German equal as official languages of Bohemia. Previously, the province's bureaucracy was required to answer supplicants in their native languages as long as their nationality made up at least 20 percent of a given region. But internal bureaucratic business had been carried out exclusively in German, to which Czechs strenuously objected. The Badeni Ordinances required all Bohemian officials to be competent in both Czech and German. This posed little problem for typically bilingual Czech officials, but it threatened to displace a large number of Germans who could not or would not learn Czech by the deadline of 1901. Following the promulgation of the Ordinances, German nationalists rioted in Prague and Vienna. Both the *Reichsrat* and the Bohemian Diet came to a standstill, as nationalists on both sides threw inkpots, attacked their opponents, and generally obstructed business. The Badeni government quickly fell, but the crisis continued until a new Prime Minister, Manfred Count Clary-Aldringen (1852–1928), rescinded the Ordinances entirely in 1899. For Bohemian nobles, the years 1897 to 1900 seemed a centennial *Götterdämmerung*.

The Feudal Conservatives generally backed the Badeni Ordinances, though they deplored the nationalist melee that followed. Karl/Karel IV Schwarzenberg wrote to Aehrenthal in 1899 indicating his support for the ordinances, but out of concern for the survival of the Empire and not for the Czechs in particular. "For our internal peace," he elaborated, "it would perhaps be useful, if one were to consider oneself as a legal subject more of a territory than of a language or a nation." The main goal of both foreign and domestic policy, he argued, was the preservation of the Monarchy. In contrast with Aehrenthal and the Constitutionals, he believed federalism and conciliation of the non-German nationalities to be the best hope for the Monarchy's survival. To counter the centrifugal forces of nationalism, it was up to the Foreign Office to nurture an Austrian patriotism.[86]

Another longtime Feudal Conservative, Rudolf Count Czernin (1855–1927), expressed in 1895 frustration that "national slogans" were preventing a compromise between Czechs and Germans in Bohemia. In a letter to prominent Constitutional Loyalist Prince Max Egon Fürstenberg (1863–1941), Czernin noted that he had considered voting for the Constitutionals out of protest against Czech tactics, but he could not bring himself to go against family tradition. Instead, he chose not to vote at all in the 1895 election.[87] Like so many of his fellow aristocrats, Czernin could not stomach either the democratic radicalism or the national chauvinism of the new generation of Czech politicians. As the Conservative mouthpiece, *Vaterland,* asserted in 1870, the party's members were loyal, above all, to the Monarchy. The Bohemian Kingdom (and its traditional estates) came next in their hierarchy of importance, followed by "the idea of nationality" and individual freedom.[88] The Young Czechs, many nobles distrustfully pointed out, had these priorities backwards.

Constitutionally Loyal Large Landowners

Like the Feudals, the Constitutionals claimed that their primary loyalty belonged to the Monarchy, but they disagreed over how best to preserve the Monarchy and their own position within it. Instead of devolving power to the fractious nationalities, they favored political centralism, and stressed the Monarchy's basic German character. Aligning themselves with German liberals, who shared their German cultural orientation and commitment to centralism, Constitutionals too found themselves drawn ever deeper into nationality politics. As Ernst Rutkowski points out, they "stood on the side of Germandom, whose interest they advocated less out of purely national grounds, but because they saw in Germandom an essential bond for the survival of the Empire."[89]

Rutkowski's mammoth collection of Constitutional political correspondence from 1880 to 1904 amply illustrates the faction's German sympathies, and party members repeatedly referred to themselves as German. The party's electoral manifesto of 1895, for example, declared: "As Germans in Bohemia we will stand by German representatives from the town and country in the Diet in their efforts to protect their national property (*nationaler Besitzstand*) and in their cultural efforts."[90] In the aftermath of Bedřich Schwarzenberg's pro-Czech speech in the Diet a year later, members of the electoral committee expressed similar sentiments.

"In yesterday's debate," the committee reported, "all agreed unanimously on the preservation of the imperial idea, the pursuit of religious instruction in the schools, the learning of the Czech language, but above all for the promotion of German-dom and for the manifestation of a rigid German attitude (*Gesinnung*)."[91]

At the same time, the Constitutionals repeatedly emphasized the primacy of their imperial loyalties. As the head of the party, Oswald Count Thun (1849–1913), noted on a number of occasions, "Our nationality has distinct limits in our patriotism."[92] As the party's name implied, the Constitutionally Loyal Large Landowners were dedicated to the constitution of 1867 and the Austro-Hungarian compromise (*Ausgleich*) that engendered it. With the compromise, the Emperor effectively made a deal to share power with the Hungarian and the Austro-German elites; the noble Loyalists pledged themselves to uphold this bargain, in exchange, as they saw it, for a share of power. But even when excluded from government, they maintained their loyalty to the Monarch and the Austrian state. As the electoral committee of the party declared in 1895, strict adherence to the constitution was the only hope for "the reinvigoration and strengthening of our Austrian fatherland."[93]

After the unrest following the Badeni language ordinances in 1897, Max Egon Fürstenberg wrote to Feudal Conservative Karl/Karel IV Schwarzenberg that it was time for "all hearts loyal to the Empire (*reichstreu*) to join ranks in order to save what could still be saved of our Monarchy." With Franz Joseph's fiftieth jubilee fast approaching, "Whether we celebrate our Emperor in German, Czech, Polish or Croatian, it should make no difference.... We all can survive, only if we rally around our Emperor *viribus unitis*."[94] At the same time, Thun and other leaders of the party expressed frustration with the Emperor's occasional willingness to abandon his stalwart German loyalists in order to placate the Empire's Slavs. As far as nationality questions went, Franz Joseph had no consistent strategy, sometimes yielding to national demands if he thought it would bring some domestic peace, sometimes standing fast against nationalists.

The Loyalists saw the Badeni Ordinances as a case in point. The Emperor had long insisted that the internal language of bureaucracy must remain German throughout Cisleithania, in order to emphasize the unity of the Austrian lands. But in 1897 the Monarch allowed Badeni to appease the Czechs by requiring bilingualism in the Bohemian Lands. When the Constitutional Loyalists objected that the change had no basis in the Constitution of 1867, the Emperor rejected their counsel. In a letter to Alain Prince Rohan (1853–1914), Oswald Thun vented his frustration: "It is sad that no human being knows what the Monarch really wants and what the government should thus do. Patriotic today means merely that one does not make a scandal.... We are patriots only when we are blind and dumb."[95] The Constitutionally Loyal Large Landowners found themselves in the sorry position of steadfastly supporting an often-ignored constitution, of loyalty to a ruler who rarely returned their affection, and of devotion to an imperial idea that had little content beyond the person of the venerable Franz Joseph.

Nor could they find solace in the German national camp. As early as 1883, Aehrenthal was complaining of nationalism's ill effect on politics: "I am certainly not mistaken in attributing this unruliness (*Verwilderung*) of politics to the exaggeration of the nationality-idea to the point of absurdity."[96] Aehrenthal was observing what Carl Schorske has described as a "politics in a new key" in fin de siècle Austria. It was, in Schorske's words, "a sharper key," more confrontational, with an appeal to feeling above reason. The most abrasive of its practitioners was Georg von Schönerer (1842–1921), a Pan-German and radical nationalist with a substantial following in North Bohemia.[97] For the nobility, accustomed to deference and genteel politics, the new style was disconcerting. In 1896 Guido Count Dubsky (1835–1907) announced his withdrawal from politics, bemoaning the "sharper pitch (*Tonart*)" of politics that was "driving the imperial idea into the background" and favoring national interest groups.[98]

In the wake of German riots over the Badeni language ordinances, Alois Aehrenthal wrote to his father, "The Germans degrade themselves, when they follow the example of the Czechs and anti-Semites. The nation of Goethe is becoming more and more a nation of beer consumers with stableboy manners (*Hausknechtmanieren*)!"[99] Alain Rohan echoed this sentiment in a letter to Fürstenberg a few years later, as the Badeni furor refused to go away. He wrote scornfully, "I personally will not sign a ballot on which a radical stands. I want to have nothing to do with the German national radicals of Schönerer's ilk. I consider this movement more damaging to the position of the Germans in Austria than all the national opponents."[100] Oswald Thun rejected the nationalists' extra-parliamentary tactics, writing in his diary, "It is a disgrace for the people (*Volk*) that it recognizes a traitor like Schönerer as its leader."[101]

But given new electoral realities, the nobles could not do without their nationalist allies, at least not the moderates. "One simply cannot separate from a national party, once an alliance is entered," Aehrenthal wrote to Karl Count Buquoy (1854–1911), "without being thrown in among the political corpses."[102] Some nobles in the party also emphasized their Germanness in order to satisfy their more German-national colleagues within the party. At a party congress in mid-1897, Karl Moritz Count Zedtwitz (1830–1915) urged such an attitude, because "it makes a good impression on a part of our voters, for whom one can never be German enough."[103] Indeed, Oswald Thun commented in a letter a few months later that in closed meetings, most Constitutionals emphasized their Austrian patriotism. But "as soon as we step out before the public, patriotism gives way to nationality, because our so-called political allies (*Gesinnungsgenossen*) these days tolerate patriotism only in homeopathic doses."[104]

For many in the party, identification with German nationalists was a painful compromise, but one that had to be made on the principle that enemies of one's enemies are one's friends. Constitutionals faced a range of no-win choices. On the one hand, an ungrateful and uncreative Emperor did little to build the imperial identity they hoped for. The only other unifying force in the Empire appeared to be its German-speaking bureaucracy and army, but even these were under attack by non-German nationalists. In standing firm against these attacks, the Constitutionals' only allies were German liberals, already on the ropes, and the more radical German nationalists. But the intransigence of German nationalists only further undermined efforts to find a compromise with the Czechs.

The hopelessness of the Loyalists' political position left Oswald Thun disillusioned and ill. Writing in 1898 from his winter retreat in Beaulieu on the French Riviera, Thun described how at ease he felt by the sea, knowing that the waves rolling over his feet could do him no harm. "If only I could have this feeling towards all the elements that so easily inflict upon me discomfort and nausea!" he continued.

> I am thinking about my good old Austria, and about our group, which was deluded enough to believe unshakably that ancient traditions and a certain spirit (*Geist*), which we carefully cultivated when we were children, could not be lost. Almost in tears, I have to say that in Austria the impossible has happened—Austria is crawling out of her skin, and nothing remains to us other than to lay ourselves down to sleep on her discarded hide.... The moment is coming, with giant strides, when the national element alone will prevail—We will be crippled, because, duty bound, we feel ourselves to be more Imperial than the Emperor (*kaiserlicher als der Kaiser*).[105]

Thun managed to hold on for eight more years as head of the party, but they were trouble-filled years and he was often sick. By 1906, with his eyes failing him, his heart and lungs weak, he retired from politics. Though his early death in 1913 was officially caused by "paralysis of the lungs,"[106] he had also long suffered from psychosomatic illnesses. The forces tearing the Empire apart tore at Thun as well; he bore in a symbolic sense the pain and unease of an entire class, unable fully to comprehend or assimilate a nationalist mindset that had conquered politics and would soon upend the empires of Europe.

Loyal to the End: Nobles and the Downfall of the Habsburg Monarchy, 1900-1918

Already in 1890, with the Czech-German language dispute roiling Bohemian and imperial politics, the two main noble political parties had begun to find some common ground in pursuit of a Bohemian compromise. The resulting "*punktace*" would have divided the province into national districts, and the Diet into national curia (with the exception of a nonnational landowners' curia similar to the one adopted in Moravia in 1905). The *punktace* failed when the Young Czechs rejected its concessions to the Germans; the two landowner parties would not find common cause again for a decade.[107]

In 1900, nobles tried once more to facilitate a Bohemian compromise. In a series of meetings with leaders of both Czech and German parties in Bohemia, the two noble groups served as mediators in the search for a solution to the province's linguistic impasse.[108] Though the discussions again foundered, they began a tentative cooperation between the parties that would expand when the demise of curial voting for the *Reichsrat* appeared imminent in 1906. In 1910, Conservatives and Constitutionals again came together to try to broker a Bohemian agreement along the lines of the Moravian Compromise of 1905. Fearing the loss of their powerful curia in the Bohemian Diet, the noble parties sought, like their Moravian counterparts, to retain a nonnational landowning curia in addition to separate Czech and German cadasters. As their joint program concluded, "national division of the large landowners [is] not desirable." In addition, "any nationalization of the bureaucracy is to be avoided."[109] This attempt too failed, as neither Czechs nor Germans were willing to yield on their basic positions: for the Czechs, the indivisibility and fundamental Czech character of Bohemia; for the Germans, autonomy for German regions of the province.

Nor did granting universal suffrage to the *Reichsrat* make governing Austria any easier, as the Emperor had hoped. Members of both noble parties began to raise the possibility of an authoritarian solution, according to which Franz Joseph would simply dissolve the *Reichsrat* permanently and appoint Imperial governments. Already in 1898, Karl/Karel IV Schwarzenberg had written that

> the increasing awareness that the parliamentary form of government has outlived its usefulness can cause satisfaction for us true conservatives.... In my opinion, Austria can no longer be held together in any other way than by a modernized absolutism.[110]

Many other nobles, both Feudal and Constitutional, quietly adopted this viewpoint, which was most prominently held by Archduke Francis Ferdinand in the years before the First World War. In 1913–14 Austria became a de facto autocracy when Count Karl Stürgkh dissolved both the Bohemian Diet and the *Reichsrat,* seemingly for good.[111] Once the war began, a noble clique would rule both Bohemia and the entire Austrian half of the Monarchy until the new Emperor Charles reconvened the *Reichsrat* in 1917.[112]

The war both united and divided the two leading factions of the Bohemian nobility. In the first few years of the war, both groups stressed their loyalty to the Emperor, and distanced themselves more than ever from nationalist politicians. Even Bedřich Schwarzenberg, who gave the impassioned pro-Czech speech in the Bohemian Diet in 1896, claimed in a 1916 letter to Otto Harrach, "I always was of the standpoint that our party should not become national."[113] One Conservative, recently returned from the front in 1915, reportedly said, "I no longer understand my compatriots (the Czechs)."[114] The lack of Czech enthusiasm for the imperial cause during the war drove a wedge between the Czechs and most of their former Conservative allies. In a 1916 meeting in Prague, the Conservative leadership called on all provinces, parties, and nations to "stand enthusiastically behind the Empire and army." While the party remained "warm" towards the "Bohemian people" (meaning the Czechs here), the continuation of "the old friendship" required that "the Bohemian people remain loyal to the Dynasty and to their ties to the Empire, which alone offers a guarantee for their national existence and cultural development."[115]

The Constitutional Loyalists too remained as loyal as ever, with some members exploring the possibility of an overhaul of political arrangements in Austria in order to give Germans a lasting control of government. In a report to the party leadership in June of 1915, the up-and-coming young landowner Wilhelm von Medinger (1878–1934) argued that the only way to make "order in our own house" was to "create a parliamentary majority of state-supporting and dynastic-loyal elements." The only truly loyal citizens, Medinger argued, were German Austrians. To ensure that they held a majority in the *Reichsrat,* he proposed that the Emperor grant Polish Galicia full autonomy, thus removing one-fifth of the representatives from parliament. The Austrian half of the Monarchy would then be predominantly German in character, with German as the sole parliamentary and bureaucratic language.

Medinger criticized Conservatives for their earlier alliance with the Czechs, who were pan-Slavs masquerading as Austro-Slavs:

> In their supposed impartiality, the (Conservatives) were against every national struggle; in this they did not understand that the battle of the Germans was a defensive struggle, while that of the non-Germans was offensive.... Now these gentlemen themselves shudder in the face of the movement they once supported.

By no means, he declared, should "our current parliament with its collection of traitors" meet again. Instead, "the most important reforms (such as electoral reform) can only be carried through by means of an octroi." He urged the Constitutionals to pursue this goal with all their power and to prove that they were "His Majesty the Emperor of Austria's truest officers" on the "battlefield of politics."[116]

There were also, to be sure, a few radical Czech nobles during the war, just as before it. Vladimír Count Lažanský (1857–1925) was the representative of an ancient Czech noble family, though his forebears had sided with the Habsburgs at White Mountain and were amply rewarded afterwards. During the nineteenth century, the Lažanskýs were active state's rights Conservatives, and Vladimír became known as a dedicated Czech patriot. Though he never mastered Czech, he regularly contributed poetry (translated from German) to the Prague literary journal *Zlatá Praha* (Golden Prague). The writer Karel Čapek, who had been a tutor for Lažanský's son during the war, called him "one of the strongest Czech nationalists ... right up to a passionate hatred of all things German and especially the Habsburg Dynasty." When Čapek came to apply for the job in 1916, Lažanský asked him, "Tell me, Herr Doctor, will we be victorious or the others?" Surprised, Čapek responded, "Which we, Herr Count? Do you mean Austria?" To which Lažanský replied, "But no! We Russians. We French." His opposition to the Habsburgs was an isolated case, and he remained an outsider in noble society. As Čapek later wrote, Lažanský's poems were "classical elegies of a sad and lonely man."[117]

As the war ground on, a substantial faction of the Conservative Party went the opposite direction from Lažanský and came increasingly to support Medinger's vision of a German-oriented Monarchy, or at least opposed Czech aspirations to a wide autonomy.[118] In May of 1918, after the Conservative Foreign Minister Ottokar Count Czernin (of an old Czech family) made comments critical of the Czechs, a group of Czechophiles, led by Bedřich Schwarzenberg (of an old German family) signed a public protest against Czernin.[119] With that, the so-called "utraquist" (a-national) wing[120] of the party split off to form the "Imperial Party (*Reichspartei*)," which backed Czernin and the Prime Minister Heinrich Count Clam-Martinic. The Conservative "Right" now openly sought autonomy for the Czechs within the Empire, while the new *Reichspartei* sided momentarily with the German centralists of the Constitutionally Loyal "Left." In a 1916 letter to Alfred Prince Windischgrätz (1851–1927), Ferdinand Prince Lobkovicz (1850–1926) illustrated the fundamental differences behind the split: "We are not agreed on everything, because I am an imperial-loyal Bohemian and you are Bohemian-friendly Austrian."[121] With the Monarchy itself on the verge of cracking up, nobles too fragmented along the national and political fault lines that deepened as the war wore on.

Amid a spate of proclamations of all sorts in 1918, Clam-Martinic issued a declaration of his own on October 22, a few days after the Czechoslovak declaration of independence. In it he proclaimed that "to the last breath we will remain loyal to our dynasty."[122] Clam's words became infamous among the Czechs, who quoted them again and again as an example of noble perfidy. If this scion of the Feudal Conservatives chose the Monarchy over Bohemia, they would argue, did that not cast into doubt the Conservatives' motives in their earlier alliance with the Czechs? This ignored, of course, the divide in the Group of the Right; Clam-Martinic was a member of the *Reichspartei* faction. But in any case, the Czech attacks were symbolic. With the declaration of independence, the Czechs would begin building their own state; nobles and Habsburgs would now become symbolic enemies, the antithesis of the new middle-class nation-state.[123]

Conclusion

Almost twenty years ago, Arno Mayer advanced the provocative thesis that the Old Regime—authoritarian monarchies, a preindustrial economic order, feudal social relations, and nobilitarian values—retained a powerful influence in Europe up until 1918, and perhaps beyond. Many historians have since criticized Mayer for understating the relative importance of bourgeois social and political forms at the end of the nineteenth century.[124] Even so, his work has sparked a much-needed reconsideration of the position of the nobility in the half-century before World War I. Without making any claim to total aristocratic dominance, historians are now providing a more nuanced portrait of late imperial nobilities.

In order to understand the nature and the role of the nobility in late nineteenth-century Europe, we need to unpack the terms Old and New Regime. In economy, Old Regime refers to nonindustrial economic sectors such as agriculture and artisanal manufacturing. Socially, the Old Regime was hierarchical and patriarchal;

society was organized by occupational sector rather than class. Personal relationships were supposedly more important than purely economic relationships, and religion was an ever-present influence in political and social life. The political Old Regime reflected the social; the top levels of the hierarchy held privileged voting rights and, in concert with monarchies, dominated government. In contrast, New Regime implies industrial capitalism, egalitarianism, and democracy.

These are, of course, ideal types. Much of the drama of late nineteenth-century European history lies in the clash of Old and New Regime forces, of landed wealth and industrial capital, quality and quantity, traditional notables and tribunes of the people. Less dramatic, but equally important, was the intermingling of the two, the development of hybrid economic, social, and political forms that frustrated the expectations of sympathizers of both Old and New.

The Bohemian nobility became just such a hybrid class in the nineteenth century, an important part of the broader mix of Old and New that so marked the late Habsburg Empire. In many ways, the emerging New Regime forced nobles to rethink the essence of their nobility. Though few would willingly cast off their traditional privileges, most realized they could survive, even flourish, in a capitalist and meritocratic world. Nobles could, after all, boast substantial capital, education, and social resources. During the course of the nineteenth century, they diversified their income by investing in industry and finance. They modernized their estates to compete on the capitalist world commodities market. In politics, nobles took advantage of the convoluted constitutional structure of the Monarchy to survive as a powerful political class. On the other hand, the Bohemian nobility resisted social change, successfully closing ranks against the threat of rising *nouveaux riches*. Nobles changed so as to conserve, but not more than they had to.

Perhaps uniquely, the Bohemian nobility allows us insight into the place of nationalism in the clash and hybridization of the Old and New Regimes. To Arno Mayer, nationalism and Social Darwinism became tools of Old Regime forces, who manipulated mass nationalist organizations for their own conservative political purposes. But as Geoff Eley and others have shown for Germany, and as this article has shown in the case of Habsburg Bohemia, the relationship of old elites to nationalism was not so simple.[125] In Bohemia, nationalism was a New Regime force, an assertion of popular sovereignty in opposition to authoritarian tendencies of the monarch and bureaucracy. Nationalists wanted power for themselves and for a broad population they claimed to lead; they were not tools of the aristocracy or a reactionary conservative cabal. Nationalism in fact made a mess of the political spectrum. Many liberals were nationalist; many conservatives were nationalist; even socialists were nationalist. Nationalism was, above all, a language of politics and interests. Nobles too tentatively employed a nationalist vocabulary in the late nineteenth century, sensing that without it they would be doomed to political impotence. This was another noble accommodation of the New Regime. But nobles had enough of the Old Regime left in them to chafe at the stridency and coarseness of their national allies. Caught between empire and nation in the last years of the Monarchy, nobles were conflicted and profoundly ambivalent about where they fit in the evolving old-new order.

Notes

1. Oswald Thun to Max Ego Fürstenberg, 28 December 1898, in Ernst Rutkowski, ed., *Briefe und Dokumente zur Geschichte der österreichisch-ungarischen Monarchie unter besonderer Berücksichtigung des böhmisch-mährischen Raumes. Teil I: Der Verfassungstreue Grossgrundbesitz 1880–1899,* 2 vols., vol. I (Munich, 1983), 580.
2. Anthony Cardoza, *Aristocrats in Bourgeois Italy: The Piedmontese Nobility, 1861–1930* (Cambridge, 1997), 10, 219.
3. On national-imperial identity, see Jeremy King, *Budweisers into Czechs and Germans: A Local History of Bohemian Politics, 1848–1948* (Princeton, 2002).
4. On the Junkers and democratization, see Hans Rosenberg, "The Pseudo-Democratisation of the Junker Class," in *The Social History of Politics: Critical Perspectives in West German Historical Writing since 1945,* ed. Georg G. Iggers (Dover, NH, 1985), 81–112.
5. By modernization, I mean the processes of industrialization, urbanization, and expansion of political awareness and participation to middle and lower classes, and the emergence of mass national consciousness.
6. See Eric Hobsbawm, *The Age of Revolution, 1789–1848* (New York, 1996 [1962]).
7. Arno Mayer, *The Persistence of the Old Regime in Europe* (London, 1981).
8. David Higgs, *Nobles in Nineteenth-Century France: The Practice of Inegalitarianism* (Baltimore, 1987).
9. Cardoza, *Aristocrats.*
10. See Josef Macek, *Česká středověká šlechta* (Prague, 1997), ch. 1.
11. Hannes Stekl, "Zwischen Machtverlust und Selbstbehauptung: Österreichs Hocharistokratie vom 18. bis ins 20. Jahrhundert," in Hans-Ulrich Wehler, ed., *Europaeischer Adel 1750–1950* (Goettingen, 1990), 151.
12. Nobles financed one-third of the Kreditanstalt in 1857. Stekl, "Zwischen Machtverlust," 157. Herman Freudenberger points out that nobles also put up two-thirds of the capital for the Chartered Bank of Vienna (also known as the Schwarzenberg Bank) in 1788. It collapsed after the Habsburg state bankruptcy of 1811. Herman Freudenberger, "The Schwarzenberg Bank: A Forgotten Contributor to Austrian Economic Development, 1788–1830," *Austrian History Yearbook* 27 (1996): 41–64.
13. Milan Myška, "Der Adel der böhmischen Länder," in *Der Adel an der Schwelle des bürgerlichen Zeitalters 1780–1860,* ed. Armgard von Reden-Dohna and Ralph Melville (Stuttgart, 1988), 182.
14. C.A. Macartney, *The Habsburg Empire, 1790–1918* (New York, 1969), 622.
15. Jerome Blum, *Noble Landowners and Agriculture in Austria, 1815–1848* (Baltimore, 1948).
16. Landowners received 70 million gulden as compensation. See Alfred Maria Mayer, "Die nationalen und sozialen Verhältnisse im böhmischen Adel und Grossgrundbesitz," *Čechische Revue* 2 (1908): 352. See also Alois Brusatti, ed., *Die wirtschaftliche Entwicklung,* vol. I, *Die Habsburgermonarchie 1848–1918* (Vienna, 1973), 410–415.
17. Myška, "Der Adel," 180. See also Solomon Wank, "Aristocrats and Politics in Austria, 1898–1899: Some Letters of Count Alois Lexa von Aehrenthal and Prince Karl Schwarzenberg," *Austrian History Yearbook,* vol. 19/20, pt. 1 (1983–1984), 136.
18. Milan Myška, "Šlechta v Čechách, na Moravě a ve Slezsku na prahu buržoazní éry," *Časopis Slezského muzea* Series B, no. 36 (1987): 46–65.

19. Mayer, "Die nationalen," 349–51. Note that Mayer's statistics are from 1908 or before, while Medinger's are from 1917 or before. Both sets of statistics are similar, as there was little change in large estate holdings from 1900 to 1918.

20. Wilhelm Medinger, *Grossgrundbesitz, Fideikommiss und Agrarreform* (Vienna, 1919), 32. In Moravia, fourteen landholders owned 13 percent of the province; in Silesia, four owned 25 percent.

21. Statistics from ibid., 34.

22. Ibid., 48–49.

23. Ibid., 16–17.

24. Ibid., 13, 20–21.

25. The only exception was noble political privileges, which will be considered below.

26. Citing Benedict Anderson, Anthony Cardoza notes that nobilities had "concrete, rather than imagined solidarities … the products of kinship, friendship, and personal acquaintance." Cardoza, *Aristocrats,* 8.

27. Ibid., 127. David Higgs notes a similar phenomenon among the French nobility in the nineteenth century. See Higgs, *Nobles in Nineteenth-Century France.*

28. Medinger, *Grossgrundbesitz,* 13.

29. Hradek foundation document, 1841. Quoted in Inge Rohan, *Sychrov Castle: Monument of the Rohan Family* (Turnov, 1996), 19.

30. Ibid., 26–27.

31. Members of the Schwarzenberg secundogeniture used both German and Czech forms of their first names in different contexts. To emphasize this important dualism, I use both as well.

32. Zdeněk Bezecný, "Karel V. ze Schwarzenberku," *Opera Historica* 4 (1995): 286. Schwarzenberg's take was nothing compared to Emperor Francis Joseph's, whose lists numbered over 800,000 beasts shot over his long lifetime.

33. Dominic Lieven, *The Aristocracy in Europe, 1815–1914* (New York, 1991), 157.

34. Gary B. Cohen, *The Politics of Ethnic Survival: Germans in Prague, 1861–1914* (Princeton, 1981), 75–76.

35. Mayer, "Die nationalen," 584.

36. Rita Krueger documents this democratic sociability in "From Empire to Nation: The Aristocracy and the Formation of Modern Society in Bohemia, 1770–1848" (Ph.D. diss., Harvard University, 1997).

37. On curial voting, see table 18 in Bruce Garver, *The Young Czech Party and the Emergence of a Multi-Party System, 1874–1901* (New Haven, 1978), 349. The curias were 1) large landowners, 2) chambers of commerce, 3) municipalities, 4) rural communes, and after 1896, 5) universal.

38. Wank, "Aristocrats and Politics," 137. See also Gerald Stourzh, "Die Mitgliedschaft auf Lebensdauer im österreichischen Herrenhaus 1861–1918," *Mitteilungen des Instituts für österreichische Geschichtsforschung,* no. 73 (1965): 63–117.

39. Garver, *Young Czechs,* 346. In 1908, 17 percent of Bohemian Diet representatives were high nobles. See Robert Luft, "Die Mittelpartei des Mährischen Grossgrundbesitzes 1879–1918," in *Die Chance der Verständigung: Absichten und Ansätze zu übernationaler Zusammenarbeit in den böhmischen Ländern 1848–1918,* ed. Ferdinand Seibt (Munich, 1987), 191f.

40. For more on the Moravian Diet and the particular importance of the nobility there as powerbroker, see ibid., 187–243.

41. Daniel Miller, *Forging Political Compromise: Antonín Švehla and the Czechoslovak Republican Party, 1918–1933* (Pittsburgh, 1999), 25.

42. Adam Wandruszka and Peter Urbanitsch, ed., *Die Habsburgermonarchie 1848–1918, vol. 2, Verwaltung und Rechtswesen* (Vienna, 1975), 281. On 1848 and its legacy, see also Ralph Melville, *Adel und Revolution in Böhmen: Strukturwandel von Herrschaft und Gesellschaft in Österreich um die Mitte des 19. Jahrhunderts* (Mainz, 1998).

43. Wank, "Aristocrats and Politics," 139.

44. Stekl, *Zwischen,* 163–164. See also Medinger, *Grossgrundbesitz,* 51–53.

45. Wank, "Aristocrats and Politics," 138.

46. N. von Preradovich, *Die Führungsschichten in Österreich und Preussen 1804–1918* (Wiesbaden, 1955); cited in Stekl, "Zwischen Machtverlust und Selbstbehauptung" 161.

47. William Godsey, *Aristocratic Redoubt: The Austro-Hungarian Foreign Office on the Eve of the First World War* (West Lafayette, IN, 1999), 31.

48. William Godsey, "Quarterings and Kinship: The Social Composition of the Habsburg Aristocracy in the Dualist Era," *Journal of Modern History,* no. 71 (March 1999): 64.

49. Ibid., 62, 94–104.

50. For a summary of some of this debate, see Gary Cohen, "Neither Absolutism nor Anarchy: New Narratives on Society and Government in Late Imperial Austria," *Austrian History Yearbook* 29 (1998): 37–61.

51. Wank, "Aristocrats and Politics," 139.

52. On liberalism in Austria, see in particular Pieter M. Judson, *Exclusive Revolutionaries. Liberal Politics, Social Experience, and National Identity in the Austrian Empire, 1848–1914* (Ann Arbor, 1996).

53. The two noble factions were parties in the sense of *Honoratiorenparteien,* which they remained until 1918. Given their very small constituencies, they had a minimal administrative apparatus and did not run campaigns in the normal sense. On the two noble political parties, see Lothar Höbelt, ""Verfassungstreue" und "feudale": Die beiden österreichischen Adelsparteien 1861–1918," *Études Danubiennes,* vol. 7, no. 2 (1991): 103–114.

54. Cisleithania denotes the lands of the Austrian half of the Austro-Hungarian Empire after 1867, when the *Ausgleich* effectively gave Hungary autonomy. Technically, Cisleithania was known as the "lands represented in the Reichsrat," or the Austrian provinces, Bohemia, Moravia-Silesia, and Galicia and Bukovina.

55. Bruce Garver, *Young Czech Party,* 51.

56. Technically, Czech Social Democrats shared a party structure with their German-Austrian counterparts until 1911. But national interests divided Czech and German socialists long before then. See Macartney, *Habsburg Empire,* 683–685, 803–804.

57. In another context, Rogers Brubaker writes of "the nationalization of narrative and interpretative frames, of perception and evaluation, of thinking and feeling. It has involved the silencing or marginalization of alternative, nonnationalist political language. It has involved the nullification of complex identities by the terrible categorical simplicity of ascribed nationality." Rogers Brubaker, *Nationalism Reframed: Nationhood and the National Question in the New Europe* (Cambridge, 1996), 20.

58. King, *Budweisers,* 48–49.

59. King, *Budweisers,* 132–139.

60. Gerald Stourzh, "Ethnic Attribution in Late Imperial Austria: Good Intentions, Evil Consequences," in *The Habsburg Legacy: National Identity in Historical Perspective,* ed. Ritchie Robertson and Edward Timms (Edinburgh, 1994), 71.

61. Stourzh, "Ethnic Attribution," 74. King documents a similar compromise, brokered by the Crown, in Budweis in 1913. See King, Budweisers, 277–280.

62. Karl/Karel III Prince Schwarzenberg, 1871 speech in the Reichsrat. Quoted in Milan M. Buben, "Česká zemská šlechta: Schwarzenberkové sekundogenitura [The Bohemian nobility: the Schwarzenberg secundogeniture]," *Střední Evropa* 12, no. 56 (1996): 106.

63. "Utraquism" had a long history in Bohemia. It originally referred to the practice introduced by Jan Hus in the early sixteenth century of delivering the Eucharist "sub utra specie," i.e., both bread and wine. This set him apart from the traditional practice of offering wine only to the clergy. During the Hussite Wars, the ultimately victorious moderate faction of Hussites adopted the name Utraquists. They rejected the radical egalitarianism of the Taborites, and were more conciliatory towards the Catholic Church. Among nobles in the nineteenth

century, Utraquism signified a moderate federalism that acknowledged the Czech and German duality of Bohemia.

64. Friedrich Schwarzenberg to Vincenc Auersperg, 8 September 1862. Reproduced in Antonín Okáč, *Rakouský problém a list Vaterland 1860–1871* [The Austrian problem and the newspaper Vaterland], vol. 2 (Brno, 1970), 129–134.

65. Robert Sak, "Der Platz der Schwarzenberger in der tschechischen Politik der zweiten Hälfte des neunzehnten Jahrhunderts," *Opera Historica Editio Universitatis Bohemiae Meridionalis* 2 (1992): 108.

66. Karl/Karel III Schwarzenberg to František Rieger, 23 April 1862. Quoted in Okáč, *Rakouský problém*, I, 77.

67. Karl/Karel III Schwarzenberg to Vincenc Auersperg, August or September 1862. Reproduced in Okáč, *Rakouský problém*, II, 125–128.

68. Quoted in Buben, "Schwarzenberkové sekundogenitura," 108. Schwarzenberg's statement has been reported in a variety of ways; Cynthia Paces adopts the following: "We see in the Hussites not celebrated heroes, but a band of bandits and arsonists, communists from the fifteenth century." Paces, "Religious Images and National Symbols in the Creation of Czech Identity, 1890–1938" (Ph.D. diss., Columbia University, 1998), 27.

69. Quoted in Jiří Rak, *Bývalé Čechové ... české historický mýty a stereotypy* [Czechs of old ... Czech historical myths and stereotypes] (Prague, 1994), 78.

70. Paces, "Religious Images," 28. The National Liberal (Young Czech) Party was founded in 1874, though they tended to group themselves in the Reichsrat with the Old Czechs until 1888. See Gordon Skilling, "The Politics of the Czech Eighties," in *The Czech Renascence of the Nineteenth Century*, ed. Peter Brock and Gordon Skilling (Toronto, 1970), 254–281.

71. This seemingly trivial issue dominated Bohemian and Imperial politics for much of the last decade of the nineteenth century. Germans opposed the change because official bilingualism would have effectively removed scores of German monolingual civil servants. Both sides rioted in the Landtag and Reichsrat over the issue, and it brought down a number of Imperial governments.

72. Bedřich Schwarzenberg speech in *Reichsrat*, quoted in *Fremden-Blatt*, Vienna, 7 November 1896, 3.

73. 6 Jan 1898, quoted in King, *Budweisers*, 98. Bedřich was the brother of Karl/Karel IV of the secundogeniture.

74. Buben, "Schwarzenberkové sekundogenitura," 107.

75. On the Staatsrecht program, see Garver, *Young Czechs*, 49–53.

76. Franz Thun quoted in Havránek, "The Development of Czech Nationalism," *Austrian History Yearbook*, vol. 3, pt. 2 (1967): 236.

77. Skilling, "Czech Eighties," 265–266. Rieger's quotation came from a letter on 23 February 1883.

78. Rieger, letter of 10 December 1889, quoted in ibid., 206.

79. Concessions included the advent of official bilingualism for the public business of the Bohemian bureaucracy (1880), the split of Prague University into Czech and German parts (1882), and an expansion of the franchise (1882).

80. Quoted in Skilling, "Czech Eighties," 266.

81. Quoted in ibid., 268.

82. Garver, *Young Czechs*, 228.

83. Ibid., 240.

84. Ibid., 309.

85. Alois Aehrenthal to his father, 5 June 1893, in Rutkowski, ed., *Briefe und Dokumente, Teil I*, 185. Schwarzenberg repeated this call for absolutism in an 1898 letter to Aehrenthal: "In my opinion, Austria can no longer be held together in any other way than by a modernized absolutism." Quoted in Solomon Wank, "Aristocrats and Politics," 170.

86. Karl Schwarzenberg to Alois Aehrenthal, 4 May 1899, Rutkowski, I, 684–685.

87. Rudolf Czernin to Max Egon Fürstenberg, 20 November 1895, Rutkowski, I, 240.
88. "Der entscheidende Punct," *Vaterland,* 9 January 1870. Cited in Okáč, *Rakouský problém,* I, 226.
89. Rutkowski, I, 17.
90. "Wahlaufruf," Prague, 6 November 1895, Rutkowski, I, 235.
91. "Bericht über die Wahlkomiteesitzung vom 16. November 1896," Rutkowski, I, 285–286.
92. Oswald Thun to Alain Rohan, 15 March 1898, in Paul Molisch, ed., *Briefe zur Deutschen Politik in Österreich von 1848 bis 1918* (Vienna, 1934), 364. See also Oswald Thun to Franz Thun, 9 March 1898, Rutkowski, I, 462. Oswald Thun was a descendent of Joseph Mathias Thun of the Klösterle branch of the family. He served as head of the Constitutionals from 1890 to 1906.
93. "Wahlaufruf," 6 November 1895, Rutkowski, I, 234.
94. Max Egon Fürstenberg to Karl Schwarzenberg, 30 December 1897, Rutkowski, I, 422.
95. Oswald Thun to Alain Rohan, 22 December 1897, Rutkowski, I, 417.
96. Alois Aehrenthal to his father, 23 August 1883, Rutkowski, I, 113.
97. Carl Schorske, *Fin-de-Siecle Vienna: Politics and Culture* (New York, 1981), 119. It was particularly galling to nobles that von Schönerer was himself noble, albeit of low rank. His father had been granted a title of nobility in 1860 in honor of his work constructing railway lines. See Schorske, 121–122.
98. Guido Dubsky to Joseph Maria Baernreither, 3 August 1896, Rutkowski, I, 261–263.
99. Alois Aehrenthal to his father, 12 May 1897, Rutkowski, I, 328–329.
100. Alain Rohan to Max Ego Fürstenberg, 10 April 1899, Rutkowski, I, 679.
101. Oswald Thun, diary entry 16 September 1897, Rutkowski, I, 90.
102. Alois Aehrenthal to Karl Buquoy, 13 December 1889, Rutkowski, I, 152.
103. Karl Moritz Zedtwitz to Baernreither, 2 July 1897, Rutkowski, I, 355.
104. Oswald Thun to Alain Rohan, 15 March 1898, in Molisch, 364.
105. Oswald Thun to Max Ego Fürstenberg, 28 December 1898, Rutkowski, I, 580.
106. Rutkowski, I, 24.
107. On the punktace, see Jan Křen, *Konfliktní společenství: Češi a Němci 1780–1918* (Prague, 1990), 230–238.
108. On the "Verständigungskonferenzen" of 1900, see Ernst Rutkowski, ed., *Briefe und Dokumente zur Geschichte der österreichisch-ungarischen Monarchie unter besonderer Berücksichtigung des böhmisch-mährischen Raumes. Teil II: Der Verfassungstreue Grossgrundbesitz 1900–1904* (Munich, 1991), 613–634.
109. "Schlussprotokol über die in Prag und in Wien von den Vertretern der beider Gruppen des Grossgrundbesitzes in Böhmen abgehalten Besprechungen über eine Reihe von den deutsch-böhmischen Streit bildenden Fragen," 1910, SOA Litoměřice (Děčín), RA Clam-Gallas, k 618, ic 2319.
110. Karl/Karel Schwarzenberg to Alois Lexa von Aehrenthal, 3 February 1898. Quoted in Soloman Wank, "Aristocrats and Politics in Austria 1867–1914: A Case of Historiographical Neglect," *East European Quarterly* XXVI, no. 2 (1992, June): 141–142. Similar thoughts seemed to be on Oswald Thun's mind when he wrote in June 1897: "The further words from the Emperor: 'We have laws with which one can not govern' give occasion to very deep reflection." Oswald Thun to Alain Rohan, 14 June 1897, in Molisch, 355.
111. Wank, "Historiographical Neglect," 142.
112. Robert Kann, *A History of the Habsburg Empire, 1526–1918* (Berkeley, 1974), 489.
113. Quoted in Höbelt, ""Verfassungstreue" und "feudale," 111f.
114. Unnamed Conservative quoted in Wilhelm Medinger, "Referat in der Versammlung des Verfassungstreuen Grossgrundbesitzes," Prague, 13 June 1915, p. 20. SOA Litoměřice (Děčín), RA Clam-Gallas, k 618 ic 2319.
115. Friedrich Schwarzenberg, report of meeting of members of the Conservative Large Landowners, 16 January 1916. SOA Plzeň (Klatovy), RA Windischgrätz, k 656 ic 4113.

116. Medinger, "Referat," 11, 13–16, 20–21, 24.
117. Karel Čapek, *Ratolest a vavřín* [Twig and laurel] (Prague, 1947), 97–98, 100, 297. See also Petr Mašek, *Modrá krev* [Blue blood] (Prague, 1994), 110–15.
118. The party was also now known as the "Right," with the Constitutionals dubbed the "Left." The Conservative Clam-Martinic, who became Prime Minister in December 1916, favored a pro-German government dictated by an Imperial octroi. See Todd Wayne Huebner, "The Multinational "Nation-State": The Origins and the Paradox of Czechoslovakia, 1914–1920" (Ph.D. diss., Columbia University, 1993), 40, 105.
119. Oswald Kostrba-Skalicky, "Die 'Burg' und der Adel," in *Die Burg,* ed. Karl Bosl (Vienna, 1974), 165. In addition to Schwarzenberg, signers of the protest included Friedrich Prince Lobkowicz, Count Bohuslav Kolowrat, and Adalbert Count Sternberg. See also Lothar Höbelt, "Adel und Politik seit 1848," in *Die Fuerstenberger,* ed. Erwein Eltz and Arno Strohmeyer (Schloß Weitra, 1994), 374–375.
120. Oskar von Parish-Senftenberg to Prince Alfred Windischgrätz, 29 May 1918. Excerpt in Molisch, 393.
121. Ferdinand Lobkovicz to Alfred Windischgrätz, 7 June 1916. SOA Plzeň (Klatovy), RA Windischgrätz, k 656 ic 4113.
122. Antonín Kubačák, "Činnost Svazu československých velkostatkářů' v letech 1919–1943 [Activity of the Union of Czechoslovak Large Landowners 1919–1943]," *Sborník archivních prací* 37 (1987): 339. In addition to Clam-Martinic, signers of the declaration included Zdeněk Lobkowicz, Jaroslav Chotek, Adalbert Schönborn, Josef Nostitz, F. Lichtenstein Jr., and Eugen Czernin.
123. On nobles and nascent Czechoslovakia, see Eagle Glassheim, "Crafting a Post-Imperial Identity: Nobles and Nationality Politics in Czechoslovakia, 1918–1948" (Ph.D. diss., Columbia University, 2000).
124. Among others, see Lieven, *Aristocracy in Europe;* and David Blackbourn and Geoff Eley, *The Peculiarities of German History* (New York, 1984).
125. See Geoff Eley, *Reshaping the German Right: Radical Nationalism and Political Change after Bismarck* (New Haven, 1980).

Chapter 5

The Bohemian Oberammergau

Nationalist Tourism in the Austrian Empire

Pieter M. Judson

In the fall of 1892, in a tiny and out-of-the-way village in southern Bohemia, the German League of the Bohemian Woods (*Deutscher Böhmerwaldbund*) laid the foundations for a modern festival theater capable of accommodating 2,000 visitors. The League, an Austro-German nationalist self-help organization, hoped thereby to transform the isolated village of Höritz/Hořice na Šumavě, into an internationally acclaimed festival site that might one day rival the Bavarian passion play at Oberammergau. Ultimately, the League gambled that a strong tourism industry could help to reverse the declining economic and demographic position of the German-speaking population in that part of southern Bohemia referred to in Czech as the *Šumava,* and known by Germans as the *Böhmerwald* or Bohemian Woods.[1]

The villagers of Höritz/Hořice presented their passion play to an international audience several times before 1914. When the First World War intervened, the play was cancelled indefinitely, and was not revived until 1923, by which time the Bohemian Woods had been incorporated into the new Czechoslovak State. After that, the villagers performed the play in three- or four-year intervals until 1938, when the region was incorporated into the Third Reich. During the Second World War the Nazi Government used the festival theater to train troops for the *Afrikakorps,* and at the end of the war, American occupation forces briefly used the theater as a dance hall. After expulsion had removed the German-speaking population from the region, Höritz/Hořice's new inhabitants actually revived the passion play in 1947 and 1948, presenting a Czech-language version of the original using the same scenery, costumes, and direction. In 1948, however, the new communist regime banned further performances, and in 1966 tore down what remained of the theater. With the fall of communism in 1989, the village's Czech-speaking inhabitants have decided to renew the passion play tradition, and they are currently raising money to build a new outdoor amphitheater.[2]

At first glance, this appears to be a story about a quaint village religious tradition revived over a century ago (and then again in the 1990s) by pious inhabitants who also hoped to benefit from tourist spending in their economically depressed village. But anyone who knows the history of nationalist movements in the region will immediately recognize the potentially more bizarre qualities to this story. First is the issue of the sponsorship of the passion play by the League in the 1890s. Why did a German nationalist organization well known in Austria for its anticlerical ideology fund an overtly Catholic religious tradition? Second is the problem of how support for the passion play could have been understood to further a specifically German nationalist interest in the region? Third is the more elusive question of what the passion play signified to its audiences and to the villagers themselves? Did the play contribute to building a stronger sense of German nationalist identity, as was hoped, either among audiences or performers? In a larger sense, my investigation of the passion play tradition is meant to shed some light on the local workings of German nationalism in Bohemia during the first half of the twentieth century.

Let us start with the *Deutscher Böhmerwaldbund,* or League.[3] A group of concerned citizens from Southern Bohemia, most of them living in the city of Budweis/České Budějovice and led by a young lawyer, Josef Taschek, founded this organization in 1884. They wanted both to raise funds for and to mobilize public interest in the economic plight of German speakers in the Bohemian Woods. The League's leaders hoped to improve the region's economy enough to dissuade its inhabitants from emigrating, and to prevent a so-called invasion of Czech-speakers into a region they themselves claimed had been originally purely German in character. The League's pursuit of German nationalist objectives was linked intimately to regional issues of economic survival in southern Bohemia.[4] Ideologically, the League proclaimed an essentially defensive stance. It aimed only to protect what it referred to as German national property (*Nationalbesitzstand*) in a region known increasingly as a *Sprachgrenze,* or language frontier, and not to intimidate or germanize the Czech-speaking population there. Such programmatic niceties were often lost in daily political conflicts, however, particularly in a region where many people had little sense of belonging to either nation and were therefore considered fair game by both Czech and German nationalist organizations.

The political importance of maintaining linguistic purity in such regions grew considerably in the 1880s, as German nationalist politicians in Bohemia increasingly adopted a strategy of seeking full administrative separation from the Czechs. Recognizing that they would always constitute a political minority in Bohemia as a whole, German nationalists now sought to delineate a specifically German

Bohemia from its Czech counterpart. Such a settlement would have given Czech and German nationalists a free hand in the separate administration of school systems, electoral politics, and welfare policies, and in some versions it would have prevented civil servants in the German districts from the obligation of having to learn Czech. Most Czech nationalists vigorously opposed any policy of administrative separation for Bohemia. They defended the administrative integrity of the historic kingdom, arguing that there were in fact Czech-speaking minority communities in every region, including those with a German-speaking majority.

Once German nationalists had adopted the goal of separation, their politicians had to face the difficult reality of linguistic demographic trends throughout the regions of Bohemia they alleged to be German. Demands for administrative separation were founded largely on census results that confirmed the overwhelmingly German linguistic character of geographic regions like the Bohemian Woods. However, in German nationalist eyes the demographic situation was changing in the Czechs' favor, as ever more Czech speakers established themselves in previously German areas. In some ways it was not so much that greater numbers of Czech speakers were invading previously German villages, as the nationalists portrayed it, but that the Czech speakers who did migrate there no longer assimilated linguistically into the larger German-speaking population. Increasingly such minority populations were supported by vigorous new Czech nationalist organizations like the National Union for the *Šumava* (*Národní Jednota Pošumavská*) that performed comparable functions to those of the Germans' League of the Bohemian Wood.[5] Organizations like the German League were meant ideally to keep local populations alert to the dangers of Czech "penetration" into their region. In fact, however, their greater task was to convince or teach the locals about the importance of belonging to a German national community in the first place. One could not argue for vigilance against the Czechs if the local population did not see itself in terms of nationalist identity.

The model for this new type of nationalist self-help organization among German nationalists in Austria was the German School Association (*Deutscher Schulverein*), the first of several German nationalist associations founded in the 1880s. This organization raised money to support German language schools and kindergartens in linguistically mixed localities where the small number of German-speaking children did not qualify for a state-supported German-language school. The School Association organized branches in villages, towns, and cities in every region of the Empire, from Vorarlberg in the West to the Bukovina in the East, from Silesia in the North to Dalmatia in the South. Its structure was meant to coordinate the diverse needs of specific localities with the resources collected by an interregional umbrella organization. The School Association swiftly grew to become one of the largest voluntary associations in Central Europe. In 1886, only six years after its founding, it already boasted 107,000 members. The founders of the German League for the Bohemian Woods modeled their own modest organization on this successful marriage of local concerns with interregional fund-raising. Taschek tirelessly promoted his new organization in tiny villages and towns across southern Bohemia. He encouraged local branches to report back to the central organization about demographic conditions and economic needs in their localities. And given the rudimentary nature (by Bohemian standards) of transport in Southern Bohemia at the time, the poor condition of roads, and the absence of many railway links, this kind of organizational structure made good sense.[6]

There were of course some dangers involved in founding an organization that gave too much leeway to the initiative of local branches. School Association leaders had themselves learned this the hard way when their organization was ripped apart by a controversy over the issue of anti-Semitism in the mid-1880s. Some local branch leaders had wanted to bar Jews from joining the organization, while the umbrella leadership had promoted Jewish membership and aid to Jewish schools as a good alternative to local Slav schools. Although the leadership won this particular battle, several members led by Georg von Schönerer and his wife resigned from the organization in 1885 to set up a rival (and unsuccessful) German School Association for anti-Semites. Taschek seems to have kept firm control over the League through his more than fifty years as its leader and moving force, and the issue of Jewish membership was never raised within his organization. Nevertheless, after 1890 the League faced increasing competition for funds and members from other newer organizations, especially the anti-Semitic League of Germans in Bohemia (*Bund der Deutschen in Böhmen*).[7]

All of these and other regional nationalist organizations founded in Austria in the 1880s and 1890s hoped to mobilize an ever-greater number of local activists for the nationalist causes. To do so, however, required convincing people that this cause held some deeper significance to local society in the first place. Interest in German nationalism was not particularly high in southern Bohemia, when compared to that in urban centers like Prague or Reichenberg/Liberec in the North. While more urban-centered organizations focused their rhetorical efforts completely on nationalist politics, the League decided on a different set of tactics. It directed its attention more to the economic issues of specific concern to local farmers and artisans. The League engaged several traveling teachers (*Wanderlehrer*) who held local courses and workshops on matters of interest to the peasant and artisan populations of the region. The organization helped found credit cooperatives to help farmers purchase tools, livestock, fruit trees, or even land. Unlike any other comparable organization in the Austrian Empire, however, the League also promoted tourism to the region, and lobbied the government heavily for the development of roads and railroads to link the region more effectively to the outside world.[8]

Why Taschek saw tourism as a potential savior of the Southern Bohemian economy at such an early date is difficult to say. In the 1880s, Austria's tourism industry was only just being organized, and mostly in well-traveled destinations with good railway connections like the Tyrol, the Bohemian spa towns, or the Imperial capital of Vienna.[9] Yet from the start, leaders of the League asserted that the tourist industry offered the Germans of the Bohemian Woods a viable economic solution to many of their problems. In particular, the rising popularity of the *Sommerfrische* (summer vacation) in the countryside among the urban middle classes in the rest of Austria and neighboring Bavaria appeared to present a potentially rich source of economic stimulation.[10] The extremely low prices of accommodation and board made the region attractive to middle-class vacationers who could not afford long-term visits to the more fashionable summer resorts. The landscape and quality of the air was indeed legendary. But developing a tourism industry turned out to be more difficult than was originally imagined. The region was unknown, was difficult to reach, and had bad internal roads. It was hard to persuade people to come to such an out-of-the-way region, and it often turned out to be even harder to persuade the locals to participate in the venture that promised them a better livelihood.

The League addressed these problems by publishing guidebooks, advertising at travel agencies and exhibitions in Austria and Germany, and lobbying the government to improve railway connections. The second problem, how to get the locals to cooperate more fully, took a great deal of the League's energy, and was never fully solved. Early travelers to the region often complained about the poor quality of local food, accommodations, and sanitary conditions.[11] Few of the locals saw much value in making the tourist experience as comfortable as possible. As late as 1908, a newspaper in the comparatively well-traveled town of Prachatitz/ Prachatice complained that locals charged too much for rooms and meals, that shopkeepers treated tourists with a brusqueness bordering on rudeness, and that shops were dirty and displayed their wares unattractively. These problems, it was believed, drove tourists into the arms of the apparently more polite and cleaner Czech shopkeepers.[12]

To nationalists in the League, the economic desirability of bringing in great numbers of German-speaking tourists to help revive an economically impoverished area was inseparable from the demographic need to populate a threatened German landscape with even more German speakers. The ambivalence around the question of promoting a general tourist industry that was at the same time a specifically nationalist tourism remained visible in the League's literature. Was it more important to ensure local Germans a livelihood through tourism, or to bring in as many specifically German speakers as possible as tourists? When Czech nationalists in the National Union for the *Šumava* began to promote the region as a tourist destination for Czechs from Prague and other cities, the German League reacted with bitterness. "The Czechs frequently organize trips to the Bohemian Woods, and strive to promote its Czechification through mass tourism," complained Taschek at a League convention in 1902. "The only way to respond to this policy is through a mass immigration of as many German summer vacationers as possible." Elsewhere Taschek accused "Czech summer vacationers and tourists [of choosing] to come to our Bohemian woods not for love of nature or forest beauty, but with the intention of engaging in anti-German agitation and disturbing the national peace in our *Heimat.*"[13]

With this background in mind, we can now approach the actual setting of our story. The village of Höritz/Hořice sits 679 meters above sea level on a steep hillside, in a rolling landscape that remains bucolic even today. In 1900 the village (or *Marktfleck,* as such regional marketplaces were traditionally called) counted a population of 1,232 inhabitants with 146 houses covering 500 hectares. Its layout has not changed much during the past century. Most of the buildings still surround a long, narrow square built into the side of a hill. At the bottom of the square stands a small Gothic church, fully renovated in 1892–93 and renowned for its Grödener carved wood statuary. According to the Austrian census of 1900, an overwhelming majority of Höritzers (1,222) claimed German as their language of daily use (*Umgangssprache/obcovací řeč*), while ten individuals claimed the Czech language. Twelve individuals in the village were listed as Jews, and the rest Catholics.[14] Most villagers farmed and raised sheep, although some did work at the graphite works in Schwarzbach/Černá v Pošumaví, almost an hour away. One kilometer below the village, about a ten-minute walk from the tiny main square, lies the railroad station. In 1891, the completion of the Budweis-Salnau line suddenly linked Höritz/Hořice to Krummau/Krumlov and Budweis/Budějovice to the north, as well as to Schwarzbach/Černá v Pošumaví to the south. As was so often the case in rural Europe at the start of the twentieth century, the arrival of a railway played a critical role in determining the particular trajectory of the village's development. In this particular case it is clear that without the new railway connection, the League would not have invested so many resources in developing the town, and Höritz/Hořice's passion play might never have gained world-wide attention.

Figure 5.1. The Town of Höritz/Hořiče in the Bohemian Woods at the Turn of the Century. Postcard from the author's personal collection.

Among the villagers were several German nationalists of the more liberal rather than radical or anti-Semitic variety. They had founded a local branch of the League as early as August 1884, and by 1888 they numbered 178 members (15 percent of the total populace). Their president, Francis Mugrauer, ran the local inn, the *"Zum Teufel."* The League held its local meetings here, and it was also here, ironically given the inn's name, that rehearsals for the passion play took place in 1893 before the theater's completion.[15] Höritz frequently earned an honorable mention in the League's magazine, the *Mittheilungen des deutschen Böhmerwaldbundes.* One story from Höritz/Hořice involving the activities of the local priest helps to explain why German nationalists there and in the region did not fear that their support for the local passion play would somehow subsidize the politically reactionary or alleged pro-Czech activities of the Catholic Church. Most German nationalists in Bohemia considered parish priests to be unofficial, yet highly effective "national fifth columnists," men who could be considered part of the Czech nationalist movement. Both the Church's political opposition to the liberals' secular school system and the increasing tendency of local priests to speak Czech rather than German or both languages (given the changing make-up of recruits to the clergy in Bohemia), made all Church institutions suspect to German nationalists. Yet Höritz/Hořice reported a more cordial relationship between its parish priest and its local German nationalists.

In 1886 the village council decided to erect a monument to Emperor Joseph II. Such statues became something of an industry for civic-minded German nationalists in late nineteenth-century Bohemia, even in rural areas like the Bohemian Woods. The local branch of the League shared the costs with the village council, and in August of 1887 the town dedicated the statue. Interestingly, it was reported that the parish priest had helped with the preparations for the celebration and had participated at the unveiling. He had even decorated the parish house with both the imperial black/yellow flag and with a German nationalist black-red-gold flag. "These flags prove," noted the League's magazine, "that the priest in this parish is no enemy of the German people and of his own parishioners, but a priest who fulfills the duties of his office as a good Austrian should, and who remains loyal to his nation of origin." Most parish priests would, of course, have boycotted such a ceremony, not so much for its arguably German nationalist aspects but because they rightly perceived the anticlerical nature of the cult of Joseph II in Bohemia.[16]

Around the time of the railroad's completion, a young gymnasium professor from nearby Krummau/Krumlov, Josef Johann Ammann, began researching passion play traditions among peasants in southern Bohemia. Höritz/Hořice was the only village that had maintained the tradition from the seventeenth century through the 1880s. The village also had an 1816 text written by linen weaver Paul Gröllhesl, who had adapted it from seventeenth-century counterreformation texts by Cistercian monks in the region. During the course of the nineteenth century, peasant groups had performed the Gröllhesl play at irregular intervals, generally dressed in their Sunday best, and at a local inn for mostly peasant audiences. In the 1830s the play had flourished under the guidance of a particularly forceful parish priest, Father Bruno. He had tried, with mixed results, to professionalize the venture. Bruno's caustic marginal remarks cover the original Gröllhesl manuscript, and his severely disapproving comments tell us much about how peasants treated the work in the 1830s. Repeatedly Bruno admonished the performers to inject more seriousness into the venture: Mary Magdalene should be presented as a loyal follower of Christ, and not as a lovesick schoolgirl; the taunting of Christ should induce pity in the audience, and not hysterical laughter.[17]

New elements were added to the performances over the years. In 1851, for the first time, women played the female roles of Eve, Mary, Mary Magdalene, and Veronica.[18] At around that time, some players also began to create what they imagined were historically authentic costumes for themselves. In the 1880s a local theater group took over the production. On learning of a travelling production of the play in the winter of 1889, Ammann rushed to make the arduous two-hour trip on a stormy day from Krummau/Krumlov to the village of Kalsching/Chvalšiny, a trip that today takes a matter of minutes. In Kalsching/Chvalšiny he was able to witness a production firsthand. According to Ammann, the piece had a powerful effect on local peasant audiences. By the end there was not a dry eye in the house, especially among the women. And both intentional and unintentional comedic touches helped to hold the attention of the audience during the long hours it took to perform the piece.[19] Although at first Ammann had never dreamed the play might compete with Oberammergau's passion play, the completion of the new rail line and the subsequent financial support of the League for a real festival theater in Höritz/Hořice excited his ambitions.[20]

For their part, Taschek and the other leaders of the League saw in the passion play a golden opportunity to introduce far more tourists to the Bohemian Woods than had been previously thought possible. Once the tourist had come to Höritz/Hořice to see the play and had been exposed to the surrounding landscape, he would want to return for summer relaxation, to enjoy the good clean air, and perhaps in the winter he would come to ski, skate, and toboggan.[21] So in 1892 the League concluded an agreement with the village of Höritz/Hořice to provide the financing both for a festival theater and for the production itself.[22] The village would provide the actors (some 350 strong), while the League hired designers, a musical director, and a theatrical director from Budweis/Budějovice, Ludwig Deutsch, who claimed, at least, to be experienced in passion play productions.[23]

Problems soon arose regarding the League's relationship with Ammann. Ammann considered that the text was his legal property (he owned the copyright), and he planned to publish an annotated version soon after the play had received its first performances. Although happy to allow the League and the town of Höritz/Hořice full usage rights to the text, he kept ultimate ownership. This did not present any difficulties at first, according to Ammann's account, until Deutsch joined Ammann for actual rehearsals in Höritz/Hořice in March 1893. The relationship between these two men was not a happy one, and we have only the author's account of the problems that then developed. Deutsch, it turned out, had no experience directing the passion play at Brixlegg, as he had claimed, but had appeared once as Christ in a travelling production. Moreover, Ammann claimed that Deutsch treated the villagers with arrogance, and soon lost their trust. Worst of all, Deutsch engaged a Moravian priest, Provost Landsteiner of Nikolsburg/ Mikulov, to improve upon Ammann's lyrics for several of the songs. Ammann agreed to small changes, but at the end of the 1893 season the League invited Landsteiner to rewrite the text entirely, and to prevent Ammann from publishing his version. Ammann brought a lawsuit against the League that was eventually settled out of court. The League gained the rights to his version, but Ammann could publish his text. After this, Landsteiner was generally, if misleadingly, presented as the author of the revived text. Two Höritzers quit the production in protest, given Ammann's work in reviving the play and the fact that the town had granted him honorary citizenship. Deutsch, for all of his problems, remained on the job and celebrated much success over the years as director of the production. For the most part, this teapot tempest seems to have paled in comparison to the enormous changes the festival brought to the people of Höritz/Hořice.[24]

Construction of the theater proceeded apace on a hill above the town, and by the spring of 1893 the largely wood structure on a granite foundation was ready. The theater held some 2,000 spectators, and was the first building in the Bohemian Woods to use electricity.[25] When the play opened in June, it took two steam engines worth of coal to generate enough electricity for one performance. The village also hastily erected some refreshment stands to satisfy the visitors, who would sit through an eight-hour performance with few intermissions. The performances were timed so that visitors could catch an evening train back to Krummau/Krumlov or Budweis/Budějovice, but many people were known to sneak out before the final tableau for fear of missing their connection. Most visitors preferred not to chance actually spending a night in Höritz/Hořice, something the 1908 Baedeker guide to Austria strongly advised against. And, despite the best efforts of the League to improve conditions for tourists, one Viennese feuilletonist caused a media uproar with a bitingly satiric account of the small-town boredom and boorishness he encountered on a 1908 trip to Höritz/Hořice.[26]

The first half of the play, performed in the morning, consisted of *tableaux vivants* depicting biblical scenes from the creation and the fall, then skipping ahead to scenes from the life of Christ, and ending with his entrance into Jerusalem. In the afternoon the passion play itself was performed. The production was designed and performed in a style that could be characterized as nineteenth-century international historicist. Anyone who has seen a D.W. Griffith film set in ancient times or an early Cecil B. DeMille production would immediately recognize several of its design elements.[27]

Responses to the passion play varied. Most newspapers and critics, particularly the German nationalist ones, gave it enthusiastic reviews, praising both the technological marvels (electric lights, organ) and the convincing, simple acting style of the Höritz/Hořice villagers. Several Catholic conservative papers conceded that the play was both powerful and emotional, although they deplored its

Figure 5.2. The Last Supper, as depicted around 1900 at the Höritz Festival for a local guide: *Der Böhmerwald und das Höritzer Passionsspiel,* published by the Deutscher Böhmerwaldbund, Budweis, 1908.

connection to anticlerical German nationalism and the League. Grumbling was to be heard in the more radical German nationalist and anti-Semitic papers. They complained that by sponsoring the passion play, the nationalist movement was playing into the hands of clerical reactionaries. What is interesting, however, is the degree to which the most radical nationalist of German nationalist organizations (like the *Südmark,* headquartered in Graz) decided to close ranks behind the League. Instead of seizing this opportunity to discredit moderate nationalists and to split the nationalist movement further (their usual strategy for obtaining political and financial support), these groups focused on the positive publicity the play might bring to local German nationalists.

In August 1893 the conservative *Vaterland* did report that Czech nationalists had managed to gain access to the play's text, and with the support of local clerical conservatives, were planning their own rival passion play. This report turned out later to be groundless, and may even have been planted by German nationalists attempting to stir up greater sympathy for the play among those hard-core nationalists who hated the idea of working with the Church on a cultural project. Repeatedly throughout the 1890s, some clerical conservative anti-Semitic newspapers launched thinly-veiled attacks on the play.[28]

Not only did German nationalists and foreign tourists flock to see the passion play in the early years, but soon it began to draw the interest of prominent citizens, of the nobility, and of the Habsburg family as well. The Bishop of nearby Budweis/Budějovice was a frequent visitor, and his presence did much to diminish attacks on the venture by the conservative media. After the first month of performances, members of the Schwarzenberg family who owned a good chunk of the Bohemian Woods reserved several blocks of tickets. Later the family erected its own refreshment pavilion for the exclusive use of its guests. A week after the first Schwarzenberg visit in 1893, the Governor of Bohemia, Count Francis Thun, bought tickets for a gala performance. And in mid-August the local papers reported that the play had even piqued the interest of Archduke Ludwig Victor, the Kaiser's transvestite younger brother, known in intimate circles as "Luzi-Wuzi," whose scandalous behavior eventually required his being kept in the countryside around Salzburg for long stretches. In 1895 Crown Princess Widow Stephanie attended a performance as a guest of the Schwarzenberg family. Despite terrible weather, several hundred people showed up to greet Stephanie and her daughter Archduchess Elizabeth. Along with a performance, the audience heard Taschek thank the Crown Princess Widow in person for ensuring that the passion play would be included in the volumes of the *Österreichische ungarische Monarchie in Wort und Bild* being prepared under her patronage. In 1896 it was the turn of the heir to the throne, Archduke Francis Ferdinand, to attend. After a French and American coproduction filmed a short version of the play in 1897, an American entrepreneur even tried unsuccessfully to organize a tour in the United States.[29]

In May of 1895, at the instigation of the League, the village, together with the League and the local savings-and-loan bank, created a limited liability corporation known as the Höritzer Folk-Theater (*Volksschauspiele*). The League contributed 6,000 florins, and the bank 9,000 florins, for shares of the corporation. This way the festival could be placed on a financially more secure footing, and could gain access to capital itself through loans, instead of depending on generosity of individuals or the League. The Board of Directors of the corporation elected by its members included Taschek, Mugrauer, the mayor and vice-mayor of Höritz/Hořice, the mayor of Krummau/Krumlov, a representative of the actors, and several notable citizens of Budweis/Budějovice. The latter included the lawyer Dr. Israel Kohn, a Jew, a close associate of Taschek's, and a longtime Board member of the League.[30]

In 1912, the last time the passion play was performed before the First World War, the villagers of Höritz/Hořice erected a granite obelisk to Joseph Taschek, the man who more than anyone else had brought them and their village international renown as the Bohemian Oberammergau. The monument stood above the town near the theater, and was sculpted by Jordan Wiltschko, the stonemason who played Jesus from 1894 through 1912.[31]

The First World War and the immediate postwar period brought unimaginable suffering to the Bohemian Woods. Several leading actors in the passion play fell in battle, and economic hardship reached terrible proportions. The tourist economy that had been so carefully nurtured before the war was ruined. In addition to the usual postwar problems of inflation, shortage, and disease, many families could hardly survive without the additional income that lodging the *Sommerfrischler* had brought them. Furthermore, with the breakup of the Habsburg Monarchy,

Figure 5.3. The theater in Höritz/Horiče as it appeared in 1912 at the time of the final pre-war performances of the Passion Play. The obelisk erected to honor Joseph Taschek's support for the play appears at the lower left. Postcard from the author's personal collection.

the League lost many of its non-Bohemian members and over half its revenues. Although the organization reconstituted itself under the new Czechoslovak State, it was never able to attain the level of activism (and the budget) it had achieved before or even during the war years.

So it was not until 1921 that the village council even considered attempting to revive the passion play, after a series of town meetings demonstrated the continued interest of the villagers in doing so. The council agreed to produce the play again, but on the condition that the Höritzer Folk-Theater corporation assume the full responsibility for the play from the League. After a year of negotiations, the village elected a new passion play committee, chose new dramatic and musical directors, and developed a brand-new production. The *Südböhmische Volkszeitung* reported in democratic fashion that the new committee included representatives of every class, the clergy, teachers, *Bürger,* and workers, and several members of the League. On the morning of the reopening, in the spring of 1923, the village council, the play committee, and all the actors assembled in the square before entering the church to hear the village chorus sing a German mass. Then everyone proceeded on foot to the theater above the town. The local papers reported that people crowded the square as far as the eye could see. This time most visitors came from near rather than far, from Bavaria, Bohemia, and the neighboring Austrian Republic rather than Great Britain or the United States.[32]

The production, noted the *Südböhmische Volkszeitung*, was a great success, moving more swiftly than in the prewar years, and requiring fewer intermissions. The actors proved that even after the war the village remained a wellspring of thespian talent. Some names were familiar. Marie Kienzl played the Virgin Mary, as she had before the war. According to the paper, Frau Kienzl was not one to be seduced by the latent potential for excessive drama in her role. Instead she eschewed tearful histrionics for a natural and dignified style. The village schoolteacher, described as a worthy successor to the recently deceased stonemason Wiltschko, now played the role of Christ.[33]

In 1923 the German-language newspapers stressed the unity of village society, the apparently seamless cooperation of church, secular educators, burghers, farmers, and workers in the face of what they liked to describe as a hostile Czechoslovak State. If there were any internal conflicts in Höritz/Hořice (and there had been a few before the war), they were well hidden both from the public and from the Czech administrators. The differences between pre- and postwar nationalist attitudes appeared subtle, but were in fact substantial. The rhetoric had not changed much, but its effects ran deeper. Before the war each German nationalist organization or party had stressed the importance of maintaining unity in the face of the Czech nationalist challenge. Since there had been no singular German nationalist interest before the war, but rather several competing ones, any German unity had been far more rhetorical than actual. Now the a-national and impartial imperial governmental superstructure was gone. It had been replaced by that of a government that privileged the Czech nation, however democratic it might have been on paper and in practice. The villagers had experienced the violence and humiliation of incorporation into what often seemed to them an alien state. Their own politicians had demanded inclusion in the new German Austrian State, but their region had been assigned by the Peace Settlement to Prague. Whether or not they wanted a German national identity, those who spoke German and not Czech were forced into a position as outsiders in the new Czechoslovak national society. Whether or not they had ever thought much in terms of a German national identity before the war, the law now assigned them such an identity. For this reason, the most ludicrous prewar claims made by German nationalists suddenly seemed to make a kind of sense to the larger German-speaking public. And the constant prewar complaints about Czech nationalist incursions into regions that were not theirs were transferred to the new Czechoslovak government, whose existence, especially in its founding years, seemed driven by unreasonable efforts to make life as difficult as possible for the newly orphaned German nationals of the Sudetenland.[34]

So it should not surprise us that a few weeks before the opening of the play, the *Südböhmische Volkszeitung* complained bitterly that the revival of the passion play had caused the state to recategorize Höritz/Hořice as an official tourist destination. This recategorization was understood to be a kind of nationalist punishment, since it required that bilingual signs now mark all restaurants and inns, that each such establishment be equipped with bilingual menus, and that each hostelry employ at least one person who spoke the Czech language. In some contexts, such a requirement might seem practical, even useful for promoting tourism, but in this case it was viewed as unjustified meddling by a hostile state.[35]

In the interwar years the organizers of the play viewed it perhaps less ambitiously than had their pre-1914 predecessors. Under the Monarchy it had seemed a viable ambition to build a successful tourist and vacation industry in the Bohemian Woods based on the natural beauty of the region and anchored by the growing fame of the passion play. After the war, the general collapse of local economies doomed the budding tourist industry. The mutual suspicions that governed relations among the new neighboring states also made travel and tourism far more difficult in the postwar years than they had been before 1914. And while the world-famous spas of Bohemia, or the ski regions of the Tyrol continued to attract their traditionally upper bourgeois clientele, even in reduced circumstances, bargain destinations like the Bohemian Woods saw their business evaporate. A brochure published by the League in the early 1930s made what reads today as a desperate plea for outsiders to return to the unfortunate region, so hard-hit by war and now by economic depression.[36]

Let me conclude this essay with a few thoughts about the relationships between German nationalist politics and this passion play. An examination of the passion play and its history in light of its promoters' nationalist intentions suggests that the goals of the latter could not easily be realized through the institution of the former. The play certainly served the economic ambitions of local and regional nationalist activists, and there is no question that it promoted the region by bringing in more tourists. In their public statements, at least, both German and Czech nationalist leaders did treat the play's nationalist significance as self-evident. Yet whether tourists themselves actually returned home with a more distinct consciousness about the national struggle on the so-called language frontier is harder to evaluate. Personal testimonies by visitors to the passion play all emphasize the profoundly moving nature of the experience, rather than its profoundly Germanic qualities (whatever those might have been). Visitors do not seem to have left believing they had witnessed something particularly German, but rather something impressive in its rural simplicity.

Did the institution of the passion play increase the nationalist consciousness of the villagers themselves? Actually, the passion play seems to have strengthened the villagers' consciousness of themselves more as Höritz/Hořic'ers than as anything else. Recollections and anecdotes confirm that their participation in the passion play was of central importance to the villagers' lives. Already in the 1890s, for example, male Höritzers were known to wear extremely long hair and full beards in order to recall Old Testament scenes, especially in the years when the play was not performed. The village did everything in its power to market itself as a kind of goal for cultural pilgrims, especially in those off years. Nor did the fact that the nationalist League had contributed so much to Höritz/Hořice's newfound fame create a stronger sense of nationalist identity. Rather, as elsewhere in southern Bohemia, villagers seem to have considered the League to be something of a local welfare organization, its German nationalist identity secondary to its important economic self-help functions.

Of course, a nationalist identity became far more compelling to the villagers after 1918 than it had been under the Monarchy. Before 1918, when local nationalists had complained loudly about the occasional incursions of Czech nationalist administrators at the district or regional level, the complaints had been made to an imperial umpire who, it was believed, would ultimately set things right. After 1918, when the umpire vanished, German speakers faced an apparently hostile state. This change alone made the nationalist worldview far more compelling in its logic to otherwise a-national villagers. Now nationalist activists could link the dire economic and social problems experienced by the village more convincingly to the nationalist workings of the new self-proclaimed Czechoslovak nation-state. And whether or not German speakers had previously thought much about a German national identity, the state forced them to adopt such an identity by categorizing them as a minority population outside the nation with specific rights and duties. Even in Czechoslovakia, a state that arguably treated its national minorities with less violence and more respect than did any other successor state in the interwar period, German speakers remained conscious of their status as outsiders. This alone made it much easier for its organizers to depict a cultural production like the passion play as a transparently nationalist undertaking.

Notes

1. I would like to thank Jeremy King and Tara Zahra for their generous advice and assistance with this essay, and to thank the staff of the Internationales Forschungszentrum Kulturwissenschaften in Vienna for its support. In this essay the term Austria refers to the Austrian half of the Dual Monarchy, what is often referred to as *Cisleithania*. The term German Austria refers to the post-1918 Austrian State. I have included both the German and Czech names for all Bohemian places mentioned. From the start, the organizers and promoters of the passion play in Höritz/Hořice compared it self-consciously to the play in Oberammergau. Even the official program to the passion play in 1893 referred to Höritz as the "Oberammergau of the Bohemian Woods." *Höritzer Passionspiele. Ein Volkschauspiel im Böhmerwalde* (Budweis, 1893), 14.
2. The play was presented in the following years: 1893–98, 1903, 1908, 1912, 1923, 1927, 1930, 1933, and 1936. After the war, a Czech version was presented in 1947 and 1948. Petr Jelínek, *Mysterium Hoericense-Das Höritzer Passionsspiel im Böhmerwald*, trans. Ivan Slavik (Krumlov, 1991), 7–8. Jelínek claims erroneously that the play was performed in 1913 rather than in 1912. On the postwar institution of a Czech version of the play, see Jeremy King, *Budweisers into Czechs and Germans* (Princeton, 2002), 202; *Jihočech*, 11 January 1946, 2; 4 April 1947, 1. I thank Professor King for sharing these citations with me.
3. On the founding, goals, and early growth of this organization, see the Festschrift *Fünfzig Jahre Deutscher Böhmerwaldbundes* (Budweis, 1934).

4. On Taschek's career in Budweis/Budějovice (he served as the last German national mayor), see King, *Budweisers*, chapters 2–4. See also the retrospective on his leadership and a 1934 interview with him in *Fünfzig Jahre Deutscher Böhmerwaldbundes*, 3–4.

5. For the goals and activism of the *Národní Jednota Pošumavská*, see *Zpráva o činnosti Národní Jednoty Pošumavské za devátý Rok 1892–1893* (Prague, 1893), especially 1–3.

6. On the history, structure, and membership of the *Schulverein*, see Pieter M. Judson, *Exclusive Revolutionaries. Liberal Politics, Social Experience, and German Nationalism in the Austrian Empire, 1848–1914* (Ann Arbor, MI, 1996), 207–215.

7. Judson, *Exclusive Revolutionaries*, 225–234, 258–262.

8. "Fünfzig Jahre Deutscher Böhmerwaldbund. Aus den Erinnerungen des Gründers und Bundesobmannes Josef Taschek (ein Interview)" in *Fünfzig Jahre Deutscher Böhmerwaldbund*, 3–4.

9. On early tourism in the Monarchy, see the exemplary brief study by Laurence Cole, "The Emergence and Impact of Modern Tourism in an Alpine Region: Tirol c. 1880–1914," in *Annali di San Michele*, no. 15 (2002): 31–40. See also, Rainer Amstäder, *Der Alpinismus. Kultur—Organisation—Politik* (Vienna, 1996); Günther Burkert, "Der Beginn des modernen Fremdenverkehrs in den österreichischen Kronländern. Föderalistische und nationale Elemente als bestimmende Faktoren," in *Schriftenreihe der Arbeitsgemeinschaft für Wirtschafts- und Sozialgeschichte* (Graz, 1981), 1–72; Cole, *"Für Gott, Kaiser und Vaterland. Nationale Identität der deutschsprachigen Bevölkerung Tirols 1860–1914* (Frankfurt/New York, 2000); Pieter M. Judson, "Tourism, Travel, and National Activism in the Böhmerwald, South Tirol, and South Styria Around 1900," in *Geschichte und Region/Storia e Regione*, 10/2 (2001): 59–90; Arthur Müller, *Das Problem des Fremdenverkehres in Österreich. Psychologisch-propagandistische Betrachtungen* (Vienna, 1909); and Josef Stradner, *Der Fremdenverkehr* (Graz, 1917).

10. There is now an explosion of literature on the rise of the *Sommerfrische* in Austrian historiography. Among the best surveys remains Hanns Haas, "Die Sommerfrische—Ort der Bürgerlichkeit," in *'Durch Arbeit, Besitz, Wissen und Gerechtigkeit.' Bürgertum in der Habsburgermonarchie*, ed. Hannes Steckl, Peter Urbanitsch, Ernst Bruckmüller, Hans Heiss (Vienna, 1992), 364–377.

11. Taschek's annual reports to the membership frequently betray concern for this problem. See "Rückschau über die zwanzigjährige Tätigkeit des Deutschen Böhmerwaldbundes. Für die 20. Hauptversammlung berichtet vom Obmann Josef Taschek," in *Mittheilungen des Deutschen Böhmerwaldbundes*, no. 47 (1904), 12; and "Bericht über die Hauptversammlung des Deutschen Böhmerwaldbundes am 27. August in Prachatitz," in *Mittheilungen des Deutschen Böhmerwaldbundes*, no. 48 (1905), 9.

12. See "Gewissensforschung," in *Deutsch Böhmerwald*, 13 September 1908, 5.

13. "Hauptbericht über die Thätigkeit des Deutschen Böhmerwaldbundes für die XVIII. Hauptversammlung am 7. September 1902 in Neuern, verfasst und erstattet von Bundesobmann Josef Taschek," in *Mittheilungen des Deutschen Böhmerwaldbundes*, no. 45 (1902), *Beilage*, 10.

14. For population statistics, see *Gemeindelexikon der im Reichsrate vertretenen Königreiche und Länder. Bearbeitet auf Grund der Ergebnisse der Volkszählung vom 31. Dezember 1900, herausgegeben von der K.K. statistischen Zentralkommission*, vol. IX, *Böhmen* (Vienna, 1904), 756. For further descriptions and statistics see *Durch Deutschböhmen* (Eger and Vienna, n.d., 1909?), 34–36; *Grieben Reiseführer. Band 99, Bayerischer u. Böhmerwald* (Berlin, 1939), 200. The village population seems to have remained stable until the Second World War. In 1939 *Grieben* listed the population as 1,157.

15. For the founding date of the Höritz/Hořice association, the membership and president, see *Mittheilungen des Deutschen Böhmerwaldbundes*, no. 15 (1888): 177. On Mugrauer and the rehearsals at his inn, see *Deutsche Böhmerwald Zeitung*, 18 May 1893, 158.

16. *Mittheilungen des Deutschen Böhmerwaldbundes*, no. 11 (August 1887): 135. On the German nationalist deployment of a cult of Joseph II in Bohemia, see the essay by Cynthia Paces

and Nancy M. Wingfield in this volume as well as Wingfield, "Statues of Emperor Joseph II as Sites of German Identity," in *Staging the Past. The Politics of Commemoration in Habsburg Central Europe, 1848 to the Present,* ed. Nancy M. Wingfield and Maria Bucur (West Lafayette, IN), 2001, 178–205.

17. Johann Josef Ammann, *Das Passionsspiel des Böhmerwaldes. Neubearbeitet auf Grund der alten Überlieferungen* (Krummau, 1892). Ammann gives a detailed history of the Gröllhesl text as well as of its colorful performance history, iv–viii, and he offers a useful discussion of how the Höritz/Hořice text differed from the text for the Oberammergau play.

18. Ammann, vii.

19. Ammann, viii, xi.

20. Ammann, xi–xv. Ammann noted that before the completion of the railroad connection, return trips from Krummau/Krumlov to Höritz/Hořice "were trying tours" that could take up to six hours.

21. *Mittheilungen des Deutschen Böhmerwaldbundes,* no. 35 (October 1893), *Beilage,* "Hauptbericht der neunten Hauptversammlung," 239–240.

22. *Mysterium Hoericense,* 6. The final cost of the theater to the League surpassed 60,000 Gulden. See "Das Böhmerwald-Passionsspiel in Höritz," in *Mittheilungen des Vereines Südmark,* 1912, 132.

23. Ammann, xv, xxi–xxii.

24. For a detailed account of the controversy and the lawsuit, see Ammann, xxi–xxx; for the League's terse version of events, see *Mittheilungen des Deutschen Böhmerwaldbundes,* no. 37, *Beilage,* 9.

25. One guidebook claimed that through the 1908 production, some 65,000 people had seen the play in each year it had been produced. *Durch Deutschböhmen,* 35. This figure seems exaggerated, since the theater accommodated only two thousand spectators, it was not always sold out, and the play was performed ca. seventeen times in a given season. In its first three years the play was presented fifty times to a total audience of 95,000 people (ca. 32,500 annually had seen it). *Mittheilungen des Deutschen Böhmerwaldbundes* no. 37, *Beilage,* 9.

26. Karl Baedeker, *Österreich (ohne Galizien, Dalmatien, Ungarn und Bosnien)* (Leipzig, 1910), 328. See also the biting satiric account of a visit to Höritz and the Bohemian Woods in Raoul Auernheimer, "Auf der Reise nach Höritz," in *Neue Freie Presse,* 2 August 1908, 2. *Heimat* author Peter Rosegger was one of the many angry readers who felt the need to defend Höritz/Hořice from what they termed an unfair attack.

27. Ammann pointed out that director Deutsch designed costumes according to his own taste, and that the production could not be said to express historic truth in its particular look. Ammann, xvi.

28. "Höritzer Glossen," in *Deutsche Böhmerwald Zeitung* (Krummau), 24 August 1893, 270.

29. *Mitteilungen des Vereines Südmark,* 1912, 133; *Mysterium Hoericense,* 6; Andreas Brunner and Hannes Sulzenbacher, *Schwules Wien. Reiseführer durch die Donaumetropole* (Vienna, 1998), 120–121; on Crown Princess Stephanie's visit and the Schwarzenberg's private pavillion, *Mittheilungen des Deutschen Böhmerwaldbundes, Beilage,* no. 37, 9.

30. *Deutsche Böhmerwald Zeitung,* no. 38, 19 September 1896, 304.

31. *Deutsche Böhmerwald Zeitung,* no. 26, 21 June 1912, 287. Taschek's wife, Marie Taschek, had been named the "godmother of the flag" (*Fahnenpathin*) of the Höritz corporation at the time of the flag's dedication (*Fahnenweihe*). *Deutsche Böhmerwald Zeitung,* no. 26, 27 June 1896, 208.

32. On the negotiations surrounding the revival of the passion play, see *Südböhmische Volkszeitung,* no. 1, 7 January 1923, 3. On the ceremonies surrounding the reopening of the play, and for a review of the performance, see *Südböhmische Volkszeitung,* no. 24, 12 June 1923, 9.

33. *Südböhmische Volkszeitung,* no. 34, 26 August 1923, 1.

34. For an excellent general picture of the difficult period of transition and adjustment to a new regime in Southern Bohemia, see King, *Budweisers,* ch. 5, especially 160–164.
35. *Südböhmische Volkszeitung,* no. 18, 6 May 1923, 7.
36. *Der Böhmerwald. Ein Paradies für Naturfreunde das Jedem etwas bietet* (n.d., ca. 1930).

Chapter 6

THE SACRED AND THE PROFANE

Religion and Nationalism in the Bohemian Lands, 1880–1920*

Cynthia Paces and Nancy M. Wingfield

In his famous 1882 lecture "What is a nation?" the French historian Ernst Renan demanded a sharp division between religious and national identity: "Religion cannot supply an adequate basis for the constitution of a modern nationality." He asserted that over the course of the nineteenth century, religion had become "an individual matter" and had "ceased almost entirely to be one of the elements which serve to define the frontiers of peoples."[1] Liberal nationalists in the last years of the Habsburg Monarchy tended to agree in principle with Renan's separation of religion from political discourse. Yet, in Habsburg Central Europe, religious ritual, discourse, and symbolism were never entirely divorced from nationalist practice. In the Bohemian lands, Czech nationalists associated Roman Catholic religious symbols with autocratic Austrian power in the region. They replaced Catholic icons with the medieval religious reformer, Jan Hus. German nationalists in the Bohemian lands in turn revered Emperor Joseph II, who was credited with secularizing the region, with almost religious fervor. Religious monuments then became political symbols, and political figures took on sacred significance.

The dissolution of Austria-Hungary in 1918 exacerbated the situation. Of all the successor states of the Habsburg Monarchy, none stands out as more progressive, modern, and secular than interwar Czechoslovakia. A close examination of the attempts to build a new "Czechoslovak" national identity in the first years of the Republic, however, calls this characterization into question. In addition to the necessary creation of national symbols, including flags, stamps, and coins, Czechoslovakia also witnessed the destruction of a variety of markers that failed to fit the new "nation-state" identity of this multinational state. In particular, Czech nationalists no longer tolerated those symbols of Roman Catholicism that served as reminders of Habsburg dominion. Thus, in a country that was more than 90 percent nominally Roman Catholic, symbols of Catholicism were nonetheless unwelcome. After 1918, radical nationalists used the newfound statehood both to remove statues of Catholic saints and to integrate further Hussite imagery into the state iconography. In fact, in the early years of the Czechoslovak Republic, religious symbols were central to the contentious debate over Czechoslovak identity in a post-Habsburg Central Europe. From the major urban spaces of Prague to the market squares of the border regions, nationalists attempted to obliterate evidence of the former Habsburg presence by removing monuments, statues, signs, and symbols—above all, the ubiquitous double-headed eagle. In this atmosphere, the "life cycle" of Bohemian monuments—their unveiling, their politicization, and their destruction—reflected the strong link between religion and nationalism in post-Habsburg Central Europe. In the First Czechoslovak Republic, religion could never be the purely individual matter that Renan described.

"Monument Fever" in the Bohemian Lands

By the mid-nineteenth century, secular monuments and statues had begun to replace religious ones in the public spaces of the Bohemian lands, reflecting the popularity of public figural monuments—one of the preferred art forms of nineteenth-century culture.[2] The appearance of numerous images of the ruling Habsburg dynasty and other historic figures paralleled an increase in popular political manifestations and national festivals that competed with traditional dynastic and religious ceremonies for the hearts and minds of the people. Statues of Habsburg monarchs and officials joined the Virgin Mary and Bohemian saints in the squares of the towns and cities throughout Habsburg Austria. Czech nationalists resented these reminders of Roman Catholic victory in the Thirty Years' War and responded to the frenzy of new statues of Habsburg and other German figures by making plans to build their own. The last decades of the nineteenth century and the first decades of the twentieth were an era of "monument fever" in Bohemia. Soon after statues of Joseph II started appearing throughout the Bohemian lands and Upper Austria in the early 1880s, Czech nationalists began organizing committees to build statues to honor their national heroes. Following twenty years of fund-raising, Czech national organizations unveiled statues of the nineteenth-century nationalist historian František Palacký in 1911, the tenth-century Bohemian King Wenceslas in 1912, and the medieval church reformer and martyr Jan Hus in 1915 in some of the most important public spaces of Prague.

Just as religious statues had played a role in the church rites of earlier times, when secular martyrs replaced saints, some of the new temporal monuments became associated with contemporary, secular rituals. Many of these new rituals

Figure 6.1. Statue of Emperor Joseph II standing before the Deutsches Haus in Brünn/Brno. (Courtesy of the Archiv města Brna.)

borrowed heavily from the folk traditions of Roman Catholicism. This was certainly the case with the rituals associated with the statues of enlightened absolutist Emperor Joseph II, which would be linked with German nationalism in the Bohemian lands.

Numerous statues of Emperor Joseph II were put up in the decade following his centenary in 1881. From the time of their unveiling, the commemorative discourse around these centenary monuments fulfilled more than the straightforward functions of celebrating the abolition of *Leibeigenschaft* (serfdom) or the issuance of the *Tolerenzpatent*. Both the ceremonial installation of statues of Joseph II and the cults that grew up around the emperor in the late nineteenth century reflected changing political ideologies and commitments. The commemorations of the emperor incorporated broader issues of the politics of collective memory and national identity. These statues became repositories for multiple meanings, and invited a variety of interpretations, which often ran at cross-purposes with one another. They were religious and secular; modern and traditional; mournful and triumphant.

Although they sometimes borrowed elements from earlier celebrations, particularly the religious terms used to exalt Joseph II, these commemorations were modern, secular events. Mass participation reflected the expansion of the political franchise and general social mobilization in Cisleithanian Austria. The religious imagery the Germans employed in laying claim to Joseph II as a German national hero and attempting to legitimate the national goals they espoused is all the more striking, because organized religion does not appear to have played a role in the overwhelmingly secular rites. Nor do church groups seem to have been among the numerous organizations to have sent wreaths to be laid ceremoniously at the bases of the newly unveiled statues. Apparently, the only religious organization to participate in the commemorations was the occasional Jewish community that contributed a wreath.[3] Indeed, outside the celebratory masses, there is little mention of religious identity in connection with the commemorations. While rejecting apparent Czech assertions that "masses of Jews" had participated in the festivities connected with the unveiling of the statue in Budweis/České Budějovice in 1883, one local German-language newspaper commented: "The Jews certainly have good reason to hold Joseph II in high regard since he gave them their human rights…"[4]

In the eighteenth century the absolutist, reforming Emperor Joseph II sought to organize his domains more rationally, by creating a centralized and unified bureaucracy to serve a well-organized state with obedient subjects. Joseph II abolished *Leibeigenschaft,* introduced religious tolerance, relaxed censorship, established educational uniformity, and instituted linguistic standardization. In his attempt to build an essentially unitary, standardized, and uniform state, he sought to remove privilege. The Emperor's chief target was the largest, wealthiest, and most privileged corporate group in the Monarchy—the Roman Catholic Church.[5]

A century later, German nationalist speakers employed religious imagery at unveiling ceremonies of statues of Joseph II in laying claim to the emperor as

Figure 6.2. Crowd Gathered at the Statue of Emperor Joseph II in Aussig/Ústí nad Labem. (Courtesy of the Muzeum města Ústí nad Labem.)

their national hero and in invoking his legacy to legitimate their national goals. The language of religion gave power to a supposedly secular discourse as the speakers argued that although clerical fanatics enthusiastically represented Joseph II as an enemy of religion, it was not religion he fought, rather he was a relentless opponent of zealots who hid their ambitious goals behind the mask of religion. Germans also stressed that the emperor was the great enemy of the Jesuits and their Black Army.[6]

Indeed, German commemorations of Joseph II reflect Katherine Verdery's assertion that in arresting the process of a person's bodily decay, "a statue alters the temporality associated with the person, bringing him into the realm of the timeless or the sacred."[7] The Germans endowed their reforming emperor, who had offered his people the "Gospel of the Enlightenment," with the characteristics of a national saint. Recalling Joseph II's visit to Kostenblatt/Kostomlat pod Milešovkou near Teplitz/Teplice in northern Bohemia during the famine of 1771, one of the town fathers recounted the words of a local pastor: as if in answer to his prayers, "like a second Egyptian Joseph, the good Emperor Joseph II appeared in Bohemia." The Emperor was still fondly remembered for donating food and funds to help the starving poor of the town.[8] Reports on unveiling of another Joseph II statue in northern Bohemia commented that the morning of the exalted festival was indeed extremely overcast, but the weather improved during the course of the day. Soon the sun was laughing in the blue sky, as if to say that there was also joy in heaven over the triumph of a German people celebrating their saint.[9] One speaker noted that while the Slavs flocked to Rome to thank the Pope for giving them the Slavic apostles Cyril and Methodius as their national saints, it was not necessary for Rome to provide the Germans with a saint. The Emperor Joseph was their saint, and they were consecrating a monument to him.[10] Another speaker chided other national groups in the Monarchy—and a few fanatical clericals—for failing to be thankful to the noble *Volkskaiser,* whom he called a second messiah, "since, as once the savior freed us from sin and blame, Joseph II freed us from the chains and bonds of bodily and spiritual servitude."[11] Perhaps the best example of the messianic language that would be increasingly connected with Joseph II was the telegram a German student organization in Prague sent to the unveiling ceremonies of a statue of the emperor in a small town in Bohemia in late October 1881: "Our parents placed Joseph, the unforgettable, under the gods. We, however, want him to be honored at least as a deity carrying blessings, as a national saint! Holy Emperor Joseph, pray for us, for your downtrodden German *Volk.*"[12]

German employment of Joseph II for nationalist ends reflects their success in transforming this cultural icon from *Volkskaiser* to *Kaiser des deutschen Volkes,* to a national saint. In fact, Germans cited Joseph II himself in the claims they laid to him: "With head bared, Joseph II spoke once before the statue of [French King] Henry IV on the Pont Neuf in Paris: 'I covet such a title; there is nothing more beautiful than to be named father of one's people.'"[13] German nationalists asserted that the peoples he governed had rewarded Joseph with ingratitude. But now, a century later, his dearest wish was being fulfilled: the "people," if only the Germans, bestowed upon him the title "Father," and at the same time honored him as saint.

The "Joseph II Movement" developed soon after the German liberals lost political power in 1879, in an era when many Germans believed that imperial concessions to Slavic nationalities under the Taaffe government threatened the position of German culture and language in the Monarchy. (Count Eduard Taaffe, the Austrian minister president from 1879 to 1893, headed the hated coalition known as the Iron Ring, which generally favored agrarian, clerical, and Slavic interests.) Throughout the Bohemian lands, the defensive and self-consciously nationalist language of this culture of commemoration reflected bravado in the face of what many Germans perceived as demographic and political losses to the increasingly nationally conscious Czechs. The centenary statues reflected disgruntled Germans' experiences of loss, and Joseph II became a mnemonic symbol for an imagined past golden era of German predominance in the Monarchy. Both German liberals and nationalists revered the emperor for "recognizing" German cultural and linguistic superiority. The statues thus became sites of symbolic exchange where the living acknowledged their debt to the long-dead emperor that they could never fully discharge.[14]

Statues of Joseph II soon became the secular equivalents of shrines as the Germans located a sacred part of their national identity in their representations of him. The unveilings of these statues took on the significance of secular holy days. Participants in the daylong celebrations, which were similar throughout the Bohemian lands, took symbolic possession of the local public sphere in the name of the German nation.[15] Local notables and associations organized the celebrations and mobilized the German public to take part. Like most secular celebrations in the Monarchy, they were meticulously choreographed by the city fathers and were performed almost exclusively by male actors for an audience that also included women and children. The official program often began at dawn with reveille, which might be followed by a celebratory mass. Waving flags and singing national songs, marchers then paraded through some of the most significant public spaces in the community. The rhetoric surrounding the unveiling often included religious terminology, demanding, for example, that Emperor Joseph II's exalted spirit must fill the hearts of those in attendance. Not only was Joseph II immortal, he had also become "the Apostle of truth and light."[16]

The dedication ceremonies both incorporated the rural peoples' traditional veneration of Joseph II as their liberator and "friend," and registered contemporary German-national protest against the clerical sympathies of the Habsburg dynasty and the Slavophile nationalities policies of Emperor Franz Joseph. The abolition of *Leibeigenschaft* had freed Germans and Slavs alike. And, many of these statues went up in small farming communities, where the peasants had been among the last to choose a specific national identity. The erecting of Joseph II statues and the unveiling ceremonies constituted a political pedagogic device that the dominant bourgeoisie employed, in the attempt to mobilize those villagers whose identity had heretofore not been explicitly national to create an imagined community of Germans.[17]

Czech nationalists observed the German sanctification of the emperor with growing concern. Many of them believed that the statues symbolized the combative posture of the Germans in their battle against the Czechs on what Czechs considered Slavic soil. They noted that while Joseph II might initially be praised as someone who valued humanity, during the course of a speech, he would become the father of his people or a [German] national saint.[18] Although Czechs warned them not to "misuse the name and memory of Emperor Joseph for political demonstrations and stirring up trouble,"[19] the German nationalists in Bohemia especially employed the image of Joseph II in their battles against the attempts of the imperial government in Vienna to extend limited language rights to non-German speakers during the late nineteenth century.

The issue of national rights in the Monarchy was at the heart of the decision to erect another statue in the Bohemian lands. In 1889, Czech nationalists formed a committee to raise funds for a memorial in Prague dedicated to Jan Hus, the reform-minded Prague priest whom the Roman Catholic Church burned for heresy in 1415. Czech nationalists particularly esteemed Hus for his insistence on employing the vernacular language in Mass. Hus preached in Czech, and translated many Catholic rites and prayers into Czech. Moreover, he codified much of the Czech written language. Hus became the preeminent symbol of Czech nationalists in their political debates about language rights in the Monarchy during the second half of the nineteenth century.

The importance of Hus as a religious figure, however, made him a contested choice for national hero. Following his martyrdom, the Bohemian lands had erupted in civil war, which resulted in converting a majority of Bohemians to Hussitism. Although the Habsburgs succeeded in reconverting the Bohemian Protestants to Roman Catholicism during the seventeenth-century Counter-Reformation, Hus remained a Czech folk hero. During the nineteenth century, Czech nationalists revived his memory, recreating him as the first Czech patriot. These secular nationalists might overlook the religious element of the Hus legacy, but devout Roman Catholics were unwilling to venerate a heretic.

Like Emperor Joseph II, a secular figure who was fêted with religious fervor in the era of heightened nationalism, Hus too embodied an ambiguous space between political and religious meaning. Hus was undeniably a religious figure; yet Czech nationalists stressed only his contributions to the Czech language and to national pride. While German nationalists sanctified the secular Joseph II, Czech nationalists attempted to de-emphasize Hus's religious connections.

Although it was downplayed, Hus's religious heritage did not sit well with Czech Catholics, even those who sympathized with nationalist goals. After the Prague municipal government announced its support of a Hus Memorial, Catholics protested vehemently. Canon M. Karlach explained the Catholic opposition to the Hus Memorial: "This statue will stand as a disgrace and insult to the Catholic Church and its people, humiliating this Catholic city."[20]

Figure 6.3 Jan Hus Memorial on Old Town Square, Prague. (Photograph by Cynthia Paces).

The proposed Hus Memorial was particularly troubling to Prague Catholics because of its location on Old Town Square. This central square was already home to the baroque Marian Column, which had stood since 1650. A monument to the Habsburg victory over the Swedish invaders during the Thirty Years' War, the Marian Column became for Czech nationalists a symbol of the defeat of the Protestant Bohemian lands at the Battle of White Mountain in November 1620, and the subsequent loss of political and religious freedom there. During the Counter-Reformation, the Habsburgs sponsored the building of new baroque churches, Marian Columns, and other religious statues throughout Central Europe as a way to bring Protestants back into the Roman Catholic fold. By the nineteenth century, Czech nationalists viewed baroque art as a sign of their political subjugation to the Monarchy. As the historians Zdeněk Hojda and Jiří Pokorný have explained, these religious statues became "monuments against their own will" as their meanings shifted from religious to political.[21]

Nonetheless, Czech Catholics, many of whom had nationalist sympathies, became enraged when the Prague City Council determined that a new Jan Hus Memorial would share the site of the Marian Column. The Catholic press responded vehemently to the proposal: "The Catholic Czech nation will not permit Old Town Square, which is reigned over by our Marian Column—the monument which represents our return to glory—also to contain a Hus Memorial, that symbol of insult, heresy, and rebellion against the Catholic Church and faith!"[22] In protesting the site, the Catholic press declared itself part of the nation, while still objecting to a symbol many nationalists held dear.

The leadership of the Hus Club insisted that honoring Hus was not meant to disparage the Roman Catholic Church. Hus Club member Václav Březnovský defended the Club's position at a meeting of the Prague Board of Aldermen. "The Hus concept is not a religious idea," he insisted.[23] Throughout 1897 and 1898, Catholic organizations such as the "Marian Nation," Catholic men's and women's clubs, and Catholic workers' organizations staged demonstrations on Old Town Square to protest the proposal to place the Hus Memorial across from the Marian Column. In June 1898, more than 4,000 people participated in a procession to honor the Marian Column and to oppose the future Hus Memorial.[24] Conflict over the proper monument for Old Town Square would continue in the Bohemian lands for decades.

Different groups throughout the Bohemian lands erected statues to create, reflect, and strengthen their shared cultural identity in the region. Just as the Catholic Church erected religious statues during the Counter-Reformation to create central public spaces for worship, in the nineteenth century various socio-political interest groups—whose identity often had a linguistic component—used symbols to evoke a sense of shared history. These symbols became representative of the contested geography of the Bohemian lands.

The Statue War

The "era of monument fever," which lasted from the 1890s through the First World War, cast in stone—and metal—a series of conflicts in the Bohemian lands: German versus Czech, Catholic versus secular, Habsburg versus nationalist. These tensions did not vanish with the declaration of the Czechoslovak Republic in 1918. Czech nationalists had succeeded in convincing the international community of their right to self-determination. Now they sought to redesign the landscape of their new state to conform to the nationalist goals that founded it.

Radical nationalists believed that official actions to create the symbolic space of Czechoslovakia—a new flag, national anthems—had not gone far enough. Four centuries of Habsburg rule had imprinted the Czechoslovak landscape with numerous reminders of the past. Some Czechs determined that the most vexing of these remains had to be removed. And, as with the unveiling of statues to Emperor Joseph II and Jan Hus, the destruction of monuments blurred the distinction between the religious and the political. Certainly, the desecration of a statue is part of the larger history of iconoclasm, because pulling it down both removes that specific body from the landscape and deprives it of its sacredness and timelessness.[25]

The most dramatic example of nationalists' penchant for destroying Habsburg religious-cum-political monuments was the toppling of the Marian Column in Prague. Despite twenty-five years of protests by Czech Catholics, the Hus Memorial had been unveiled in 1915. For three years, Jan Hus and the Virgin Mary had shared what was perhaps the most important public space in the

Bohemian lands. This symbolic tension, which existed so briefly in Old Town Square, was too great for the most passionate Czech nationalists to bear. On November 3, 1918, one week after the proclamation of Czechoslovak independence, a crowd returning from a commemoration of the Battle of White Mountain, the scene of Habsburg victory over Bohemian Protestant nobles, gathered at Old Town Square to destroy the Marian Column. "Down with it, down!"[26] a frenzied mob cheered. Now they would get revenge. "Down with it, down!" the crowd insisted. Finally, above the shouts, the onlookers heard a loud crack, and then a crash. The Marian Column came tumbling down onto the Square. The seventeenth-century baroque column broke into three large chunks, and the delicate statue of the Virgin Mary shattered into pieces on the cobblestones. A group of the most radical nationalists in Prague had finally achieved their goal: the removal from Old Town Square of an unambiguous reminder of Habsburg dominion over the Bohemian Lands. Announcing that they were heirs to the medieval Hussite warriors, these nationalists had purified this public space for the Czech national and historical tradition.

The destruction of the Marian Column reflected the revolutionary mood in Prague in the liminal period in which a Czechoslovak state was established. When a delegation from the provisional government, the National Council, arrived on Old Town Square in an attempt to prevent the destruction of the Marian Column, František Kysela-Sauer, the mob's leader, exclaimed, "You are the National Council; we are the Nation!"[27] Indeed, those who participated in pulling down the Marian Column viewed their deed as an act of national defiance

Figure 6.4. Residents gather at Old Town Square, the site of the toppled Marian Column. (Courtesy of the Archiv hlavního města Prahy).

against a Monarchy that had oppressed their people for centuries in a so-called "prison house of nations."[28]

The Marian Column, argued Kysela-Sauer, was a "political symbol," not a religious one. True Catholics followed Christ, he wrote, not the "international, political clerical movement, whose central committee sat in Rome."[29] Although Kysela-Sauer admitted that the Column did not directly commemorate Habsburg victory at White Mountain, he warned that this did not render the monument harmless. Any memorial from the Thirty Years' War, he suggested, represented the defeat of Czech culture, which was characterized by political, religious, and class liberty.

The state did not condone, but did tolerate, the Marian Column's disappearance. Catholic leaders demanded the charge of "criminal damaging of foreign property," but the state declared that this charge did not apply to an "era of revolution." Instead, Kysela-Sauer was charged with a vandalism misdemeanor in February 1919, three months after the "crime," but the charges were swiftly dropped because the statute of limitations had already run out. Another one of the ringleaders, Senator Ferdinand Šťastný, won parliamentary immunity.[30] Even the press paid little attention to the Marian Column's fate, burying the story in the middle of the daily newspapers.

The destruction of Habsburg-era religious monuments did not end with this dramatic event, which can be almost explained away by the revolutionary mood in the new capital city. A few days before the Marian Column's felling, Catholic politician Moric Hruban uncannily presaged the event. "In Prague one observed the appearance of two main trends of thought: the social revolutionary and the anti-Catholic. The casual observer could not recognize the real situation because everything around was hidden under flags and flowers and covered by a mood of rejoicing for the newly won state and national independence."[31]

Popular attacks on statues continued well into the 1920s. The statues destroyed during this period fell into two categories: the religious and the political. These categories cannot, however, be neatly separated. Religious statues carried strong political messages, and statues of political heroes became sacred spaces to members of new minorities in Czechoslovakia.

Another incident—less familiar than the Marian Column destruction—illustrates the complex politics surrounding religious statues in Bohemia. In August 1920, a baroque statue of St. John of Nepomuk (Jan Nepomucký) was removed from the town square of Dobrovice, an industrial town fifty kilometers northeast of Prague. Nationalists particularly vilified statues of St. John of Nepomuk, since the seventeenth- and eighteenth-century Jesuit counter-reformers promoted St. John of Nepomuk as a symbol of Bohemian Catholicism. John of Nepomuk was used as a foil for the popularity of the heretic Jan Hus in Bohemia. A priest in the court of King Wenceslas IV, John of Nepomuk had been martyred in 1369. When the Counter-Reformation Jesuits searched for a local Catholic hero to displace the popularity of Hus, John of Nepomuk seemed ideal. Both were priests and martyrs, both lived within fifty years of one another, and both were even named

Jan. Yet, by the twentieth century, nationalists viewed him as an agent of Habsburg cultural domination. Throughout Bohemia and Moravia, St. John of Nepomuk statues fell victim to nationalist mobs, in spontaneous or privately planned acts.[32] What is different about the Dobrovice case is that numerous branches of the government became involved in the decision to remove this St. John statue. Debates about the statue occurred in the city council, the mayor's office, the regional administration of Mladá Boleslav/Jungbunzlau, the chief of police's office, the Bureau of Monuments in Prague, the Regional Bureau of Monuments, the Ministry of Education and National Enlightenment, the Ministry of the Interior, and the Ministry of Justice.

In July 1919, representatives of the Regional Political Assembly in Mladá Boleslav discussed the potential consequences of having a prominent John of Nepomuk statue in their jurisdiction. The local Czechoslovak National Socialist Party and the Social Democratic Party petitioned the Dobrovice City Council to remove the statue. Branches of the national government, including the Bureau of Monuments, Ministry of Education, and Ministry of Interior, implored the local city council to "use all means to prevent the spontaneous removal of the monument."[33] The Bureau of Monuments further emphasized that the statue was a valuable piece of baroque art from 1645. However, the issue of spontaneous removal—and its potential danger—seemed more important than the artistic merit of the statue.

Prague's attempt to intervene appears to have made local branches of the government more eager to remove the statue. Local authorities sought to prove that they reflected the new state nationalism. The City Council decided not only to remove the statue, but also to replace it with a new monument that represented "the history of the liberation of the nation, which was now emptied of Austria and Rome."[34] A modern town monument would affirm Dobrovice's place in the new state; retaining John of Nepomuk would cast doubts as to where Dobrovice's real allegiances lay.

Immediately following the July 1920 decision to remove the statue, local Roman Catholic leaders began to protest the decision. Not only did the Church remind the town council of the region's predominantly Roman Catholic population, but it also argued that religious art technically belonged to the Church. The question of property was now at the heart of the debate. The town fathers retorted that Count Maxim Valdštejn (Wallenstein) had given the statue to the Dobrovice in 1645, and the town had since taken care of cleaning the monument. It therefore was town property. The Bureau of Monuments in Prague in turn responded that the statue could be considered a national treasure, and thus belonged to the state. The town council compromised with the Bureau of Monuments and agreed to carefully remove the monument and send it to Prague's sculpture museum, which housed the Marian Column fragments and other victims of the recent statue wars.[35]

The mayor's office chose 28 October 1920, the second anniversary of the Czechoslovak state, to remove the statue. Members of local government insisted they picked this date "so as not to harm the religious feelings of Roman Catholics."[36] Choosing a national holiday, they implied, de-emphasized the religious nature of the conflict. The issue was not religious beliefs, but a former regime that used religious symbols to oppress Czech nationalism. Like Kysela-Sauer, leader of the Marian Column mob, the local government insisted that John of Nepomuk was not a religious symbol, but a political one.

During the summer of 1920, the small Dobrovice town square became the site of daily protests by angry Roman Catholics who demanded that the statue remain there. Unmoved, the mayor's office rescheduled the statue's removal for two months earlier than the original date, citing public safety. On the morning of 27 August 1920, a huge crowd gathered at the square, some to celebrate the felling, others to prevent it. What happened next is unclear, but the scaffolding around the monument suddenly gave way, killing two bystanders (a worker and a nine-year-old boy) and critically injuring two middle-aged women.[37]

While six members of the crowd faced charges of "endangering life," the Ministry of the Interior confirmed the town's right to remove the statue. A subsequent report explained, "The statue of St. John in Dobrovice stood on the square in Dobrovice and belonged to the town."[38] Local authorities had every right to remake their public space in a way more suitable to the "spirit of the present era."[39]

This incident found its way into the archives primarily because of the loss of lives in Dobrovice. What the paper trail shows us, however, is how important public space had become to every level of the new government. In particular, regional authorities desired to demonstrate their membership in the nation, even when the national government itself frowned on this method of demonstrating it. Furthermore, the Dobrovice case shows how religious symbols become political monuments in key historical moments.

Unsurprisingly, political symbols met fates similar to those of the Marian Column and the statue of John of Nepomuk. In addition to the removal of Habsburg coats of arms from buildings, statues of Habsburg monarchs and their loyal servants disappeared from town squares. Likenesses of the late Emperor Franz Joseph disappeared from the landscape and Field Marshal Josef Radetzky, the hero of the Battle of Custozza, was removed from Prague's Lesser Town Square (Malostranské náměstí/Kleinseiter Ring).

Given the enormous popularity, and even near-religious devotion, that Emperor Joseph II had acquired among German nationalists, it is no surprise that statues of Joseph II became particular targets of Czech wrath in the immediate postwar era. These statues had gained high visibility and precise, national meaning in the Czech-German clashes in the decades that preceded 1914. Following sporadic attacks on these statues in the wake of the Great War, they became the targets of Czech nationalists in the full-scale statue war that broke out in autumn 1920. Attacks on statues in the German-dominated border areas, often instigated by the Czech Legionnaires and other soldiers, resulted in deadly clashes and violent protests throughout the region, as Germans retaliated against the disrespect shown their emperor by attacking Czech property and images of the state.

The first volleys in the "Statue War" of autumn 1920 were fired in Teplitz/Teplice on 28 October 1920, the second anniversary of Czechoslovak independence. Following a gathering that day, members of Teplitz's Czech minority and Legionnaires stationed there produced a series of demands, including the removal of the city's bronze Joseph II statue within three days. Rather than meet Czech demands of getting rid of the statue altogether, officials attempted to conceal the source of aggravation by boarding it up. The longer the statue remained encased, the angrier the Germans of Teplice became at the indignity the Czechs had inflicted on "their" emperor. During the night of 5 November, the wooden covering was removed. Although the central government sent troops to maintain the peace, local Czechs took matters into their own hands on 11 November, and pulled down the statue. After a brief sojourn at the city construction-supply site, it was taken to the city museum.[40]

The successful removal of Joseph II in Teplitz produced a chain reaction. On the Czech side, there were anti-German protests throughout Bohemia and attempts on other statues of the emperor. On the German side, city councils and cultural organizations protested the Legionnaires' actions in Teplitz and the government's failure to prevent them.

The ensuing conflict in Eger/Cheb would have the most spectacular repercussions throughout the Bohemian lands. Two days after the events in Teplitz, the Czechs in Eger, who had sporadically attacked the city's Joseph II statue since the war's end, struck again, this time successfully. In the early hours of the morning of 14 November, some 200 armed Czech soldiers marched to the marketplace. After blocking access to the area and preventing the German watch from interfering, they knocked the statue off its pedestal, stole the arm of the emperor, which had broken off in the process, and then went on their way. Nearby residents heard the noise, observed the damage, and sounded the alarm. Germans gathered in response to the pealing of church bells and the cries of "Emperor Joseph has been overturned! Everyone to the marketplace." There was unrest throughout the night. Around 4:30 in the morning, about 200 Germans assembled outside the Hotel Continental where Czech officers were quartered and tried to force their way in. Shots were fired, with injuries to both sides.[41]

When the Germans again gathered at the marketplace later that morning, the statue of Joseph II, which had been restored by dawn, sported a sash in the German-nationalist colors of black-red-gold. Banners in the same colors hung from some of the houses around the square. About 100 of the demonstrators, mainly children and adolescents, badly damaged the town's recently opened Czech-language school.[42]

The Czech response to the damage to the Czech school in Eger was immediate. Anti-German protests in Prague beginning 16 November resulted in some of the worst ethnic violence of the interwar period. Reflecting the common practice of collapsing German and Jewish identities, Czechs attacked both German and Jewish residents as well as communal buildings and other symbols of German and Jewish culture.[43]

Following the example of Prague, there were anti-German demonstrations in Czech-dominated cities and towns across the Bohemian lands. Unrest spread throughout predominantly German northern and western Bohemia, as local Czechs damaged or destroyed statues of Joseph II as well as those of other figures of cultural and historic importance to the Germans, and the Germans there responded to the Czech attacks. Some local officials placed their statues of the emperor and other Habsburg figures under the authority of Prague. Elsewhere, German residents spontaneously, but peacefully restored their towns' statues of Joseph, which had been removed earlier.

The future of the statues, which had in some cases been taken to court, would not be settled until the mid-1920s, when destruction of reminders of the Habsburg past was codified into law in 1923 and justified as an essential act for the protection of the Republic.[44] In their attempts to have the statues removed, the Czechs utilized earlier German rhetoric against the statues, arguing the existence of a Joseph II "cult." Moreover, German claims in the wake of the statue war, that the "old statue doesn't talk politics, neither does it intrigue, nor protest the Czechoslovak state" begged the question.[45] From the time they were unveiled, the Germans had employed the statues of Emperor Joseph II as symbolic sites of German iden-

Figure 6.5. The one-armed statue of Emperor Joseph II standing in the courtyard of the Státní okresní archiv Cheb. (Photograph by Nancy M. Wingfield).

tity. And, they had constructed this identity not only in opposition to imperial policy coming out of Vienna, but also in opposition to the Czechs, in their losing battle for political supremacy in the Bohemian lands. It is thus no surprise that statues of Joseph II became emblematic of German politics, intrigue, and opposition to the Czechs and the Czechoslovak state.[46]

A blurring of the sacred and the profane marked the eras of monument fever and statue wars in Bohemia. Although Czech nationalists may have insisted that their objection to the Marian Column or the St. John of Nepomuk statues was political, not religious, devout Czech (and Slovak) Roman Catholics were unwilling to separate these categories so easily. Moreover, merely insisting that a symbol like the early Protestant Jan Hus was political, not religious, did not appease Catholics, who viewed him as a heretic. The interwar period featured dueling religious-cum-political festivals, devoted to Czech martyrs of the past, as disparate groups battled over the correct meaning of their national identity.

While Czechs and Slovaks could not agree on the meaning of Czechoslovak identity, German citizens did not feel they had an equal stake in the new state, and they attempted to maintain their own national and cultural symbols. It is ironic that the pre-national, enlightened-absolutist emperor became a national figure celebrated with the increasingly apocalyptic and martyred religious rhetoric of German nationalists. The German nationalists of the Bohemian lands, however, believed themselves caught up in a life-or-death battle for survival. And just as Joseph II had been misunderstood in his time, so too were the Germans of the Bohemian lands misunderstood in theirs. From the outset, there were contemporary political undertones in much of the rhetoric surrounding the Joseph II centenary statues. Local German bourgeois politicians employed these statues in their national-linguistic battles with the Czechs to mark as German (and middle-class) the public spaces they still dominated.

Why did sites devoted to political figures become sacred while sacred symbols became political? In his landmark study of French national identity, *Realms of Memory: Rethinking the French Past,* the historian Pierre Nora distinguishes between *imposed* and *constructed* national symbols. Official institutions impose certain symbols whose meanings are meant to be straightforward and clear. In the modern era, new and newly independent countries have invented a variety of symbols to evoke patriotism and trust in government. While these attempts might not always succeed, the symbols are intended to have simple and direct meanings for the citizenry. Constructed national symbols, however, appear more gradually and accidentally. Their meanings contain "various layers of memory."[47] The values different groups ascribe to various symbols often result in conflicts about the identity of the entire nation.

In both the late Habsburg period and the early years of the First Czechoslovak Republic, the diverse population widely disagreed on these constructed national symbols. A small group of Czech nationalists competed with other constituencies in the Bohemian lands for the predominance of their symbols. These symbols, which emerged from a variety of historical sources, contained contradictory meanings. Although liberal nationalists—Czech and German—proclaimed secular intentions, the historic heroes and symbols available to them emerged from a history in which religion had been a key indicator of loyalties and differences. Thus, in the Bohemian lands, constructed symbols with political intentions also evoked religious meanings and interpretations. Of course, the very phenomenon of erecting statues as sites of national memory has its roots in religious tradition. Like religious shrines, national sites of memory become places where people could prove their devotion by visiting, lighting candles, and laying wreaths. In the heavily charged atmosphere of the multinational and multi-confessional Bohemian lands of the late nineteenth and early twentieth centuries, it is no surprise that competing definitions of the nation became layered with one of human society's most personal and potent identity markers: religion and spirituality.

Notes

* Research for this article was funded in part by the Fulbright-Hays Doctoral Dissertation Abroad Fellowship and the International Research and Exchanges Board (IREX) with funds provided by the National Endowment for the Humanities, the United States Information Agency, and the United States Department of State.

1. Ernst Renan, "What is a nation?" in Geoff Eley and Ronald Grigor Suny, eds., *Becoming National. A Reader* (Oxford, 1996), 50–51.
2. Sergiusz Michalski, *Public Monuments: Art in Political Bondage 1870–1997* (London, 1998), 7–8.
3. See, for example, Carl Richter, *Geschichte der Kaiser Josef-Denkmäler in Böhmen, Mähren, Niederösterreich und Schlesien* (Reichenberg, 1883), 360.
4. *Budweiser Kreisblatt,* 28 October 1883, 2.
5. T.C.W. Blanning, *Joseph II* (New York, 1994), 92–93.
6. Richter, *Geschichte der Kaiser Josef-Denkmäler,* 80.
7. Katherine Verdery, *The Political Lives of Dead Bodies* (New York, 1999), 5.
8. For the "Gospel of the Enlightenment," see the *Leitmeritzer Zeitung,* 24 November 1880, 1037; for the "Egyptian Joseph," see Richter, *Geschichte der Kaiser Josef-Denkmäler,* 168–169.
9. Richter, *Geschichte der Kaiser Josef-Denkmäler,* 74.
10. Ibid., 81.
11. Ibid., 76.
12. Ibid., 69.
13. *Budweis Kreisblatt,* 27 October 1883, 1.
14. See Peter Hogan's comments on the relationship between mourning and monuments as well as on group reaction to the destruction of its monuments. *The Ability to Mourn: Disillusionment and the Social Origins of Psychoanalysis* (Chicago, 1989), 270–282. The phrase "sites of symbolic exchange" is from Jay Winter, *Sites of Memory, Sites of Mourning: A Cultural History of the Great War* (Cambridge, 1995), 94.
15. See "The Celebration: Bequeathing Local and National Memories," in Alon Confino, *The Nation as Local Metaphor: Württemberg, Imperial Germany, and National Memory, 1871–1918* (Chapel Hill, 1997), 40–51.
16. Státní okresní archiv České Budějovice, [Hereafter SOA-ČB] sign. K 1071, Fest-Gedicht zur Enthüllungsfeier des Kaiser Josef-Denkmals in Strodenitz am 25 Juni 1889; Richter, *Geschichte der Kaiser Josef-Denkmäler,* 78.
17. The term, imagined communities, belongs to Benedict Anderson, *Imagined Communities: Reflections on the Origin and Spread of Nationalism* (London, 1983). On statues as pedagogic devices, see William Cohen, "Symbols of Power: Statues in Nineteenth-Century Provincial France," *Comparative Studies in Society and History* 3 (1989): 491.
18. SOA-ČB, sign. K 1071, Program slavnostní odhalení pomníku císaři Josefovi v Rožnově (Celebratory program for the unveiling of the Joseph II statue in Rožnov); *Moravská orlice,* 18 November 1892, 1.

19. A Czech deputy made these remarks in the Bohemian Diet in the early 1880s (Richter, *Geschichte der Kaiser Josef-Denkmäler,* 36). See also *Národní listy,* 30 October 1881, 1, on the German nationalist use of Emperor Joseph II.

20. Archiv Hlavního Města Prahy [Hereafter AHMP], Spolek Zbudování Pomníku Husova, Carton 13, Stanislav Forman, *Dějiny spolku pro vystávení pomníku Mistra Jana Husi v Praze* [History of the Club for the Building of the Master Jan Hus Memorial in Prague] (Prague, 1903), 5. This source is the official, self-published history of the Club for the Building of the Jan Hus Memorial in Prague.

21. Zdeněk Hojda and Jiří Pokorný, *Pomníky a zapomníky* [Monuments and Forgetting] (Prague, 1996).

22. Quoted in Forman, *Dějiny spolku,* 21.

23. Forman, *Dějiny spolku,* 25.

24. Forman, *Dějiny spolku,* 25.

25. Verdery, *The Political Lives of Dead Bodies,* 5.

26. Quoted in Libor Gottfried, "Kterák socha Mariánská byla stržena," [How the Marian column was demolished], *Dějiny a součastnost* 5 (1994): 29–30.

27. Quoted in Sauer-Kysela's memoir of the event: František Sauer-Kysela, *Naše luza, jesuité a diplomaté* [Our Mob, the Jesuits, and the Diplomats] (Prague, 1923), 8. Also quoted in Ferdinand Peroutka, *Budování státu: Československá politika v letech popřevratpvých* [The Building of the State: Czechoslovak Politics in the First Post-Revolutionary Years], vol. 1: *1918–1919,* reprint ed. (Prague, 1991), 117; and in the Catholic newspaper *Lidové listy,* 11 November 1923. Peroutka was a journalist with connections to the political leaders of the new Czechoslovak state. His four-volume work is a firsthand account of the political activities surrounding the building of the Czechoslovak state, and is considered by Czechoslovak historians to be the best source on the politics of this era.

28. The phrases, "prison of the peoples" and "prison house of nations," were often employed by nationalists throughout Austria-Hungary during the late Monarchy.

29. Kysela-Sauer, *Naše luza,* 24.

30. Gottfried, "Kterák socha Mariánská byla stržena," 30.

31. From Moric Hruban, *Z Času nedlouho zaslých* [From the Recent Past] (Rome, 1967), 199. Quoted and translated in Frank Hajek, "Jan Šramek and the Czechoslovak People's Party. Catholics and Politics in Czechoslovakia, 1918–1929" (Ph.D. diss., Emory University, 1974), 39.

32. See especially, Vít Vlnas, *Jan Nepomucký, Česká legenda* (Prague, 1993).

33. Statní ústřední archiv [Hereafter SÚA], Presidium ministerstvo vnitra [Hereafter PMV], 1919–1924, IV/P/47 (Pomníky). Report of the Regional Political Board in Mladá Boleslav to the Provincial Political Board in Prague, č. 33255, 27 August 1920.

34. SÚA, PMV, Minutes of the Meeting of the Town Council of Dobrovice, 14 July 1920. 1919–1924, IV/P/47.

35. Ibid.

36. Ibid.

37. Report of the Regional Police Bureau for Bohemia in Prague, Mladá Boleslav office, no. 24. A Report from the Presidium of the Regional Political Administration in Prague reported the age of Jan Matura as six, but most sources give his age as nine. See *Presidium zemské správy politické v Praze Presidiu ministerstva vnitra č. 28.305* [Presidium of the Regional Political Administration in Prague to the Ministry of the Interior] (2 September 1920), SÚA, PMV 1919–1924, IV/P/47.

38. SÚA, PMV 1919–1924, IV/P/47, no. 10, Ministerstvo vnitra, Oddělení N. č. 18.465 pres. 1920, "Zpráva o snešení sochy svatého Jana v Dobrovici." [News about the removal of the St. John Statue in Dobrovice.]

39. SÚA, PMV 1919–1924, IV/P/47, no. 10, Ministerstvo vnitra, Oddělení N. č. 18.465 pres. 1920.

40. For a complete record of events in Teplitz, see SÚA, PMV 1920–1924, sign. IV/P/47, file 225/159/4, Zápis o jednání parlamentní vyšetřující komise v Teplicích-Šanově [Record of the proceedings of the parliamentary inquiry commission in Teplitz-Schönau/Teplice-Šanov], 15 November 1920. See also *Teplitzer Zeitung,* 31 October–21 November 1920.

41. On the situation in Eger, see Státní okresní archiv Cheb, okresní úřad Cheb (fond 437), carton 47, cat. no. 558.

42. Ibid.

43. On the demonstrations in Prague, see SÚA, PMV 1920–1924, sign. IV/P/47, file 225/159/3 and SÚA, PP 1916–1920, D/6/30. See also the report of German Ambassador Samuel Saenger from 17 November 1920, in Manfred Alexander, ed., *Deutsche Gesandtschafts-berichte aus Prag,* vol. 1: *Von der Staatsgründung bis zum ersten Kabinett Beneš 1918–1921* (Munich, 1983), 350; and the discussion of the Prague city council, AHMP, Protokol schůzí rady městské, listopad-prosinec 1920, Zápis o mimořádne schůzi rady meštské, 17 November 1920.

44. In their legal complaints, Czech nationalist groups employed Paragraph 23 of "Zákon na ochranu republiky" [Law for the defense of the republic], *Sbírka zákon a naízení státu Čes-koslovenského,* 50/1923 (Prague, 1923), 207–17. This law called for the removal from public view of statues, inscriptions, and memorials of antistate character, or of members of the Habsburg Monarchy or the Hohenzollern Dynasty.

45. *Tetschen-Bodenbacher Volks-Zeitung,* 27 November 1920, 5.

46. SÚA, MPV, sign. IV/P/47, file 225/159/6, Decision of the High Court in Prague, 18 April 1923. On previously bland images—which the Emperor Joseph II had never been—acquiring "precise meanings and sudden, high visibility" in times of political upheaval, see Marina Warner, *Monuments & Maidens: The Allegory of the Female Form* (New York, 1985), 23; and Verdery, *The Political Lives of Dead Bodies,* Introduction.

47. Pierre Nora, *Realms of Memory. The Construction of the French Past,* vol. 3: *Symbols,* trans. by Arthur Goldhammer (New York, 1993), xi.

Chapter 7

ALL FOR ONE! ONE FOR ALL!

The Federation of Slavic Sokols and the Failure of Neo-Slavism

Claire E. Nolte

Historians have recognized the major role that the gymnastic club Sokol (Falcon) played in the Czech national movement.[1] Founded in Prague in 1862, the organization had over 100,000 adherents in more than 1,000 clubs by the time of its fiftieth anniversary in 1912.[2] A major reason for this success was the ideological foundation laid by the organization's founder, Miroslav Tyrš, who held the post of gymnastic director (*náčelnik*) of the Prague Sokol until his death in 1884. At a time when the national divide in the Bohemian lands was still fluid, Tyrš emphasized the club's Slavic identity to distinguish it from the older German *Turnverein*, its obvious model.[3] The new organization expressed its Slavism in the club symbol of a falcon, a feature of South Slav and Polish folklore, and in the elaborate club uniform, a hybrid of styles that was understood to be "Slavic," although at least some of its elements were Hungarian.[4] As the Sokol idea spread to other Slavic nations, Tyrš dreamed of a time when "all of the diverse Slavic youth will find themselves under one flag, the Sokol flag."[5] Although Tyrš was never able to create his Slavic Sokol union, his successors sought to carry out this aspect of his program with the formation, in 1908, of the Federation of Slavic Sokols. Despite the great hopes surrounding its inauguration, the Federation was short-lived, its troubled history a testimony to the difficulties of forging unity out of the diversity of the Slavic world.

The Sokol had always promoted itself as the "birthplace of Slavic gymnastics," although in the early years of the club, this rather meant "Austro-Slavic gymnastics," since other Austrian Slavs, that is, Slavs living in the Habsburg Empire, were the first to emulate the Czech example.[6] One year after the creation of the Prague Sokol, the first Sokol club outside the Bohemian Crownlands was founded in Ljubljana in direct emulation of the Czech model. The Sokol idea had been carried to the area by South Slav students who had studied in Prague and joined the Sokol there. The club they founded, *Južní Sokol,* copied much of the Prague Sokol's uniform, and became a center of national life, counting many prominent political and cultural leaders in its ranks.[7] Inspired by the example of Ljubljana, a Croat Sokol club was founded in Zagreb in 1874.[8]

Although the Czechs and South Slavs maintained a close collaboration, not only gymnastically, but also politically in the empire, that was not the case with the Poles. In 1866, a Sokol club was founded in Lemberg/Lwów, whose leaders resisted, at first, using the name "Sokol" and adopting the "Slavic" gymnastic system that had been developed in Prague.[9] Polish reluctance to embrace the Czech model reflected basic political and cultural differences between these two Slavic nations. While the mostly bourgeois Czech politicians hoped to form a Slavic bloc in the empire to promote their cause, the aristocratic leaders of Galicia supported the regime in Vienna in return for concessions that allowed them to continue their domination of the province and contain the aspirations of the mostly Ruthene peasant class there. In addition, the Poles distrusted Czech Russophilism, given the history of conflict between Poles and Russians and the fact that the Russian tsar was ruling over most of what had once been Poland. These issues complicated the relationship between the Polish and Czech Sokol movements, despite the efforts of club leaders on both sides to ameliorate them. Nevertheless, in the early years of the movement, the clubs in Lemberg, Ljubljana, and Zagreb requested, and received, gymnastic trainers from Prague, a practice the Czech leaders hoped would lead to closer coordination among them.[10]

Sokol headquarters in Prague attached great importance to the nascent Sokol movements of the other Slavic peoples. Tyrš tracked their growth in the statistical handbooks he published about the organization, and in 1882, on the occasion of the twentieth anniversary of the founding of the Prague Sokol, he invited them to the gymnastic festival he was organizing to commemorate the occasion.[11] Although this anniversary celebration only lasted one day and was a relatively modest affair in light of those that followed, it became a landmark in the history of Czech gymnastics, and was the birthplace of the gigantic gymnastic displays called "Slets," from the Czech word for a flocking of birds. Several practices that became Slet traditions were inaugurated at the 1882 event, including the ceremonial greeting of foreign guests at the train stations in Prague, the march through Prague of Sokol clubs in full regalia carrying their club flags and led by leaders on horseback, and a mass calisthenic display of hundreds of gymnasts performing in unison, sometimes to musical accompaniment.[12] The participation of Croat and Slovene Sokols in the first Slet encouraged the Czech organization to undertake more aggressive efforts to promote "Slavic" gymnastics. A few months later, the first Czech Sokol outing to a destination outside the Bohemian Crownlands brought over 1,200 Czech gymnasts to Cracow, a practice that continued with visits to other Slavic capitals, while at the same time trainers from other Slavic clubs began to attend gymnastic courses in Prague.[13] Although limited in scope, these early Austro-Slavic gymnastic efforts allowed club leaders in Prague to employ expansive rhetoric about the "Slavic mission" of the Sokol movement.

By the turn of the century, sports and physical activity had become popular ways to occupy the expanded leisure time of an increasingly urbanized population. The older Sokol organizations of the Poles, Czechs, and South Slavs experienced a rapid rise in membership, and several newer groups were established, including a Polish Sokol movement in Prussian Poland that became a junior partner to the larger organization in Galicia.[14] A Serbian Sokol was founded in Belgrade in 1882, a Ruthene Sokol club appeared in 1892 in Cracow, and a gymnastic movement called Junak, created in 1884 at the behest of the Bulgarian government, gravitated into the Sokol arena by the early twentieth century.[15] Elsewhere, the Hungarian government banned the Sokol in Slovakia, and the tsarist regime forbade the name "Sokol" in the Russian Empire until after the Revolution of 1905, although the clubs remained illegal in Russian Poland even after that time.

These Slavic gymnastic efforts acquired a new ideological direction with the appearance, following the Russian Revolution of 1905, of "Neo-Slavism," a reformulation of old-style Pan-Slavism with its overtones of tsarist imperialism into a new program that emphasized cultural cooperation among all the Slavic nations.[16] Although the Czech Sokol was declared to be "above politics," its leaders were closely aligned with the Young Czech Party, a once-influential alliance of liberal elites that had lost ground to newer parties of interest. The Young Czechs eagerly embraced Neo-Slavism as an issue that could galvanize support in an era of popular suffrage. Although Neo-Slavism only lasted a few years and was officially apolitical, many Habsburg officials feared it was a new Pan-Slav effort to destroy the Monarchy. The new movement held two congresses, the first in Prague in 1908 on the sixtieth anniversary of the 1848 Slav Congress there, and the second two years later in Sofia, along with smaller meetings to promote the economic and cultural cooperation of the Slavic peoples. Many projects were on the agenda of these gatherings, including the formation of a Slav bank and a Slav news service, but the first concrete manifestation of the Neo-Slav effort was the creation of the Federation of Slavic Sokols in 1908.

Slavic solidarity through gymnastics was a project dear to the heart of the president of the Czech Sokol Union (*Česká obec sokolská*, or Č.O.S.), Josef Scheiner.[17] A prominent Young Czech and distant relative of Tyrš's wife, Scheiner had risen through the ranks of the Sokol, becoming Č.O.S. president in 1906, a post he held until his death in 1932. He expressed his hopes for Slavic solidarity through gymnastics in a speech at the 1907 Slet in Prague:

> [I]n place of a monument to past glory, let us build a new monument on the powerful shoulders of men who are self-aware, a living monument, on whose foundations we can cultivate a grand pavilion of freedom and liberty for all Slavic people without exception! In defiance of all coercion, in defiance of all that strives for our death, in

defiance of all that has for centuries pounded against the Slavic fortress, we want to stand upright and, with a determined mind and a strong chest, defend our national patrimony with equality, liberty, and freedom for all![18]

Indeed, the 1907 Sokol Slet had attracted a record number of foreign guests, most of them Slavic, although in a sign of future trouble for the Neo-Slav effort, the presence of over 100 Russian guests had caused the Polish Sokol to boycott the event.[19] The Slet was a forum for the Neo-Slav effort, when plans were made for the upcoming Neo-Slav Congress, and Slavic brotherhood was extolled in private meetings and dinners. For example, at one celebration during the Slet, a Serb declared that the Sokol had a positive impact on other Slavs, "Our enemies in the South and the West know this very well, as do the enemies that live among us. But it is hopeless to try to hold back the flood of Pan-Slav solidarity."[20] His colleague from Montenegro seconded this idea, adding "that we stand strong and on guard against our common enemies. We are resolved to offer everything, everything, even our lives, for the sacred Pan-Slav cause."[21] At a private dinner for Slavic guests, Ivan Hribar, the mayor of Ljubljana and a key figure in the Neo-Slav movement, declared "When not only we Slavs, but also our non-Slavic friends are convinced of the danger of Pan-German expansion, then we will all have to work together to find a way to fight this dangerous enemy."[22] In addition, a Bosnian urged the world press to publicize the wild regime of the Austro-Hungarian military in his homeland, and a Polish Sokol from Posen (Poznań), who was attending the Slet privately, bemoaned the fact that his fellow-nationals from Galicia were boycotting it:

> We Poles in Poznań do not sit by full plates courtesy of the government's goodwill, as do our aristocratic comrades in Galicia, and we therefore feel our membership in the great Slavic family all the more, and are hurt that much deeper by the absence of the Poles at this Sokol Slet.[23]

Tributes to Czech cultural leadership of the Slavic world echoed throughout these events. At a meeting hosted by the Czech politician Václav Klofáč, a Russian declared that the Slavs were now looking to the Czechs as they had once looked to the Russians, and at a dinner at the Slavic Club, the Czechs were hailed as the "teachers, pioneers, and apostles of the Slavic idea," Prague was dubbed the "Slavic Athens," and the mayor of Zagreb declared that the Czechs were the model for all Slavdom.[24]

In February 1908, the Federation of Slavic Sokols was inaugurated at a meeting in Vienna by leaders of the three constituting organizations: the Č.O.S., the Slovene Sokol Union, and the Croat Sokol Union.[25] The agenda included proposals for Slets, Slavic language courses, and even a dictionary of all Slavic languages. The new organization was loosely structured and dominated by Czechs, with the two top positions of president and gymnastic director held by Josef Scheiner and the Č.O.S. *náčelník*, Jindřich Vaníček, respectively. On the tricky issue of the organization's language, the proposal to institute "all Slavic languages" was rejected in favor of "that Slavic language, which is common in the headquarters of the organization," a formula that effectively mandated Czech since the federation's headquarters was defined as "the current abode of its president."[26] Although representatives from both the Bulgarian and the Serbian gymnastic movements were present at this founding meeting, the Poles, still suspicious of Czech motives, did not attend.

Thanks to this new federation, Scheiner could confidently inform the 1908 Neo-Slav Congress in Prague that the Sokol was "without opposition the most powerful organization in Slavdom," and further assert that it "is on the way to become the link joining all Slavic men together on the basis of the noble idea of brotherhood, equality, and freedom for all, for the purification, ennobling, strengthening, and growth of Slavdom."[27] In addition, the Sokol presented an exercising display at the Congress that so inspired the Russian delegates, they donned Sokol uniforms and one of them exclaimed, "The Sokol is the medicine that Russia needs the most!"[28] The Neo-Slav Congress concluded with a resolution to promote Slavic solidarity in five areas, one of which was Sokol gymnastics.[29]

Russian enthusiasm for the Sokol at the 1908 Neo-Slav Congress was the culmination of a drive to spread the movement in Russia that Josef Scheiner, dubbed the "Apostle of the Sokol in Russia," regarded as his special mission.[30] Although Czech émigrés had founded a few Sokol clubs in Russia in the 1870s, they had remained isolated.[31] After the Č.O.S. had raised the international profile of the organization by winning medals at a gymnastic meet at the 1889 World's Fair in Paris, Russian schools began to request Czech trainers. When these émigrés went on to found clubs on the Sokol model, the movement established a foothold in the vast Russian hinterland.[32] After the Russian Revolution of 1905 lifted many restrictions on club life, including a ban on the name "Sokol," the movement grew more rapidly, reaching 40 clubs, while the number of Czech trainers, estimated at 20 in 1905, topped 200 by 1914, creating a shortage in the Czech lands.[33]

Czech cultivation of the Russian Sokol alienated the Poles, especially since the ban on Sokol clubs in Russian Poland remained in place even after the 1905 Revolution. The Polish Sokol Union in Galicia sent a message to the constituting meeting of the Federation of Slavic Sokols in 1908, explaining that they would join the federation once they were convinced that Slavic brotherhood truly existed. Seeking to lure the Poles into membership, Scheiner opened an investigation into another area of contention, the nationally mixed area of Teschen in Silesia, where it was reported that Polish workers were being forced to join Czech Sokol clubs. Negotiations on this issue resulted in the creation of a joint arbitration board to moderate the dispute.[34] In addition to Teschen, Czech Sokol leaders also outraged the Poles by encouraging a nascent gymnastic movement among the Ruthenes of Galicia, where two gymnastic movements had taken root. The older of the two, called "Sokil-Bat'ko," was officially apolitical, but the other organization, a gymnastic and firefighting movement called, in a Cossack reference, "Sič," was promoted by the Radical Party and was strongly anticlerical.[35] By 1912, however, the two Ruthene groups were working toward a merger, and Czech Sokol writers were waxing enthusiastic about "this marvelous 'Ukrainian-

Ruthenian Sič' active among the simplest folk, in the popular spirit of gymnastics and uplift, very close to that of the Sokol."[36]

In February 1910, the Board of Directors of the Federation of Slavic Sokols voted to recommend the Galician Polish Sokol Union to membership, with final admission to be approved by the Federation's Executive Council, a large body that was scheduled to meet during the Neo-Slav Congress in Sofia later that year.[37] The Poles had set forth three conditions for joining, two of which, that the Board of Directors be broadened to give each national organization one vote and that the Federation communicate with each member organization in its native language, were intended to undermine Czech domination of the organization. The final condition, that no member union be required to participate in gymnastic events outside of its homeland, was ultimately rejected at Sofia, but the Poles joined anyway, bringing 218 clubs with almost 25,000 members into the Slavic Sokol organization.[38]

The same meeting that recommended the Poles for membership also considered the application of the Serbian Sokol organization. The first Serbian Sokol had been founded in Belgrade in 1882, but it was poorly organized, despite the efforts of the Czech trainer hired as its *náčelník* in 1894, and the movement languished.[39] One reason for this unpromising development was the presence of a rival gymnastic organization called "Dušan Silný." Founded in 1896, it propagated the Greater Serbia program and practiced what was purported to be a more "Serbian national" style of training, which emphasized military exercising, along with light athletics and some sports.[40] In 1908, a Czech trainer arrived in Belgrade in response to a request from the Sokol club to lead its training sessions.[41] Others followed, so that by 1913, there were an estimated fourteen Czech gymnastic teachers in the Serbian Kingdom.[42] Josef Scheiner went to Belgrade in 1909 to negotiate an end to the rivalry between the Sokol and Dušan Silný and, with the help of the Serbian King Peter, who supported the gymnastic effort, the two organizations united to form the Union of Serbian Sokol Clubs Dušan Silný, with the Czech *náčelník* of the Belgrade Sokol as its gymnastic director. By 1913, after Serbian Sokol clubs inside the Habsburg lands, from the Banat, Croatia, Slavonia, Hungary, and Bosnia-Herzegovina, joined this new union, it encompassed an estimated 122 clubs with 8,000 members.[43]

The first gymnastic festival of the newly created Union of Serbian Sokol Clubs Dušan Silný was scheduled to take place shortly before the second Neo-Slav Congress in Sofia in 1910, and a large contingent of Czech Sokol members en route to Sofia stopped in Belgrade to participate in it.[44] In his speech at this event, Scheiner praised the Serbs for their "history, which is rich in great heroic deeds and famous battles [waged] to cast off the yoke of slavery and establish freedom and independence for the country," while the mayor of Belgrade declared the Czechs to be "the teachers of the Serb nation" and thanked them "for all they have done for the edification of Slavdom."[45]

Proceeding on to Sofia, the Czech contingent took part in the mass exercising display that had been arranged to coincide with the Neo-Slav Congress there.

At a time when Neo-Slavism was in decline, the public exercising display of over 4,000 Sokols in Sofia was the most successful event of the Congress.[46] Representatives from the three original member unions of Czechs, Croats, and Slovenes, along with Polish and Serbian candidate members and Bulgarian and Russian observers, attended the meeting of the Federation's Executive Council where, to demonstrate the scope of the organization, the minutes were read in five languages.[47] With both Bulgarians and Russians expressing an interest in joining, the Federation's secretary ended his presentation with the following prediction:

> The Sokol movement will be the cement joining together all of the branches of the Slavs as brothers—the home of each is home to the other, not a foreign land. The Slav will be called noble, steadfast, and free, and will bear the message of mankind's renewal on the basis of equality, brotherhood, progress, and an unshakeable love for homeland. To this great future Slavdom, in which the Sokol movement will be the forward guard of victory—*Nazdar!*[48]

At the next meeting of the Federation's Executive Council in Zagreb in 1911, the Bulgarians were formally accepted into membership.[49] Although some short-lived gymnastic clubs had been founded by Czech émigrés working in Bulgaria in the 1870s, the Bulgarian gymnastic movement began only in 1894 when Swiss gymnasts, hired to teach physical education in the schools, launched a movement called "Junak" (Hero).[50] Representatives of this organization made contact with the Czech Sokol at Slets in Prague, and Bulgarian trainers began to enroll in Č.O.S. gymnastic courses. Nevertheless, at the time the Bulgarian Junak Union brought its more than 4,000 members into the Federation of Slavic Sokols, its training program was still led by Swiss gymnastic instructors.[51]

The years 1910 and 1911 marked the high point of Slavic solidarity in the Sokol movement, when it was still possible to dream of the day when the Sokol Federation would bring all Slavic gymnasts together in a gigantic union of over 120,000 members. Of the older member organizations, the Č.O.S., with 78,000 members in 1910, had the largest membership, while the Slovene Union had just over 6,000 members and Croats around 12,000.[52] To celebrate these growing numbers, the leadership of the Federation of Slavic Sokols decided to hold a grand Slet in Prague in 1912, that would commemorate the fiftieth anniversary of the founding of the first Sokol club in Prague, and also highlight Slavic gymnastic achievements. As preparations for the Slet began, however, the Federation was seriously divided. The Poles were outraged by the proposed entry of the newly created Russian Sokol Union into the Federation, as well as by the proposal to invite Ruthene clubs to the Slet.[53] In the course of a fiery debate at the 1911 meeting of the newly expanded Board of Directors, the Poles demanded that Russian Sokol leaders press their government to allow Sokol clubs in Russian Poland. When a Bulgarian countered by accusing them of political bias, one of the Polish representatives responded, "it is not possible to separate the national from the political."[54] Ignoring the Polish protests, Josef Scheiner traveled to Rus-

Figure 7.1. Slavic Sokols at the 1912 Slet in Prague. From left: 2 Ruthenes, a Bulgarian Junak, a Slovene, a Czech, a Russian, a Serb, and a Croat. Photo reproduced with permission of the Tyrš Museum of Physcial Education and Sport in Prague.

sia personally to invite leaders of the Russian Sokol to the 1912 Slet.[55] Their presence caused the Polish Sokol organization to boycott the event.

The grand Slet took place over several weekends, beginning in May and continuing through the first week in July, with the main events scheduled for the end of June, and it attracted record-breaking crowds, estimated as high as 300,000 over the course of the event.[56] Appropriately for the first All-Slav Slet, most of the foreign guests were Slavs, not all of them gymnasts, since many came to attend the corollary events scheduled to coincide with the Slet, such as a meeting of Slav journalists, or the ceremony to dedicate the monument to the Czech national leader, the historian František Palacký. One of the more impressive groups, almost 750, arrived from Russia, among them 250 students from Russian schools who arrived together with their Czech gymnastic teachers.[57] Southern Slavs made up the other major gymnastic representation, including 555 Slovenes, 658 Croats, 336 Bulgarians, and, most impressively, 1,169 Serbs. Ruthenes and Montenegrins sent small gymnastic delegations, while Slovaks attended as observers.[58] All of these colorful uniforms and flags and national traditions heightened the impression of the traditional Slet parade through the streets of Prague, which featured almost 18,000 Slavic Sokols marching shoulder to shoulder in apparent solidarity.

Another traditional high point of the Slets, the men's mass calisthenic display, broke all previous records for participation, featuring over 11,000 Czech gymnasts in a coordinated display performed to musical accompaniment that attracted sold-out crowds, and was repeated the next day, when the Czechs were joined by members of the Serbian Sokol in a gesture of solidarity with clear political overtones. The gymnastic display of the Serbian Sokol itself was equally tendentious. A mere four years after Austria-Hungary and Serbia had almost gone to war in the Annexation Crisis, the Serbs came to Prague from seven countries under six governments to perform as one group under the leadership of the Czech gymnastic director of the Union of Sokol Clubs Dušan Silný.[59]

To unify these disparate elements, the Slet committee had given the event an overriding theme based on fifth-century BC Greece that was to be manifested in the architecture, decoration, and style of the Slet grounds. This Greek theme had its clearest expression in a mass theatrical event on the exercise field that, along with the parade through Prague and the men's calisthenic display, formed the third high point of the 1912 Slet. This peculiar type of display, a combination of *tableaux vivants* with traditional theater, had first appeared at the 1907 Slet, when the Hussite victory at Německý Brod in 1422 had been reenacted in the form of a gigantic chess game, complete with horses and cannon and a cast of over 400. The success of this effort led to the even more elaborate theatrical scene at the 1912 Slet, when 1,292 men, women, and children reenacted the events surrounding the Battle of Marathon.[60] Incorporating a pentathlon competition as well as original music and choral singing, it was repeated three times in the course of the Slet, to great acclaim. As a description of the Battle of Marathon in the club paper makes clear, the play was intended as a metaphor for Slavic solidarity.

> The world historical significance of this battle … lies especially in the fact that it manifested for the first time the driving force behind a common, military effort by several tribes of the same national and ethnic origins, who were divided and separated by domestic fights, [that force being] the national idea, which united divided Hellas. Consciousness of their national and ethnic identity allowed them to function as one force in defense of their common national interests.[61]

In the end, however, the realities of the Slavic world undermined the solidarity exhibited on the exercise-field. At a meeting during the Slet, the Executive Council of the Federation of Slavic Sokols reprimanded the Poles for their failure to attend the Slet, declaring:

> The Executive Council … having discussed the lack of Polish participation, regrets the step [the Poles] have taken, which they see as belittling and threatening the efforts to overcome the conflicts among the Slavic nations through a common effort based on conscientious and consistent training of a sort best exemplified by our Slet.[62]

At that same meeting, Federation leaders voted to consider the application of the Russian Sokol Union for membership. The subsequent admission of the Russians prompted the Galician Polish Sokol Union to withdraw from the Federation, and they were soon followed by the Bulgarians, angered at Czech support for the Serbs in the Second Balkan War.[63] For this reason, one historian has concluded,

The functioning of the Federation of Slavic Sokols ended for all practical purposes in 1912, ... and so, from Scheiner's conception, which he propounded in 1912 over the skepticism of many Slavic Sokol activists, there remained some months later only chauvinistic attitudes and an often unqualified support for the Russian monarchy.[64]

The failure of the Federation of Slavic Sokols demonstrates some of the contradictions of Czech Slavism. Although the Pan-, Austro-, and Neo-Slav movements all originated in the Bohemian lands, their propagators often lacked an understanding of the true conditions of the Slavic world.[65] This was especially true of the Czech "Awakeners," the scholars and writers of the late eighteenth and early nineteenth century who laid the foundations for the Czech national movement. Inspired by the predictions of a glorious future for the Slavic peoples in the writings of the German philologist Johann Gottfried von Herder, they made Slavic solidarity a cornerstone of Czech identity. However, as the future president-liberator of Czechoslovakia, Thomas Garrigue Masaryk, pointed out in his 1895 book, *The Czech Question,* the Slavism of the Awakeners was often "false, superficial, and unwholesomely fantastic" because its proponents had no direct knowledge of other Slavic nations.[66]

As war loomed in Europe, a new generation of Czech leaders attempted to unify the Slavic world in the face of a perceived Pan-German threat. By this time, however, the contradictions of Czech Slavism had become more pronounced. The economic development of the Bohemian lands had produced a modern and confident national society, the most "westernized" of the Slavic peoples, whose artists and writers were internationally recognized. The disparity between the Czechs and most of the other Slavs was evident in the selection of a Greek theme for the 1912 Slet, whereby Prague became the "Slavic Athens," a center of cultural life like Athens in ancient Greece, and the Czechs became the teachers of the other, more backward, Slavic peoples.[67] Josef Scheiner expressed these sentiments in his speech at Old Town Square on the day of the Slet parade:

> After five years our Sokols have again flocked to our golden, Slavic Prague in untold numbers to demonstrate our success and progress in the healthy education and ennoblement of the Slavic people.... Today with uplifted heart and a deep consciousness of our great mission, all Slavdom stands here in uniform rows in an open manifestion of its pure intentions and goals, which are animated by a deep, honest love for its people, this dear Slavic people, whom we want to lead up out of oppression and humility into the light of learning and freedom worthy of man, worthy of the beautiful spirit and innate nobility of the Slavic race, which has always been the carrier and protector of humanity, brotherhood and equality of all.[68]

But these assumptions were not shared by the other Slavic nations, not even those in the Federation of Slavic Sokols, as an incident at the 1911 meeting of Executive Council of the Federation demonstrates. The Federation secretary, who was Czech, had submitted a formal complaint against Č.O.S. leaders for creating the Slet committee without consulting the other member organizations, declaring, "By this, the brotherly member organizations could be deeply pained and the one-sided action of the Č.O.S. interpreted as a breach of the equality of all members represented in the Federation."[69] His stand outraged the Č.O.S. leadership, especially Josef Scheiner, who forced him out a few months later over the objections of the representatives of the other Slavic Sokol organizations.[70]

The Czech presumption of leadership of the Slavic world reflects the conundrum of supranational identities, which have often been the unsustainable inventions of a group claiming dominance, either culturally or militarily, over others.[71] In fact, there could be no such thing as "Slavic solidarity" as long as Russia controlled Poland, Polish lords ruled over Ruthene peasants, Czechs and Poles fought over Teschen, and Serbs and Bulgarians could not agree on Macedonia. These hostilities ultimately destroyed the dream of Slavic solidarity through gymnastics expressed in the slogan over the main tribunal of the 1912 All-Slav Sokol Slet, "All for One! One for All!"

Notes

1. A recent history described the Sokol as "[p]robably the most influential, and certainly the most celebrated of popular Czech patriotic organizations"; Hans Kohn called it "the greatest inspiration to the Czech national movement"; R.W. Seton-Watson claimed, "What the Czechs are today they owe in very large measure to the Sokols"; Bruce Garver wrote that it "made the greatest contribution to reviving Czech patriotism and self-confidence"; and Friedrich Prinz warned that "their meaning for the development of national cooperation and mass consciousness can not be overestimated." Derek Sayer, *The Coasts of Bohemia: A Czech History* (Princeton, 1998), 105; Hans Kohn, *Pan-Slavism: Its History and Ideology* (Notre Dame, IN, 1953), 184; R.W. Seton-Watson, *A History of the Czechs and Slovaks* (London, 1943), 212; Bruce Garver, *The Young Czech Party 1874–1901 and the Emergence of a Multi-Party System* (New Haven, 1978), 31; and Friedrich Prinz, "Die böhmischen Länder von 1848 bis 1918," *Handbuch der Geschichte der böhmischen Länder*, ed. Karl Bosl (Stuttgart, 1967–1968), Vol. 3, 86.

2. In 1912, there were 119,183 adult members in Czech Sokol clubs in the Empire. If adolescents and children are counted, the number was 168,260. Men's and women's clubs, which were still separate at that time, totaled 1,156 in that year. "Statistika České obce sokolské za rok 1912," *Sokol: časopis věnovaný zájmům tělocvičným* [hereafter: *Sokol*], Vol. 40 (1914), 219.

3. The origins of the Sokol and its traditions, some of them drawn from *Turnverein* practice, are discussed in Claire E. Nolte, *The Sokol in the Czech Lands to 1914: Training for the Nation* (Basingstoke, England, 2002), 39–55. Writing in 1895, the future president of Czechoslovakia, Thomas Garrigue Masaryk, described the Sokol as a "purely German concept, of German origins, which was transferred to us and decked out with national eclecticisms." Tomáš Garrigue Masaryk, *Česká otázka: Snahy a tužby národního obrození* (Prague, 1895), 104.

4. The understanding of "original Czech" dress among nationalists at this time was unclear, and many styles thought to be Czech were really Hungarian or Polish adaptations. Renata Tyršová, *Jindřich Fügner: paměti a vzpomínky na mého otce* (Prague, 1927), Vol. 1, 121. That confusion about "national dress" occurred elsewhere is evident from Hugh Trevor-Roper, "The Invention of Tradition: The Highland Tradition of Scotland," *The Invention of Tradition,* ed. Eric Hobsbawm and Terence Ranger (Cambridge, 1992), 15–41.

5. "Zprávy spolkové," *Sokol*, Vol. 1 (1871), 41.

6. Austro-Slavism meant cooperation among the Slavic nations of the Habsburg Empire. See, Hugo Hantsch, "Pan-Slavism, Austro-Slavism, Neo-Slavism," *Austrian History Yearbook,* Vol. 1 (1965): 23–37; and Stanley B. Winters, "Austroslavism, Panslavism and Russophilism in Czech Political Thought, 1870–1900," *Intellectual and Social Developments in the Habsburg Empire from Maria Theresa to World War I,* ed. Stanley B. Winters and Joseph Held (New York, 1975), 175–202.

7. The history of the Ljubljana Sokol is described in "Dodatky k návštěvě slovanských hostí," *Památník sletu slovanského Sokolstva roku 1912 v Praze* [hereafter: *Památník sletu 1912*], ed. A. Očenášek, et al. (Prague, n.d. [1919]), 296–297; and Wolfgang Kessler, "Der Sokol in den jugoslawischen Gebieten (1863–1941)," *Die slawische Sokolbewegung: Beiträge zur Geschichte von Sport und Nationalismus in Osteuropa,* ed. Diethelm Blecking (Dortmund, 1991), 198–218. See also, M. Šesták, "Češi a Jihoslované v habsburské monarchii v letech 1850–1890," in Václav Žáček, et al., *Češi a Jihoslované v minulosti* (Prague, 1975), 485–486.

8. The Croat Sokol is discussed in František Hochmann, "Tělocvik v Chorvatsku," *Památník vydaný na oslavu dvacetiletého trvání tělocvičné jednoty Sokola pražského* [hereafter: *Památník Sokola pražského*] (Prague, 1883), 283; "Dodatky k návštěvě slovanských hosti," 400–401; and Kessler, "Der Sokol in den jugoslawischen Gebieten," 198–218.

9. Background on the Polish Sokol is in Przemysław Matusik, "Der polnische 'Sokoł' zur Zeit der Teilungen und in der II. Polnischen Republik," *Die slawische Sokolbewegung,* 104–135; and Bernard Woltmann, "Der polnische 'Sokol' 1867–1914," *Sokol, jeho vznik, vývoj a význam: Sborník příspěvků z mezinárodní konference, Praha, září 1997,* ed. Marek Waic (Prague, 1998), 123–124.

10. In 1871, the Czech gymnast Jan Veselý was dispatched by Prague Sokol leaders to serve as the gymnastic director of the Ljubljana club, and in 1873, another trainer, František Hochmann, became the gymnastic director of the Polish Sokol in Lemberg/Lwów. He later held the same position in Zagreb. Both chronicled their experiences in the club paper. J.Z. Veselý, "Vzpomínky českého Sokola," *Sokol,* Vol. 2 (1872), 122–124, 130–132, 138–140, 146–148, 154–156, 162–164, 170–172, and 186–187; and "Zprávy spolkové," ibid., Vol. 3 (1873), 77–78, 103, 131–132; Vol. 4 (1874), 38–39, 48, 69, and 85; Vol. 5 (1875), 55; and Vol. 6 (1876), 85.

11. Tyrš published three statistical studies of the movement: *Statisticko-historický přehled jednot sokolských pro rok 1865,* comp. Miroslav Tyrš (Prague, 1866); *Statistický přehled jednot Sokolských pro rok 1866,* comp. Miroslav Tyrš (Prague, n.d.[1867]); and *Sborník sokolský pro rok 1868,* comp. Miroslav Tyrš and František Čermák (Prague, n.d. [1869]).

12. The first Slet in 1882 featured 1,600 in the Slet parade and 720 in the gymnastic display. It is described in František Kožíšek and Josef Müller, "Jubilejní slavnost Sokola Pražského r. 1882," *Památník Sokola pražského,* 138–142.

13. Statistics on the participation of gymnastic trainers from other Slavic clubs in Prague Sokol training courses are given in A. Očenášek, "Rozvoj tělocvičné věci pod vedením České Obce Sokolské," *Věstník sokolský,* Vol. 13 (1909), 184–186.

14. The first Polish Sokol club in Prussia was founded in 1884. Information about this movement is in Matusik, "Der polnische Sokoł," 114–120; and "Přehled tělocvičných jednot sokolských v Polsce (t.j. Haliči a Velikém Knížectví v Prusku)," *Sokol,* Vol. 15 (1889), 116.

15. See notes 35, 39, and 50 below.

16. The Neo-Slav movement is examined in Paul Vyšný, *Neo-Slavism and the Czechs 1898–1914* (Cambridge, 1977). See also, Hugo Hantsch, "Pan-Slavism, Austro-Slavism, Neo-Slavism," 23–37; and K. Herman, "Slovanství v českém životě v době nástupu imperialismu," *Slovanství v národním životě Čechů a Slováků,* ed. V. Šťastný (Prague, 1968), 301–327.

17. Scheiner's foreign policy initiatives are chronicled in Karel Vaníček, "Starosta ve styku slovanském a mezinárodním," *Svému milému starostovi Bratra Dr. Josefa Scheinerovi Sokol Pražský* (Zvláštní příloha časopisu *Sokol,* Vol. 37, [1911]), unpaged.

18. Quoted in "Pátý slet všesokolský," *Sokol* (1908), 35.

19. The Slet attracted the following delegations: 117 from Russia, including many Czech *émigrés;* 55 Serbs from the Kingdom of Serbia and 74 from the Habsburg lands; five Montenegrins; 422 Slovenes; 800 Croats; five Slovaks; nine Hungarians; 16 Ruthenes; 188 Bulgarians; 85 French; 24 Belgians; 7 English; 11 from Luxembourg; 2 from French Algeria; and 1 each from Scotland, Greece, and Spain. *Pátý slet všesokolský pořádaný v Praze Českou obcí sokolskou ... 1907,* ed. Josef Scheiner (Prague, n.d. [1908]), 121–143.

20. Quoted in a police report, entitled "V. Sokolkongress in Prag," Státní ústřední archiv v Praze [State Central Archives in Prague, hereafter: SÚA], *Collection of the Police Director,* PP (1900–1907) V/58/18/1907.

21. Quoted in ibid.

22. Quoted in ibid. Hribar led the Ljubljana Sokol since 1879. His role in the Neo-Slav movement is discussed in Irena Gantar Godina, "Slovenes and Czechs: An Enduring Friendship," *Slovene Studies,* Vol. 17.1.2. (1995): 102–104; and Irena Gantar-Godina, *Neoslavizem in Slovenci* (Ljubljana, 1994).

23. Quoted in "V. Sokolkongress in Prag." Sixteen Sokol members from Prussian Poland attended the Slet privately.

24. Quoted in "V. Sokolkongress in Prag," and in "Pátý slet všesokolský," *Sokol,* Vol. 34 (1908), 39.

25. "Schůze výboru Svazu slovanského Sokolstva konaná dne 2. února r. 1908 v Vídni," *Sokol,* Vol. 34 (1908), 60–63; and Minutes of Executive Council, Federation of Slavic Sokols, February 2, 1908, Tyršovo muzeum tělesné výchovy a sportu v Praze, oddělení archivní documentace [Archive of the Tyrš Museum of Physical Education and Sport in Prague, hereafter: MTVS], *Sokol Collection,* Box 53.

26. A copy of the revised constitution, with the changes regarding language, is in MTVS, *Sokol Collection,* Box 53.

27. Quoted in "Sokolstvo na sjezdu slovanském," *Sokol,* Vol. 34 (1908), 173.

28. Quoted in ibid., 197.

29. The five areas were culture, economy, tourism, journalism, and the Sokol. The deliberations of this gathering are discussed in Vyšný, *Neo-Slavism,* 91–124. See also, Jan Hájek, "Novoslovanský sjezd a společenské akce v Praze v létě roku 1908," *Pražské slavnosti a velké výstavy: Sborník příspěvků z konferencí Archivu hlavního města Prahy 1989 a 1991,* ed. Jiří Pešek (Prague, 1995), 283–303.

30. Scheiner was given this title in Nikolaj Manochyn, "Tyrš a Rusové," *Památník IX. sletu všesokolského pořádaného na oslavu stých narozenin Dr. Miroslava Tyrše za účasti Svazu "Slovanské Sokolstvo,"* ed. Rudolf Procházka (Prague, 1933), 134.

31. Around 1870, a Czech community in Mirhošt, in the western Ukraine, planted the first seeds of the Sokol movement in Russian soil when they founded two Sokol clubs, one of them equestrian. Hopes that the movement would spread, however, were dashed when the tsarist regime, concerned about the club's political tendencies, instituted a ban on the creation of further Sokol clubs that remained in effect until after the Russian Revolution of 1905. Information about these early clubs is in Karel Kareis, comp., *Srovnávací statistický výpis jednot sokolských ... dle sčítání počátkem ledna 1871* (Prague, 1871), 21, 64. See also, Manochyn, "Tyrš a Rusové," 135, and Ladislav Jandásek, *Tyršovo slovanství* (Prague, 1947), 98–99.

32. The first Czech gymnast to go to Russia was Julius Grumlík, a Prague Sokol trainer who answered a request from the Czech director of a *Gymnasium* in Tiflis in 1889. A philologist by training, he also taught academic courses, as did most of the Czech gymnasts who followed him. Antonín Roček, "K některým otázkám česko-ruských sportovních a tělocvičných styků do r. 1918," (Unpub. manuscript, MTVS, Apr. 1974–Nov. 1977), 42–43; and Vladimír Belfín, "K působení sokolských tělocvikářů v carském Rusku," *Teorie a praxe tělesné výchovy a sportu,* Vol. 15 (1967), 600–601.

33. F.K. Šnepp, "Náš úkol, směr a cíl," *Sokol*, Vol. 32 (1906), 88; Josef Scheiner, "Sokolstvo," *Slovanstvo: Obraz jeho minulosti a přítomnost*, ed. J. Bidlo, et al. (Prague, 1912), 720; and "Co bylo v roce 1910?" *Věstník sokolský*, Vol. 14 (1910), 651. Belfín has documented 203 Czech gymnastic teachers in Russia in 1914, but feels there were most likely more. Belfín, "K působení sokolských tělocvikářů," 600.

34. The Czech claim that Poles willingly joined Czech Sokol clubs to advance their social position echoed the German explanation for why Czechs enrolled their children in German schools. J. Kavalír, "Z ślązkeij ziemi," *Sokol*, Vol. 36 (1910), 229–232; J. Kavalír, "Z ślązkeij ziemi," *Věstník sokolský*, Vol. 14 (1910), 512–514; František Zelený, "Z vévodství slezského," *Věstník sokolský*, Vol. 15 (1911), 689–691; and Meeting of Board of Directors, Federation of Slavic Sokols, 9 June 1908, MTVS, *Sokol Collection*, Box 53.

35. Information on these clubs is in "Zprávy spolkové—Rusini," *Sokol*, Vol. 28 (1902), 233; and Jindra Duchoňová, "Ukrajinské sokolstvo," *Věstník sokolský*, Vol. 17 (1913), 264–265.

36. "Dodatky k návštěvě slovanských hostí," *Památník sletu 1912*, 414.

37. "Svaz Sokolstva slovanského," *Věstník sokolský*, Vol. 14 (1910), 105–107.

38. The Galician Sokol organization had 24,688 members in 1910. Scheiner, "Sokolstvo," 717.

39. Information on this club is in Václav Žáček and Růžena Havránková, "Srbové a Češi v době řešení 'východní krize'," *Češi a Jihoslované v minulosti*, 396; Scheiner, "Sokolstvo," 718; and Kessler, "Sokol in den jugoslawischen Gebieten," 209–210. On the Czech trainer, see "Různé," *Sokol*, Vol. 20 (1894), 23.

40. See "Slavnost svěcení praporu 'Dušana silného' a veřejné cvičení v Bělehradě srbském ve dnech 13. a 14. června t.r.," *Sokol*, Vol. 23 (1897), 191.

41. The trainer was František Hofman, the *náčelník* of the Liberec/Reichenberg Sokol, who also took a position at the military academy in Belgrade. He subsequently adopted the Serbian name Miroslav Vojinovič. Kessler, "Sokol in den jugoslawischen Gebieten," 210. See also, K. Miffek, "Sokolství v Srbsku," *Věstník sokolský*, Vol. 17 (1913), 677; and "Dodatky k návštěvě: Srbové," *Památník sletu 1912*, 398.

42. "Čeští-Sokolové do Srbsku," *Sokol*, Vol. 38 (1912), 96.

43. Kessler, "Sokol in den jugoslawischen Gebieten," 210. See also, Laza Popović, "Srbská sokolská župa Fruškogorská," *Sokol*, Vol. 38 (1912), 193–194.

44. Czech Sokol members made up the bulk of the participants, some 620 of the 975 marching in the Slet parade. A. Heller, et al. "V Bělehradě a Sofii," *Věstník sokolský*, Vol. 14 (1910), 374.

45. Ibid., 375.

46. Vyšný, *Neo-Slavism*, 209; and Kohn, *Pan-Slavism*, 196. Nevertheless, the delegates attending the Neo-Slav Congress ignored the Sokol display. "V Bělehradě a Sofii," 374.

47. The five languages were Czech, Slovene, Serbo-Croatian, Russian, and Bulgarian. "Výbor Svazu slovanského Sokolstva v Sofii," *Sokol*, Vol. 36 (1910), 203–206.

48. Quoted in ibid., 206. "Nazdar!" (Good luck!) was the official greeting of the Czech Sokol movement.

49. "Za Svazu Slovanského Sokolstva," *Věstník sokolský*, Vol. 15 (1911), 528–530.

50. On these early clubs, see Losan Mitev, "Die Entwicklung der Turngesellschaften 'Sokol' und 'Junak' in Bulgarien bis zum Jahr 1914," *Die slawische Sokolbewegung*, 175–177; Vašek Roubal, "Balkánský Sokol," *Památník Sokola pražského*, 284–286; and "Telocvično-střelecké spolky ve Východním Bulharsku," ibid., 286–287.

51. Scheiner, "Sokolstvo," 719. One source claims that the Junak Union had 4,400 members in 1910, and another that there were 56 clubs with 9,000 members in 1912. "Svaz Sokolstva slovanského," *Věstník sokolský* (1910), 106; and Mitev, "Die Entwicklung der Turngesellschaften in Bulgarien," 178. See also, "Dodatky k návštěvě: Bulhaři," *Památník sletu 1912*, 413–414.

52. Membership statistics are in "Svaz Sokolstva slovanského," *Věstník sokolský* (1910), 103–107.

53. Minutes of Meeting of Board of Directors of the Federation of Slavic Sokols, 20 December 1911, MTVS, *Sokol Collection,* Box 53.

54. Ibid.

55. Nikolaj Manochyn, "Ruské Sokolstvo," *Památník sletu 1912,* 411.

56. Information on the Slet is in *Památník sletu slovanského Sokolstva roku 1912 v Praze,* ed. A. Očenášek, et al. (Prague, n.d. [1919]).

57. Karel Heller, "Sletová setba—sletová sklizeň," *Památník sletu 1912,* 362.

58. Ibid., 362.

59. See above, note 41. The exercising display of the Serbs is described in A. Očenášek, "Pondělí 1. července," *Památník sletu 1912,* 308–309. The six "governments" were Austria, Hungary, Croatia, Serbia, Montenegro, and the Ottoman Turkish Empire. Together, they controlled seven "countries" where the Serbs had Sokol clubs, including Dalmatia, Hungary, Croatia, Bosnia-Herzegovina, Serbia, Montenegro, and Ottoman areas of southeastern Europe. Some Sokol sources assert that the Serbs arrived from "ten countries," counting territories like the Banat, Kosovo, and Macedonia separately. See ibid., 308; Kessler, "Sokol in den jugoslawischen Gebieten," 198–215; and "Dodatky k návštěvě slovanských hosti: Srbové," *Památník sletu 1912,* 398–399.

60. Written by the playwright and Sokol activist, Karel Domorázek, the Marathon play was performed only one other time in 1927 at a celebration in the French city of Toulouse for the *Fédération Régionale des Societés de Tire et de Préparation Militaire.*

61. Dr. Kadeřábek, "Marathon," *Sokol,* Vol. 38 (1912), 165.

62. "Ze svazu slovanského Sokolstva," *Věstník sokolský,* Vol. 16 (1912), 478. The Russian representative at this meeting argued against a harsher punishment, like expulsion, for the Poles.

63. "Poslání z Svazu slovanského Sokolstva," *Věstník sokolský,* Vol. 16 (1912), 345; "Z Svazu slovanského Sokolstva," ibid., Vol. 17 (1913), 806-807; and Police Report, 20 August 1914, SÚA, *Collection of the Governor's Office,* PM (1911–1920) 8/5/43/25/1914/No. 19706.

64. Roček, "K některým otázkám," 31.

65. Pan-Slavism in a general sense refers to all forms of Slavic consciousness and cooperation, but it also acquired a specific meaning as a movement for Slavic political unity under Russian leadership. It is examined in S. Harrison Thompson, "A Century of a Phantom: Panslavism and the Western Slavs," *Journal of Central European Affairs,* Vol. 11 (1951), 57–77; and Václav Šťastný, "Vliv tzv. slovanské politiky Ruska v českém prostředí," *Slovanství v národním životě Čechů a Slováků,* ed. V. Šťastný (Prague, 1968), 256–265. Czech Slavism is explored in Vladimír Macura, *Znamení zrodu: České národní obrození jako kulturní typ.* 2nd ed. (Jinočany, 1995), 156–168; and Jiří Rak, *Bývali Čechové: České historické mýty a stereotypy* (Jinočany, 1994), 113–126. See also, notes 6 and 16 above.

66. Masaryk, *Česká otázka,* 44.

67. Prague was referred to as the "Slavic Athens" in the album of the 1912 Slet. *Památník sletu 1912,* 56.

68. Quoted in František Mašek, "Průvod sokolstva a hold jeho král. hlav. městu Praze," *Památník sletu 1912,* 285–286.

69. Letter of Antonín Novotný to Federation of Slavic Sokols, 21 December 1910, attached to Minutes of Meeting of Board of Directors, Federation of Slavic Sokols, 27 January 1911, MTVS, *Sokol Collection,* Box 53.

70. Minutes of Meeting of Executive Council, Federation of Slavic Sokols, 2 July 1912, MTVS, *Sokol Collection,* Box 53.

71. In an essay examining the supranational identities of "Czechoslovak," "Yugoslav," and "Soviet," Hans Lemberg questions whether artificial "Greater Nations" (*Großnationen*) can exist in an age of nationalism. Hans Lemberg, "Der Versuch der Herstellung synthetischer Nationen im östlichen Europa im Lichte Theorems vom Nation-Building," *Formen des nationalen Bewußtseins im Lichte zeitgenössischer Nationalismustheorien,* ed. Eva Schmitt Hartmann (Munich, 1994), 160.

Chapter 8

STAGING HABSBURG PATRIOTISM

Dynastic Loyalty and the 1898 Imperial Jubilee[*]

Daniel Unowsky

One cannot easily or immediately banish entirely from the world this factional striving for much greater autonomy—enthusiasm for independence—, but one certainly must endeavor to use all permissible and promising means to defeat such strivings, to render them harmless, or even to channel them in better directions....

Just as Our House will also offer the most tenacious resistance against such tendencies, so it will want neither to overlook nor to overestimate those manifestations which national feelings—whether German, Slavic, Hungarian, Romanian, or Italian—have been able to bring to pass over the course of the centuries, but most especially in the last decades.

Franz Joseph to Francis Ferdinand, 7 February 1903[1]

Habsburg historians often describe the last decades before the First World War as a period in Habsburg history dominated by the nationalities' conflicts. Scholars award much less attention to efforts made in these years to foment Habsburg patriotism. The letter quoted above suggests that Franz Joseph himself believed (or at least hoped) that nationalism and separatism, while serious, could successfully be countered. The Habsburg court, the government of the Austrian half of the Monarchy (Cisleithania), the Joint Army, the Catholic Church, and elements of the aristocracy responded to the political crises of the late Habsburg Monarchy by reasserting the importance of the Habsburg ruler as a symbol of stability and as a focus for a common supranational identity. No Department of Information coordinated a systematic program of Habsburg patriotic propaganda. Yet, during extraordinary imperial celebrations, like the emperor's seventieth, seventy-fifth, and eightieth birthdays, and, above all, the great jubilee festivities planned for 1898 and 1908, the fiftieth and sixtieth anniversaries of Franz Joseph's 2 December 1848 accession to the throne, the Habsburgs and their closest supporters reminded the population of the common bond to the emperor and "Austria." Under Franz Joseph, Habsburg political ritual, imperial ceremony, and public celebrations promoted dynastic patriotism and, if with more limited success, fostered support and loyalty for the state he ruled.

This article will focus on efforts by the Habsburg court and the Joint Army to overcome national tensions, "to channel them in better directions," by filling the 1898 jubilee celebrations in Cisleithania with patriotic content.[2] Political strife, including the German-Czech conflict in Bohemia and the parliamentary obstruction in Vienna that followed the propagation of the Badeni Language Ordinances, marred the 1898 jubilee year.[3] Official jubilee festivities and publications addressed such divisions by presenting Franz Joseph in his various roles: head of state; leader of a modern great power; commander in chief of the armed forces; prince of peace; patron of economic and cultural progress; and father of all the peoples.

Father of the Peoples: The Court and the 1898 Jubilee Theater Production

In the summer of 1897, Franz Joseph broke with his often-stated reluctance to approve of extravagant and ephemeral festivities. The Office of the Court Master (*Obersthofmeisteramt*), one of the four traditional divisions of the Habsburg court, began planning a series of official celebrations for the 1898 jubilee.[4] Franz Joseph continued to call on his subjects to celebrate him and his House "with acts of charity" even as he set in motion court preparations and specifically approved of court and government promotion of the 1898 jubilee.[5]

The program developed by the Court Master was to commence on the morning of 29 November with a mass and Te Deum in the Cathedral of St. Stephen. A special jubilee theater production was scheduled for the evening of 1 December. The jubilee itself, 2 December, was to begin with the "Homage of His Majesty by the Imperial Family" in the Marble Hall of the imperial palace. Later in the day at a less than spontaneous "Homage of the Peoples" in the Spanish Riding School, Francis Ferdinand, Franz Joseph's nephew and heir, would praise the emperor in the name of the peoples of the Monarchy before silent representatives from the provinces. The court celebrations were to end with a "soiree at court" in the Court Opera Theater.[6]

Of the official jubilee celebrations, which were all canceled after the murder of Empress Elisabeth on 10 September, the jubilee theater production was the single court-controlled event designed to be witnessed by the largest audience.

Due to its public character, the theater production offered an opportunity to make a definitive jubilee statement. The organizers hoped to bolster state patriotism and to agitate against ethnic and social division by blending together traditional elements of Habsburg legitimacy with reminders of concrete achievement in the present. The court intended the production to be performed a minimum of five or six times in the Court Opera Theater, since "a great portion of the population of Vienna will want to see the production."[7] More than two thousand people would attend each performance in this great opera house. For the first presentation of the play, the court reserved the central boxes for the imperial family and selected aristocrats, high government officials, and bureaucrats.[8] The potential audience was not limited to residents of and visitors to the capital. Seats were set aside for Viennese and provincial journalists, ensuring that the reading public would find detailed descriptions in provincial newspapers. The play would also be published and made available for purchase all over the Monarchy. Presumably, in the years ahead, schools and local communities would perform it on the emperor's October 4 name-day and other imperial occasions.[9]

The evolution of the 1898 jubilee theater production will remind those familiar with Robert Musil's unfinished modernist masterpiece, *The Man Without Qualities,* of the Parallel Action.[10] In the novel, Ulrich, the title character, joined a committee seeking to organize festivities for the upcoming (and never realized) seventieth jubilee of Franz Joseph's reign. Ulrich's unfocused committee failed to develop a convincing central idea that would instill the Parallel Action with meaning. The actual court committee that produced the 1898 jubilee production had an even more daunting task than the mere creation of a patriotic play. The court and the government of Cisleithanian Austria sought to praise Franz Joseph and the Imperial House without making references that could exacerbate national tensions or be used by political factions for partisan advantage.

Special theater performances had marked previous Habsburg celebrations.[11] However, court and government officials took a much more active role in the development of the 1898 jubilee theater production. In August 1897, Francis Ferdinand requested that the Office of the Court Master "bring to production a *patriotic play* that should correspond to the sublime occasion, and in which living scenes from the past of the Most High Imperial House should be presented, and on which the entire membership of the court theater, opera house, and ballet was to collaborate." The production was to take under two hours to perform, and was to include dance intermixed with dialogue and *tableaux vivants*.[12] The court solicited proposals for the production from several professional patriotic playwrights, but rejected all submissions due to their apparent failure adequately to represent the glorious development of the Habsburg state.

Court and government officials then intervened directly in the creative aspects of the proposed production. In an extraordinary meeting, attesting to the perceived importance of the proposed theater presentation, the Court Master Rudolf von und zu Liechtenstein, the Second Court Master Prince Alfred Montenuovo, the Common Minister of Foreign Affairs and of the Imperial House

Agenor Gołuchowski, the Cisleithanian Minister President Francis Graf von Thun und Hohenstein, and the General Intendant of the Court Theaters August Freiherr Plappart von Leenheer met on 22 March 1898 to determine the "disposition" for the jubilee theater production. They began by evaluating a list of great moments in "Austrian state history" and the "history of the House of Habsburg" drawn up by Plappart and Joseph Alexander von Helfert, a prominent patriotic historian.[13] These moments were to serve as the inspiration for a series of *tableaux vivants* to be incorporated into the theater production:[14]

1) The 1282 investment by Emperor Rudolf von Habsburg of his sons with his Austrian lands.
2) The acquisition of Tyrol by Duke Rudolf IV in 1365.
3) The 1515 double marriage of the grandchildren of Maximilian I.
4) The joining of the crowns of Hungary and Bohemia to those of the Austrian hereditary lands by Ferdinand I, 1526–27.
5) Emperor Rudolf II's Court at Prague, 1576–1612.
6) Ferdinand II during the Thirty Years' War.
7) Leopold I and the lifting of the Turkish siege of Vienna in 1683.
8) Maria Theresa, holding her infant son Joseph, asking for and receiving Hungarian promises of assistance at the Hungarian *Landtag* in 1741.
9) The declaration of the Victory of Kolin and the founding of the Order of Maria Theresa in 1757.
10) Maria Theresa with Francis Stephen in the circle of the Habsburg family, servants of the state, soldiers, and scholars.
11) Kaiser Joseph II at the plow, the lifting of *Leibeigenschaft*, the Edict of Toleration, and the founding of the Burgtheater.
12) Emperor Francis I's entrance into Vienna after the First Paris Peace in 1814; Congress of Vienna.
13) The wedding of Emperor Francis in 1830.
14) Ferdinand the Good riding in an open coach through the streets of Vienna to the acclamation of the public on 15 March 1848.
15) Arrival in Nußdorf of the steamship bearing Princess Elisabeth of Bavaria in 1854.
16) Emperor Franz Joseph: Vienna World Exhibition in 1873; the 1879 Makart Procession in honor of the silver wedding anniversary of the imperial couple; unveiling of the Maria Theresa monument in 1888.
17) Final Tableau; Apotheosis; the expansion of the imperial palace; City Regulation and Greater Vienna.

According to the minutes of the meeting, Cisleithania's Minister President Thun led the ensuing "lively discussion" about the "meaning" of the scenes. After carefully weighing "political and other considerations" with regard to the "prevailing trends of the day," the committee chose a handful of scenes with "the greatest subtlety." Most of the suggestions were quickly rejected as undignified or unpoetic. Foreign Minister and conservative Polish magnate Gołuchowski opposed the inclusion of Joseph II at the plow, and convinced the committee to present instead the less radical Maria Theresa together with her more radical son. Gołuchowski also pushed for the inclusion of the Congress of Vienna, an event of "world historical importance" when Austria "constituted the political center of Europe if not the world" and which had ushered in an "epoch of peace." At Thun's insistence, the committee deemed unacceptable all references to Franz Joseph's poor predecessor Ferdinand, the revolutions of 1848, and "historical moments of recent and the most contemporary times."[15]

In the end, with Plappart basing his views on artistic criteria, Foreign Minister Gołuchowski hoping to portray the Monarchy as a great (and conservative) power, and Cisleithanian Minister President Thun eager to avoid stirring up ethnic tensions, the committee agreed on an opening and six tableaux. The chosen scenes reflected, in the view of the committee, the proper dignity of the moment and conveyed the proper message of imperial patriotism: the late thirteenth century investment of the sons of Rudolf, the first Habsburg Holy Roman Emperor, with the Austrian lands; the double wedding of 1515 in Vienna's St. Stephen's Cathedral; the second siege of Vienna in 1683; the Pragmatic Sanction; Maria Theresa and Joseph II; Francis I and the Congress of Vienna. The final scene would "allegorically glorify the Ruling Majesty and bring an Apotheosis that in a certain sense illustrates the crowning achievements and deeds of the Habsburgs fulfilled by Emperor Franz Joseph I." The Apotheosis, a great metaphor of unity and harmony of the peoples of the Monarchy, would present Franz Joseph as the benevolent father of his subjects and as patron of art, culture, and industry.[16]

After this meeting, the Court Master contracted Christiane Gräfin Thun-Salm, an author of light fiction and patriotic one-act plays, to craft a melodramatic narrative to knit together the chosen scenes.[17] Thun-Salm's play, *The Emperor's Dream*, was sure to remind its viewers of Franz Joseph's annual participation in the Holy Thursday Foot Washing and the Corpus Christi Procession, ritualized displays of Habsburg self-sacrifice, humility, piety, and concern for others.[18] The author centered the play on Emperor Rudolf I, familiar to her audience through the legend of his encounter with the Host. Before he was crowned emperor, Rudolf was alleged to have offered his horse to a priest bearing the Eucharist to the home of a dying person. Another priest later prophesied on the rise of the Habsburg dynasty to world monarchy based on Rudolf's demonstrated qualities of piety and charity, qualities Franz Joseph and all members of the House of Habsburg supposedly shared.[19]

The production opened with nobles flocking to the imperial palace in Vienna to pay homage as Rudolf invested his sons with his Austrian lands in 1282. Concerned about the fate of his lands, Rudolf sleeps fitfully. Future appears to him and guides him through the succession of brief scenes from the Habsburg past. During each scene, soldiers, burghers, and tavern keepers explain the importance of the historical moment and, after the dialogue sets the tone, a *tableau vivant* is revealed in the background as the orchestra plays appropriate music or the choir sings of battles, peace, and Habsburg glory. The first Habsburg Holy Roman emperor remains unsatisfied, however: he has not yet seen what he holds most important:

All the peoples united by my scepter
I have loved as only a father can.
The Ruler who has the love of the people,
He is the best and such a one I wish to be.
Let me see if also in future days
The distant grandchildren feel as do I.[20]

In response, Future sings the praises of Rudolf's future heir:

It glitters in the golden light of fifty years
The crown, that your noble offspring bears,
Beloved by the people, as never was another ruler
When you hear the jubilation that envelops him,
Coming from thousands and thousands of hearts—
Then lay down your tired head in peace!
What you have planted, you see it bloom again.
The love, that once founded the power of Habsburg,
This love also binds people and ruler.[21]

Love and Loyalty, played by members of the company of the court theater, would then bring Rudolf to the celebration of Franz Joseph's imperial jubilee. Modern cities, art, science, handicrafts, trade, and commerce flourish under this emperor's steady hand, and all the people of the monarchy "Thank our Kaiser, whom we all love!/Hail to him and to beloved Austria!" Pleased and moved, Rudolf gestures to the Imperial Loge, convinced that his great descendant would fulfill his dreams for his people and his House.

As Rudolf sinks back into sleep, the play culminates in the final tableau, the magnificent Apotheosis. This final scene blended together decorations and "allegorical figures of the present" like *Bohemia, Hungaria,* and *Galicia* wearing provincial colors and bearing the shields of the Habsburg provinces. This vision of the Monarchy as a harmonious mosaic of peoples and cultures moving into the future with confidence, guided by the experience of the sacred House of Habsburg, reaches a crescendo with the collective singing of the state hymn.[22]

Like all other court celebrations, the December performances were canceled after the murder of Elisabeth. Still, *The Emperor's Dream* was published and recommended for sale by newspapers including the *Neue Freie Presse,* which noted that the play stood out from among the many jubilee publications due to Thun-Salm's "meaningful verses, lovely language, and the fresh living image of folk scenes."[23]

The narrative of Habsburg family and state history contained in the final version of the play, developed with the assistance of a professional historian, tailored to properly address issues of the day by politicians like Gołuchowski and Thun, and penned by the author of popular patriotic publications, couched the Habsburg answer to current problems in the form of a traditional allegory of dynastic glory. The theater production associated Franz Joseph with his great predecessor, Rudolf. In the production, Franz Joseph became the symbol of an idealized monarchy of harmony, national cultural fulfillment, and economic progress. This play, like all the official court events, was designed to depict the emperor as a ruler who cared for the needs of all citizens, irrespective of social status or self-designated national/ethnic affiliation. In 1898, the Monarchy did not seek to supplant nationality with state identity, but to project dynastic loyalty as an essential aspect of ethnic identity within a harmonious Austria.

In order to display the emperor, the dynasty, and the Monarchy in a harmonious image of ethnic peace and cultural progress, however, this panegyric play had to lift Franz Joseph out of time: the decade of neoabsolutist rule following the revolutions of 1848–49 could not be emphasized in a constitutional era when Franz Joseph was father and patron of the peoples and guarantor of civil rights; the emperor could not be associated with policies and governments considered anathema by competing ethnic and political factions. Only by distancing Franz Joseph from the actions taken by his governments over the course of his reign could the message of tolerance and unity be conveyed in a way appropriate to maintaining imperial dignity and to avoiding an exacerbation of ethnic passions. Franz Joseph became, then, a focus for popular dynastic loyalty and a symbol of an idealized Austria existing above the compromises and complications of the real world.

The Pillar of the Regime: The Armed Forces and the Jubilee

Court promotion of the jubilee aimed to remind the population of the glory and traditions of the imperial house, the personal qualities of the good emperor, and the importance of the unity of the state for the development of each ethnic and social group in the Monarchy. The most ubiquitous of all common institutions of Austria-Hungary, the Joint Army, also appealed for increased loyalty to emperor and fatherland during the 1898 jubilee.

Throughout his long reign, Franz Joseph never forgot that the Habsburg army had defeated revolution and ensured the existence of the Monarchy in 1848–1849. Franz Joseph constantly displayed his preference for a military lifestyle. He surrounded himself with military advisors and insisted that the formal aspects of military discipline be strictly adhered to. Military discipline became part of the ceremony that regulated all aspects of his public life. Like Joseph II, Franz Joseph appeared in public almost exclusively in military uniform, with the rare exception of his many hunting trips and visits to foreign countries. Franz Joseph even participated in the Foot Washing and the Corpus Christi Procession dressed as First Soldier of the realm, uniting his roles as holy Habsburg ruler and commander-in-chief of the armed forces.[24]

The 1867 Compromise creating Austria-Hungary provided for a common Ministry of War to oversee the Joint Army under the direct control of the emperor-king. The emperor-king possessed the sole power of command over the military, but the provisions of the Compromise concerning the Joint Army and the Hungarian, Austrian, and Croatian National Guards had to be renewed each decade, by definition subjecting military matters to political debate.[25] Every ten years, Hungarian politicians agitated for increasing the role of the Hungarian National Guard and for the use of Hungarian as the language of command in units of the Joint Army recruited from Hungarian soil. Czech factions repeatedly called for the creation of a Bohemian National Guard. Still, the Common Army was a very visible symbol of state unity. The officer corps was supranational in ideology and multiethnic in personnel. Loyalty to the person of the emperor was at the core of the dynastic patriotism drilled into the members of the armed forces. Though the rank and file spent less time in this school of dynastic loyalty than did the officers, the Joint Army was, as Oscar Jászi wrote, "the chief supporter and maintainer of the monarchy."[26]

The Joint Army played a very prominent and public role in all of the 1898 jubilee celebrations. As was the case every year, military bands paraded through the streets of towns and villages, awakening the population (as early as 4:30 a.m.) with the sounds of military marches on the emperor's 18 August birthday. At the request of the military command, the Court Master integrated into the court jubilee program the unveiling of a monument to the late Archduke Albrecht, the victor at Custozza in 1866 and General Inspector of the armed forces. Contributions from officers and enlisted men funded the construction.[27] The military leadership also developed its own jubilee program for 2 December. On the morning of the jubilee itself, all members of the armed forces, aside from those on watch, were expected to attend religious services in churches and other houses of worship. The commander of the Second Corps ordered that "also those military persons who participated in the parade in Olmütz on the occasion of the accession of the emperor on 2 December 1848 attend [the religious services] as a corporation."[28] After religious services, the soldiers and officers, dressed in parade uniforms, gathered in their garrisons all over the Monarchy for the distribution of the Jubilee-Commemorative-Medal. The military handed out more than three million of these tokens of the supposed bond between soldier and emperor-king.[29]

At these solemn ceremonies, during which the soldiers wore reminders of the ongoing official mourning for the murdered Empress Elisabeth and received their jubilee medals, the Joint Army also distributed the thirteen-page *Commemorative Pamphlet for the Soldiers on the Occasion of the Fiftieth Jubilee of His Majesty Franz Joseph I*, "dedicated by the officers to the enlisted men." This pamphlet was written before the assassination of the empress and, according to the *Fremden-Blatt*, was published "in every provincial language."[30] Rank-and-file soldiers served in active service for only three years, too short a time to imbibe the corporate and supranational ethos of the career Habsburg military officer.[31] This pamphlet, like the jubilee medal, was intended to instill in enlisted soldiers and noncommissioned officers a sense of corporate identity and supranational dynastic loyalty. The pamphlet was, in effect, an attempt to immunize the Joint Army against the threat of radical nationalism.

The pamphlet depicted Franz Joseph as the patron saint of the armed forces. The emperor cared for the welfare of his soldiers, had relied on this most loyal institution to suppress revolution and defend the state from foreign threats, and trusted the armed forces to meet future challenges. Sitting on the "God-entrusted throne" of the Habsburgs, the "first soldier of the Monarchy" understood and worked to meet the needs of his beloved soldiers. The brochure credited the emperor with improvements in armaments, uniforms, pay, and benefits, and with the reduction of harsh punishments. Franz Joseph raised the reputation of the military in the greater society by creating medals honoring valor and service and by ensuring that veterans had priority for employment in government and government-supported institutions. Franz Joseph, himself a veteran, directed the government to found homes for war invalids, and institutions to provide financial assistance to families left behind by the fallen. Out of benevolence, Franz Joseph had reduced active service to three years from eight, instituted universal conscription thereby eliminating (at least in theory) exemptions for the wealthy and highborn, and created an army based on duty and bravery and merit:

> Just as each enjoys the benefits of his fatherland, each person has the duty to defend the monarch and the fatherland to the last drop of blood, and rank and wealth frees none from this obligation. Whether born in a palace or in a hovel, son of a prince or of a poor day laborer, all are equal when it is time to defend the fatherland.[32]

The pamphlet did not limit its stated justifications for an intensification of devotion to Kaiser and fatherland to practical matters that affected the daily life of the ordinary soldier. National separatism had the potential of reducing the effectiveness of a multinational military force, and opposition to separatism and radical nationalism was the chief focus of the military's jubilee message. The pamphlet urged the soldiers to retain their loyalty to emperor and fatherland gained during their active duty after the end of their service, and to teach this patriotism to their children:

> Hold tight to your duty, do not let yourself be led astray by demagogues, by coarse agitators and rebels, who only lie to you and deceive you!...

> Our exalted ruler's protection and care encompasses all of his people; like children to a father, each is as near to his heart as the other. He will bring right and justice to each, no matter how great the hindrances, but, like a father, our Emperor and King must be able to count on the loyalty of His [subjects]—irrespective of language and nation, of tribe (*Stamm*) and confession—in the face of any danger, at any time![33]

After the death of the empress, many parades, concerts, and other activities planned for the jubilee week were canceled.[34] The 2 December program of religious services and distribution of jubilee medals and pamphlets, however, was carried through, and delivered a message of dynastic loyalty. The pamphlet handed out that day by the armed forces to millions of soldiers all over the monarchy exhorted them to resist the lure of nationalism and to maintain their discipline and loyalty to Kaiser and fatherland after the end of their service. The military portrayed the emperor as a model of dedication to duty, who alone promised to ameliorate the dangers threatening the Monarchy and to assure the welfare of each individual citizen.

The court program of celebrations and the army jubilee program, medals, and pamphlet must be seen in the context of a wide range of efforts by the court, the Cisleithanian government, and the Joint Army to rouse patriotic sentiment throughout the jubilee year. The government of the Austrian half of the Monarchy encouraged the populace to honor the benevolent emperor by donating to charities that benefited the public welfare. Habsburg citizens, communities, and voluntary associations contributed tens of millions of gulden to commemorate the 1898 jubilee.[35] The court and Cisleithanian government produced and handed out tens of thousands of jubilee medals, which, like the three million produced by the army, were distributed in ceremonies across Habsburg Austria on 2 December.[36] The Ministry of Religion and Education encouraged schools to stage pageants and concerts, and directed school boards to cancel classes, arrange for pupils to attend appropriate religious services, and hold school assemblies featuring patriotic speeches and the singing of the state hymn.[37] Government newspapers bombarded readers with articles and editorials that emphasized the character of the emperor and important moments from the history of the imperial family.

Consistent with the themes of the jubilee play, after the death of Elisabeth, official and unofficial publications increasingly defined the emperor-martyr as the living embodiment of an idealized Austria that deserved the loyalty and sacrifice of its citizens.[38] Bolstering this message, the Catholic hierarchy produced a special pastoral letter, authored by Cardinal Schönborn of Prague, signed by every member of the episcopate of Cisleithanian Austria, and meant to be read in every Catholic pulpit in late November. The pastoral letter compared the widower Franz Joseph implicitly with Christ.[39] At the same time, the government defended the dignity of the living symbol of state unity by preventing manufacturers from gracing wrapping paper, rubber balls, cigarettes, and tortes with the image of the emperor.[40]

Of course, even during the jubilee year of 1898 it was clear that imperial celebrations could not paper over deep divisions in Habsburg society. The death of the empress underscored Franz Joseph's image as a long-suffering and well-intentioned martyr to peace and harmony, but the 1898 anniversary of Franz Joseph's accession to the throne was not spared from partisan bickering. Throughout the year, Karl Lueger and his anti-Semitic Christian Social Party used their control of Vienna's city institutions to promote party interests. While Lueger's city government organized a march of more than 70,000 schoolchildren around the Ringstrasse to commemorate the occasion, Christian Social journalists attacked liberals, socialists, Jews, and Pan-Germans for their alleged lack of patriotism.[41] For their part, Pan-German members of the *Reichsrat* (Cisleithanian parliament) walked out of the parliamentary chamber just before the special jubilee sitting on

25 November. Pan-German leader Georg von Schönerer raged against the alleged pro-Slav and anti-German orientation of the government:

> I and my colleagues in conviction will not be present at the next so-called Jubilee-Meeting, since in our opinion men with German national convictions cannot participate in declarations of loyalty and manifestations of homage at this time and for as long as the illegal coercive [Badeni] language ordinances exist.[42]

The Social Democratic representatives also absented themselves.[43]

The day before the jubilee meeting, Galician peasant, Jewish, and Social Democratic deputies traded charges and countercharges for some ten hours over the state of emergency that had been instituted in the western counties of Galicia during the summer and fall months in response to a wave of anti-Jewish riots.[44] The day after the jubilee meeting, negotiations on renewing the Compromise dominated the headlines. Although Hungarian soldiers and government officials received jubilee medals, religious services were held in Hungarian towns to honor Franz Joseph, and *Hungaria* figured prominently in the court's jubilee play's depiction of state unity, for the most part the Hungarian half of the Monarchy treated the 1898 celebration of Franz Joseph's fiftieth anniversary as *emperor* as a holiday occurring in a neighboring state. Franz Joseph was, after all, crowned Hungarian *king* only in 1867.

Yet, despite political conflicts and national rivalries, court, government, and army efforts to foment patriotism in the late nineteenth and early twentieth centuries were not without popular resonance. In the last decades of Franz Joseph's reign, millions of Habsburg subjects participated in imperial celebrations. Huge crowds attended local festivities and packed churches, mosques, and synagogues to capacity for special ceremonies. Clergy praised the qualities of the ruler and the ruling house, equating patriotism and dynastic loyalty with religious duty. Millions of Czech, Polish, German, and Ruthenian speakers offered prayers for the emperor's health and sang the *Gott erhalte,* the state hymn, in their own languages. Newspapers narrated the heroic history of the dynasty and called for an increase in devotion to the ruling house. Portraits of the emperor, often purchased during imperial jubilee or birthday festivities, hung in mansions, middle-class homes, and peasant huts, reminders of the benevolent imperial personage, the father figure who aimed to satisfy the needs of all of his faithful subjects.[45] On 2 December 1898, throughout Cisleithania, "Bengali" lighting illuminated town centers and special jubilee decorations. From Galicia to Vienna, "from palaces to the most humble little houses,"[46] millions of Habsburg subjects set candles in their windows, displaying "glowing signs of their heartfelt sympathy for the Jubilee Kaiser."[47]

In 1898, a year in Habsburg history characterized by "politics in a new key," official celebrations and publications distanced the emperor from divisive government decisions and associated him instead with economic and cultural progress. Imperial celebrations memorialized the emperor as the aging and steadfast emperor-martyr, the (grand)father of all the peoples. The court, army, and Cis-leithanian government presented Franz Joseph as the symbol of an ideal Austria yet to be achieved, an Austria achievable only if Habsburg citizens could reconcile competing economic and national interests through a shared devotion to the aging emperor and a common "Austrian patriotism" assumed to exist above and beyond nationalism.

Notes

* This article is based on research supported in part by grants from The University of Memphis Faculty Research Grant Fund, the Joint Committee on Eastern Europe of the American Council of Learned Societies and the Social Science Research Council, the International Research and Exchange Board, and the Austrian Exchange Service (ÖAD).

1. This letter directly addressed Francis Ferdinand's fear that Hungarian nationalist politicians threatened the unity of the army. Haus-, Hof-, und Staatsarchiv (HHStA), Francis Ferdinand Nachlaß, ct. 1, Folder Kaiser Franz Joseph I. 1900–1907, Franz Joseph to Francis Ferdinand, 7 February 1903.

2. Imperial celebrations in the Hungarian half of the monarchy (Transleithania) are not considered in this article. Dualism complicated efforts to promote Franz Joseph as a symbol of unity. Imperial celebrations in Cisleithania presented *emperor* Franz Joseph as father of all his peoples (including those of Hungary) and as the binding force within the Monarchy as a whole. Hungary recognized only anniversaries of Franz Joseph's 1867 coronation as Hungarian *king*.

3. Carl Schorske termed the new interest politics of the era of suffrage expansion "politics in a new key." Schorske, *Fin-de-Siecle Vienna* (New York, 1981). Among many others, see Pieter Judson, *Exclusive Revolutionaries: Liberal Politics, Social Experience, and National Identity in the Austrian Empire, 1848–1914* (Ann Arbor, 1996); John Boyer, *Culture and Political Crisis in Vienna. Christian Socialism in Power, 1897–1918* (Chicago, 1995); Boyer, *Political Radicalism in Late Imperial Vienna: Origins of the Christian Social Movement, 1848–1897* (Chicago, 1981); Gary Cohen, *The Politics of Ethnic Survival: Germans in Prague* (Princeton, 1981); Bruce Garver, *The Young Czech Party, 1874–1901, and the Emergence of a Multi-Party System* (New Haven, 1978); Berthold Sutter, *Die Badenischen Sprachen-Verordnungen von 1897*, 2 vols. (Graz and Cologne, 1965). On the new politics in Galicia, see Harald Binder, "Polen, Ruthenen, Juden. Politik und Politiker in Galizien 1897–1918" (Ph.D. diss., University of Bern, 1997).

4. The Court Master's was the largest division of the court administration. The Court Master oversaw production of imperial celebrations and ceremonies, enforced court rankings, and presided over the various imperial guards. The High Chamberlain (*Oberstkämmerer*), the Marshal of the Court (*Obersthofmarschall*), and the Master of the Stables (*Oberststallmeister*) led the other three departments of the Habsburg court. The most comprehensive overview of the structure of the Habsburg court remains Ivan Žolger, *Der Hofstaat des Hauses Österreich* (Vienna, 1917). See also Margit Silber, *Obersthofmeister Alfred Fürst von Montenuovo. Höfische Geschichte in den beiden letzten Jahrzehnten der österreichisch-ungarischen Monarchie (1897–1916)* (Ph.D. diss., University of Vienna, 1987).

5. Franz Joseph expressed this preference on many occasions, including his 1888 fortieth jubilee. See HHStA, AR, 1888, F1, ct. 39, Circular from 15 December to all missions.

6. Other events scheduled from 29 November to 2 December included a military gala-dinner as well as family and state dinners. A number of events were later added to the official program: the unveiling of a monument dedicated to Archduke Albrecht (discussed below),

official receptions of deputations from the provincial legislatures, the two capitals, and Bosnia and Herzegovina on 29 November; and an illumination of the city of Vienna on 2 December. On the preparations for the events, see HHStA, Neue Zeremonial Akten (NZA), 1898, ct. 143, Protokoll der am 17. und 20. Dezember 1897 stattgehabten Sitzungen betreffend die Hoffestlichkeiten....

7. HHStA, Obersthofmeisteramt (OMeA), 1898/r. 19/a/22, ct. 1369, Protocol, 31 May 1898.

8. The Ministry of War and the Cisleithanian Minister President each received half of the tickets to the second performance to distribute to government officials and army officers not invited to the first performance. HHStA, NZA, ct. 143, Sitzung am 20/6 1898.

9. Local communities and voluntary associations often produced this type of patriotic pageant for imperial occasions. According to the *Neue Freie Presse* (*NFP*), for example, Sidonie Heindl-Purschke and Leonie Schwenger's *Hoch Österreich!* was performed "on many Austrian stages" and was provided free to amateur theaters and voluntary associations. *NFP* (morning edition), 26 July 1898, 7. The Ministry of Religion and Education's *Verordnungsblatt für den Dienstbereich des Ministeriums für Cultus und Unterricht* brought plays, pageants, books of songs, and patriotic pamphlets like Dr. Leo Smolle's *Funf Jahrzehnte auf Habsburgs Throne. 1848–1898* and Franz Karl Graf Marenzi's *Jubelhymne zum fünfzigjährigen Regierungs-Jubiläum Seiner Majestät des Kaisers Franz Joseph des Ersten* to the attention of public schools all over Cisleithania.

10. Robert Musil, *Der Man ohne Eigenschaften* (Berlin, 1930–1943).

11. In 1879, for example, the Habsburg family and the court sponsored two theatrical performances to commemorate the imperial couple's twenty-fifth wedding anniversary. The 1879 celebrations included a pageant of scenes from the Habsburg past chosen by a historian tied together with poetry and music, and performed by and for the Habsburg family. The Court Master also arranged a special showing of a short play performed by the cast of the Court Theaters in the Court Opera House before an audience selected by the Office of the Court Master. The Office of the Court Master assigned seating based on court rankings to previous theater productions controlled by the court and honoring the imperial house. This was the case for the theater production associated with the unveiling of the Maria Theresa monument in 1888, part of the celebrations of Franz Joseph's fortieth jubilee. More than two thousand invited guests filled the theater, transforming the Court Opera Theater into a physical manifestation of the ideal social structure of the monarchy as defined by the court, updated to reflect at least some of the changing social reality of the late nineteenth century. HHStA Zeremonial Akten (ZA) Prot. 112, Ceremonial Protocol 1888, Anhang zum Ceremoniel-Protokoll II.

12. HHStA, General-Intendanz (GI), 1897, ct. 167, Z. 1082; HHStA, GI, 1897–1898, ct. 169, Z. 48; HHStA, OMeA 1898/r. 19/a/22, ct. 1369. Francis Ferdinand's role was very limited. He set out the framework for the production, but most details were approved directly by Franz Joseph himself.

13. As undersecretary in the Ministry of Education from 1848–1861, Helfert had pushed the ministry to adopt educational materials that would use the Habsburg dynasty as a binding force in the state. Helfert was also president and a founding member of the Österreichische Volksschriften-Verein, dedicated since 1848 to promoting "love of fatherland."

14. HHStA, OMeA 1898/r. 19/a/22, ct. 1369, Pr. 2773. Protocol, 22 March 1898; HHStA, Gen. Int., ct. 169, 1898, ad. Z. 48.

15. HHStA, OMeA 1898/r. 19/a/22, ct. 1369, Pr. 2773. Protocol, 22 March 1898; HHStA, Gen. Int., ct. 169, 1898, ad. Z. 48.

16. HHStA, OMeA 1898/r. 19/a/22, ct. 1369, Pr. 2773. Protocol, 22 March 1898; HHStA, Gen. Int., ct. 169, 1898, ad. Z. 48.

17. Thun-Salm authored a number of one-act plays and collections of stories, including *"Was die Grossmutter Erzählte." Märchen und Erzählungen* (Vienna, 1906). Thun-Salm delivered her corrected manuscript to the director of the Court Theater on 6 May. He sent a copy to

Francis Ferdinand. On 28 May, Liechtenstein, Plappart, Gołuchowski, and Thun met and approved Thun-Salm's work. HHStA, GI, 1897–1898, ct. 169, Z. 48.

18. Daniel Unowsky, "Reasserting Empire: Habsburg Imperial Celebrations after the Revolutions of 1848–1849," in Maria Bucur and Nancy Wingfield, eds., *Staging the Past: The Politics of Commemoration in Habsburg Central Europe, 1848 to the Present* (West Lafayette, IN, 2001), 13–46; James Shedel, "Emperor, Church, and People: Religion and Dynastic Loyalty during the Golden Jubilee of Franz Joseph," *Catholic Historical Review* (January 1990): 71–92.

19. On the legend of Rudolf, see Anna Coreth, *Pietas Austriaca. Österreichische Frömmigkeit im Barock* (Vienna, 1982).

20. Christiane Gräfin Thun-Salm, *Des Kaisers Traum* (Vienna, 1898), 58.

21. Ibid., 59.

22. HHStA, 1898/r. 19/a/22, ct. 1369, Prot. 2773. Protocols, 22 March and 31 May 1898.

23. *NFP* (morning edition), 30 November 1898, 5. The even more spectacular court celebrations for the 1908 sixtieth jubilee were carried through, and included a shortened version of Thun-Salm's piece—most of the dialogue connecting the scenes was eliminated and the final scene was altered and simplified.

24. On Franz Joseph's attachment to military life, see István Deák, *Beyond Nationalism. A Social History of the Habsburg Officer Corps* (Oxford, 1990); Jean-Paul Bled, *Franz Joseph*, trans. T. Bridgeman (Oxford, 1987); Egon Caesar Conte Corti, *Vom Kind zum Kaiser: Kindheit und erste Jugend Kaiser Franz Josephs I. und seiner Geschwister* (Graz, 1950).

25. On the renewal of the military provisions, see Deák, *Beyond Nationalism*, 55–58.

26. Oscar Jászi, *The Dissolution of the Habsburg Monarchy* (Chicago, 1929), 141; Deák, *Beyond Nationalism*, 4.

27. Franz Joseph insisted that no undue pressure be exerted on his famously underpaid officers and soldiers. Yet, the lists of contributions made from a number of military formations were strangely uniform: each soldier of a particular rank "voluntarily" contributed the exact same amount, and this sum was often deducted from military pay over the course of several months. For example, all officers of the Infantry School of Budapest "volunteered" to have six percent of one month's salary automatically deducted in order to demonstrate their patriotic feelings and love for the deceased army inspector and archduke. Kriegsarchiv (KA), 1895, ct. 934 contains the lists of contributions. The monument was placed on the grounds of the imperial palace complex in the center of Vienna. The army leadership feared that any other location chosen in the city would have prompted Hungarian complaints that such a location was a direct attack on Hungarian autonomy and, therefore, on the provisions of the Compromise. KA, 1895, ct. 934, Pr. 2600, 1896; 2845, 1896.

28. *NFP* (morning edition), 22 November 1898, 6.

29. Already in the first half of November, newspapers reported on the plans made by the Joint Army for 2 December. See *NFP* (morning edition), 10 November 1898, 5.

30. *Fremden-Blatt* (morning edition), 2 December 1898, 51. Kriegshammer sent copies of this pamphlet to the minister of Religion and Education. Allgemeines Verwaltungsarchiv (AVA), Ministerium für Cultus und Unterricht (MCU), Präs., 1898, ct. 264, Z. 3090, Pr. 31 December, 1898. Kriegshammer to Arthur Bylandt Rheydt, minister of religion and education.

31. Deák, *Beyond Nationalism*.

32. *Gedenkschrift für die Soldaten anlässlich des 50 jährigen Regierungs-Jubiläum S. M. des Kaisers Franz Joseph I* (Vienna, 1898), 4.

33. *Gedenkschrift für die Soldaten*, 12–13.

34. Alone among the items listed in the official court program for the 1898 jubilee, the unveiling of the Albrecht monument was postponed, not canceled. The monument was revealed in an elaborate ceremony on 21 May 1899. Events commemorating the unveiling included a theater production in the Opera and a reception at court attended by almost 1600 persons. HHStA ZA, Prot. 123, Ceremonial Protocol 1899, Anhang IV.

35. According to the list compiled by the Ministry of the Interior for the emperor, the population contributed at least 39,621,600 gulden and 9.5 crowns to charity in honor of the jubilee. HHStA, Kabinettskanzlei (Kab. Kanz.), Korrespondenz-Akten (Korr. A.), ct. 197, ad. Corr. 47, 1899. The figures underestimate the charitable actions. The *NFP* reported that more than twenty million gulden were donated for charitable purposes in Vienna and Lower Austria alone. *NFP* (morning edition), 4 December 1898, 6.

36. The *NFP* estimated that three million medals would be handed out to active and retired members of the armed forces, and 40,000 for state bureaucrats. *NFP* (morning edition), 15 November 1898, 4–5. The *NFP* estimate was very conservative. Over 100,000 medals were distributed to government employees in the Hungarian half of the monarchy alone. HHStA, Ministerium des Äussern (MA), Administrativ-Registratur (AR), F1, 1898, ct. 36, Kaiser Franz Josef folder 11, Z. 1577, Pr., 9 January 1899. Bánffy to Goluchowski, 4 January 1899.

37. AVA, MCU, Präs., 1898, ct. 257, Z. 1469. Pr. 31 May 1898. After the death of the empress, festive events were canceled, but all the Monarchy's pupils were still required to listen to patriotic speeches delivered by teachers and school directors. For examples of these school celebrations, see *XXI. Jahresbericht des K.K. Rudolf-Gymnasiums I Brody* (Brody, 1899); *Jahres-Bericht des Gymnasiums der k.k. Theresianischen Akademie in Wien* (Vienna, 1899).

38. See, among many others, *Kaiser Jubiläums Festblatt der Wiener Zeitung*, 2 December 1898; Max Herzig, ed., *Viribus Unitis. Das Buch von Kaiser* (Vienna, Budapest, Leipzig, 1898).

39. For comments on the letter, see *NFP* (morning edition), 16 November 1898, 1. The *Reichenberger Zeitung*, 17 November 1898, 1, rejected the Catholic hierarchy's vision of the Monarchy as a "mosaic" of the peoples, and criticized the bishops for supporting the Catholic political parties; *Glos Narodu*, 17 November 1898, 2. The letter itself was printed in full or in part in many newspapers throughout the Monarchy. See *Wiener Diöcesanblatt*, nr. 22, 1898.

40. The requests to use the imperial image, the rejection of these requests, and the reasons given for the rejection can be found in the archives of the Interior Ministry. In 1898 and again in 1908 the Interior Ministry issued regulations to ensure the use of the imperial image on "items of daily use" such as "unsuitable, throw-away packaging, paper products of lower quality, envelopes, labels, and the like is not to be approved." AVA, Ministerium des Innern (MI), Präs. 1/J, 1908, ct. 1210, Prs. 4262, 1 May 1908.

41. Christian Socialist journalists often equated liberals, socialists, and Jews. For a few examples of Christian Socialist anti-Semitism and attacks on Pan-German rivals during the jubilee year, see *Reichspost*, 14 January 1898, 1; *Reichspost*, 10 March 1898, 9–10; *Reichspost*, 25 June 1898, 5; *Österreichische Volkszeitung*, 28 June 1898, 2.

42. *Alldeutsche Tagblatt*, nr. 24, 1898; *Unverfälschte Deutsche Worte*, nr. 11, 1898.

43. The Social Democrats did not attempt to counter the jubilees, nor did the central committee of the party recommend that party members distance themselves from imperial celebrations. In fact, the central committee of the party voted 7–3 in favor of participation in the official mourning session of the *Reichsrat* after the murder of the empress. Social Democratic Archives (SDA), Sozdem. Verband (Klubprotokolle) 25.3.1897 bis 25.9.1903. Heft 1, Meeting, 24 September 1898.

44. Social Democrats and the conservative Polish nobles, the *stańczycy*, blamed the anti-Semitic radical priest, newspaper editor, and peasant organizer Stanisław Stojałowski, his new Christian People's Party, and the United Peasant Party for the riots. Binder, "Polen, Ruthenen, Juden;" Krzysztof Dunin-Wąsowicz, *Dzieje Stonnictwa Ludowego w Galicji* (Warsaw, 1956); Dunin-Wąsowicz, *Jan Stapinski. Trybun ludu wiejskiego* (Warsaw, 1969). For an example of anti-Semitic rhetoric printed in peasant-oriented newspapers at the time of the outbreak of these riots, see *Związek Chłopski*, 11 May 1898.

45. Daniel Unowsky, "The Pomp and Politics of Patriotism: Imperial Celebrations in Habsburg Austria, 1848-1916" (Ph.D. diss., Columbia University, 2000).

46. *Dziennik Polski,* 4 December 1898. On illuminations in Galicia, see also *Slowo Polskie,* 3 December 1898.

47. *Linzer Volksblatt,* 4 December 1898. On Vienna's decorations and illuminations, see, among many others, *Das Vaterland* (evening edition), 1 December 1898; *Neues Wiener Abendblatt,* 1 December 1898; *The Times,* 3 December 1898.

Chapter 9

ARBITERS OF ALLEGIANCE

Austro-Hungarian Censors during World War I

Alon Rachamimov

"A New Era of Human Co-Existence"

One of the most common experiences in World War I was the experience of captivity. During four years of fighting, an estimated 8.5 million soldiers had been taken captive, or roughly one out of every nine men in uniform.[1] Among the warring countries, none had a greater POW problem than Austria-Hungary: out of 8 million soldiers mobilized by the Dual Monarchy during the war, an estimated 2.77 million wound up in captivity, the great majority (2.1 million) in Russia.[2] The last prisoners—some 430,000—returned to Central Europe only after the end of the Russian Civil War and only after sufficient funds were allocated by the newly-formed League of Nations.[3]

It might not come as a complete surprise to learn that during the war the Dual Monarchy developed a very significant censorship apparatus to examine what these POWs were writing from captivity, and to intercept or blot out correspondence deemed objectionable for various reasons. One such letter, for example, sent from Russia on October 7, 1917 caught the eyes of the censors in Vienna, who seized it because of its "Zionist" content before it reached the addressee in Prague, the young Jewish intellectual Robert Weltsch.[4] In the letter, POW officer Hans Kohn, the future historian of nationalism and Weltsch's close collaborator in various publications, reported about his political activity in Russia during the Jewish High Holidays of 1917:

I have addressed an audience of 160 Jewish [POW] officers during the services of both the Day of Atonement and Sukkoth held here for them. Because many people have not yet heard a Zionist speech, the effect was great. I have held also many conversations in private or in small groups, and our success in agitation is superb from a numerical, intellectual and social point of view. I was especially fortunate in influencing the Zionism of "old Zionists" and many are now well-disposed toward the names of Buber, Bar Kochba, and Weltsch. You would be astounded by the Zionist vigor here. For me these past 14 days have gone by ecstatically. I have also noticed how much I have learned in captivity, and how thankful I should be for my 15 months in captivity in terms of maturity and thoroughness [*Durcharbeitung*].[5]

Later on in his letter, Kohn impatiently implored Weltsch to write him more often, declaring that "here in captivity one's vision becomes sharper, more nostalgic and impartial. Today I think differently about most questions (not only Zionist ones), becoming more radical and resolute than three years ago. We all hope here that everything would not be in vain and that a new era of human co-existence will arrive, in which all coercion and unconscious self-deception crumble."[6]

Kohn's elated words did not reach Weltsch in Prague, and were eventually consigned to the files of the Austro-Hungarian POW censorship. Nonetheless, even five decades later, when Kohn decided to write his memoirs and reflect on the many twists and turns of his life and career, he still felt that captivity had provided him with his most important formative experience.[7] His imprisonment in various places in Russia, Siberia, and Turkestan (today the countries of Central Asia) gave him a deeper appreciation of the Russian language and culture, while introducing him to non-Western cultures and mentalities. According to Kohn, the years of internment between 1915 and 1920 "changed my outlook and redirected my life into paths I could hardly have foreseen in 1914."[8]

From the perspective of the Austro-Hungarian POW censorship, however, Kohn's near-messianic yearnings sounded suspiciously unpatriotic. Surely, this was not what the Habsburg Monarchy expected of its loyal soldiers who had the misfortune of being captured by the enemy. Nevertheless, for officials in Vienna, Kohn was of less importance as a person than as a putative representative of wider political attitudes among Austro-Hungarian prisoners of war. Could Kohn's pacifist-sounding longings for "a new era of human co-existence" reflect the opinions of broader groups among the prisoners? Were these just the ramblings of an odd intellectual, unappreciative of the fact that Austria-Hungary's arch-enemy was falling apart before his very eyes? The unpleasant fact that so many Habsburg soldiers became prisoners of war during the First World War made this very question a crucial one, resulting in the creation of a remarkable intelligence-gathering system in Vienna based on captivity correspondence. By employing over a thousand censors simultaneously and by reading millions of letters and postcards, the Habsburg military authorities tried to gauge the loyalty and political attitudes of their own troops. The main goal of this chapter is to look at various opinions and forms of behavior that the censors tagged as "patriotic," as well as those they designated "suspicious," "disloyal," and "unpatriotic." I would like to argue here that beyond noticing when soldiers venerated the emperor/king, or expressed a sense of personal suffering and hatred of the enemy, the censorship struggled to define the meaning of "patriotism" and "loyalty." It preferred to lump a wide array of actions and opinions as "suspect" and "disloyal." In doing so, it utilized a double standard regarding perceived "loyal" nationalities and perceived "disaffected" nationalities, and failed to recognize genuine support for the state that found expression in many of the letters.

Patriotism and the Multinational State

The expanding nature of warfare during the nineteenth century created throughout Europe a sense that the size of a country's military was crucial to maintaining (or enhancing) its international standing.[9] Consequently, broadly-conscripted, reserve-based armies were gradually added to smaller professional cores, bringing with them a new kind of soldier into the center stage: the citizen soldier.[10] Serving now only a limited number of years in active duty (three in Austria-Hungary), these citizen soldiers were expected to mobilize quickly upon the threat of war and fight willingly for their country.[11] The fact that in their civilian lives these men were not under constant supervision of the army meant that it was impossible to motivate them exclusively by negative means. Rather, these civilian-soldiers needed to bring with them a sense of serving and fighting for a common cause, or develop such notions in the military, which would be "a school for the fatherland."[12]

The difficulties of convincing soldiers that the state as a whole was their *patria* are well documented even in such self-described "nation-states" as France, Italy, and Imperial Germany, where linguistic, cultural, and emotional attachments were predominately local at least until the last decades of the nineteenth century.[13] After the embarrassing defeat in Abyssinia in 1896, the Italian Education Minister, Ferdinando Martini, was famously quoted as saying "we have made Italy: now we must make Italians."[14] The task of creating emotional bonds with the state was even more daunting in a dynastic multinational state, such as the Habsburg Monarchy, where the state was the patrimony of its ruling house and not the embodiment of popular sovereignty.[15] In other words, in contrast to the evolving nation-states of Western Europe, the Habsburg Monarchy lacked a self-evident collective "us," into which many separate identities could be intertwined. The seemingly rational western European progression of identities from individual to village/town to region to nation and finally to the nation-state, a progression that aimed to mobilize every person on behalf of the state, did not flow smoothly in multinational Austria-Hungary even in theory. Thus, individuals might indeed have had strong attachments to their native region and to a nation within the Monarchy, but another European state might claim to embody their national project (e.g., Germany, Romania, Serbia, or Italy). Conversely, Habsburg subjects might have felt a sense of belonging to the multinational state, yet still long for an imaginary nation-state, at times without really resolving—or wishing to resolve—the contradictions inherent in such a position. A Czech nationalist from Bohemia might dream about an independent Czech homeland, yet at the same time support a strong, viable Austria-Hungary as a necessary bulwark against German and Russian expansionism. This was indeed the attitude of the father of Czech nationalism, František Palacký, and the influential approach known as "Austro-Slavism."

For the Habsburg Chief of Staff, General Franz Conrad von Hötzendorf, these entangled threads of loyalty were especially disturbing. An advocate of centralizing the monarchy along dynastic and linguistically-German lines, Conrad had little patience for the demands of Czech or Magyar nationalists.[16] Even before his appointment as Chief of Staff in 1906, Conrad became convinced that vigorous military action was the only way to combat enemies from within and outside the Monarchy.[17] In the years prior to World War I, Conrad bombarded the Foreign Office with memos about "corrosive nationalist elements especially in Bohemia, Bosnia-Herzegovina, Galicia, and the South Tyrol," and suggested a preemptive war against Austria's "congenital foes" (Italy and Serbia) as the only way to disentangle this problem.[18] "Only an aggressive policy with positive goals," wrote Conrad, "can save this state from destruction."[19] A successful war would send a clear message to those subjects within the Monarchy who were not sufficiently *kaisertreu*, while simultaneously strengthening the Dual Monarchy's international standing. In any case, he confided to his lover Gina on 28 June 1914, an unsuccessful war was preferable to a slow decline, "because such an ancient monarchy and such an ancient army cannot perish ingloriously."[20]

Yet, despite Conrad's oft-expressed pessimism regarding the future of the Monarchy and the loyalty of some of his troops, Austro-Hungarian citizens mobilized in the summer of 1914 without any difficulties whatsoever.[21] The willingness of these Habsburg citizen-soldiers to fight for their country, and the apparent widespread support for the initial war effort, attest to the existence and even the depth of imperial loyalties among the population. Pictures of excited crowds in the major cities of Austria-Hungary are not markedly different from the pictures of elated masses in France, Russia, and Germany. Whether these crowds indeed signified widespread "war enthusiasm" or just "bourgeois war enthusiasm," as some historians have recently argued, they do nonetheless express staunch support for their warring countries, be it a nation-state or a multinational one.[22] The reports of the Austro-Hungarian Army High Command (*Armeeoberkommando* or AOK) show that contrary to pessimistic prewar assessments, general mobilization proceeded smoothly, and almost no resistance was encountered even in "problematic" military districts in the Czech-speaking areas.[23] If "patriotism," then, in Carlton Hayes's basic definition, is the "love of country or native land," and if the willingness to sacrifice one's life for one's country is an indication of this love, then Austro-Hungarian citizens appear in the summer of 1914 to be just as patriotic as their counterparts in other parts of Europe.[24]

Still, as an anticipated short war became a long and costly one, as military setbacks piled up, and as a significant part of the Austro-Hungarian imperial army found itself in Russian, Serbian, and Italian captivity, the Army High Command reverted to its prewar mistrust of sections of the recruited citizenry, suspecting that lack of heart or even worse might have caused military setbacks.[25] It was through careful examination of letters and postcards that the Austro-Hungarian military leadership attempted to make sense of this apparent "unpatriotic" and "disloyal" behavior.

The Austro-Hungarian POW Censorship

During the long years of captivity, letters and postcards were the principal means of communication between POWs and their families and friends back home. It was this correspondence that enabled POWs to keep in touch and share some of their experiences in captivity: to notify their families that they had fallen captive, to complain, to give instructions, vent their frustrations, express homesickness, request money, or gossip about an acquaintance who, for example, had been cheating on his wife.[26] POW Majer Freund wrote to his wife Rachela in Galicia on 30 August 1916: "I am sick of Jacob Eisler. He is living here with a Christian woman and wants to go to America with her. I want you to tell this to his wife Beily."[27] Occasionally, letters contained rumors that circulated among the prisoners and fuelled their fears and anguish.[28] POW Ivan Rom wrote on 24 February 1915 to his mother Ivana in Carniola (present-day Slovenia):

> I must inform you what kind of news we received from Austria. It is said that every fifth prisoner, who is currently in Russia, will be shot upon returning to Austria. We, who fought 3 months in bloody battles, certainly do not deserve this. Whether this would actually take place remains to be seen. Perhaps it would be so upsetting that our soldiers would prefer to stay in Russia, rather than return.[29]

It was the sheer number of Austro-Hungarian POWs in enemy hands and the similarly huge number of captive enemy soldiers in the Habsburg Monarchy that made the volume of this POW correspondence astonishingly great.[30] The *daily* average of incoming and outgoing POW mail reached a robust 8,000 pieces in September 1914, rising to 75,000 pieces a day in the beginning of 1915, 266,000 in the beginning of 1916, and 455,000 in November 1916, a level that remained constant until the Bolshevik Revolution a year later.[31] Each letter would typically take at least a month before reaching its addressee, dallying at times as much as six months en route. Thus, for example, between 23 February and 7 October 1915, Miss Sascha Kronburg of Vienna sent 147 articles of mail to her fiancé, Lt. Alfred Mayer, interned in the far-eastern camp of Rasdolnoe. Having some connections abroad, she sent some of this mail via England, Romania, and the United States (the latter two countries neutral at the time), using simultaneously also the official Red Cross route via Sweden. As perhaps only someone in love might do, she compiled detailed statistics of the average duration each route required: Sweden an average of 105 days, the United States 55 to 65 days, England

45 days, and Romania 30 days. Beyond the sheer quantity of letters written by Miss Kronburg, it is astonishing that in the midst of a world war, almost all the articles of mail sent from Vienna to the Russian Far East arrived at their destination.[32]

The reason for the relative delay in the official Red Cross route was the wartime practice of censorship, primarily the Austro-Hungarian POW censorship. In contrast to the Russian military authorities, who read samples of mail, the Austro-Hungarian POW censorship was instructed to read all incoming and outgoing mail. It grew into a sizable and surprisingly efficient institution, considering the task at hand.

The practices of censorship in wartime Austria-Hungary were shaped (like many other political practices in the Dual Monarchy) by a combination of legal, quasi-legal, and illegal measures, as well as by a host of political considerations. The legal basis for censorship went back to the *Ausgleich* and to a series of laws passed in the years 1867–1869 in both halves of the Monarchy that allowed for the suspension of certain civil liberties during wartime. Most important in this context was the expected suspension of the right to secrecy of correspondence. The authorities viewed this suspension as a temporary measure, with ultimate control resting with the parliaments of Austria and Hungary.[33]

The institutional contours of censorship were sketched in 1912 in a series of secret meetings between officials in the Austro-Hungarian War Ministry (*Kriegsministerium*), the joint Ministerial Council (*Ministerrat*), and members of the General Staff. Josef Redlich, the Austrian constitutional historian and liberal statesman, viewed the meetings and ensuing top secret *Dienstbuch J-25a* as "completely unlawful," and estimated they were designed to give the army broad powers under the guise of preventing critical information from reaching the enemy.[34] Thus, *Dienstbuch J-25a* called for the establishment of a War Supervisory Office (*Kriegsüberwachungsamt* or KÜA) within the Austro-Hungarian War Ministry with jurisdiction—it was hoped—in both halves of the monarchy. The KÜA had the assignment to implement military and other measures appropriately and quickly in order to prevent espionage, sabotage, and the circulation of unauthorized information. As the Austrian historian Gustav Spann has pointed out, the KÜA was in name and purpose a completely new entity within the legal framework of the *Ausgleich,* although its sponsors attempted to conceal it within the recognized joint *Kriegsministerium.*[35]

The quasi-legal status of the KÜA became apparent during the first weeks of the war, when the Hungarian government of Count Tisza successfully blocked its full operation in Hungary, while defining precisely what it could and could not do on Hungarian territory. Specifically, all political and press matters were separated from the supervision of the KÜA in Vienna and were handled separately from Budapest. As a result, Hungarian newspapers reported much more freely and broadly on the war than did their counterparts in the Austrian half of the Monarchy. Moreover, since the Hungarian parliament continued to meet throughout the war, while the Austrian *Reichsrat* was adjourned until May 1917, the activities of the KÜA in Hungary were monitored by the legislature in Budapest, whereas in Vienna the KÜA became an unencumbered military-bureaucratic tool.

The KÜA was divided into five main groups. Group II—"The Censorship"—was further divided into three sections: *Press Censorship, Telegram Correspondence Censorship,* and *Letter Censorship,* in which *POW Correspondence* constituted a separate subsection. For all official purposes the POW censorship apparatus was not acknowledged as a part of the imperial bureaucracy, but rather as part of the Central Information Bureau of the Red Cross (*gemeinsames Zentralnachweisbureau des Roten Kreuzes-Auskunftstelle für Kriegsgefangene* or GZNB).[36]

The POW censorship was considered by far the best-organized subsection within the Austro-Hungarian Letter Censorship. What made it unique from the very beginning of the war was its centralized structure. In contrast to subsection *Foreign Correspondence,* which operated from twenty-two different locations until the fall of 1916, subsection *Inland Correspondence,* which focused on perceived "problem areas" and read only samples, and subsection *Field Post,* which delegated authority to junior officers in the units themselves, the GZNB processed all incoming and outgoing POW mail in one place: Vienna. This enabled the POW censorship to function simultaneously as both a gatekeeper and an intelligence-gathering unit. The thoroughness and versatility of the GZNB censorship not only won it accolades within the Austro-Hungarian censorship apparatus, but also led it to serve as a model for the 1916 reform of the *Zensurdienst* in Germany (to the considerable delight and pride of General Max Ronge, head of the Intelligence Bureau—*Evidenzbureau*—in the AOK).[37]

Under the direction of a career officer—Major Theodor Primavesi—the GZNB grew very quickly in size, employing in the beginning of 1916 more than 1,150 censors who read mail in more than thirty-five different languages, divided into fifteen language groups (see Table 1).[38] The KÜA's personnel guidelines instructed the censorship to use "as a rule persons unfit for front-line service (*felddienstuntaugliche Personen*).… In case of emergency, also rank-and-file soldiers fit for front-line service could be recruited, whose civilian occupation and social and civil status (*soziale Zivilstellung*) would guarantee proper fulfillment of their assignments (professors, governmental officials, bank clerks, etc.)." Thus, according to the War Supervisory Office, the desired profile of an Austro-Hungarian censor included linguistic, intellectual, and social credentials. Still, political considerations were even more important: censors were required to be absolutely trustworthy from a political point of view. A special group within the GZNB—the *Hyperzensur*—assessed the reliability of each individual censor. In addition, each language group commander had to review regularly the political tendencies of his censors, and report "Slavophiles," "Austrophobes," "irredentists," or any other case of "questionable" opinions. Judging by the constant complaints of the GZNB command, the army rarely allocated enough personnel qualified to meet the many qualifications and the heavy workload.[39] Thus, the GZNB turned to civilians, who worked for a small honorarium or as volunteers, and who eventually constituted almost half of the people employed in the GZNB.

Table 9.1. The Personnel of the GZNB Censorship, 21 January, 1916

Department	Officers	Rank-and-File	Civilians	Total
Command	4	4	6	14
Information	1	5	0	6
Blotting out & interception	0	19	0	19
Supervisor (*Hyperzensur*)	1	5	1	7
Post	2	92	0	94
Other depts.	7	73	3	83
Balkan group	0	2	7	9
Czech*	11	78	49	138
German	11	90	92	193
English/French	2	5	11	18
Hebrew	0	6	3	9
Italian	11	66	65	142
Croat	2	22	8	31
Polish	16	44	24	84
Romanian	2	11	11	24
Russian	4	25	152	171
Serb	3	20	15	38
Slovak	1	9	8	18
Slovene	1	3	5	9
Ukrainian	6	19	25	50
Hungarian	3	5	6	14
TOTAL	88	593	491	1,172

* Some language groups were divided into subgroups (e.g., six Russian subgroups, three German, two Czech, etc.) that have been combined here. The surprisingly small number of Hungarian censors reflected the paucity of POW correspondence in that language. In many cases, Magyar POWs in Russia were specifically prohibited from writing in their mother tongue due to the lack of qualified censors in Russia able to read Hungarian fluently.
Source: 'Übersicht über den gesamten bei der Zensurabteilung in Verwendung stehenden Personalstand,' KA/AOK (1915)/GZNB/Kart. 3734/Akt.2438 ad January 21, 1916.

Every article of mail sent by or to Austro-Hungarian prisoners of war or to POWs held in Austria-Hungary was first handled by the *Sortiergruppe* (Sorting Group). The *Sortiergruppe* would sort out the correspondence into languages, creating bundles of 1,000 articles of mail. The *Sortiergruppe* was also responsible for conducting a first search for the correspondence of "suspicious people," or conversely marking "suspicious-looking" correspondence written by people not identified yet as "suspicious." From the *Sortiergruppe* the mail would be forwarded to the heart of the GZNB operation—the Language Groups (*Sprachgruppen*). It was there that all the POW mail was read, assessed, analyzed, and subsequently forwarded to the appropriate groups (see Figure 1). The great majority of letters—a monthly average of 95 percent–98 percent—processed by the language groups proceeded smoothly to the *Auslaufgruppe* (Outgoing Mail), where they received

Figure 9.1. The Mail Sorting Process at the GZNB

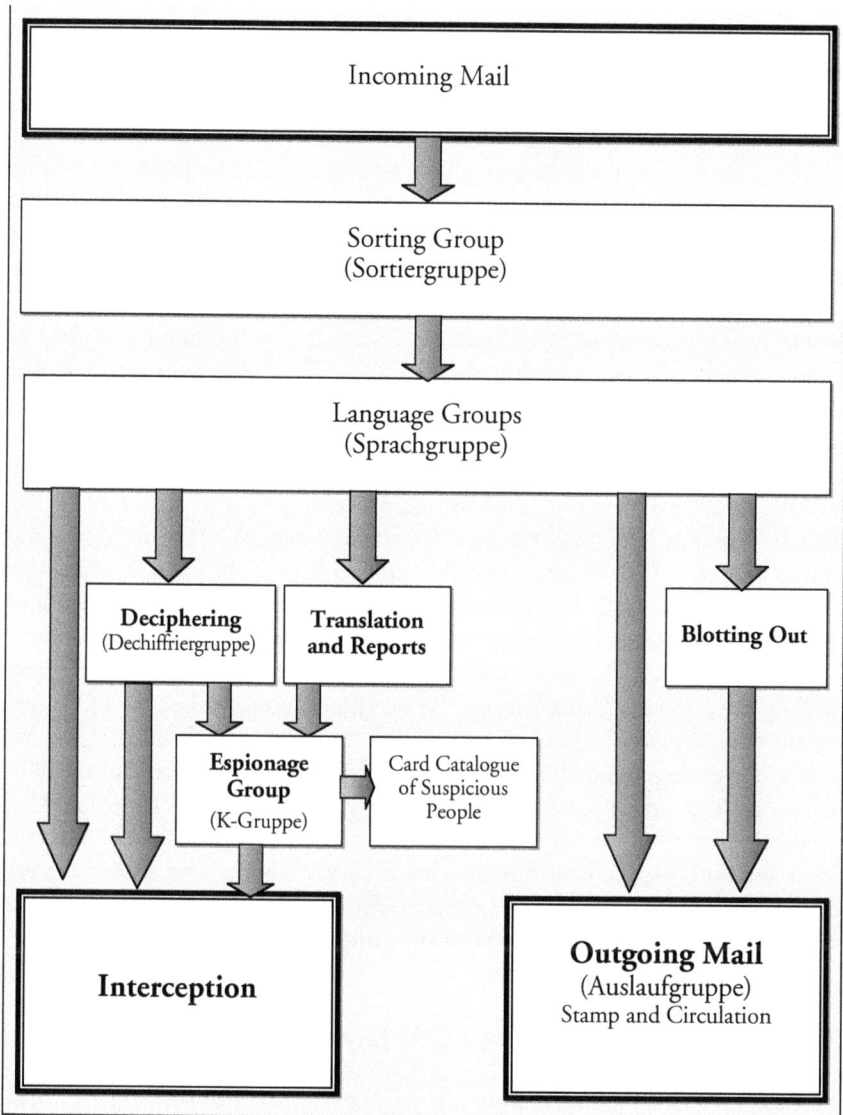

a censorship stamp and were released from GZNB control. In dealing with letters that appeared problematic, censors could choose one of two options: they could intercept them or blot out problematic sections. In the first case, the letters would be translated and transferred to the Espionage Group (*Kundschaftgruppe* or K-Gruppe). The K-Gruppe took particular interest in espionage, sabotage, treason, and desertion, and created a card catalogue with the names of all those suspected of such activities.[40] The K-Gruppe also received periodic and special reports from the individual language groups, evaluating the letters handled by that group.

When the *Sortiergruppe* or the language groups encountered letters that attempted to convey information surreptitiously, they would forward them for deciphering to the *Dechiffriergruppe.* The codes handled by the censors ranged from the naively simple (e.g., talking about 'Uncle Willi' when discussing Germany), through the elusive (marking with tiny dots the letters meant to carry the real message), to the sophisticated (writing between lines with invisible ink that appears when the letter is ironed). In the case of letters that required blotting out, the problematic sections would be translated into German and sent to the K-Gruppe (or integrated into reports). The blotted-out letter would then be forwarded to the *Auslaufgruppe,* stamped, and released. The blotting-out techniques caused much satisfaction within the GZNB. Utilizing what historian Gustav Spann termed an "artisanal approach" to this task, the GZNB censors devised a system of blotting out text by applying the same writing material in which the letter had been originally written. Thus, the censored parts would be submerged in a background of graphite or ink (of various colors and shades) and made illegible. An attempt to remove the censored section would result in the removal of the original text. The GZNB Command took pride in the fact that other belligerent countries (especially Russia) seldom showed the same sophistication in blotting out text, thus making it possible sometimes to read the censored sections.[41]

At first the GZNB focused on traditional censorship duties, primarily controlling the flow of information. Yet, the fact that censors read all the POW mail meant that they were in an excellent position to gather valuable information and assess its meaning. Besides mining POW correspondence for specific pieces of intelligence (e.g., about the formation of the *Česká družina* in 1914 or regarding epidemics and food shortages in Russia), the censors increasingly began to integrate and synthesize information into broad survey reports. The issue of the perceived loyalty (or disloyalty) of the Austro-Hungarian prisoners in Russia stood at the very heart of these efforts from the earliest stages of the war.

Censorship and the Issue of POW Loyalty

During the first six months of the war, one of the most interesting assignments handled by the GZNB was the request "to provide a certain picture of the political and military reliability" of Austro-Hungarian POWs in Russia and Serbia.[42] To do so each language group collected a sample of POW letters and counted how many POWs reported being wounded while being captured. Specifically, the POW censorship was interested in pinpointing particular regiments "that had been compromised through a significant number of unwounded prisoners of war."[43] The underlying assumption here was that only wounds could automatically justify a soldier's capture and clear him from suspected cowardice or treason. In other words, only through individual suffering could Austro-Hungarian

POWs make an uncontestable claim for not failing their duties as "patriots." Dr. Burghard Breitner, a noted surgeon and future head of the Austrian Red Cross Society, entitled his wartime memoirs *Captured Unwounded* to indicate his sense of his own dishonorable conduct.[44] It should be emphasized, though, that this perception was very common in all armies during World War I. Canadian historian Jonathan Vance has shown that the British Army during the Great War was also deeply imbued "with the nineteenth-century military ethos, which held that to be captured could have resulted only from some personal failing on the part of the soldier."[45] This ethos was inextricably bound up with the emphasis placed by European general staffs on personal and collective bellicosity (the much discussed "cult of the offensive"), as well as by the contemporary cultural link between élan and manliness.[46]

Thus, wounds constituted a conclusive test for the loyalty and patriotism of individual prisoners. For the Austro-Hungarian AOK, however, wounds were far more important on a collective than on an individual level. Therefore, the reports produced by the POW censorship emphasized "the percentages of wounded POWs among the various nations represented in the army."[47] In December 1914 the GZNB listed the following percentages of wounded Austro-Hungarian POWs:[48]

Germans	about 85%
Poles	about 85%
Slovaks	about 90%
Slovenes	about 80%
Italians	about 70%
Magyars	about 95%
Ruthenes	about 70%
Serbs	about 30%
Czechs	about 50% (in the previous month only 30%)
Romanians	about 95%

It is important to emphasize that these and similar figures produced by the POW censorship during the first six months of the war are almost certainly exaggerated. Not only were the samples upon which these figures were based rather small, but there was a serious discrepancy between the very high percentage of wounded men and the relatively lower mortality rate among the prisoners. The estimated overall mortality rate for Austro-Hungarian POWs in Russia was 17.6% according to official Austrian statistics, and the medical attention received by Austro-Hungarian POWs in Russia was usually insufficient, especially during the chaotic first year.[49] It seems highly unlikely that so many POWs were injured, yet still managed to survive the ordeal. What seems more likely to have happened is that in their letters POWs overstated their wounds in order to appear more patriotic and more manly, and perhaps out of fear of retribution from the state. The need to exaggerate one's wounds may have been felt more strongly by soldiers from certain national backgrounds (such as Magyars), but in reality had little relevance in explaining how these soldiers became prisoners. Habsburg soldiers usually fell into enemy hands when entire sections of the front collapsed and in situations where individual soldiers had no control whatsoever over their fates.[50]

It seems also that censors within the individual language groups attempted to exculpate "their" POWs and present them in a favorable light. A case in point is the figures attributed to Czech POWs in Russia. During the winter of 1914–1915 the head of the *böhmische Zensurgruppe A,* Dr. Kolinsky, made two attempts to put the Czech wounded figures in context. The first was in mid-December 1914, when he wrote a correction to the figures presented above, in which he stated that the percentage of wounded Czech POWs in Russia was actually 60 percent and not 50 percent and that most of the unwounded belonged to specific *Landsturm* battalions and did not represent Czech soldiers in general. The second and more serious attempt was in March 1915, when Kolinsky assembled a collection of letters from unwounded Czech POWs, explaining the circumstances in which they had been captured. This collection demonstrated, he argued, that "although these soldiers fell into enemy hands healthy and unwounded, the accompanying circumstances (*Begleitumstände*) suggest they held out heroically until the last moment."[51] This last attempt by Kolinsky resulted in a letter of reprimand from the head of the POW censorship—Major Theodor Primavesi—that forcefully reiterated the prejudices against Czechs held by the Austro-Hungarian High Command. "An attempt has been made," wrote Primavesi, "to present this nation [i.e., the Czechs] as virtuous, and their notorious Austrophobe statements as the work of individual agitators.… The fact is that one *never* finds Germans, Croats, and Magyars serving in enemy camps. These soldiers would rather hunger and die than let themselves be coerced into serving our mortal enemies."[52] In his condemnation Primavesi was undoubtedly raging against the creation in Russia of a Czech Company (*Česká družina*) to fight against Austria-Hungary. However, at that point in time—the spring of 1915—the Czech Company contained only a few hundred soldiers, the vast majority Russian citizens of Czech ancestry and not prisoners of war.[53] This anti-Czech bias found further expression in Primavesi's report from March 1915, which stated that "one feels revulsion that there is a nation that shakes the entire structure of our proverbial dynastic, brave, and loyal army; this incidentally has already been demonstrated through many years of intensive subversive activity (*Wühlarbeit*)."[54]

The matter, however, was not resolved with this reproach due to a surprising increase in the percentage of unwounded Magyar POWs detected by the censorship during the first months of 1915.[55] As a result, the POW censorship had to choose between three different courses of action: label Magyar POWs as "disloyal," reassess its conclusions regarding the loyalty of Czech POWs, or repudiate this method as a faulty indication of loyalty. The absence of data on the subject from the spring of 1915 and onwards suggests that the GZNB chose the third option, that is, they relinquished the method altogether. Still, Primavesi's report made a valiant effort to explain why "the large number of unwounded [Magyar] POWs is not connected in any way with the proven soldierly qualities of the Magyars."[56] Ironically, to make this point he relied on Kolinsky's method of collecting letters that explained "accompanying circumstances" such as hunger, lack of clothing, freezing weather, and lack of ammunition.[57]

For the GZNB, two additional motifs were solid indicators of patriotism among the POWs: veneration of the emperor/king and hatred of the enemy. Both of these figured prominently in a collection of "patriotic letters" assembled by the GZNB in the years 1915–1916.[58] An example of such a "patriotic letter" came from the Polish-speaking POW Jakob Skiba, who wrote home on 16 August 1916 from a work detail near the city of Perm:

> In two days we celebrate the birthday of our "old master." This is how we call our emperor. We would like to organize some sort of celebration in his honor, but don't know if it's going to be allowed. Love and reverence are really owed this monarch whose life goal was the preservation of peace. All the peoples of Austria love their old master, [and] even in Russia one utters his name with respect. His whole life was full of suffering for sins he did not commit. We Poles have a special reason to love and appreciate him. In the Russian area of Poland we are dispossessed, our property is confiscated, we cannot speak or sing in Polish. Only in Austria do we enjoy full freedom.[59]

The fact that the censorship expected prisoners to love their monarch and dislike their captors is not at all surprising. However, beyond these two commonly accepted motifs, there were additional indications understood to be "patriotic" by the various language groups. A comparison between them uncovers a noticeably different standard of patriotism for different nationalities. As a rule there was a marked difference between what was accepted as "patriotism" among Magyar and Polish POWs and what was accepted as "patriotism" among Czech and Slovak prisoners.[60] Magyars and Poles could indeed combine *kaisertreu* feelings with expressions of nationalism, but Czechs and Slovaks were restricted to the three essential indications of patriotism: love of monarch, hatred of the enemy, and anguish over being POWs. Thus, for example, a Polish POW officer, Seweryn Kisielewski, could be considered a patriot by the GZNB although his letter waxed poetically about "Our future Poland ... this eternal sufferer ... who waits for the final victory to restore her lost freedom."[61] In contrast, the GZNB did not recognize indications of Czech national sentiments as congruent with dynastic patriotism. The kind of letters that were put in the file of Czech "patriotic letters" were restricted to apologetic formulations such as the one written by POW Havlíček to his fiancée Rosa Jandl in June 1915:

> I am really jealous of all the comrades who were lucky enough to die for the fatherland, but there was no other option to escape this awful situation. I am so miserable that I have lost you, since you would never give your hand to a person who allowed himself to be taken captive. I regret that I dodged this terrifying bullet storm, and that no bullet found me.[62]

Most illuminating perhaps were the observations made by the head of the Slovak language group regarding the patriotism of Slovak POWs: "He [i.e., the Slovak] knows that he is fighting for a just cause for his master and emperor, and [he] has the conviction in his childish and humbly-preserved soul that God would not forsake him in this just battle. Further he knows that … he must bring the greatest sacrifices; he perceives the matter as a Christian martyr, approaching resolutely our righteous, holy cause like a deeply devout man who believes in the immortality of his soul.…"[63] Thus, "patriotism" in the Hungarian and Polish cases was a broader and more malleable concept than in the Czech and Slovak cases. It recognized a fuller range of opinions and identities, and allocated them a legitimate place within multinational Austria-Hungary. In the Czech and Slovak case "patriotism" was a rigid and restrictive concept that delegitimized national identities and opinions.[64]

As mentioned above, during the war the GZNB created lists of POWs whose opinions and forms of behavior were deemed particularly objectionable or suspicious. These included POWs who volunteered for anti-Habsburg units or expressed support for the Entente and various irredentist causes.[65] They included also POWs who insulted the emperor in words the censors occasionally found "too coarse to repeat on paper," POWs exhibiting suspicious economic behavior (e.g., a POW divulging that he "gained possession of ten gold rings" or POWs demanding higher wages from their Russian employers), and POWs expressing contentment with their status as prisoners. Although the POW censorship did not regard all these activities and opinions as equally severe, it did view all of them as undesirable from the perspective of the state, requiring accountability after the war.

Among the most fascinating collections of "suspicious" correspondence is a file containing 411 letters composed by Habsburg POWs who had formed close personal relationships with women in Russia and had announced their matrimonial intentions.[66] Most of these letters were written by speakers of various Slavic languages (mainly Czech, Polish, and Ukrainian) as well as by Jewish POWs. The Slovene POW N. Pongratschitsch wrote to his mother in Styria: "I have found a little wife, whom I married here in Russia. I will return home so you can see your Russian stepdaughter. Please tell Hani she shouldn't think about me anymore, because I have heard a lot about her."[67] In another letter Klaudia Andreieva wrote from Omsk to Josef Srb of Dolní Slivno near Mladá Boleslav/Jungbunzlau in northern Bohemia:

September 22, 1916

Praised be Jesus Christ!

I regret to inform you the following sad news. Your son Josef has converted to the Greek-Orthodox church because he wanted to marry me, a Russian. We could not get married in church until the conclusion of peace, and we decided to wait. In the meantime I had his child. God made it that we would be afflicted by a grave illness, and your son, Josef, died from it leaving me a child and no means whatsoever. We ask you in Christ's and the Holy Mother's name, to forgive your son and not to deny support for his child. The child is not to blame for our offence. Please write me in Russian. I love the child and will never leave him.... The child received the name Vladimir at his baptism.[68]

In the case of Jewish POWs, relationships with local women often resulted from close contacts between Austro-Hungarian Jewish soldiers and local Jewish communities in Russia. The Hebrew memoirist Avigdor Hameiri described in detail how Jewish families would "adopt" certain prisoners of war and invite them for holiday and Sabbath meals.[69] This interaction resulted at times in betrothal or marriage, as was the case with R. Judkowycz, who informed Rachela Lea Freund of Przemyśl: "I have become engaged to a very educated girl from a very good house, I also live with her, and I am treated very well by the people."[70] Adele Schwarzbach suggested to her brother interned in Simnik near Omsk "if you have a pretty girl there, bring her back with you. If, however, you can marry her there, do so and stay there."[71] On a certain level it was clear to the censors that these relationships did not constitute political or military acts. The head of the GZNB censorship was even asked whether a specific Austrian law prohibited such marriages.[72] Still, the increasing number of reported marriages in the years 1916–1918, and the presumably much greater number of extramarital relationships, induced the censorship authorities to characterize them as *"Vaterlandsflucht"* (fleeing the fatherland). Moreover, the mood expressed in many of these letters reflected a longing to end the war and a wish to return to normalcy. Thus, until the very last days of war the GZNB continued to track marriages of prisoners in Russia and report them to the proper authorities. The case of POW Ludwig Vacek preoccupied the attention of both the *Kriegsministerium* in Vienna and the Governor's Office in Prague as late as 26 October 1918, i.e., two days before the proclamation of the first Czechoslovak republic.[73]

The increasingly chaotic conditions in Russia during the years 1917–1918 brought with them a lax regime within POW camps and greater interaction between prisoners and the Russian civilian population.[74] This relaxed atmosphere was accompanied by increasing efforts to recruit POWs to anti-Habsburg units, and greater contacts between prisoners and various socialist organizations. Since the POW censorship had already developed before 1917 a broad definition of "disloyalty," it regarded these new developments with great alarm. The increasing willingness of Austro-Hungarian POWs to write with little restraint and express their opinions frankly, "as though there is no censorship and no avenging justice," according to mortified words of the Czech language censor Carl Ritter von Eisenstein, worked to confirm preexisting suspicions about the prisoners.[75] General Max Ronge, the head of the Intelligence Bureau in the AOK, thought that a considerable number of POWs had been infected in Russia by the "Bolshevik bacillus" and warned that "what awaits returning POWs [*Heimkehrer*] is not a jubilant welcome but a thorough examination of heart and conscience."[76]

Thus, when Austro-Hungarian POWs began returning from Russia in the winter of 1917–1918, a restrictive repatriation system had been set up as a "prophylactic political device."[77] Before being granted a four-week leave, returning

POWs (*Heimkehrer*) were required to undergo a sorting process in "reception stations," spend at least a fortnight in medical quarantines, complete successfully ten days of "disciplinary re-education" (*disziplinäre Nachschulung*), report for duty at their reserve units and, most importantly, account (*rechtfertigen*) for their behavior in captivity in "justification proceedings." Only then, and only after their conduct in captivity had been cleared, did the prisoners receive their furlough. POW officer Gottfried von Scotti felt humiliated by this reception, and told the interrogating officer: "I feel the fatherland had let me down."[78] Nevertheless, even the data of the Austro-Hungarian War Ministry regarding the loyalty of the returnees suggests that relatively few committed themselves to an openly anti-Austrian course: out of the 120,272 POWs who were screened by May 1918, only 1,620 could not justify their behavior in captivity; 514 *Heimkehrer* were labeled 'suspect of disloyal activity' (i.e., no conclusive proof was found), while 603 returnees deserted from their reserve units before their investigations could be completed (and of course may have deserted for a variety of reasons).[79]

Official fear and widespread distrust of Austro-Hungarian POWs had short and long term consequences: First, it added unnecessary hardship to the lives of the returning POWs, who had spent between two and four years in Russian camps and who returned home before Austria-Hungary disintegrated in the fall of 1918. Second, the series of large-scale mutinies that broke out among Austro-Hungarian reserve units in the Spring and the Summer of 1918, in which returning POWs played a prominent role, was sparked most probably by the restrictive policies and rough treatment towards the *Heimkehrer*. Thus, if the mutinies did indeed constitute an important milestone in the breakup of the Habsburg Monarchy—as most historians writing on the subject agree—they were triggered primarily by the miscalculations and perceived fears of the Austro-Hungarian military authorities.[80] These fears were the outcome of prewar prejudices against certain nationalities, as well as the manner in which the GZNB interpreted the opinions and behavior of prisoners in Russia. Third, the narrow definition of "patriotism" and the broad definition of "disloyalty," adopted by the GZNB, demanded from POWs passivity, self-sacrifice, and uncritical parroting of official slogans. This attitude contradicted four decades of efforts to turn, in the words of Eric Hobsbawm, "subjects into citizens" and to win over their loyalty.[81] By doing so, the censorship failed to recognize a real attachment to the Habsburg state that found expression in many of the letters:[82] it underrated the strong sense of grief expressed by POWs when Emperor-King Franz-Joseph died in November 1916, it distrusted the generally constructive suggestions of POWs regarding how to alleviate material conditions in captivity, and, most importantly perhaps, it seriously exaggerated the willingness of POWs in Russia to volunteer to fight against Austria-Hungary long before this was actually a problem. Thus, although the GZNB censorship became during the war a highly sophisticated intelligence-gathering organ, it remained nonetheless firmly attached to preconceived notions and prejudices.

Notes

1. For estimates of the numbers of prisoners during World War I, see Alon Rachamimov, *POWs and the Great War: Captivity on the Eastern Front* (Oxford and New York, 2002), ch. 1; Niall Fergusson, *The Pity of War: Explaining World War I* (New York, 1998), Table 42, 369; A. Klevanskii, "Voyennoplennye tsentral'nykh derzhav v tsarskoi i revolyutsnoi Rossii," in M. Birman, ed., *Internatsionalisty v boyakh za vlast' Sovetov* (Moscow, 1965), 22–25; Gerald H. Davis, "The Life of Prisoners of War in Russia, 1914–1921," in *Essays on World War I: Origins and Prisoners of War*, eds. Samuel Williamson and Peter Pastor (New York, 1983), 165, 190, note 1; and *In Feindeshand: Die Gefangenschaft im Weltkrieg in Einzeldarstellungen*, eds. Hans Weiland and Leopold Kern, 2 vols. (Vienna, 1931), statistical appendix.

2. This estimate was made by Leopold Kern based on *Kriegsministerium* data. See *In Feindeshand*, statistical appendix; Rachamimov, *POWs and the Great War*, ch. 1.

3. Rachamimov, *POWs and the Great War*, ch. 6.

4. Österreichisches Staatsarchiv (ÖStA)/Kriegsarchiv (KA)/Armeeoberkommando (AOK) 1918/ Gemeinsames Zentralnachweisbureau des Roten Kreuzes-Auskunftstelle für Kriegsgefangene (GZNB)/Kart:3757/Akte 5003. On Hans Kohn's Zionist period, see Hagit Lavsky, "Leumiut Bein Teoria le-Praktika: Hans Kohn ve-Hazionut," [Nationalism in Theory and Praxis: Hans Kohn and Zionism], *Zion*, 67, #2 (2002): 189–212.

5. KA, AOK(1918)/GZNB/ Kart. 3757/Akte 5003.

6. Ibid.

7. Hans Kohn, *Living in a World Revolution: My Encounters with History* (New York, 1964), 89–90.

8. Ibid., 90.

9. The North German Confederacy, for example, in 1870 fielded 1,200,000 soldiers, twice as many soldiers as Napoleon had led into Russia and fifteen times more than the largest of the eighteenth century's armies. Michael Howard, *War in European History* (Oxford, 1975), 99. See also, John Keegan, *The Face of Battle: A Study of Agincourt, Waterloo and the Somme* (London, 1976); and John Keegan, *A History of Warfare* (New York, 1993), 359–366.

10. The armies of the French Revolution were the first to demonstrate the tremendous potential of a "people's army," although establishing a smoothly functioning system of recruitment was by no means an easy task. See Isser Woloch, *The New Regime: The Transformations of the French Civic Order 1789–1820s* (New York, 1994), ch. 13.

11. István Deák, *Beyond Nationalism: A Social and Political History of the Habsburg Officer Corps 1848–1918* (New York and Oxford, 1990); Gunther Rothenberg, *The Army of Francis Joseph* (West Lafayette, IN, 1976).

12. On the development of disciplinary techniques in modern society and on the role of the military, see Michel Foucault, *Discipline and Punish: The Birth of the Prison* (New York, 1979); Eugen Weber, *Peasants into Frenchmen: The Modernization of Rural France, 1870–1914* (Stanford, 1976), 298.

13. Alon Confino, *The Nation as a Local Metaphor: Württemberg, Imperial Germany and National Memory 1871–1918* (Chapel Hill, NC, 1997), part 2. See also Celia Applegate, *A Nation of Provincials: The German Idea of Heimat* (Berkeley, 1990); Eric Hobsbawm, *Nations and Nationalism since 1780: Programme, Myth, Reality* (Cambridge, 1990), ch. 3; Eugen Weber, *Peasants into Frenchmen*.

14. Quoted in Confino, *The Nation as a Local Metaphor*, 15.

15. Oscar Jászi, *The Dissolution of the Habsburg Monarchy* (Chicago, 1964; orig. 1929), 436. On the emotional bonds of one group of Habsburg soldiers—the Jews—to the army and to the multinational state for which they fought, see Marsha L. Rozenblit, *Reconstructing a National Identity: The Jews of Habsburg Austria during World War I* (Oxford and New York, 2001).

16. Rothenberg, *The Army of Francis Joseph*, 144–145.

17. Rothenberg, *The Army of Francis Joseph*, 144.

18. Holger Herwig, *The First World War: Germany and Austria-Hungary 1914–1918* (London, 1997), 10.

19. Ibid., 9–10.

20. Ibid., 11.

21. Ibid., 33–37; Manfried Rauchensteiner, *Der Tod des Doppeladlers: Österreich-Ungarn und der Erste Weltkrieg* (Graz, 1993); Z.A.B. Zeman, *The Break-Up of the Habsburg Empire 1914–1918: A Study in National and Social Revolution* (London, 1961), 42–44.

22. See Peter Fritzsche, *Germans into Nazis* (Cambridge, MA, 1998); Niall Ferguson, *The Pity of War*; and Jean-Jacques Becker, *The Great War and the French People* (Leamington Spa, 1985).

23. Zeman, *The Break-Up of the Habsburg Empire*, 42.

24. In contrast to the extensive theoretical literature on nationalism, written in the past two decades, there is relatively little on patriotism. See, for example, Hubertus Jahn, *Patriotic Culture in Russia during World War I* (Ithaca, 1995), introduction; Hobsbawm, *Nations and Nationalism since 1780*, ch. 3; Carlton Hayes, *Essays on Nationalism* (New York, 1937).

25. Graydon Tunstall, *Planning for War against Russia and Serbia: Austro-Hungarian and German Military Strategies, 1871–1914* (New York, 1993), chs. 7–8.

26. KA, AOK 1916/ GZNB/Kart. 3745/Akte 4117/2.

27. KA, AOK 1916/ GZNB/Kart. 3745/Akte 4117/2.

28. The renowned French historian Marc Bloch was also struck by the prevalence and potency of rumors on the front during World War I. One of his first forays into the analysis of mentalities was his "Réflexions d'un historien sur les fausses nouvelles de la guerre," *Revue de synthèse historique* 33 (1921); see also Marc Bloch, *Memoirs of War 1914–1915*, trans. Carole Fink (Cambridge, 1988).

29. "Kroatisch-Slovenisch Gruppe-Separat Bericht," KA, AOK (1914–1915)/GZNB/Kart. 3726/Akte 418.

30. According to official Austrian figures, there were 1,861,000 enemy soldiers in the Habsburg Monarchy. The two largest groups were Russian POWs (1,269,000) and Italian POWs (369,600). See *In Feindeshand,* statistical appendix.

31. The deteriorating political conditions in Russia, however, reduced the flow of mail to a trickle in the spring of 1918, and from the summer of 1918 onwards mail could be sent back home only in convoluted or makeshift ways.

32. "Statistik über Sicherheit und Schnelligkeit verschiedener Routen für die Gefangenschaft nach Russland," KA, AOK (1915)/GZNB/Kart. 3737/Akte 2965.

33. "Die Zensur der Kriegsgefangenenkorrespondenz: Merk- und Handbuch für den Zensurdienst bei der Zensurabteilung des GZNB," KA, AOK (1915)/GZNB/Kart. 3733/Akte 2196. The only in-depth study of Austro-Hungarian censorship during World War I is Gustav Spann, *Zensur in Österreich während des I. Weltkrieges 1914–1918* (Ph.D. diss., University of Vienna, 1972).

34. KA, AOK (1915)/GZNB/Kart. 3733/Akte 2196; Spann, *Zensur,* 51–52.

35. KA, AOK (1915)/GZNB/Kart. 3733/Akte 2196; Spann, *Zensur,* 51–53.

36. KA, AOK (1915)/GZNB/Kart. 3733/Akte 2196; Spann, *Zensur,* 53–56, 113–123.

37. Spann, Zensur, 113–123.

38. KA, AOK (1915) GZNB/Kart. 3734/Akte 2438ad. The GZNB processed correspondence in the following languages: German, Russian, Italian, Czech, Polish, Slovak, Slovenian, Ukrainian, Serb, Croat, Romanian, "Bessarabian" (today Moldavian), Hungarian, French, English, Swedish, Hebrew, Yiddish, Ladino (or Spaniolit, the language of Sephardic Jews, especially in the Balkans), Spanish, Lithuanian, Estonian, Latvian, Bulgarian, Greek, Albanian, Arabic, Turkish, Persian, Cherkessian, Finnish, and occasional letters in Chinese, Japanese, and various Caucasian and Central Asian languages. See Heinrich von Raabl-

Werner, "Oesterreich-Ungarns offizielle Kriegsgefangenenfürsorge," *In Feindeshand,* Vol. 2, 325.

39. At times, these complaints had a touch of the absurd: some censors were reported to experience 'insanity fits,' others had 'limited thinking abilities,' while there were complaints of 'bums' (*Galgenvögel*), and even criminals. See Spann, Zensur, 154–155.

40. Since this card catalog no longer exists today, it is unclear how extensive it was. What is clear, however, is that many types of offenses were deemed suspicious and could land a person on the list of suspect POWs.

41. Spann, *Zensur,* 126–127.

42. KA, AOK (1914/1915)/GZNB/Kart. 3726/Akte 44, p. 3.

43. Ibid.

44. Burghard Breitner, *Unverwundet gefangen: Aus meinem sibirischen Tagebuch* (Vienna, 1921).

45. Jonathan Vance, *Objects of Concern: Canadian Prisoners of War through the Twentieth Century* (Vancouver, 1994), 26. On the AOK's predilection to look for collective scapegoats, see Rachamimov, *POWs and the Great War,* ch. 1. See also Tunstall, *Planning for War,* chs. 7–8; Richard Plaschka, "Zur Vorgeschichte des Überganges von Einheiten des Infantrieregiments Nr. 28 an der russischen Front 1915," *Österreich und Europa: Festschrift für Hugo Hantsch zum 70. Geburtstag* (Graz, 1965), 455–464.

46. See Keegan, *The First World War,* ch. 2; J.M. Winter, "The Generals' War," *The Experience of World War I* (London, 1988), 70–101.

47. KA, AOK/GZNB/Kart. 3728/Akte 1385. The GZNB used the language of a letter as an indication of the national identification of the writer. Although in most cases this assumption was probably true, it was not always the case. There were POWs who spoke several languages fluently and who used them interchangeably, and there were languages such as Magyar and Yiddish, which POWs preferred in many cases not to use, the former because of a dearth of Magyar-speaking Russian censors, which resulted in logjams and delays, and the latter because it was usually prohibited by the Russian military authorities.

48. KA, AOK/GZNB/Kart. 3728/Akte 1385.

49. *In Feindeshand,* statistical appendix.

50. An estimated number of 100,000 Austro-Hungarian soldiers were captured during the first Russian offensive, 119,000 Austro-Hungarian soldiers were taken captive when the fortress of Przemyśl surrendered, about 100,000 Austro-Hungarian POWs were taken during the ill-fated Black and Yellow offensive (August 26–October 13 1915), and an astounding 300,000–380,000 Austro-Hungarian soldiers were estimated captured during the Brusilov Offensive in 1916. Because of extreme weather in the Carpathian Mountains, it was never determined how many prisoners were among the 793,000 men lost during the Austro-Hungarian Winter Offensive (23 January–30 April 1915). On one day alone, 27 February 1915, 40,000 men from the Austro-Hungarian Second and Third Armies were reported missing, either captured by the enemy or lost in the snow. For an in-depth discussion of this issue, see Rachamimov, *POWs and the Great War,* ch. 1.

51. "Böhmische Zensurgruppe A, 7. Spezialbericht: Einige Schilderungen über die Situation bei der Gefangennahme," KA, AOK (1914/1915)/ GZNB/Kart. 3726/Akte 630.

52. Ibid. Emphasis in the original.

53. On the history of the Czech Legion, see an excellent survey by Josef Kalvoda, "Czech and Slovak Prisoners of War during War and Revolution," in *Essays on World War I: Origins and Prisoners of War,* eds. S. Williamson and Peter Pastor (New York, 1983), 215–238.

54. KA, AOK (1915)/GZNB/Kart. 3728/Akte 1385, Section E-3.

55. Due to the paucity of letters written in the Hungarian language, it is not clear how many letters were used or whether this conclusion had been reached by another method (family names, place of origin, etc.). KA, AOK (1915)/GZNB/Kart. 3728/Akte 1385, Section E-3.

56. KA, AOK (1915)/GZNB/Kart. 3728/Akte 1385, Section E-3.

57. Regarding the ways Austro-Hungarian POWs viewed and interpreted their capture, see Rachamimov, *POWs and the Great War,* ch. 1.
58. KA, AOK (1915)/GZNB/Kart. 3731/Akte 1746. These letters were most probably collected for propaganda purposes.
59. "Meldung von 17. Oktober 1916," Polnische Zensurgruppe, KA, AOK/GZNB/Kart. 3731/Akte 1746 letter #1.
60. Interestingly, the files of the GZNB do not contain "patriotic letters" written in German. There are letters in Hungarian, Ukrainian, Polish, Czech, and Slovak, and a couple of examples in Slovene and Serbian. It is not clear whether letters in other languages were not collected or simply not preserved.
61. "Kostroma, Kgf. Offizier Seweryn Kisielewski an Sofie Kisielewska in Krakau," 22 November 1915, KA, AOK (1915)/GZNB/Kart. 3731/Akte 1746, patriotische Briefe, letter #8.
62. KA, AOK (1915)/GZNB/Kart. 3731/Akte 1746.
63. "Patriotische Briefe der slovakischen Kriegsgefangenen," KA, AOK (1915)/GZNB/Kart. 3731/Akte 1746, p. 1.
64. For the Czech language censors it was probably inconceivable that Czech national motifs would be accepted by the AOK as anything but expressions of separatism and disloyalty. It mattered little in this respect that until May 1917, only a tiny minority of the Czech-speaking POWs in Russia (7,273 out of an estimated 250,000, or 2.9 percent) volunteered for the Czech Legion and committed themselves unequivocally to a separate Czech state. Kalvoda, "Czech and Slovak Prisoners of War in Russia," 223.
65. For example, a letter in Italian written on 30 July 1915 by POW Antonio Vedovalli in Omsk to Erminia Vedovalli in Breguzzo, South Tyrol: "These German barbarians have certainly brought misery upon you. But God knows how to punish these dogs. With my friend I am waiting to be transported to my new fatherland, sunny and beloved Italy, where I will enlist and perhaps fight against these arrogant Germans and liberate our villages." KA, AOK (1916)/GZNB/Kart. 3743/Akte 3880/1, p. 2.
66. The language distribution of the letters was the following: 199 in Czech (47 percent), 73 in Polish (17.5 percent), 55 in German (13.1 percent), including many from Jewish POWs, 31 in Ukrainian, 14 in Slovak, 12 in Serbian, 10 in Russian, 8 in Hungarian, 3 in Romanian, 3 in Slovene, and one each in Croat, Italian, and Yiddish.
67. All names are spelled as they appeared in the original censorship report: thus Pongratschitsch instead of Pongračić. "Sonderbericht September 21. 1916," Slovenische Zensurgruppe, KA, AOK (1916)/GZNB/Kart. 3745/Akte 4117/1.
68. Russische B. Gruppe, Gruppenleiter Hermann Safir, "Spezialbericht: Eheschliessung und Tod eines österr. kgf. in Russland," KA, AOK (1916)/GZNB/Kart. 3745/Akte 4117/4.
69. Avigdor Hameiri, *Begehenom shel Mata* [Hell on Earth] (Tel Aviv, 1932).
70. Zensurgruppe Deutsch C., Gruppenleiter Oblt. Beran, March 12 1917, KA, AOK (1916)/GZNB/Kart. 3745/Akte 4117.
71. Ibid.
72. Böhmische Zensurgruppe B., 11 July 1916, in Ibid.
73. KA, AOK/GZNB/Kart. 3745/Akte 4117-6.
74. See Rachamimov, *POWs and the Great War,* ch. 3.
75. R.v.Eisenstein, "Die nationalpolitische Bewegung der Tschechen (Oktoberbericht)," Referat XIV/19, 6 November 1917, KA, AOK (1917)/GZNB/Kart. 3755/Akte 4871, p. 1.
76. Quoted by Hannes Leidinger and Verena Moritz, "Österreich-Ungarn und die Heimkehrer aus russischer Kriegsgefangenschaft im Jahr 1918," *Österreich in Geschichte und Literatur,* Vol. 41, #6 (1997), 394.
77. Otto Wassermair, *Die Meutereien der Heimkehrer aus russischer Kriegsgefangenschaft bei den Ersatzkörpern der k.u.k. Armee im Jahre 1918* (Ph.D. diss., University of Vienna, 1968). See also Rachamimov, *POWs and the Great War,* ch. 5.

78. "Aufzeichnungen von Obst. Gottfried Scotti über der Kriegsgefangenschaft in Rußland," KA, Nachlaß Mühlhofer, B/231:16.

79. Wassermair, *Die Meutereien der Heimkehrer,* 87–88.

80. See Leidinger and Moritz, "Österreich-Ungarn und die Heimkehrer"; Herwig, *First World War,* 364–373; Rauchensteiner, *Der Tod des Doppeladlers,* ch. 24; Richard Plaschka, Arnold Suppan, and Horst Haselsteiner, *Innere Front: Militärassistenz, Widerstand und Umsturz in der Donaumonarchie* (Vienna, 1974), vol. 2.

81. Hobsbawm, *Nations and Nationalism,* 88.

82. Rachamimov, *POWs and the Great War,* ch. 6.

Chapter 10

SUSTAINING AUSTRIAN "NATIONAL" IDENTITY IN CRISIS

The Dilemma of the Jews in Habsburg Austria, 1914–1919

Marsha L. Rozenblit

The Jews of the Habsburg Monarchy always constituted an unusual category. Regarded by the authorities as members of a religious confession and not as one of the *Völker* of the multinational Monarchy, Jews nevertheless behaved in ways that led at least some people to consider them an ethnic group, a *Stamm*, perhaps even one of the nationalities of the realm. Habsburg Jewry, which in 1910 numbered over 2,000,000, including 932,458 in Hungary, and 1,313,687 in the Austrian half of the Monarchy,[1] was an extraordinarily diverse group, ranging from traditional, pious, Yiddish-speaking, often poor Jews in Galicia and in some parts of Hungary to the modernized, Germanized, Magyarized, or Czechified Jews in other parts of Hungary, Bohemia/Moravia, and Vienna, some of whom were no longer poor, no longer religious, and no longer isolated from the societies and cultures in whose midst they lived. Whether they practiced all, some, or none of the rules and regulations of the religion of their ancestors, and whether they believed that they had assimilated successfully, most Jews continued to regard themselves as a distinct group in Habsburg society. Most other subjects of the Monarchy, not only the anti-Semites, agreed.

Indeed, Jews in the Austrian half of the Monarchy in the last decades before the First World War developed what I have labeled a tripartite identity.[2] They espoused a fervent Austrian political identity, supporting the multinational empire with genuine conviction, believing only it could guarantee their legal and civil rights, only it could protect them adequately from the anti-Semitism rampant in many of the nationalist movements, and only it allowed them the latitude to develop Jewish identity as they saw fit. This political identity found expression in what Robert Wistrich has called the cult of Franz Joseph.[3] Jews praised the emperor (rather than the German liberal parties) for having granted them emancipation and freedom, glorifying him as the embodiment of decency, and middle-class virtue, and in the words of the Hungarian Jew Charles Fenyvesi, for having "made our world whole."[4] Alongside this patriotic political identity, one shared just as fervently by modern, acculturated Jews in Vienna and Prague as by traditional, small-town Jews in Galicia (who affectionately called the emperor Froyim Yossel),[5] modernizing Jews also adopted one of the cultures of Habsburg Austria, often embracing German, but sometimes also Czech or Polish culture. Those who adopted German culture—largely the Jews of Bohemia and Moravia, the Jews who immigrated to Vienna, and many Jews in Bukovina—saw themselves as members of the German *Kulturnation* and identified with the rational, humanistic values of the Enlightenment. Their sense of the superiority of German culture notwithstanding, they did not regard themselves as members of the German *Volk*. They were Germans both by culture and by identification with the Austrian supranational state, but they did not see themselves as Germans in the same way as German nationalists saw themselves as Germans. To a very significant extent their German identity was cultural, not ethnic or national. The same can surely be said about the relationship of Polonized Jews in Galicia to Polish culture.

Finally, most Jews in the Austrian half of the Dual Monarchy found that this relatively tolerant, multinational society gave them room, far more room than nation-states would have given them, to espouse a Jewish ethnic identity, one characterized by religion for some and by full-blown nationalist dimensions for others. Jews in Habsburg Austria felt comfortable asserting that they were Jews, a people with a common history and common destiny. True, not all Jews felt intense ethnic loyalties. Many Jews did try to assimilate utterly into the nations whose cultures they had adopted. But most Jews felt emotional ties to a Jewish people that transcended the bonds of religion. They lived their lives within the comfort of a largely Jewish social universe of Jewish family, friends, neighbors, business associates, and organizational cronies;[6] and they appreciated that the state allowed them the luxury of adopting German or Czech or Polish culture while still maintaining Jewish ethnic loyalty. Some Jews went further. The Zionists and the diaspora nationalists argued that the Jews were a nation like all other nations, and demanded that the Austrian state recognize the Jews legally as one of the nations of the realm. They sought Jewish cultural autonomy within a future Austria that would be reorganized as a federation of autonomous nationalities.[7] Most Jews did not share this nationalist vision, but like the Zionists, they understood that a multinational state was far more hospitable to Jewish ethnicity (at least in principle) than any nation-state with its much more rigid definition of the nation ever could be.

What was the national identity of the Jews of Cisleithanian Austria? The Jews were famous, and deservedly so, for their Austrian identity, an identity artfully memorialized in Franz Czokor's 1936 play, *3 November 1918,* in which the Jewish doctor, having no homeland when the Monarchy falls apart, places earth in the name of "Austria" on the grave of his colonel who has killed himself because he too no longer has a homeland.[8] But this Austrian identity was not "national" in the sense in which that word is used east of the Elbe. Social scientists today generally divide national identity into two types: the civic nationalism of the United States, England, and France, which, at least in theory, creates the nation out of the community of citizens, those people who participate in the life of the polity; and the ethnic nationalism of Central and Eastern Europe, in which the "nation" is the ethnocultural community of descent, which in turn seeks political sovereignty over a territory in which *Volk* and state are congruent.[9] Although they did not use the term, Jews imagined Habsburg Austria as a "civic" nation, to which they could be loyal. This Austrian state upheld the rule of law and guaranteed its impartial administration, a fact that the Jews deeply appreciated, worried as they always were about the impact of anti-Semitic agitation, especially among the radical nationalists. This Austria guaranteed that the Jews could exercise their rights as citizens. The Jews may have adulated Franz Joseph as the personification of this state, but they were not old-fashioned dynastic loyalists. Rather, they espoused a vigorous Austrian patriotism and an Austrian identity, a framework that enabled them to avoid the pitfalls of ethnic nationalism. They did not have to embrace membership in a nation, many of whose members rejected them anyway, and they had more space in which to develop their multiple identities. They could be Austrians, and Germans (or Czechs or Poles), and Jews all at the same time.

World War I provided the Jews with the perfect opportunity to assert this Austrian identity. Jews greeted the outbreak of the war in August 1914 with great enthusiasm because the war allowed them to display simultaneously their Habsburg and Jewish loyalties. Like Jews all over Europe, Habsburg Jews could demonstrate with their *Gut und Blut* their absolute loyalty to the state in which they lived and hope that Jewish valor would dispel anti-Semitic notions about Jewish cowardice.[10] But unlike Jews elsewhere, Habsburg Jews experienced no dissonance between their state patriotism and their Jewish loyalties. Focusing on the Eastern Front and the conflict with Russia, Jews fervently believed that Austria-Hungary's war was a Manichean struggle between the forces of good and evil, of culture and barbarism, of light and dark. They regarded Russia not simply as an enemy that had invaded Austrian territory, but as the oppressor and persecutor of the Jews of Eastern Europe. Thus World War I became a *Rachekrieg für Kischinev,* a war of revenge for the pogroms, a war to liberate the Jews of occupied Galicia and of Russia itself.[11] One soldier, whose letter was reprinted in the Jewish press, presumably because it expressed Jewish wartime ideology so well, insisted:

> It is a very sweet feeling … to be able to go to war against an enemy like Russia. Oh may we be able to take revenge for the mutilated bodies of Kishinev, for the most shameful atrocities of Zhitomir, for the eyes put out in Bialystok, for the defiled Torah scrolls, for the pogroms, and for the innumerable murdered innocent children.[12]

The fact that hundreds of thousands of Jews fled from the invading Russian armies in Galicia and Bukovina only underscored the need for victory against the evil empire. Jews understood that the war on the Eastern Front was simultaneously a war to defend the fatherland, to liberate fellow Austrian Jews in distress, and to free the Jews of Eastern Europe from czarist oppression.

The Jews cared deeply about the war in the East. They expressed profound disappointment with Austro-Hungarian setbacks, and reveled in Austro-Hungarian victories in Galicia in 1915 and 1916.[13] The editors of the Prague-based Zionist newspaper *Selbstwehr,* for example, declared the "overwhelming joy" of "we Austrian Jews," noting: "Lemberg conquered. These two words encompass the enormous measure of our happiness that no one will forget his whole life long."[14] In his war diary, army medic Teofil Reiss from Vienna gleefully described how the Austrian troops were "hunting [the Russians] like dogs" in Russian Poland in the summer of 1915. Stationed on the Eastern Front for most of the war, Reiss was always eager to get back to the front after convalescing behind the lines for illness or wounds. Despite his grim realism about the terrible conditions of the fighting war, Reiss wanted to serve in the war against Russia.[15] When Russia was defeated, most Jews felt that the Dual Monarchy had won the war.[16] The rest of the fighting, the struggle with Serbia, and the standoff with Italy (which found widespread support in Austria generally) frankly did not interest them at all. Serbia and Italy were not enemies of the Jews. Jews did their duty at the Isonzo Front and elsewhere, but not with the same commitment with which they fought against Russia. The same Teofil Reiss, for example, who was always eager to re-

Figure 10.1 Jewish Soldiers Celebrating the Holiday of Simchat Torah on the Isonzo Front, 1917. Courtesy Central Archives for the History of the Jewish People, Jerusalem, Au 258/11

turn to the front in the East, seemed less interested in the fighting war when he was posted to Italy in 1918. Moreover, when the army tried to reassign him to the front after he had recovered from some wounds, he noted "naturally I reported that I was sick."[17]

The Jewish press was filled with articles and letters from people of widely disparate political and religious viewpoints who regarded Austria's war with Russia as a Jewish holy war. W. Reich, a rabbi in Baden bei Wien, for example, wrote a series of articles in the Viennese liberal Jewish newspaper *Österreichische Wochenschrift* in the summer and fall of 1914 in which he depicted Russia as a land of robbery, rape, murder, brutality, and pogroms in contrast to Germany and Austria, bastions of culture, progress, and humanity. He concluded that "this war is a holy war for us Jews." Using biblical images, and evoking a mood of messianic urgency, he insisted that the Central Powers would emerge victorious because God would help Austria defeat the "Cossacks," a term he surely chose to invoke the anti-Jewish pogroms.[18] Similarly, articles in the Zionist newspaper *Selbstwehr* in Prague asserted that the purpose of the war was to liberate the Jews of Russia from "barbarous despotism." "For us," one writer in this paper noted, "the battle for the Fatherland is at the same time a battle for the just cause and also a holy war against the hereditary enemy of the Jews."[19]

The course of the fighting in 1914 and 1915 only encouraged Jewish spokesmen to continually draw the equation between Austrian and Jewish interests. The Jewish press regularly presented gruesome reports of Russian atrocities against the Jews in Galicia, many of them exaggerated, and used inflated language to depict Russian policy as a "war of annihilation against all that is Jewish."[20] Heinrich Schreiber from Vienna declared in May 1915 in the *Österreichische Wochenschrift* that "we struggle bravely for the ideals of our Fatherland, and we feel as one with the masses of our fellow Jews who are threatened by the enemy hordes and their pogroms."[21] A writer for the Brünn/Brno-based Zionist newspaper *Jüdische Volksstimme* likewise noted in March 1915 that "we do not forget that we are fighting against the descendants of Esau," against a country that murders and tortures Jews, for the liberation of millions of Jews, and for the creation of a new, more moral world.[22] Jewish spokesmen also insisted that Jewish refugees who fled from Galicia and Bukovina suffered both as Jews and as Austrians. They had fled from the Russians out of fear of Russian anti-Semitism and worry that the Russians would punish them for their Austrian patriotism.[23] Indeed, the Jewish press emphasized that Russia persecuted the Jews of Galicia and Bukovina (thus inducing them to flee) precisely because of "their Austrian sympathies, their loyalty to the Kaiser, their love and respect for His Majesty Kaiser Franz Joseph."[24] In the summer of 1915, after the German and Habsburg armies drove the Russians out of most of Galicia, Rabbi Moritz Güdemann, the elderly chief rabbi of Vienna, noted in his diary: "Oh great, obstinate, impenitent Russia of terror and pogroms, how dearly you and your czars must still pay for your persecution of the Jews."[25]

Jewish participation on the home front also bolstered the Austrian and Jewish loyalties of Jews. As good Austrian citizens, Jews contributed to the war effort, buying war bonds and donating time and money to various charities that helped soldiers, their widows, and their orphans. Despite a genuine concern for the general war effort, however, Jews focused the bulk of their wartime charitable work on helping fellow Jews: providing for the religious needs of Jewish soldiers in the army and aiding the hundreds of thousands of Jewish refugees from Galicia and Bukovina who flooded into Bohemia, Moravia, and Vienna.[26] Indeed, aiding the refugees became the most important war work done by Austrian Jews, and in particular by Austrian Jewish women. They understood their refugee work—work often characterized by an attitude of condescension and cultural superiority toward the objects of their charity—as simultaneously supporting both their own distressed community and the larger Habsburg war effort. After all, the refugees were citizens of Habsburg Austria, victims of Austria's war with Russia who suffered, at least in part, because of their Austrian loyalties. At the same time, the refugees were Jews, and helping them both reflected and encouraged Jewish solidarity.[27] Jews in Bohemia, Moravia, and Vienna recognized that the anti-Semitic, anti-refugee sentiment, which grew enormously during the difficult last two years of the war, endangered the situation of all Jews, and they strove valiantly, albeit without much success, to combat it.[28] They also understood that only the multinational state could protect them from the ravages of this anti-Semitism.

Jewish participation at the battlefront reinforced the complex identity of Austrian Jews. Those who fought for the Monarchy—and they numbered over 300,000[29] during the course of the war—did so as loyal Habsburg subjects, devoted to Kaiser and Reich.[30] That so many Jews earned medals for their wartime heroism, that so many Jews fell in battle, gave all Jews a sense of pride in Jewish participation in the war effort, even if it did not dispel anti-Semitic myths about Jewish cowardice. Moreover, the reality of ultra-orthodox Galician and Hungarian Jewish soldiers valiantly marching off to battle provided an effective visual image of the utter loyalty that Habsburg Jews, including the least assimilated, felt for the Monarchy. At the same time, the refusal of Habsburg army authorities to abide official anti-Semitism in the service made all Jews appreciate the multinational state. In Germany, where Jews had hoped that their wartime service would lead to full acceptance in the German nation, the army succumbed to anti-Semitic pressure to take a military census that deeply humiliated the Jews.[31] In Austria-Hungary, as István Deák has shown, not only did many Jews serve as officers in the army, but the army also considered itself to be above national and confessional strife, valuing loyalty to the fatherland and dynasty above all else. The Austro-Hungarian military assumed that the Jews were a profoundly loyal element and saw no reason to bow to anti-Semitic demands for a similar census.[32] Jews felt that both the army and the multinational state deserved their unreserved support and affection, and they fervently hoped for their survival.

During the last two years of World War I, Jews in Habsburg Austria experienced a growing sense of alarm when it seemed increasingly possible that the multinational empire that protected them and allowed them the latitude to assert their comfortable tripartite identity, might dissolve. They watched in dismay as the increasingly vituperative nationality conflict escalated, especially after the reopening of parliament in 1917. They feared the growth of anti-Semitism. They worried that Galicia might become part of an independent Poland that would persecute the Jews. They fervently upheld the continued existence of the Austrian *Gesamtstaat* even as they developed and supported plans to reconfigure that same state to conform to twentieth-century demands for greater democracy and national self-determination. This intense commitment to the multinational state endured to the very last moments of the Monarchy and beyond. The final years of the war also witnessed a deepening of Jewish ethnic solidarity and a growth in Jewish nationalism, both developments that only fortified the devotion of Jews to the multinational state. After all, Zionist plans for Jewish national autonomy would only work within the context of a federation of nationalities, not in the context of nation-states. Ordinary Jews also understood that the multinational state provided more room to express Jewish ethnicity than a nation-state would, especially those that might be created if Austria-Hungary were to disintegrate.

Kaiser Franz Joseph's death in 1916 presented Jews with a moment to reflect on the larger dilemma they faced. In his memoirs, Manès Sperber recalled that his father sobbed on the day the emperor died, declaring to his son that "Austria has died with him. He was a good emperor for us. Now everything will be uncertain! It is a great misfortune for us Jews."[33] Jews genuinely mourned the Kaiser's passing. Rabbi Adolf Altmann in Meran, Tyrol, delivered a sermon praising the emperor as a virtuous, just man, a loyal and good father to all his peoples. The Jews, he declared, would continue to love the emperor for all eternity.[34] Austrian Zionists likewise saw the death of the Kaiser as a "misfortune" and declared that Franz Joseph had been "the standard and the model ... of how one can be a good and true Austrian."[35] With the passing of the Kaiser, Jews felt nervous about the future. They became alarmed about the implications of rising anti-Semitism and the inability of the state to curtail it.

The issue of Galicia, perhaps more than any other, strengthened Jewish commitment to the multinational empire. In theory, Jewish spokesmen supported the demands of the Polish national movement in occupied Russian Poland. They feared, however, that the newly independent Poles would attack the Jews if the Austrian authorities were not there to prevent anti-Semitic depredations, and they hoped that Galicia would remain in Austrian hands no matter what official plans were afoot to create an independent Poland. In an article in November 1916, after the Central Powers had created the so-called "Kingdom of Poland," a puppet state under their control, Josef Samuel Bloch, the Galician-born editor of the *Österreichische Wochenschrift*, reminded the Poles that their new state must be based on "justice and humanity for all."[36] Jewish nationalists especially sought to keep Galicia Austrian, arguing that the Poles would violate the rights not only of Jews, but also of Ukrainians in the province.[37] One writer in Prague's *Selbst-wehr* reminded his readers that only a united Habsburg Austria, which did not represent the interest of any particular nation, could guarantee the civil and political rights of all the citizens; only the centralized state could protect national minorities.[38] All Jews reacted with alarm when pogroms broke out in Galicia in the spring of 1918[39] and especially in the fall and winter of 1918–1919, when large numbers of Jews were killed in Lemberg/Lwów/L'viv and elsewhere in East Galicia during the Polish-Ukrainian conflict there.[40] If, in the words of Joachim Schoenfeld, "the birth of Poland was accompanied by rivers of Jewish blood,"[41] then surely Polish nationalism, and by extension nation-states in general, were less congenial to Jews, indeed, to all ethnic or religious minorities, than the old multinational Monarchy had been.

In the last two years of the war, Jews increasingly believed themselves to be not only the most loyal supporters of the Monarchy but also the "only unconditional Austrians in this state." They feared that most of the nationalist politicians no longer remained committed to "the concept of Austria."[42] By the summer of 1918, one writer in the *Österreichische Wochenschrift* noted that the Jews were "the only Austrians loyal to the state left in the Monarchy."[43] Perhaps he exaggerated, but Jews really did sense their increasing isolation at the hands of nationalist agitation. Jews of all political and religious persuasions from the Zionists to the Orthodox continued to plead for the "inviolability of the whole Monarchy." As Robert Stricker, the leader of Austrian Zionists, intoned, "We nationally-conscious Jews want a strong Austria. Only it can provide a home to its nations. We believe that an Austria must exist. If there were no Austria, it would be a misfortune for the entire world."[44] After all, "the idea of the Austrian state is an indubitable necessity," noted another spokesman.[45] Zionists, of course, wanted to reorganize Austria as a democratic federation of nationalities, and this goal required a multinational state. But all Jews feared the consequences of the collapse of the Monarchy and the creation of nation-states.

When World War I ended and the Habsburg Monarchy collapsed, the Jews faced a genuine crisis. For the most part they genuinely mourned the death of the old state. Heinrich Schreiber of Vienna wrote:

> We acknowledge openly and honestly the deep pain in our hearts about the gloomy and painful transformation and upheaval. It is with ... deep sadness ... that we bid farewell to the united fatherland, and we stand shocked before the grave of old, familiar, honorable memories and feelings ... that a day of calamity has dashed into ruins. Our only comfort is the thought that we are not guilty for it.[46]

At the same time, with some important exceptions, Jews worried about life in the successor states, fearing that anti-Semitism would grow dangerous without the Habsburg authorities to hold it in check. Other Austrians—Czechs, Poles, South Slavs—rejoiced in their newly declared national sovereignty and freedom from Habsburg domination, but Jews felt uncertain about the future. They not only worried about anti-Jewish persecution, but they felt anxiety about how they would reconstruct a national identity in states that now demanded that they adhere to the dominant national community even while anti-Semitic national leaders declared Jews unfit for membership in the national community. The old Austrian identity had fit the Jews so well. They could be Austrians politically, Germans (or Czechs or Poles) culturally, and remain Jews. The new states might not tolerate such a complex identity as they worked to construct their own national identities and to nationalize their populations. Jews of course understood that it would do them no good to go into permanent mourning for Habsburg Austria, and they declared their allegiance to the new states in which they lived. In most cases, though, it was very difficult for them to adopt the national identities of those states, and occasionally legally next to impossible. Jews responded to this crisis of national identity by insisting even more vigorously on their Jewish ethnic identity and by imagining that somehow the new states would be the functional equivalents of the old Monarchy.

In many ways the case of Czechoslovakia was the most interesting. The Czechs may have considered their new state to be a Czech nation-state, but in fact Czechoslovakia was a multinational state composed of Czechs, Slovaks, Germans, Magyars, Ukrainians, and Jews. Jews in Czechoslovakia ranged from the German-speaking or Czech-speaking Jews in Bohemia and Moravia, to the German- or Magyar-speaking Jews in Slovakia, to the Yiddish-speaking Jews in eastern Slovakia and Sub-Carpathian Rus.[47] In late 1918 and early 1919, the former Habsburg Austrian Jews among them (i.e., the Jews in Bohemia, Moravia, and Silesia), most of whom adhered to German culture, felt themselves in a quandary. They did not think that they were Czech, yet to maintain a German identity seemed problematic. They asserted their loyalty to the new regime, but they imagined this regime to be an improved version of the old multinational Monarchy, complete with a beloved, wise, and elderly ruler. Indeed, they had unbounded faith in Thomas Masaryk to neutralize the anti-Semitism of the Czech national movement and to create a tolerant and just society.[48] They hoped that in the new state they could somehow be Czechoslovak by political loyalty, German (or Czech or Magyar) by cultural affiliation, and Jewish all at the same time.

Interwar Czechoslovakia did, more or less, allow the Jews the luxury of this identity, although the new state preferred the Zionist solution, that is, loyalty to the state as members of the Jewish nation rather than as Germans or Czechs. Unlike most of the other successor states, Czechoslovakia allowed the Jews to register officially as members of the Jewish nation, and surprisingly large numbers of Jews did so, especially in Moravia, Silesia, Slovakia, and Sub-Carpathian Rus.[49] In the 1921 census, 54 percent of the 354,342 Jews in the Czechoslovak Republic declared Jewish nationality. In Bohemia, only 16 percent of the Jews registered as members of the Jewish nation, but 48 percent of the Jews in Moravia and 64 percent of the Jews in Silesia did so. At the same time, 50 percent of the Jews in Bohemia registered as "Czechoslovak" and 35 percent as German, while in Moravia/Silesia, 16 percent registered as "Czechoslovak" and 35 percent as German.[50] The political leaders of Czechoslovakia may have wanted Jews to register as Jews by national affiliation in order to dilute the number of Germans, but the Zionists too urged Jews to register as members of the Jewish nation because they had long espoused a Jewish national self-definition. Moreover, such registration allowed the Jews to declare their neutrality in the nationality conflict altogether.[51] The Zionist press regularly announced that a Jewish national identity best suited the Jews in Czechoslovakia. Such an identity allowed them to be loyal citizens of the state, staunch adherents of Czech or German culture, and energetic defenders of the Jewish people. The *Jüdische Volksstimme* in Brünn/Brno, for example, insisted that "only a strong, honorable, manly national politics can actually protect the interests of all Jewry." Professing membership in the Jewish nation allowed Jews to avoid the nationality conflict and assert their loyalty to the new state. Moreover, many believed that only by declaring a Jewish national identity could they overcome Czech resentment of Jews for their traditional affiliation with the Germans, and thereby cause anti-Semitism to subside.[52] Many non-Zionists agreed. Dr. Theodor Sonnenschein, the president of the Jewish community of Troppau/Opava, Silesia, firmly believed in the necessity of a Jewish national identity in Silesia. In nationally unified states, he argued, Jews had to identify with the dominant nation, but in mixed-language countries Jews had to declare themselves a separate nation "if they did not want to suffer the same fate as the Jews in Lemberg or Slovakia."[53]

Elsewhere in the territories of the former Monarchy the situation was far more complicated. In the rump state of *Deutschösterreich* (German Austria) Jews should in theory have experienced no problems. After all, Jews here, essentially the Jews of Vienna (and after 1922 those of the Burgenland as well), had long since adopted German culture. The problem was that Viennese Jews did not understand their Germanness in the same way as did other Germans. They were Viennese, Austrian, Jewish, but not necessarily members of the German *Volk,* a concept increasingly understood in racial terms in this period. At a time when nearly everyone in the Austrian Republic sought *Anschluss* with Germany, the Jews did not support such a move.[54] The Jews in German-Austria certainly professed their loyalty to the new state as well as their affiliation with German language and culture, but they could not bring themselves to adopt a German national identity that had the same meaning for them as it did for other Germans. The virulence of anti-Semitism in the new state did not make their task of adopting a German-Austrian national identity any easier. Although they did not view the new state as a reincarnation of old Austria, they nevertheless hoped that they could continue the old Austrian tripartite identity: loyal to the state and its culture, yet also functioning as a separate ethnic group. The new political logic dictated that they retain a German national identity, but in fact more Jews turned to Jewish ethnicity and even to Jewish nationalism than ever before. Zionists lobbied vigorously for the kind of national recognition that Jews sought all over Eastern Europe in this period, even though there was not the remotest chance of ever winning national rights. They hoped Austria would not be a real nation-state, and acted as if it would allow them the status of a separate nation.[55]

Non-Zionists too struggled with the issue of their identity and came to the conclusion that they were not Germans in the way German nationalists understood the term, but rather Jews, loyal citizens of German-Austria, committed to German culture. Although they eschewed Jewish nationalism and militant ethnicity, ordinary Jews in Vienna hoped that the new nation-state would tolerate their desire to separate the political, cultural, and national strands of their identity. The same Heinrich Schreiber, for example, who had eloquently mourned the passing of the Monarchy in the pages of the *Österreichische Wochenschrift,* could not bring himself to say that he was a German in the national sense. For him, Germanness remained cultural and Jewish identity primary. He concluded: "We are Jews, we are Austrians, and when that is too little we are German-Austrians, by birth and customs, education and culture, attitude and feeling."[56] Similarly, A. Schwadron insisted in the same newspaper in January 1919 that Jews were German, not in a *völkisch* sense but in a cultural one.[57] Jews did not form a separate nation, but they did belong to the Jewish people. A spokesman for the Austrian-Israelite Union likewise noted in the spring of 1919 that the Jews were not primarily a *Volk* but a religious community whose members shared the same ethnicity (*Stamm*) and blood.[58]

The German-speaking Jews of former Habsburg Austria persisted in the identity they had developed during the Monarchy because they felt comfortable with it even if it was not appropriate in the new political situation. They responded to the collapse of the Monarchy with the hope that somehow the new states would allow them to adhere to their old identities. Czechoslovakia did give the Jews the opportunity to recreate a new tripartite identity. Austria proved less hospitable, but Jews continued to adhere to their old formula for identity even if it no longer fit the new situation. This identity, which posited a political loyalty to Austria, an affinity for German culture, and a Jewish ethnic identity, may have been better suited to a multinational society than to a nation-state, but Austrian Jews clung to it because it best conformed to their traditionally held convictions.

Notes

1. *Ungarisches statistisches Jahrbuch,* vol. 19 (1911): 18–19; *Österreichische Statistik,* N.F., 1:1 (1912): 54*, 94–95. After the Compromise of 1867, which gave Hungary quasi-sovereignty, the Austrian half of the Dual Monarchy consisted of the Habsburg hereditary lands as well as Bohemia, Moravia, and Silesia, acquired in the sixteenth century, Galicia and Bukovina, acquired as a result of the partitions of Poland in the eighteenth century, plus Trieste, Istria, Gorizia-Gradisca, and the Dalmatian coast. Officially called "the kingdoms and provinces represented in the [Imperial] Parliament [in Vienna]," the non-Hungarian part of Austria-Hungary was colloquially called "Austria" or Cisleithanian Austria. This article will use the terms "Austria," "Habsburg Austria," or Cisleithanian Austria to refer to the non-Hungarian (or Austrian) half of the Dual Monarchy. To avoid confusion, this article will refer to the first Austrian Republic, formed after World War I largely from the Habsburg hereditary lands, either as German Austria (as it was known at first) or as the Austrian Republic.

2. For a full discussion of this tripartite identity, see Marsha L. Rozenblit, *Reconstructing a National Identity: The Jews of Habsburg Austria during World War I* (New York, 2001), 14–38. In the Hungarian half of the Monarchy, which fashioned itself a nation-state, most Jews identified with the dominant Magyar nation in all ways: culturally, politically, and nationally. The tripartite identity described here only applies to the Jews in multinational Habsburg Austria.

3. Robert S. Wistrich, *The Jews of Vienna in the Age of Franz Joseph* (Oxford, 1989), 175–181.

4. Charles Fenyvesi, *When the World Was Whole: Three Centuries of Memories* (New York, 1990), 112–115.

5. Joachim Schoenfeld, *Jewish Life in Galicia under the Austro-Hungarian Empire and in the Reborn Poland 1898–1919* (Hoboken, NJ, 1985), xix–xx.

6. For a full discussion of this phenomenon in Vienna, see Marsha L. Rozenblit, *The Jews of Vienna, 1867–1914: Assimilation and Identity* (Albany, 1983).

7. Rozenblit, *Reconstructing a National Identity*, 36–37; Rozenblit, *Jews of Vienna*, 161–174; Wistrich, *Jews of Vienna*, 347–493; Adolf Gaisbauer, *Davidstern und Doppeladler: Zionismus und jüdischer Nationalismus in Österreich, 1882–1918* (Vienna, 1988). For the Jewish national program, see Hermann Kadisch, *Jung-Juden und Jung-Oesterreich* (Vienna, 1912).

8. Franz Theodor Csokor, *November 3, 1918*, in *A Critical Edition and Translation of Franz Theodor Csokor's European Triology*, Katherine McHugh Lichliter, ed. (New York, 1995), 27–71.

9. See especially Anthony D. Smith, *Theories of Nationalism* (New York, 1971); idem, *The Ethnic Origins of Nations* (Oxford, 1986); idem, *Nationalism and Modernism: A Critical Survey of Recent Theories of Nations and Nationalism* (London, 1998); Ernest Gellner, *Nations and Nationalism* (Ithaca, NY, 1983); Rogers Brubaker, *Citizenship and Nationhood in France and Germany* (Cambridge, MA, 1992); Hans Kohn, *Nationalism: Its Meaning and History* (Princeton, NJ, 1955, 1965); and E.J. Hobsbawm, *Nations and Nationalism since 1780: Programme, Myth, Reality*, 2nd ed. (Cambridge, 1992).

10. *Österreichische Wochenschrift*, 31 July 1914, 529; 4 September 1914, 609; 30 October 1914, 740; *Monatschrift der Oesterreichisch-Israelitische Union*, July–August 1914, 1–2; *Jüdische Zeitung*, 31 July 1914, 1; *Jüdische Volksstimme*, 19 August 1914, 1.

11. See, for example, *Österreichische Wochenschrift*, 7 August 1914, 547–548; 14 August 1914, 561; *Jung Juda*, 21 August 1914, 213.

12. *Österreichische Wochenschrift*, 28 August 1914, 577–579.

13. *Österreichische Wochenshrift*, 21 May 1915, 381; 28 May 1915, 406; 25 June 1915, 469; 2 July 1915, 497; *Selbstwehr*, 7 May 1915, 1; *Jung Juda*, 25 June 1915, 177.

14. *Selbstwehr*, 25 June 1915, 1.

15. "Kriegstagebuch" of Sargent Teofil Reiss, Kriegsarchiv (hereinafter KA), B/1576:12; quotation on 22nd page of unpaginated manuscript.

16. *Österreichische Wochenschrift*, 14 December 1917, 781; 15 February 1918, 97.

17. "Kriegstagebuch," 81st to 86th page; quotation, 86.

18. *Österreichische Wochenschrift*, 14 August 1914, 562–563; 21 August 1914, 577–579; 28 August 1914, 593–595; 4 September 1914, 610–611; 18 September 1914, 640–643; 8 October 1914, 681–683; 16 October 1914, 697–699; 13 November 1914, 773–775; 20 November 1914, 793–795; 18 December 1914, 873–874.

19. *Selbstwehr*, 27 August 1914, 1–2, 6; 20 September 1914, 2.

20. See, for example, *Österreichische Wochenschrift*, 4 September 1914, 609–610; 18 December 1914, 891; 1 January 1915, 2–3; 12 March 1915, 200–201; 16 April 1915, 289–290, 301; *Jüdische Zeitung*, 11 December 1914, 1; *Selbstwehr*, 29 January 1915, 1–2; 12 February 1915, 1; 19 March 1915, 1; *Jüdische Volksstimme*, 29 March 1915, 3–4; *Zweimonats-Bericht … der … Bnai Brith*, vol. 18, no. 4 (1915), 114–117.

21. *Österreichische Wochenschrift*, 21 May 1915, 381.

22. *Jüdische Volksstimme*, 29 March 1915, 2.

23. See, for example, *Österreichische Wochenschrift*, 4 September 1914, 610; 25 December 1914, 895; 26 February 1915, 154; 5 March 1915, 173; *Jüdische Zeitung*, 19 March 1915, 2; *Jüdische Volksstimme*, 18 March 1915, 1; *Jüdisches Archiv*, no. 2/3 (August 1915), 1–3.

24. *Österreichische Wochenschrift*, 5 March 1915, 173.

25. Moritz Güdemann, "Aus meinem Leben," unpublished memoir, Leo Baeck Institute (NY) (hereinafter: LBI), diary entry, 4 August 1915, 232 (typescript version).

26. On the terrible plight of the refugees in Vienna, see Beatrix Hoffmann-Holter, *"Abreisend-machung": Jüdische Kriegsflüchlinge in Wien 1914 bis 1923* (Vienna, 1995). For the Monarchy as a whole, see *XLII. Jahresbericht der Israelitischen Allianz zu Wien erstattet an die XLII. ordentliche Generalversammlung am 17. Mai 1915* (Vienna, 1915), 16–19; and *XLIII. Jahresbericht der Israelitischen Allianz zu Wien erstattet an die XLIII. ordentliche Generalversammlung am 5. Juni 1916* (Vienna, 1916), 7, Central Archives for the History of the Jewish People, Jerusalem (hereinafter CAHJP), AW 2828/34, 2828/35.

27. Ibid. See also *XLIV. Jahresbericht der Israelitischen Allianz zu Wien erstattet an die XLIV. ordentliche Generalversammlung am 25. Juni 1917* (Vienna, 1917), 13–15, CAHJP, AW 2828/36; *XLV. Jahresbericht der Israelitischen Allianz zu Wien erstattet an die XLV. ordentliche Generalversammlung am 10. Juni 1918* (Vienna, 1918), 11–12, CAHJP, AW 2828/37; *Ein Jahr Flüchtlingsfürsorge der Frau Anitta Müller 1914–1915* (Vienna, n.d., but probably 1915), CAHJP, AW 2318; *Tätigkeitsbericht des Zentralbüros zum Schutze der galizischen Flüchlinge jüdischen Glaubensbekenntnisses in Brünn für die Zeit vom 15. Dezember 1914 bis 31. Oktober 1915* (Brünn, 1915). All of the Jewish newspapers regularly reported on the refugees and on the assistance extended to them. For a fuller discussion of these issues, see Rozenblit, *Reconstructing a National Identity*, ch. 3.

28. See, for example, *Österreichische Wochenschrift*, 16 February 1917, 106; 23 February 1917, 121; 2 March 1917, 136–137; 20 July 1917, 453–455, 467; 31 August 1917, 558; 14 September 1917, 582; 30 November 1917, 749–750; *Selbstwehr*, 16 February 1917, 1; 9 March 1917, 5; 16 March 1917, 5; *Jüdische Zeitung*, 23 February 1917, 1; 9 March 1917, 2; 31 August 1917, 5; 7 September 1917, 2; 5 September (sic: October) 1917, 1–2; 23 November 1917, 1–2; 14 December 1917, 3.

29. Erwin A. Schmidl, *Juden in der k. (u.) k. Armee 1788–1918, Studia Judaica Austriaca* 11 (1989), 5, 84.

30. In their diaries and memoirs, many Jews warmly described their experiences in the Habsburg army during World War I. See especially, "Kriegstagebuch" of Sargent Teofil Reiss, KA, B/1576; Adolf Mechner, "My Family Biography," unpublished memoir, LBI; Schoenfeld, *Jewish Life in Galicia.*

31. On the German military census of 1916, see Werner Angress, "The German Army's 'Judenzählung' of 1916. Genesis—Consequences—Significance," *Leo Baeck Institute Yearbook* 23 (1978): 117–137; Egmont Zechlin, *Die deutsche Politik und die Juden im ersten Weltkrieg* (Göttingen, 1969), 527–538; and Eva G. Reichmann, "Der Bewusstseinswandel der deutschen Juden," in *Deutsches Judentum in Krieg und Revolution, 1916–1923*, Werner Mosse and Arnold Paucker, eds. (Tübingen, 1971), 516–518.

32. Letter of k.k. Minister for Defense of the Fatherland to War Minister General Rudolf Stöger-Steiner, 6 September 1917, KA, KM Präs. 1917, 83-7/22; letters of Minister of War Baron Alexander Krobotin and army chief of staff Baron Franz Conrad to all units, KA, KM Präs. 1916, 34-17/3. On Jewish officers in the Habsburg army, see István Deák, *Beyond Nationalism: A Social and Political History of the Habsburg Officer Corps, 1848–1918* (New York, 1990).

33. Manès Sperber, *God's Water Carriers*, translated by Joachim Neugroschel (New York, 1987), 114.

34. Adolf Altmann, "Predigt gehalten bei den feierlichen Trauergottesdiensten anlässlich des Ablebens Sr. apostolischen Majestät des Kaisers und Königs Franz Joseph I. am 30. Nov. und 1. Dez. 1916 im israelitischen Tempel zu Meran und im israel. Soldatenbethause zu Bozen,"

special supplement to *Meraner Zeitung*, no. 276 (1 December 1916), CAHJP, Au 175/3. See also Güdemann, "Aus meinem Leben," 253; Schoenfeld, *Jewish Life in Galicia*, 158.

35. *Jüdische Zeitung*, 24 November 1916, 1; *Jüdische Volksstimme*, 22 December 1916, 3.

36. *Österreichische Wochenschrift*, 10 November 1916, 729–731; 5 January 1917, 1–2.

37. "Begrüssung des neuen Statthalters von Galizien Excellenz von Colard durch das Exekutivkomitee des österreichischen Zionisten," Jüdisches Kriegsarchiv, CAHJP, INV. 6526/1; memorandum of Austrian Zionists to the government, 25 June 1915, Central Zionist Archives, Jerusalem (hereinafter: CZA), Z3/843; *Jüdische Zeitung*, 16 November 1916, 1–2; 1 December 1916, 1; *Selbstwehr*, 10 November 1916, 1; 22 December 1916, 1; 9 February 1917, 4–5.

38. *Selbstwehr*, 10 November 1916, 1.

39. *Österreichische Wochenschrift*, 26 April 1918, 249; *Jüdische Korrespondent*, 25 April 1918, 2; *Jüdische Zeitung*, 26 April 1918, 1; *Selbstwehr*, 3 May 1918, 1; *Jüdische Volksstimme*, 3 May 1918, 2–3.

40. *Österreichische Wochenschrift*, 22 November 1918, 739–746; 29 November 1918, 756–757; 6 December 1918, 770, 772–774; *Jüdische Zeitung*, 15 November 1918, 1; 22 November 1918, 1–4; 29 November 1918, 1–4; 6 December 1918, 3–5; *Selbstwehr*, 29 November 1918, 1; 13 December 1918, 3.

41. Schoenfeld, *Jews of Galicia*, 201.

42. *Österreichische Wochenschrift*, 22 June 1917, 389–391.

43. *Österreichische Wochenschrift*, 19 July 1918, 441–442.

44. *Selbstwehr*, 23 November 1917, 4; see also, *Jüdische Zeitung*, 12 July 1918, 1; 26 July 1918, 1.

45. *Jüdische Zeitung*, 14 June 1918, 1.

46. *Österreichische Wochenschrift*, 25 October 1918, 673–675.

47. Ezra Mendelsohn, *The Jews of East Central Europe between the World Wars* (Bloomington, IN, 1983), 131–169.

48. *Selbstwehr*, 20 December 1918, 1; *Jüdische Volksstimme*, 28 March 1919, 3–4; Bertha Landre, "Durch's Sieb der Zeit gefallen. Jedes Menschenleben ist ein Roman," unpublished memoir, LBI, 119; J. Nina Lieberman, "Lost and Found: A Life," unpublished memoir, LBI, 23.

49. Hillel J. Kieval, *The Making of Czech Jewry: National Conflict and Jewish Society in Bohemia, 1870–1918* (New York, 1988), 191; Idem, "Masaryk and Czech Jewry: The Ambiguities of Friendship," in *T.G. Masaryk (1850–1937)*, vol. I, *Thinker and Politician*, edited by Stanley B. Winters (New York, 1990), 317; and Aharon Moshe Rabinowicz, "The Jewish Minority," in *The Jews of Czechoslovakia*, vol. 1 (Philadelphia, 1968), 155–265, which reproduces many of the relevant texts.

50. Franz Friedmann, *Einige Zahlen über die tschechoslovakischen Juden (Ein Beitrag zur Soziologie der Judenheit)* (Prague, 1933), 23; Mendelsohn, *Jews of East Central Europe*, 146.

51. For an interesting description of Zionist identity in the Czechoslovak context, see Max Brod, "Juden, Deutsche, Tschechen: Ein menschlich-politische Betrachtung," *Im Kampf um das Judentum* (Berlin, 1920), 7–36. See also *Selbstwehr*, 15 November 1918, 2.

52. *Jüdische Volksstimme*, 22 November 1918, 2; 1 January 1919, 5.

53. *Österreichische Wochenschrift*, 13 December 1918, 785–786.

54. See, for example, Erna Segal, "You Shall Never Forget" (text German), unpublished memoir, LBI, 28.

55. For Zionist demands, see Denkschrift, 4 November 1918, CZA, Z3/214; letter of Austrian Zionists to government of Deutschösterreich, 4 November 1918, CZA, L6/366; *Jüdische Zeitung*, 15 November 1918, 1–2. Austrian Zionists persisted in making these demands throughout the First Republic. See *Wiener Morgenzeitung*, a daily newspaper published from 1919 on by Robert Stricker, the leader of the Austrian Zionists in the interwar period.

56. *Österreichische Wochenschrift*, 25 October 1918, 673–675.

57. *Österreichische Wochenschrift*, 24 January 1919, 55–56.

58. *Monatschrift der Oesterreichisch-Israelitische Union*, vol. 31, nos. 2–4 (February–April 1919), 4.

Chapter 11

"Christian Europe" and National Identity in Interwar Hungary

Paul Hanebrink

Gyula Szekfű, the doyen of interwar Hungarian historians, began his classic survey of modern Hungarian history, *Three Generations and What Came Afterward*, with an explanation of the several calamities that had befallen Hungary in the aftermath of World War I. Writing in 1920, Szekfű took as his point of departure the revolutions of 1918–1919 that had followed the collapse of the Habsburg Monarchy, as well as the country's dismemberment in the postwar peace talks. In the preface, Szekfű presented these catastrophes as a consequence of Hungary's prewar political development, claiming: "everyone must agree that the recent liberal past was an age of deviation, from which we can only raise ourselves with organized work, and through the building of true national traditions."[1] To rebuild their country from the postwar wreckage, Szekfű argued, Hungarians had to do more than simply reject Béla Kun's short-lived 1919 Bolshevik regime or express their outrage at the partition of Hungary's historic lands. National redemption required a thorough rejection of the liberal political traditions that had dominated public life in the decades before the war. Szekfű devoted much of this historical essay to describing the "true national traditions" that had existed in Hungary before the advent of liberalism, writing Hungarian history as a slow decline away from these original values. In his book, the historian identified an antinational "Jewish spirit" as one important cause of this cultural decline, suggesting that a return to the political course envisioned by Hungary's pre-1848 conservative reformers could correct many of the ills that had arisen from Hungary's disastrous path into modern age. The implications were clear, and many in Hungary's political elite drew them: Remaking or reestablishing Hungary as a Christian nation could be therapeutic, correcting distortions in Hungarian society and restoring Hungary to a more "natural" path of development. Christian Hungary, in short, represented an alternate and better modernity.

This belief presumed that the yardsticks by which Hungarians could measure the modernity of their nation existed outside, in Europe at large. Christian Hungary, if it meant anything, had to exist within a wider notion of Christian Europe. But what did Christianity mean in this context? Catholic and Protestant Christianity both had deep historic roots in Hungarian society, and their adherents had very different understandings of how their religion had shaped national society. Religious leaders from both confessions maintained that their churches would be critical to the nation's reconstruction. Other Hungarian political leaders talked of Christian Hungary and Christian Europe, while resisting the idea that these phrases should give any particular license to religious leaders to lead the country. Thus, the notion of "Christian civilization" had several meanings within the political and intellectual debates of interwar Hungary.

There were, of course, some who rejected their nation's Christian heritage in their zeal to restore Hungary to a former glory. These radicals sought answers in the shadows of the pre-Christian past, idolizing tribal chieftains and their heroic exploits as the essence of what it meant to be Hungarian.[2] Still, for much of the 1920s and 1930s, most of Hungary's political elite steered clear of these pagan fantasies, judging them to be too radical and too isolationist in tone to be of much use to the nation's policymakers. Instead, political leaders loudly proclaimed their policies to be both "Christian" and "national," invoking their nation's Christian history at every opportunity. One of the most significant among them was the longtime Minister of Religion and Education, Count Kunó Klebelsberg.

Klebelsberg, who led the Ministry of Religion and Education for most of the 1920s, indefatigably championed a dizzying array of cultural and educational initiatives, most notably in the areas of school and curriculum reform. His success was due in large part to his ability to "sell" his policies as part of a program, which he called "neo-nationalism," designed to return Hungary to a level and direction of social progress that seemed typical of Western Europe. The minister claimed as much in the frequent submissions he made to the League of Nations defending Hungary's numerus clausus law, a law enacted in 1920 to limit the number of Jewish students enrolled in institutions of higher learning. This law, he declared in answer to Hungary's international critics, was necessary as a temporary measure "derived from our extraordinary situation, which can be set aside as soon as our social and economic life again returns to its normal course."[3] Like Gyula Szekfű, Minister Klebelsberg also saw Hungary's recent past as an "age of deviation," a period in which a supposedly "normal" course of national development had become derailed and replaced by a set of social transformations with consequences much more dire for Hungary.[4] At issue for both men was, of course, the presence or absence of a "native" middle class, a class of entrepreneurs, professionals, and burghers that naturally assumed political leadership in a modern nation. Such a middle class had formed organically, that is, from within the native population, in countries like France or England, and had been at the forefront of political and economic changes that had come to seem exemplary to the rest of Europe, and indeed the world. In Hungary, by contrast, there had been no "native" middle class. Historical circumstances, which Gyula Szekfű had described in detail, had contrived to confine "native" Hungarians either within the peasantry or within the gentry nobility, leaving it to newly (and insufficiently) assimilated Jews to perform the functions proper to a middle class. Without a truly "national" non-Jewish (or "Christian") middle class, Hungary lost and would continue to lose its way into modernity. Minister Klebelsberg conceived all his cultural policies in light of this diagnosis.

At the same time, invoking "Christian civilization" also allowed Klebelsberg to claim "cultural superiority" for Hungary within the Carpathian Basin, a central tenet in interwar irredentist politics. As in other Eastern European societies, Hungarians traditionally understood the historical presence of the Ottoman Empire and of the Islamic faith that it represented as a cultural force at odds with the political and cultural influences coming from the Christian West. Christianity typically represented the advanced West in opposition to the non-Christian and "backward" East. Hungary, Klebelsberg claimed, stood precariously on the border between the two, a claim he repeated often to underscore the urgency of his policies. In one 1927 article he wrote: "Just as we were an outpost in the battles against Turkish barbarism in the past, so too today, we who fight on the eastern border of Europe for the cultural supremacy of the Hungarian nation, want to remain among the ranks of advance-outpost nations, but now on intellectual grounds as well."[5] In the interwar period, Klebelsberg built upon this traditional dichotomy between West and East, and between civilization and barbarism, transforming it into the justification of a cultural policy compelling to most Hungarians. To regain their accustomed place within the Carpathian Basin, and within a wider modern (symbolically Christian) Europe, Hungarians would have to undertake specific political initiatives. If they did not, they would irrevocably consign Hungary to the ranks of the backward nations beyond the pale of European civilization, and irredeemably relinquish her right to lead all the peoples who lived in the historical Crownlands of St. Stephen.

Klebelsberg, it should be mentioned, was a Catholic, and by all accounts a devout one. Yet Christian culture, as he conceived it, clearly had little to do with religion. Instead, Christianity stood as a symbol for a nation that "met" the standards of European modernity and that conformed to certain sociological models of a "normal" society. To be sure, the Christian Churches had an important role to play in restoring Hungarian society to health. Parochial schools, in particular, figured prominently in Klebelsberg's plans to combat the spread of a destructive "Jewish spirit" among Hungary's youth. But Klebelsberg made it very clear to Hungary's Christian leaders that he expected their confessional interests to take a back seat to his national policies. Speaking before the annual Catholic Conference in 1927, the minister advised the Churches to voluntarily subordinate themselves to the national interest: "every Church, without waiting for the intervention of the State or of other Churches, should itself silence any screeching voices of aggressiveness in its own camp."[6] His message was clear: Christian-nationalism did not give either Church the license to pursue its own confessional agenda.

Klebelsberg's admonitions were directed above all towards a young generation of Catholic activists eager to link the redemption of Christian Hungary to the fortunes of a reinvigorated Catholic Church. This group of Church leaders took satisfaction in the knowledge that their church had aggressively defined an anti-national "Jewish spirit" already in the 1890s, and had consistently opposed true "Christian Hungarian" values to it ever since. The Catholic Church had, after all, continually described the dire consequences to the nation of extending complete civic equality to Hungary's Jews. In 1920, one prominent Jesuit publicist could thus maintain in a book revealingly titled *The Rebuilding of Hungary and Christianity,* "Catholicism is the strongest fortress of the Christian faith and morality ... and has contributed the most value in the foundation of the country's moral powers."[7] In the bracing first days of the counterrevolution, Catholic activists dreamt of exercising this moral leadership once more, hoping to instill in the nation's schools, media, indeed its whole public life, a new spirit of Christian and nationalist community. Catholic journals buzzed with plans for the "rechristianization" of "sinful" Budapest and of the nation as a whole, encompassing elements as diverse as expanding the Catholic press and organizing the laity within civil society. One bishop's remarks in his diary reveal the scale of this ambition: "we know ... that only we [i.e., the Catholic Church] can ensure pure morality. On this depends the state, society, ... order, discipline, and happiness."[8]

Such zeal ran counter to the national interest as it had been defined by government ministers like Kunó Klebelsberg, and the regime made its displeasure known. Even Admiral Miklós Horthy, the Regent himself, writing in a letter to the Cardinal Prince-Primate of Hungary, warned of "partisanship" stoking the "fires of confessional discord, ... intensifying the lack of unity in a Hungarian society already excessively disrupted, and, with this, disturbing the work of consolidation of a Christian national foundation."[9] Under this pressure, Hungary's Catholic hierarchy soon saw the wisdom in adopting a kind of nationalist ecumenism in public. Within a few years, Hungary's Cardinal Prince-Primate had placed the Church firmly on the side of public order and national unity, even at the sacrifice of some confessional zeal. In this spirit, Hungary's higher clergy frequently appeared with their Protestant counterparts in festive, government-sponsored displays of Christian-national unity. When questioned about this by Vatican officials, the Cardinal frankly confessed that the Church simply had to strike a "modus vivendi" within the political constraints of interwar Hungary.[10]

Still, the Christianity in Christian Hungary could not be reduced so easily to an anodyne expression of national unity. Despite his many personal contacts with conservative government officials, Gyula Szekfű, for example, again and again tried to give substance to the Christian legacy on which, he claimed, Hungary's political culture rested. In all his historical writings, he was particularly concerned to identify the long continuities in Hungarian history that linked foundational events in the Middle Ages to the present and revealed the liberal era to be an aberration. As he developed his interpretation, Szekfű came to place ever greater weight on the Counter-Reformation and the Catholic restoration in the Habsburg lands as the critical link between medieval European civilization and modern Christian Hungarian culture. In the multivolume history of Hungary he wrote together with Bálint Hóman, Szekfű put it this way: "[A]s the waves of Reformation and Counter-Reformation flooded medieval Hungary one after the other, these waves again stopped at the eastern borders: again Hungary was Europe's furthermost border region ... The religious movement thus again proved that Hungary was a territory of Europe, even more its outermost region, beyond which there was no more European culture nor European development."[11] Szekfű himself tried to present this argument as unpolemically as he could, taking care to acknowledge the real achievements of Reformation-era Protestants in Hungary. Yet Counter-Reformation necessarily accompanied Reformation in his conception. It was not difficult to infer from Szekfű's writings that if the Catholic restoration had failed in Hungary, then Hungarian society might well have slipped beyond the pale of European civilization.

It was thus ultimately as a Catholic state, or at least a state in which Catholicism was predominant, that Hungary would fulfill its historical mission as the border guard of Europe. Catholicism also seemed to guarantee the integrity of Hungary's traditional state borders more effectively. In another section of the same series, Szekfű noted how important medieval accounts of the Kingdom of Hungary as a land dedicated to the Virgin Mary (the Regnum Marianum) were to Hungarians during the period of Turkish occupation. "Old Hungarian memories and impressions of the miseries of the Turkish campaigns, refreshed daily, together produced the historical philosophy of the Regnum Marianum, which alongside its Catholic character, postulated an integral Great Hungary led back to its old borders, under the leadership of the crowned king and his ancient patron, the Virgin of the Hungarians."[12] To be sure, Szekfű was a careful historian, and his interpretation is clearly situated in his discussion of sixteenth and seventeenth century Hungary, when the state was divided into a zone of Turkish occupation, a region under Habsburg rule, and an autonomous Transylvania that existed uneasily between those two great powers. Yet the parallels with interwar Hungary, when the Crownlands of St. Stephen were again divided between several different powers, were not difficult to see. In effect, his history linked national fortunes to the endurance of the Hungarian state and made Catholicism the essential spiritual tie between the two. Catholicism supported the integrity of the Hungarian state as established by St. Stephen in the Middle Ages. At the same time, it linked Hungary to a civilized European culture, but one that was implicitly Catholic in its Christianity. In Szekfű's treatment, then, Christian civilization began to acquire real content.

Catholic clergy were, of course, only too happy to embrace these conclusions. Activists in Catholic Action often recalled the work of their Counter-Reformation era forebears in erasing the legacy of Turkish occupation from the Hungarian landscape and in reviving forms of cultural expression after 150 years of foreign rule. As evidence, they adduced, among other things, the many churches and chapels dotting the Hungarian landscape, many of which dated from these years of Habsburg restoration and Catholic Counter-Reformation. Such a claim had implications in the present day, since Catholics explicitly connected their past efforts in combating heresy to their present efforts to defend Hungary from political radicalism generally and atheist Bolshevism particularly. As one speaker at the closing session of the 1936 Hungarian Catholic Congress put it: "As the Church justifiably [and] with proud self-confidence remembers how powerfully it did its share long ago in the work of restoring our country, we must not forget that a new occupation [hódoltság—the word generally used to describe the period of Turkish rule] burdens us."[13] Such statements recalled those made by Catholic leaders in the immediate postrevolutionary period. Ultimately, Catholics continued to maintain, the restoration of Christian Hungary depended on the enduring strengths of the Catholic Church.

As the radical right increasingly interpreted "Christian" as a racial category in the late 1930s, religious and lay conservatives alike turned to this essentially Catholic understanding of Christian Europe. The admonition offered by Eugenio Pacelli (soon to become Pope Pius XII) at the 1938 Eucharistic Congress is emblematic. Pacelli spoke passionately about the "invincible courage of the Hungarian armies" that defended Christian civilization against the "proud Crescent" of Islam. Their deeds might inspire the present generation to "defend the [Catholic] Church and Christian civilization against the leaders of religious negation and of social revolution by opposing them, as did Hungary of the seventeenth century 'acies ordinata,' a united front resolved that no force should break it...."[14] Christianity and Christian Hungary could thus stand for social order in the face of fascism and of course Communism, even as it stood for the nation's modernity.

Protestants naturally rejected much of the substance of this vision, even if they were just as keen as their Catholic rivals to preserve social order. Instead, they argued vigorously that their confession could shape the country's moral renewal just as well as Catholicism could. Hungary's Calvinists were the most energetic in reshaping their church to fit the new "Christian-national" course. This took some doing. The links between Hungary's liberal political elite and Protestantism had remained strong throughout the nineteenth century. Moreover, Calvinist demands for religious toleration for their own faith inspired many to favor it for Hungary's Jews as well.[15] After 1918, this liberal legacy became a burden. To cast it off, Hungary's Calvinist leaders published a torrent of articles drawing distinctions between real Protestant liberalism and the false libertinism of the Dualist Era. More significantly, the Reformed Church elevated new figures to positions of public prominence. In 1921, the Church elected László Ravasz to be the bishop of the church district that included Budapest. A rising star in the Church, Ravasz had stirred controversy with a number of essays on Hungary's "Jewish question," all sharply anti-Semitic in tone. In the tumultuous climate of the early 1920s, such a record made him an ideal figure to lead the Church.[16] As the election drew near, flyers circulated among those Church members who could vote touting his opinions on the Jewish question as proof that he could lead their Church at a time when Catholics seemed intent on a "second Counter-Reformation."[17] One theologian wrote to Ravasz to persuade him to take the job: "We have need here ... of every Christian and Protestant support. The Christian course is mainly a Roman Catholic course."[18] Ravasz became bishop in 1921. With him at its head, Hungary's Reformed Church could be an effective player in the politics of Christian nationalism.

Hungary's Calvinist theologians insisted that their faith, more so even than other Protestant denominations in Hungary, could offer Hungary a vision of society as all-embracing as that proclaimed by Catholics like the Bishop of Székesfehérvár, Ottokár Prohászka. Jenő Sebestyén, a theologian at the Ráday seminary in Budapest, led this effort. Christianity, he wrote, had relevance for "social, national, and state life;" only Calvinism and Roman Catholicism, as two equally comprehensive "worldviews," offered the ethical values and the broad perspective on which a modern society must rest.[19] But Calvinism, he and his fellow Church leaders claimed, was a more appropriate base for Christian-nationalist politics than was Catholicism. In part, Calvinists looked to history to justify this view, citing their Church's long anti-Habsburg opposition as proof of their nationalist zeal. Calvinists also relied on demographic facts. Both before and after the war, the Catholic Church in Hungary was a multiethnic institution; the Calvinist Church, by contrast, was almost 98 percent ethnic Magyar.[20] Both of these facts, Calvinists believed, made Calvinism the only truly "Magyar religion," a mantle Sebestyén claimed in 1920 when outlining his version of a Christian-national program in his newly founded journal *Calvinist Review.* He wrote: "For us, this sad fact is the most important. ... Hungary was broken, and Calvinism was paralyzed, and with this, and by this, and on account of this the Hungarian nation was also ruined.... [T]his connection has always and will always exist, since Calvinism has always gripped the Hungarian soul with overwhelming force and has steeled the social force and powers of spiritual resistance of the Hungarian nation."[21] Calvinism, to Sebestyén, presented a kind of third, and more national, option in the titanic battle between liberalism and Christianity. If the former had led Hungary to ruin, the latter threatened to drown the Hungarian nation in its universal vision of a Christian Europe. Sebestyén could accept neither. Only Calvinism had the scope and force to redeem Hungary's distorted modernization and set the state on a "Christian-national course" while still preserving the uniqueness of Hungarian culture. The result would be the road into a better Hungarian modernity.

In this spirit, Calvinist intellectuals deeply resented the historical connections that Gyula Szekfű had made between the fortunes of Catholicism and the spread of European civilization in Hungary. Indeed, historians with close ties to the Hungarian Calvinist Church blasted Szekfű throughout the interwar period for writing "revisionist" history that, so they felt, defamed the nationalist legacy of prominent Reformation-era, Protestant national leaders. The reaction in Protestant quarters to Szekfű's biography of the Calvinist Prince Gábor Bethlen was typical. Bethlen had ruled as Prince in Transylvania from 1613–1629, a time in which much of Hungary was controlled by the Ottomans or the Habsburg dynasty. However, the Ottoman Sultan had granted Transylvania autonomous status, allowing Bethlen a great deal of latitude to defend the nation's interests as he understood them. Under Bethlen, Transylvania soon became an important cultural and political center of Protestantism in Europe, and a bitter rival to the Catholic Habsburg Monarchy. Because of all this, nineteenth century liberal, often Protestant, historians revered Bethlen as an ardent defender of the national cause. Szekfű, however, placed Bethlen in a broader social, diplomatic, and economic context, reducing his subject from an icon of national unity to just one of several political actors (Catholic, Protestant, and Ottoman) striving for mastery of a complex political situation. To his outraged Calvinist critics, Szekfű seemed too willing to find common interests between Bethlen and the Ottoman Turks who controlled much of Hungary at this time. As one irate Calvinist historian put it, "According to Szekfű, ... Bethlen was an instrument of Turkish interests!"[22] Calvinists took this argument for an accusation. They bitterly resented the idea that they might have contributed to the de-Christianization of Hungary, and thus to Hungary's estrangement from the civilized West, by cozying up to the infidel.

In response to this charge, Protestants emphasized the role of their Church in mediating Western culture to rest of the Magyar nation. In part, they looked back to the itinerant preachers who had played such an important role during the Reformation in spreading Protestantism—as well as a Gospel translated into the Hungarian language—to a receptive national community. However, there were also more recent evaluations of the place of Hungary's Protestant clergy in national society. For example, one turn-of-the-century novel extremely popular in Protestant circles entitled *The Silenced Bells* by Viktor Rákosi presented the Hungarian reading public with a Calvinist preacher who receives an excellent seminary education in Utrecht, Holland, but who, compelled by a sense of responsibility for his people, returns to a remote village in Transylvania where he attempts to be shepherd to a flock teetering on the edge of ethnic extinction. The novel ends tragically; the final scene has the pastor dying on the steps of his church as the last Magyars in the village go to take communion in the Romanian Orthodox Church. Still, the image of a Protestant pastor, learned in the intellectual traditions of Western Europe, yet ever willing to serve his ethnic national community, was tremendously suggestive.[23] Dezső Szabó, to take another example, took up this theme in an essay he wrote in 1926 on the "Contemporary Problems of Hungarian Protestantism."[24] He too assigned a mediating role to Hungary's Protestant clergy, seeing them as a caste of native intellectual leaders who could adapt the cultural influences of the West to the particular needs of Hungarian society. Indeed, it was precisely because they had ceased to perform this function that Hungary's modernization had gone off course in the liberal era in the late nineteenth century. In Szabó's mind, Hungary's organic intelligentsia, for whom the Protestant clergy were emblematic, had to reclaim this leading and mediating function and bring populist social reforms to their ethnonational community. Hungary's Protestant, and especially its Calvinist, clergy embraced this self-perception enthusiastically. In a country where much of the official pomp and circumstance, such as the annual celebrations of St. Stephen's Day as a national holiday, seemed to elevate the Catholic Church above the other Christian confessions, Calvinist pastors were especially keen to hold up an alternate vision of Christian Hungary, one in which they shouldered the greatest burden in bringing social and cultural progress to the most impoverished of Hungarian villages. Reformed Church leaders saw this link between Protestantism and the country's modernization most clearly in the rural education movement that began in and around Calvinist seminaries like the one in Sárospatak and then developed in the late 1930s and early 1940s into a national movement. Indeed, one Calvinist leader active in this movement, Kálmán Újszászy, drew out this thesis explicitly: "the peasant entering civil society (a polgárosodó paraszt), the modernization of Hungary: this was the main path ... with which we identified. So a Hungary whose basic foundation was the educated citizen-peasant, unromanticized. [T]his was ... the world of the Protestant peasantry in the rural towns."[25] In the same interview, Újszászy also recalled that the "village seminars" and adult education classes with which Protestant leaders tried to educate this class of Hungary's peasants attracted students from within and from outside Trianon Hungary. Protestantism thus suggested a vision of Christian Hungary every bit as expansive as that proposed by Klebelsberg and Szekfű, a vision that looked with just as much fervor across the borders to the other Magyar communities outside Hungary. Yet this version of Christian civilization placed much less emphasis on the Hungarian state as the essential link to a wider Europe, and much more on hopes for an educated and cultured ethnic nation. It was, in short, a kind of "third way" into modernity.

There were then several ways of thinking about Christian Hungarian and Christian European culture in the interwar period. All of them presumed that Hungary needed to recapture a proper or "normal" path to modernity, a road it had strayed from during the liberal era and the postwar revolutions. As a result, all could agree that embracing the culture of "Christian Europe" would lead to a solution of Hungary's "Jewish question," though of course the methods with which Hungarians might best do this was a hotly debated and ultimately fateful issue. Moreover, all could agree that Hungary's ties to a wider Christian Europe, however construed, gave the nation a right to hegemony in all the lands of pre-Trianon Hungary. There was less agreement, however, on how these ties actually bound. To some, like Kunó Klebelsberg, Christianity seemed a secular code word for modernity, authorizing reformist, but always conservative, cultural policies. But not all were so ready to empty Christian Europe of religious content. Indeed, it was precisely because figures like Gyula Szekfű or Kálmán Újszászy insisted on the specifically Protestant or Catholic substance of Christian Hungary that Christianity held such power as a symbol. In the hands of the Catholic episcopate or of sympathetic conservatives, Christian Hungary suggested a stable social order and a state firmly bound to other Christian European states through ties of culture 1,000 years old. To Protestant churchmen, but also to oppositional intellectuals who may not have been personally very devout, Christian Hungary suggested an ethnic nation tied to European civilization not by the state or an oligarchic elite, but by a progressive set of nationally-minded intellectuals. Thus even as Hungarians came to similar conclusions about their nation's place in a civilized and modern West, they could still envision very different versions of their own national identity within that wider Christian Europe.

Notes

1. Gyula Szekfű, *Három Nemzedék és ami utána következik* (Budapest, 1989), 6.
2. Gyula Szekfű discusses the attempts to ground Hungarian national identity on this pagan past—he calls these efforts "phantasms"—in *Három Nemzedék,* 479–486. See, more generally, Katalin Sinkó, "Árpád versus Saint István. Competing Heroes and Competing Interests in the Figurative Representation of Hungarian History," in Tamás Hofer (ed.), *Hungarians between "East" and "West." Three Essays on National Myths and Symbols* (Budapest, 1994).
3. Országos Levéltár (OL): K305 1922-16-6; "Klebelsberg Kunó gróf előterjesztése a numerus claususról a Nemzetek Szövetségének."
4. For a sympathetic appraisal of Klebelsberg's policies, see József Huszti, *Klebelsberg Kunó életműve* (Budapest, 1942).
5. "Előörs-nemzetek és elmaradt népek," *Pesti Napló,* 3 July 1927; reproduced in Kunó Klebelsberg, *Neonacionalizmus* (Budapest, 1928), 48.
6. "A katolikus nagygyűlés előtt," *Nemzeti Újság,* 9 October 1927; reproduced in Klebelsberg, *Neonacionalizmus,* 83.
7. Béla Bangha, *Magyarország újjáépítése és a kereszténység* (Budapest, 1920), 151.
8. Ottokár Prohászka, *Naplójegyzetek III. (1919–1927),* Zoltán Frenyó and Ferenc Szabó SJ, eds. (Szeged-Székesfehérvár, 1997), diary entry, 7 July 1919, 31.
9. Regent Miklós Horthy to Cardinal János Csernoch, 3 November 1921, Esztergomi Prímási Levéltár (EPL): Cat. B: 3511/1921.
10. Mrs. Iván Dévényi, "Csernoch János tevékénysége az ellenforradalmi rendszer első éveiben," *Századok,* issue 1 (1977), 71–72.
11. Gyula Szekfű, *Magyar Történet. A tizenhatodik század,* vol. 4 (Budapest, 1935–1936), 232.
12. Gyula Szekfű. *Magyar Történet. A tizenhetedik század,* vol. 5 (Budapest, 1935–1936), 292–293.
13. "Vargha László a falu elhagyatottságáról," *Nemzeti Újság,* 7 October 1936.
14. *Album Congressus XXXIVi Eucharistici Internationalis* (Budapest, 1938), 135.
15. See Friedrich Gottas, "Die Geschichte des Protestantismus in der Habsburgermonarchie," in Adam Wandruszka and Peter Urbanitsch, eds., *Die Habsburgermonarchie, 1848–1918,* vol. IV, Die Konfessionen (Vienna, 1985), esp. 536–541.
16. There is no scholarly biography of László Ravasz. For his memoirs, see László Ravasz, *Emlékezéseim* (Budapest, 1992).
17. Ráday Levéltár (RL): A/1.C. 1921: Az 1921-es püspökválasztással kapcsolatos levelek, nyomtatott cikkek.
18. Aladár Szilassy to László Ravasz, 8 March 1920, RL: C./141, Papers of László Ravasz, Correspondance, doboz 15.
19. Jenő Sebestyén, "Kálvinista politika," *Kálvinista Szemle,* 8 December 1923, 1.
20. Julianne Brandt, "Protestantismus und Gesellschaft im dualistischen Ungarn," *Südostforschungen* 55 (1996): 179–240. For confessional statistics, see 229.

21. Jenő Sebestyén, "Programm…," *Kálvinista Szemle*, 4 April 1920, 1–2.
22. István Rugonfalvi Kiss, "Szekfű Gyula: Bethlen Gábor," *Protestáns Szemle*, vol. 38 (1929), 128.
23. Viktor Rákosi, *Elnémult harangok*, vol. 1 of *Rákosi Viktor munkái* (Budapest, 1903).
24. Dezső Szabó, *A magyar protestantizmus problémái* (Budapest, 1926).
25. "'A szociográfusi szemlélettel el lehet jutni a legmesszebb, csak a csúcsra nem!' Huszár Tibor beszélgetése Újszászy Kálmánnal," *Újszászy Kálmán emlékkönyv* (Budapest-Sárospatak 1996), 41.

Chapter 12

JUST WHAT IS HUNGARIAN?

Concepts of National Identity in the Hungarian Film Industry,
1931–1944[1]

David Frey

Al Jolson's *The Singing Fool* premiered in Budapest in September 1929. The first sound film to play in Hungarian theaters, it sparked what eventually became a sea change in Hungarian thinking about the nature of film. For the Hungarian film establishment—a self-identified class consisting of Hungary's film professionals, cultural critics, and government officials—it soon became doctrine that the state must necessarily foster a "national" film industry. This film industry, they believed, would first develop a characteristically "national" film product, which would eventually lead to a cohesive national film aesthetic. These film elites mobilized highly charged, symbolic language in their discussions of the potential of Hungarian sound cinema. Some framed their support of sound film production in terms of a life-or-death struggle for Hungarian culture. Foreign film, they warned, besieged more than the Hungarian language, the core of the culture. It threatened Hungarian thought, Hungarian spirit, and even Hungarian political sovereignty.[2] It placed Hungary's rightful cultural standing in Europe at risk. A segment of Hungary's political and cultural vanguard saw a developed film industry and a lively film culture as signifiers, separating Hungary from the "wastelands" of the Balkans and linking it firmly to the modern Western world.[3] Film, the quintessential mass medium, thus became emblematic of Hungary's desire to prove its modernity to the West. At the same time, early Hungarian sound film also served as a barometer, a measure of Hungary's confused perceptions of itself.

The production of sound film offered new possibilities for displaying Hungary's unique "ethnological colors and external forms."[4] Some of the nation's leaders even believed the creation of sound film to be a mandate, a means of promoting a broader cultural renaissance.[5] But what, precisely, did it mean for a film to be Hungarian? Although the rhetoric of "national" and "Hungarian" became pervasive in the 1930s, few contemporaries gave real substantive thought to what the terms meant. Thus the words became potent rhetorical vessels, filled and re-filled according to whatever was politically expedient.

This article, covering the 1930s and early 1940s, investigates a few of the ways different constituencies within the Hungarian film establishment attempted to define what was Hungarian and determine how film should portray Hungarian national identity. The definitions proposed ranged from the vacuously abstract to the simplistically specific, and naturally changed over time. As Hungary's social and political situation evolved, as internationalism in the motion picture community came under attack, and as Hungary's geopolitical situation changed, the cinematic representations of Hungary also evolved, along with notions of what were legitimate Hungarian national cultural products and forms. Populist philosophies, racial nationalism, and its handmaiden, anti-Semitism, eventually came to permeate all discussions of Hungarian cultural production. Debates over the essence of Hungarian culture and national identity—what it was, who could produce it, and how best to promote it—revealed deep contradictions in Hungarian politics and society, some of which remained unsolved even beyond the conclusion of the war. Questions of "national film" and a national film style became interrogations of the nature and viability of Hungarian capitalist modernity.[6]

Act 1, Take 1: If It Sells, Then It's Hungarian

Hungary had a rich creative tradition in silent film, one that the after-effects of World War I, particularly the new Hungarian state's geopolitical isolation and its domestic political and economic troubles, effectively destroyed. Many of Hungary's top film professionals, such as Alexander Korda and Michael Curtiz, emigrated. By the late 1920s, even lesser-knowns had fled or joined the ranks of the unemployed, and most indigenous film businesses had collapsed. As a result, the broad conceptions of "national film" that emerged in cinema circles in 1930 and 1931 were rather simple. As Hungary's nascent sound film industry slogged precariously through the early Depression years, its exasperated supporters hoped they could jump-start domestic production by arguing that any motion picture that projected the "Hungarian spirit" [*magyar szellem*] or utilized Hungarian language and music was a national film. While most agreed these films needed to be made by Hungarians, economic realities meant that Hungarian capital was unlikely to be behind the efforts and that in some cases, it was even acceptable for a "Hungarian" film to be made outside Hungary. This rhetoric changed in April 1931, when Trade Minister János Bud celebrated the opening of the Hunnia studio, Hungary's first sound film studio. Bud concluded that only with the capacity to make talkies could the foundation be laid for the creation of a true Hungarian product. According to Bud: "Should Hungarian capital work in the studio, Hungarian workers and intellectuals earn their bread there, Hungarian art triumph there, and Hungarian public opinion support its creative results, Hungarian [national] film production will come into being."[7] This truism established the early parameters for what most of Hungary's elites meant when they invoked the terms Hungarian and national: a product in the Hungarian language, made by Hungarian citizens, watched by Hungarian audiences. In fact this basic, rather unsophisticated notion of Hungarian film remained a fundamental industry-wide premise from the time of Bud's speech through the end of 1944, when Hungarian feature film production ceased.

As time passed, the institutions of distribution and exhibition gained durability, and sound filmmaking developed some momentum, Hungary's film elites slowly began to venture beyond the puerile concept of a national product to the more nuanced matter of what should constitute a Hungarian national style or genre. In other words, Hungary's film establishment now wished to do more than make movies in the Hungarian language and provide jobs for Hungarians. Its leading figures wished to make identifiable pictures, which, whether by convention or content, would reveal the uncommonness of the Hungarian people. In early 1932, István Székely, the director of the first Hungarian sound smash, *Hyppolit the Butler* [*Hyppolit a lakáj*], addressed this issue in Hungary's official film trade journal, *Film Culture* [*Filmkultura*]. In contrast to Trade Minister Bud, Székely, who learned his craft in Weimar Berlin, did not believe that film professionals determined whether or not a film was Hungarian. A film made by a well-trained foreign crew and/or a famous international director could be just as Hungarian, just as national, as a film made by Hungarians in Hungary so long as its source material, though not necessarily its language, was Hungarian. Székely proposed that comedy, although successful, was based on a simple, largely foreign-influenced formula. The second stage of Hungarian film production should be to create films that transcended comedy and were designed to succeed abroad, especially in Germany. Hungarian filmmaking must move beyond military slapstick and its stable of stock characters: aristocrats, mythologized Hungarian horsemen and farmers, and gypsy musicians. The future, preached Székely, was in operettas, criminal mysteries, and melodramas based on themes selected from Hungarian literature and classical theater.[8]

While Székely and others would soon produce scores of movies according to this formula, another school of thought was winning adherents in official quarters. In December 1933, Hungary's Interior Minister József Széll and Germany's Reichsminister Joseph Goebbels exchanged letters discussing the matter of national culture. Even as large constituencies in the Hungarian film world protested against German racial nationalism, Széll declared that outside of Germany, only Hungary understood the necessity of fostering its film industry from a "national point of view." To chase internationalism is false, wrote the Interior Minister. "Film must suit each *Volk*, and each *Volk*'s film must assume a characteristic place in the market." Hungary, he declared, would film only that which could be designated a cultural product of Hungary.[9] Naturally, Széll never defined what constituted these cultural products, assuming, as many of his contemporaries did, that Hungarian culture was *sui generis*. One knew it when one saw it, and it most certainly was not the consumerist urban operetta championed by István Székely.

The emerging splits concerning the nature of the national film became more clearly demarcated when Béla Kempelen, a rightist Hungarian cultural critic, provided some of the substantive definition Széll failed to offer in late 1933. In an article in *Film Life* [*Film Élet*], Kempelen commented on the need for an indigenous industry to produce Hungarian subject films in order to prevent the degradation of Hungarian culture. Kempelen's concept of Hungarianness shared many commonalities with other nativist and religious reactions to sound film occurring around the globe in the 1930s. Hungarian films, he proposed, ought to draw from "our homeland's history, the pearls of Hungarian literature, the more beautiful of the legends of medieval Hungary, Hungarian folk traditions, etc." This would distinguish Hungarian film from the detective dramas, love stories, and the majority of modern [foreign] films. These film types, which Székely only two years earlier had argued were the future of Hungarian film production, were labeled threatening, foreign, and "distant from the spirit of the Hungarian people" by Kempelen.

> [They] only raise the viewers' level of excitement to the point of depravity, of moral destruction, of causing crime, of poisoning, of inciting addiction, of comparing serious ambitions to the possibility of easy success, of leading to fantasies, of inciting risky [adventurous] decisions and of distracting processes of thought.... [Hungarian film] should be enjoyable, scientific, educational, and informative; the Hungarian past should be reflected in it; it should teach about noble decisions, virtues, the fulfillment of obligations, honor, [and] kindness. Enjoyment is possible, indeed amusement as well, but adventure and crime should not be brought to the screen ... morality should triumph ... and radiate back to the Hungarian spirit.[10]

Numerous voices in the film establishment chimed in with similar opinions, beseeching Hungarian filmmakers to find their sources in the gems of Hungarian literature and Hungarian history, not in the universal, cosmopolitan forms mobilizing slapstick, class difference, crime, and questionable morality. Thus, even before the nation had sent its first twenty sound films from the editing room, the front lines had formed, separating those who wished to see an exportable, modern, cosmopolitan vision from those who preferred a traditional, autochthonous, morally-instructive notion of Hungary.

As Hungary's film industry developed the capability to produce independently, the attack against international, generic cinematic forms gained adherents, especially among officials. Only a few months after Kempelen's manifesto, Sándor Jeszenszky, an advisor to the Minister of Cults and Education and from 1933 on one of the top-ranking members of the National Film Censorship Committee, echoed many of Kempelen's sentiments. In the lead article of the April 1934 issue of *Film Culture,* Hungary's authoritative film trade journal in the 1930s, Jeszenszky expressed the government's point of view. He suggested that while pursuit of international audiences might be a laudable goal, it should not be the Hungarian film community's primary objective. The moving picture, explained Jeszenszky, had the potential to play a substantial role in the building of Hungary's national culture. Film was "an excellent tool ... for bringing into existence a uniform world of feelings and thought, a singular national taste [able to] penetrate the entire society." This was a task not to be taken lightly, as low-quality film production could ruin the undeveloped tastes of the majority and cause film to fail to fulfill its "cultural mission." In order properly to complete its mission, film, like other arts, must "always [be] nationalist." It must provide the average person, the crowds, with "familiarity"; its subjects must be "their lives, their problems." Features must not wantonly pursue internationalism, instructed Jeszenszky, as this would divert attention from the nation's own experience toward a totally foreign world. If the innocent minds of the Hungarian theatergoing masses became more familiar with the lives of American gangsters and the sugared lives of Berlin salesgirls than with their own culture, it would be a disaster. Hungarian audiences would lose touch with their own lives and thoughts, as well as their distinctive brand of Hungarian happiness, which Jeszenszky believed was culturally determined. To combat this danger, prescribed Jeszenszky, Hungary needed to create a nationalist masterpiece that would "win international acclaim *on the strength of its national spirit*" and "Hungarian mentality." This was not merely a rhetorical argument made by a small nation, nor a middling monetary question, insisted Jeszenszky. Rather, it was "one of the life and death questions for Hungarian culture."[11]

So, by the mid-1930s, many in government and private industry concurred: film must be national. Film establishment figures described Hungarian film production as a calling, a faith-based art form whose importance went beyond entertainment and matters of profit. Given the country's truncated condition, wrote Henrik Castiglione, the film industry's statistical guru, filmmaking in Hungary could never become a substantial factor in the economy. "Hungarian film," he wrote, "is an instrument of the nation, for which there is not and cannot be a program; rather it must be a religion, a spiritual integration into the future."[12]

This, then, was the rhetoric. Along with painting, sculpture, theater, radio, and the industrial arts, cinema became enshrined as one of the pillars of the national culture. As such, film had the patriotic obligation to serve and unify the nation. From a practical perspective, the concern was how this goal could be accomplished without first determining what comprised the Hungarian nation. Through the 1930s, some segments of Hungary's film and political elites, with progressively more force, asserted that some distinct Hungarian morality, spirit, history, and set of customs did exist. With increasing vociferousness, they insisted that it was crucial for these ideas to be imparted to the moviegoing public, especially as film became more popular among workers and peasants.

This didactic message, coming at a time when populism and racial nationalism were on the rise, was slow to trickle down. Despite all of the calls for national films grounded in Hungarian uniqueness, both the largely Jewish filmmaking vanguard and the consumers of their products, Hungarian audiences, were slow to recognize their duties as patriots and populists. Most motion picture makers from this period did not concern themselves with the day-to-day affairs of "average" Hungarians. Rather, the top-grossing Hungarian films of the early and mid-1930s, such as *Hyppolit, The Dream Car [Meseautó], Salary, 200 a Month [Havi 200 fix], 120 Kilometers an Hour [120-as Tempó], Anniversary [Évforduló],* and *Hotel Sunrise [Hotel Kikelet]* presented the liberal, cosmopolitan, consumption-oriented middle class of Budapest as the symbol of modern Hungary. Progress, liberation, and cars were often mutually reinforcing Leitmotifs. The heroine of Béla Gaál's 1934 film, *The Dream Car,* for example, was a middle-class clerk in a Budapest company who became enamored with the most technologically advanced car available in the world while her boss became enamored with her. *Salary, 200 a Month,* a 1936 film directed by Béla Balogh, also foregrounded cars and Budapest. It told a story of how a job at a car factory in Pest made marriage possible for a poor country couple. In László Kardos's 1937 hit *120 Kilometers an Hour,* a thoroughly modern banker's daughter moved through life with speed and daring, courtesy of her automobile. In the end, of course, she was lassoed and domesticated, marrying an up-and-coming young man whom she accidentally tapped with her car. Other popular films of the period featured the lives of doctors, lawyers, office workers, hotel owners, and bankers; the dancing and singing of urbane sophisticates in formal gowns and tuxedos; and the morality of those with the flexibility to marry either above or below their class.

Largely the creative efforts of Hungarian Jews trained abroad, and based on Hollywood and Weimar German models, these films drew increasing fire over the course of the later 1930s. These movies featured bourgeois values and luxury, technological and economic advance, and urban Budapest. Alluring as it was, this type of glamorization, denigrated by opponents as the "Judeo-capitalist" model of filmmaking, fell out of favor among certain audiences and segments of officialdom, particularly as nationalism, populism, and anti-Semitism flourished. The decline of this film type was also hastened as moviegoing became a more regular pastime for the lower middle classes and as the Hungarian sound film business progressed to the point where its basic survival was no longer a question. Rejecting the liberal, middle-class vision of life, well-regarded Hungarian intellectuals and lesser ones alike cast about in search of the "true" national identity. Conservative and far-right thinkers, many with links to populist organs, now took sides in the battle to control the cinematic representations of Hungary. They campaigned for the creation of positive, peasant-oriented symbols and narratives of Hungarianness as alternatives to the vision of modernity widely associated with Hungary's urban Jews. The debate over these symbols and narratives, which the historian/sociologist Miklós Lackó has termed the fight over "national characterology" *[nemzetkarakterológia],* became much more heated in the second half of the 1930s, as the din of populism became louder.[13]

Most of these debates about the national character took place on the pages of newspapers, magazines, and books. While their political impact is hard to gauge, the effect of the debates on film is not. As Hungary as a nation embraced a backwards-looking, pastoralist vision of the future, the makers of its most modern, most technically-advanced, most capitalistic form of culture, the moving picture, responded to the broader social trends. Beginning in the mid-1930s, cinematic visions of the upper middle class began to change. On screen, the urban middle classes went from heroes to scapegoats, from representative of what was Hungarian to emblems of foreign exploitation. Capitalism, Liberalism, and city life all took on greater tarnish, as did the dramas associated with them. As early as 1935, parliamentarians had begun clamoring for more films that would inform Budapest audiences about rural Hungarian lives, customs, and dances the way the famed turn-of-the-century actress Lujza Blaha had done on stage.[14] Conversely, few members of parliament showed any interest in returning the favor and providing rural audiences with glimpses of middle-class Budapest life. What Hungary's audiences needed, particularly its rural audiences, wrote the theater owner János Füki, were films rooted in the fertile soil of Hungarian literature and Hungarian history. It was not possible for theater owners in the countryside "to manage [on a diet] of 'hypermodern' films" because true Hungarians could not relate to foreign stories about the lives, loves, and adventures of the urban middle class.[15] The middle class, and by inference the creations of István Székely, Béla Gaál, and the group of Jewish directors who were responsible for nearly every Hungarian sound picture made up to that point, stood outside the "Hungarian spirit."

More radical and discontented individuals in the film industry now began to look at Hungary's own products with a more critical eye, some with vigor and some with great reluctance. Those with populist or anti-Semitic leanings criticized the predictability and staleness of Hungarian cinema. They lashed out at the industry's failure to produce a characteristically national product. In its quest for "moderate, uniform success" it has resorted to a handful of staples, wrote the film journalist András Komor, which when lumped together amounts to little more than kitsch. He scathingly continued:

> ... in every film we find an elegant jobless engineer; there is always a stupid peasant; always gypsified gentry; and [the famed comedic actor] Gyula Kabos always has to fall into water. This is why, in every film, the storyline is forced in the ugliest way. There is always one scene where we hear jokes we have heard repeated hundreds of times. This is why there are no good Hungarian films.[16]

In direct response to this sort of sentiment and to the growing popularity of mass political movements such as fascism, populism, and socialism in mid-1930s Hungary, the film industry, with explicit government support, sought to expand the national imaginary. Filmmakers, nearly all of them foreign-trained but not Jewish, began to mobilize more potent and inclusive national images. Beginning in the middle and late 1930s, novel and diverse representations of the lower middle class and working masses, especially the peasant masses, reached Hungarian screens in small numbers.[17] Producers made pictures that portrayed the masses not only as part of the Hungarian nation, but as its essence. Likewise, they appropriated folk customs and images with abandon. Films about life on the Hungarian plain, best represented by Georg Höllering's 1936 film *Hortobágy*, and films about the everyday travails of fishermen on the river Tisza such as Géza von Bolváry's 1938 film *Flower of the Tisza [Tiszavirág]* characterized this trend.

Critical comment from the late 1930s indicates that, with the exception of these and a handful of other films, most attempts to translate peasant populism into screenplay form were unsuccessful. Rather than actually develop a new national style based on some empowering populist vision, Hungarian filmmakers frequently defaulted to stock imagery. They resorted to recycling the recognizable landscapes, folk costumes, and regal aristocratic characters that had filled the closets of Hungarian directors since the silent era. They combined trite notions of peasant life with predictable outcomes in tired, operetta-like forms. Theodore Adorno has since explained that this phenomenon was entirely foreseeable. "No homeland," writes Adorno, "can survive being processed by the films which celebrate it, and which thereby turn the unique character on which it thrives into interchangeable sameness."[18]

In an article written in 1939, the critic Sándor Eckhardt explained why he, like Adorno later, believed that this typecasting was a transnational rather than a national problem. He argued that the monotony of characters and stories in Hungarian film stemmed from the fact that foreign countries needed to envision Hungary as exotic while they pursued their own nation-building programs.[19] It was for this reason, wrote Eckhardt, that international film audiences so readily consumed certain representations of Hungary: the idealized Hungarian *Puszta* cowboy, the fabulous culture and society of the nineteenth-century Hungarian aristocracy, and the enchanting Hungarian gypsy girl and her music. The world's moviegoers needed to see these images in imported Hungarian products as well as in their own films to better understand who they were not. This inflated sense of importance prevented Eckhardt from fully acknowledging that it was for this same reason that Hungarian audiences also welcomed these portraits, Hungarian producers continued to churn them out, and Hungarian censors heartily approved of them. Images of cultural distinction declared the singularity of Hungarian culture and thus its value, even if that singularity took the form of highly recognizable stereotypes. These portrayals sold tickets, which even through the 1940s remained the objective for most of the key players in the movie industry.

Act 1, Take 2: Get Those Jews Out of Here and Let's Get Serious

In the midst of this reiteration of static concepts of Hungarian identity there were increasingly vocal calls for variety, change, and for movement away from the market-based orientation of the film industry. The comments of Eckhardt,

Komor, and others were symptomatic of a nation in the late 1930s and early 1940s that had decided to overhaul its culture. The film establishment now rejected the homogenization that Adorno and Eckhardt identified, but it had not reached any agreement defining what Hungary's new, unique character and culture should be. The only agreement was that filmmakers should replace all the old styles and forms and that Hungary's distinctiveness might become manifest if its movies took up more weighty themes.[20] As a result, Hungary's motion picture business bumbled through trysts with realist social problem films and historical films in a series of failed attempts to capture and identify one set of experiences as representative of an elusive, and perhaps non-existent, national difference.

From the late 1930s on, film professionals and critics proclaimed that Hungarian audiences were now "mature enough" to see films whose subject matter was serious, films that dealt with the reality of Hungarian life, and not just "hot puszta csárdás" films.[21] This paternalist call for realism coincided with the movement to purge Jews from the film industry, and was often a rhetorical cover for anti-Semitism. Implicit in the push for realism was that Hungarianness was at its core Christian, and thus could not be accessed, or accurately portrayed in film, by Jews.

Hungarian anti-Semites drew from the Nazi example in the mid-1930s and began to promote the idea that for a film to be Hungarian, all of its important cast members and crew must be Christian Hungarians. Hungarian film journalists, themselves often Jewish, occasionally spoke out against this rising tide. Anyone who asserts that a film "is not Hungarian because its writer, director, producer, or stars are not Christian" wrote the editors of the *Hungarian Film Courier [Magyar Filmkurir]* in the summer of 1937, "deeply wounds Hungary's culture and its economic interests" and obviously had learned nothing from the German example.[22] But by 1938, these protestations were for naught, as ideology, at least at the administrative level, triumphed over economic rationality. That August, Hungary created a Film Chamber based on the Nazi *Reichsfilmkammer* model and entrusted it with the mission of Christianizing an industry densely populated by Jews. The authorities made membership in the Chamber mandatory. By vetting the religion of all employed in the business, Film Chamber leaders hoped radically to reduce the number of Jews from what was majority status in nearly all crucial industry sectors to a maximum of 6 percent of the profession by 1943. They also believed that this step would alter the nature of the film industry, ridding it of its cutthroat capitalist character and bequeathing it a more communal, national spirit.

The purge of Jews from the motion picture business was part of a larger attempt at social engineering, an effort drastically to restrict the participation of Jews in Hungarian society.[23] The purge also served as one prong in a two-pronged offensive to change the essence of Hungarian film. The second prong sought to alter the Hungarian film style, to rid it of its shallowness and its reliance on Jewish "lemonade comedies." Over the years, the most commonly prescribed antidote for the "Jewish germ" was to apply a salve of real Hungarian subjects culled from Hungarian literature and history.[24] In the late 1930s and early 1940s, for the first time, filmmakers and critics came up with specifics, something more than just rehashing the works of Ferenc Molnár, Sándor Hunyady, Frigyes Karinthy, Kálmán Mikszáth, Mór Jókai, and other celebrated Hungarian authors. Commentators suggested historical "hero" films: fawning biographical portraits of figures from the Hungarian national pantheon or idealizations of individual careers.[25] "Nations are built upon the shoulders of their great men," suggested Mihály Fetter on the pages of the new official trade magazine, *Hungarian Film* [*Magyar Film*], in August 1939. Rather than every film having a young lady in love with the company director, Hungarian films should tell stories about "scientists and scholars [*tudósok*], statesmen [*államférfiak*], and great men [*nagy emberek*]."[26] Only by making somber, reverential paeans to Hungarian historical and cultural figures and their achievements could Hungary's filmmaking elites insure that Hungarian citizens were properly informed about the "real Hungary." The central figures of the mid-1930s' commercially successful films, company directors, after all, did not build nations; they built fortunes off the backs of the people.

Another suggestion, perhaps the most frequently voiced in the early 1940s, was to make so-called "social problem" films. This genre included movies about "Hungarian life" or supposedly fact-based "stories of the people," films about the everyday experiences and travails of regular Hungarians.[27] A 1942 book entitled *This is How Hungarian Film Is Made,* by the producer and director János Dáloky, encapsulated the prevailing right-of-center thought about the need for realist problem films. Introduced and endorsed by the most powerful figure in Hungarian film at the time, the president of the National Film Committee Baron Gyula Wlassics, Jr., the text trucked out all the obligatory phrases. It denounced the "frivolous, empty, platitude-filled, stupid joke-filled [Hungarian] films prepared according to speculative business calculations of sensuality," clear references to the capitalist modernity many Hungarians blamed on the Jews. Hungary had a historic opportunity, wrote Dáloky, since the "artistic, ethical, and productive cleansing" and "renewal" of Hungarian life, to create a legitimate national film style. Hungarian film, he continued, must be true to Hungary's "national-political interests." It must be realistic, exhibiting both the "happy and traditional" side of life as well as the "growing problems associated with the Hungarian land, Hungarian race, and Hungarian workers." What Hungarian audiences clamored for, claimed Dáloky, were films that were Hungarian-made and had Hungarian content—not the false cosmopolitan content of the 1930s, but films showing the "singular, unsophisticated, and natural Hungarian," the everyday Hungarian who both "laughs and cries."[28]

World War II–era Hungary should have been the ideal time and place for a national film style to emerge. It was a period where racist and nationalist sentiment ran higher than ever before. It was a place where legislative restrictions on the definition of who belonged to the nation, in the form of a series of anti-Jewish laws, were the strictest they had been in the twentieth century. The war and German actions had relieved Hungary of motion picture competition from the United

States, Great Britain, Poland, Czechoslovakia, Austria, and, for a time, France. There was an upwelling of support in the film industry to follow an explicitly integral national course of development and to produce an accompanying national style.

Certainly, there is evidence that the trend toward more "serious" film, more movies with populist themes, and more state-inspired "persuasive" pictures was palpable, and it did change the face of Hungarian film. Hero films showing people of peasant origin gaining access to and acceptance in aristocratic ruling circles, such as *István Bors* [*Bors István*] and *Dr. István Kovács* [*Dr. Kovács István*], were blockbusters. Pictures featuring "regular" men, lower middle-class heroes who vanquished exploitative and unpatriotic capitalists such as *The Thirtieth* [*A Harmincadik*], *Black Diamonds* [*Fekete Gyémántok*], *Andrew* [*András*], and *Changing of the Guard* [*Őrségváltás*] also numbered among the most successful and honored films of the wartime period. Pictures about the Hungarian past such as *The Song of Rákóczi* [*Rákóczi Nótája*] and *Devil Rider* [*Ördöglovas*] won huge audiences. As the war radically altered the geopolitical context and Hungary's borders changed, films idealizing the organic link of Magyardom to Transylvania via its peasant national culture and its history, including *Bence Uz* [*Uz Bence*], *Silenced Bells* [*Elnémult harangok*], *People on the High Mountains* [*Emberek a havason*], and *One Night in Transylvania* [*Egy éjszaka Erdélyben*], gained critical acclaim and box office success.

But by and large, these films were exceptions. Many were problematic because either they were too costly, or they espoused themes that government officials, upon later reflection, determined were too democratic or socially inflammatory. Hungary was no closer to developing a clear national style in 1944 than it had been in 1939. As Hungary purged itself of the largely Jewish, internationally-trained core of filmmakers who had been responsible for nearly all of its pre-1939 production, moviemaking increasingly fell into the laps of inexperienced producers and directors. These men and women resorted to techniques born of the silent era and reborn in the German *Heimat* style: the repetitive showing of recognizable landscapes, locales, and historical sites. The Hungarians naturally added their own twists, stuffing films with peasant costumes, aristocratic pomp, feudal authority figures, dashing insolvent military heroes, and gentry values— the same stereotypical characters and themes to which audiences had become accustomed before the age of sound. Ironically, though understandably, the neophyte Christian film professionals plagiarized plots and stole genres from the Jews they supplanted. In some cases, the new Christian filmmaking vanguard of the early 1940s merely substituted characters, replacing urban middle-class figures that had been the focus of the "cosmopolitan" films of the mid-1930s with captivating naïfs from the villages. Instead of featuring known Jewish stars and the clerks, offices, and fast-paced life of Budapest, Christian actors and "the world of pretty young ladies from the country took possession of the screen."[29]

In his study of the motion pictures of this era, the historian István Nemeskürty concluded that stylistically few of the so-called "Christian national" features challenged the conventions of the 1930s, and, as a result, a new, durable Hungarian film form never materialized. For example, Nemeskürty determined that the "commonplace comedy" remained the dominant Hungarian film genre, accounting for 90 of the 227 films made between 1939 and 1944.[30] There were few of the so-called "serious" films that addressed the problems of the day, and most of those that did, did so in stark, simple terms. Historical and "great man" movies were even fewer in number and lesser in quality. There is no doubt that many of the films manufactured during the war were nationalistic, meaning that they promoted nationalist feeling. They were not, however, national, meaning different in form and content and representing some sort of coherent aesthetic and culture distinct from that of other national groups.

This unsuccessful attempt to put some form of elite-sanctioned national culture on celluloid was a direct consequence of Hungary's failure to come to grips with the nature of the most modern mass medium. Hungary's political elite, caught between the desire to "teach the nation how to become itself" while maintaining a vibrant, profitable film industry, could not decide on a course of action.[31] As a result, Hungary's leaders did not consolidate the national film industry under government control. Nor did they effectively loose the shackles on the industry, allowing market and creative forces to operate freely. During the war, for example, the government created new layers of bureaucracy involved in motion picture industry product regulation and creation, rather than streamlining existing ones. Yet it left these new ministries and chambers either short of funds or without real power, hampering their activities from the outset. Still another example of the haphazard course charted by the state involved professional preparation. In 1939, the state closed all film schools, because they had been run by individuals of Jewish origin. It neglected to open any replacement schools to train the new generation of Christian filmmakers until 1944. This essentially guaranteed that the industry had to rely on a black market of seasoned Jewish professionals, which in turn helped account for the lack of progress toward the goal of an innovative Hungarian national cinema form.[32]

Rather than choose a clear course of action, the state instead adopted symbolic and practically useless reforms such as Hungarianizing all movie theater names (Budapest's "City" theater became the "Szittya," for example) and the universal terms filmmakers used (mandating the use of the Hungarian *vágó* rather than the English editor/cutter).[33] It pursued strategies designed to maximize export potential, succumbing to the pressure to produce films based on a stock of stereotypes. This approach satisfied almost no one. When Hungary's film officials did take tentative steps towards promoting a national film style, their contradictory imperatives often torpedoed their own programs. István Antal, the Minister of National Security and Propaganda, admitted as much in late 1942, when he asserted that the government's own film politics undermined its goal of realizing an organic national style. The government's distaste for capitalism and cartels led it to disperse film licenses to a broad range of filmmakers. The unintended consequence, noted Antal, was unwanted garbage. "Today basically every other film is made by one or another independent business concern. This fact in and of itself should explain ... [why] an excessive number of films ... are cultivated, superficial works of entertainment, flourishing only in their fashions, written based on the newest trends. This [practice] must stop ... "[34] Pál Kolozs, in a March 1943 article in the government-financed culture magazine *Hungarian Muse [Magyar Múzsa]*, agreed with Antal. He lamented the fact that Hungarian filmmakers still had not succeeded in creating a legitimate film style rooted in the "national character." He attributed this failure to a film industry addicted to profit-making that fed its audiences a diet of the "most worthless, most indistinctive hodge-podge" hoping that the moviegoer would just "get" the charm of the national character.[35] Like Antal, he blamed the new, small moviemaking companies' orientation towards survival, not national edification.

Bureaucratic shortcomings and the desire to project Hungarian culture abroad were just the tip of the iceberg crushing the development of a specialized Hungarian film style. The most important impediments blocking the emergence of a Hungarian national form were the political contradictions embedded in Hungarian society. The divisions between urban and rural, middle-class and worker, gentry and peasant were so problematic that in order not to offend, films had to be made in a classless "vacuum" with "heroes who did not belong to a profession."[36] So great were fears of the masses, of democracy, and of radical anti-Semitism in upper officialdom, and rightly so, that they cut short the film industry's flirtation with the most promising national film style, the social problem film. In fact, after filmmakers released a handful of social problem films in 1942, Hungary's pre-production censorship board and the government-appointed head of the state-owned film studio conspired to stymie the creation of any more such films.[37] Hungary's government bureaucrats had come face-to-face with a dilemma the literary critic Homi Bhabha would describe some forty-five years later. Bhabha suggested that in the process of declaring the supremacy of a particular cultural vision, the credibility of those asserting that supremacy is simultaneously undermined. When groups enunciate cultural difference, he adds, they generally do so by appealing to intrinsically clashing justifications. On the one hand, "new cultural demands, meanings, strategies in the political present" are what prompt declarations of cultural supremacy.[38] On the other, these claims rest on notions of eternal certitude tied to tradition and ancient community, notions that culture is impervious to change. This contradiction—change versus the absence of it—was exactly that which bedeviled Hungary's motion picture elites. Afraid of undermining their own claims to authority, Hungary's government film officials could not bring themselves assertively to endorse any new type of national cultural form. Mired in war and threatened by radical politics, once they saw that their own films could empower the discontented masses, Hungarian authorities lost faith that their audiences had the maturity to digest the truth about themselves without questioning the social order.

The experiment with the historical drama, the other film type moviemakers and cultural commentators believed might lead toward a national style, was similarly truncated. This category of films, which consisted of "great man" movies, pictures featuring the exploits of Hungary's lesser heroes of the past, and features about seminal events in Hungarian history, was sunk by a profound lack of imagination and capital. The assumptions behind these films were that while Hungarian audiences would naturally be attracted to their own history, foreign audiences would have far less interest unless the stories were enhanced. This enhancement meant, at least in the case of the great man experiments, enormous casts, elaborate costumes, and fantastic scenery. For Hungary to wade into the genre of historical films, therefore, it had to be willing to invest unprecedented sums of money. And since capital was still in short supply due to the restrictions placed on Jewish activities in the film industry, not to mention the financial drag of the war, big-money productions were out of the question in the early 1940s.

This changed in late 1942, when the state signaled a willingness to underwrite such an endeavor. In the first months of 1943, employees of the state-owned Hunnia film studio, in cooperation with the National Film Committee and the Propaganda Ministry, developed outlines for a great man film series. Initially, they conceived of three major historical films, focusing on a few of the founding fathers of modern Hungary: Prince Ferenc Rákóczi, Count István Széchenyi, and Louis Kossuth. The first project to be undertaken was a massive historical costume drama about the rebellion of Prince Rákóczi of Transylvania against Habsburg rule in the early 1700s. Using a superstructure of romance girded by music, the film's wartime purpose was to put "Hungarian freedom, Hungarian communal feeling *[közösségi érzés]*, [and] Hungarian fighting spirit and love of country" on display.[39] *The Song of Rákóczi* was to be a Hungarian *Madame du Barry* meets *Dr. Robert Koch*.

In many ways, *The Song of Rákóczi* was the Hungarian *du Barry*. Similarly to *du Barry*, the costs of making *Rákóczi* were enormous, more than doubling those of the most expensive Hungarian movie made prior to 1943. Thus, despite being one of the most successful box-office smashes Hungary ever produced, the film was a colossal failure, costing its backers, the state-owned Hunnia studio and the Propaganda Ministry, over 300,000 *pengő*.[40] Even before the release of *The Song of Rákóczi*, naysayers were predicting that its genre would be stillborn. They explained that the structural obstacles that had prevented Hungary from producing historical costume dramas in the past had not disappeared. Hungary simply could not risk losing 2–300,000 *pengő* on every film it made, argued *Hungarian Film* editor Géza Matolay, who months earlier had advocated the same dramas. Hungarian historical films, he added with sadness, could not expect to recoup losses in sales abroad. Hungarian historical subjects were unknown elsewhere in Europe and there was no real market for them.[41] János Vaszary, a well-regarded director and screenwriter, was even more candid. Before *The Song of Rákóczi* debuted, he pronounced the historical genre dead. "The time of Hungarian history films," Vaszary correctly foretold, "has passed."[42]

The age of the Hungarian historical film was over before it began, consigned by Hungary's film elites to the dustbin alongside the Hungarian social problem film. With these failures, Hungarian film ironically became, by some accounts, *less* national. The historian István Nemeskürty explained the phenomenon.

> The majority of the wartime directors ... were ignorant of the very primary rules of the profession, and easily confused by any intricate story ... [This and the fact that they were terrified by war led] Hungarian film production ... [to take] refuge in the remotest past of film history in its search for stories and inspiration....[43]

Despite Nemeskürty's disparaging of the content, quality, and complexity of Hungarian wartime features, it would be unfair to blame film producers alone for the banality and shoddiness of the period. Hungary's filmmakers were constrained by shortages of raw film and by crippling limits on their expenditures and studio time. They were restricted by two distinct layers of official censorship—preproduction and postproduction—as well as meddling by the Propaganda Ministry and extensive self-censorship, all of which severely limited the range of potential topics they could address. They may also have been hamstrung, or guided, by what they believed Hungarian audiences desired. Despite all protests to the contrary, Hungarian producers had little choice but to make their films primarily for the Hungarian market.

What Hungarian moviegoers wanted was exactly that which cinema patrons the world over wanted, especially during the war: a chance to be entertained and to retreat into a world of fantasy. Some wanted hero films, others did not. Some wanted films about people resembling themselves, others had no desire to relive their day-to-day experiences in the confines of a theater. Most simply wanted a few hours of escape. Eighty percent of Hungarian movies, perhaps more since the war had begun, concluded with a happy ending, estimated the editor of the trade weekly *Theater News* [*Mozi Ujság*], Mrs. István Szentpály. This was true not only because Hungarian films sought to imitate American ones, but because Hungarian audiences demanded it be so.[44] "More comedy, light, etc. films will have to be produced to replace the propaganda or serious-theme films," remarked Nándor Jenes after his return from Italy in November 1942.[45] Whether you make serious films or comedy, wrote a crass cinema owner in Nagyvárad [Oradea], "make sure you make them with women."[46] A 1943 survey of cinemagoers by the Propaganda Ministry revealed that the majority of those polled wanted to see things they were not being offered (only 18 percent answered that they were content with the present selection). However, when asked what specific type of movie they would like to see more frequently, only 2.5 percent of the respondents felt Hungary needed more historical films. Less than 4 percent felt more films about the everyday life of the common man should be produced. Yet nearly 12 percent believed Hungary needed more comedies, although comedies were already the most common genre appearing on Hungarian screens.[47] A random survey of cinema owners conducted by a *Hungarian Film* writer in September 1944 turned up similar results. When asked what his audiences wanted, a Budapest cinema manager answered bluntly, "Give us Hungarian comedies!"[48] These surveys appear to reveal that for the average moviegoer, the syrup of the bittersweet "Judeo-capitalist" farce was perhaps not so awful a tonic after all.

In this context, Hungary's retreat from the problem film and the historical film is more understandable. Not only did Hungary's government film authorities shy away from endorsing a unified national ideal, Hungarian audiences did not want it. By 1943, some higher-ups in the Hungarian film world suggested giving up the search for a national style, or at least admitting that Hungarian national film might be better off if it were less identifiably national. In an interview with the editor of *Theater News,* the highly respected János Vaszary remarked: "I don't believe Hungarian culture should exist in-and-of itself, being only useful domestically. Thus, it would do our culture more good [to have] exportable, gleeful [*vidám*] film [as opposed to historical, propaganda, or didactic film]."[49]

This school of thought did not dissuade everyone in the film industry from continuing to pursue the quest for the holy grail of a national film style. Imre Bencsik, for example, the founder of a small, Eisenstein-influenced art film movement, offered a creative solution. In arguing for the creation of a national film style, Bencsik concluded that film was a work of art capable of reflecting the tastes, customs, and moral qualities of a people; that it "conceals in itself the notion of national art" (underline in original). "The national film style," he continued, "[was] not expressed in externalities, rather the film, as art, must hide it in itself. It is not possible to call a film Hungarian, [just because its] cowboys eat goulash on the Hortobágy plain for two hours." Concentrating on the content, on a catalogue of Hungarian stereotypes, or on a chronicling of Hungarian history was the wrong way to frame a national production. Rather, Bencsik proposed, "collective Hungarian characteristics" would materialize in a director's work if he/she focused on the rhythm of the editing:

> We must integrate the ancient Hungarian rhythm into the rhythm of the film.... As foreign examples I can only speak of Slavic films, which have some sort of monotone rhythm, [with] pictures presented in a uniform duration of somewhat too great length.
> The Hungarian rhythm guides all of the manifestations of our lives, it immediately directs our pronunciation: the stress on the first syllable, the others unstressed; in addition, for example in the *csárdás,* the "stress" on the first step to the right, the second unstressed, and this repeated to the left. We find this Hungarian rhythm in the meter of our verse, in the ancient eighth, in music, and in all our temporal arts. We must achieve this in the rhythm of film editing. We must begin scenes with longer, expressive, "stressed" pictures, which are followed by shorter, quicker, as explained above "unstressed" pictures. A stressed picture then moves the action forward again, followed again by unstressed pictures, etc.
> Consequently, our films will not only be garbed in "peasant undergarments" *[gatyás],* but the typical Hungarian films will be girded in all sorts of private ways.[50]

Whether Bencsik had put his finger on something concrete and was on his way towards developing a legitimate theoretical alternative for a Hungarian national style remains an unanswered question. In March 1944, when German troops arrived in Hungary, the country forfeited control over the destiny of its film industry. As a result, Hungary was never able to seize the opportunity to change its motion picture undergarments. The search for a national style came to an abrupt end.

The leaders of interwar Hungary sought to deal with the complications of the modern age, to paraphrase Andrew Janos, by backing in. The travails of the film industry as it sought an identity for the nation were symptomatic of this approach. Hungary's political elites welcomed sound film and its capitalist tendencies. Yet they soon determined to reject those same tendencies without understanding the full implications of such a decision. What the state and the film establishment ultimately faced was the realization that one might be able to ostracize Jews, capitalism, and the middle class on a theoretical level, but one could not escape the fact that the film industry would collapse without them. In the search for a national ideal, Hungary's filmmakers cast aside content and forms geared toward the cosmopolitan classes, but ended up resorting to those same genres when state-endorsed attempts to control the tastes of the Hungarian nation either backfired or became too expensive. Since the appearance of sound, the Hungarian film establishment had muddled through encounters with middle-class modernism, populist social problem films, and historical films. The failure of all of these experiments suggests that there is one fundamental truth about national identity: it cannot exist in a uniform, unchanging sense. It is entirely a subjective construct that is fundamentally contingent upon interpretation and time, and is always being contested or reformulated. The answer to the question "What is Hungarian?" today, inevitably, will be different tomorrow.

Notes

1. Research for this essay was supported in part by a grant from the International Research and Exchanges Board (IREX), the Fulbright-Hays Doctoral Dissertation Research Abroad program administered by the U.S. Department of Education, and an American Council of Learned Societies (ACLS) Fellowship for East European Studies. The author would like to express his gratitude to all of these organizations.
2. Gyula Gyárfás, "Magyar film—Feltámadás! [Hungarian Film—Resurrection!]," *Filmkultura* IV, no. 4 (1 April 1931): 1–2.
3. For example, see the following as an example of importance attached to film culture: "És most jöjjön az állam! [And Now the State Should Intervene!]," *Magyar Filmkurir. A magyar mozgóképszinházak és a filmkereskedelmi független lapja* III, no. 7 (20 February 1929): 1.
4. Andor Lajta, "A magyar film története. V. A magyar hangosfilm korszak első 16 éve, 1929–1944 [The History of Hungarian Film. Volume V: The First 16 Years of Hungarian Sound Film, 1929–1944]," ca. 1953, Szinháztudományi és Filmtudományi Intézet kézirat [Theater and Film Studies Institute, unpublished manuscript], Budapest, 12.
5. In an article titled "The Americans and Hungarian Film Production," the editors of *Mozivilág* claimed sound film production would bring about a flowering of not only Hungarian film but literature, acting, and culture in general. "Az amerikaiak és a magyar filmgyártás," *Mozivilág* II, no. 19 (11 May 1930): 1–2.
6. For broader English language considerations of Hungary, its Jews, and modernization/modernity, see Andrew C. Janos, *The Politics of Backwardness in Hungary 1825–1945* (Princeton, 1982), 201–323 and Ezra Mendelsohn, *The Jews of East Central Europe between the World Wars* (Bloomington, IN, 1987), 84–128.
7. "Scitovszky Béla belügyminiszter és Bud János kereskedelmi miniszter hangosfilm-üzenete a magyar közönséghez a magyar film támogatása érdekében [Sound Film Report of Interior

Minister Béla Scitovszky and Trade Minister János Bud to the Hungarian Public in the Interests of Supporting Hungarian Film]," *Filmkultura* IV, no. 5 (1 May 1931): 1.

8. István Székely, "A magyar hangosfilm új újtai [New Paths for Hungarian Sound Film]," *Filmkultura* V, no. 3 (1 March 1932): 2. While Székely may have wished to transcend comedy, it was farce and his partnership with the great comedic actor Gyula Kabos that made Székely Hungary's most successful and prolific domestic director until his self-imposed exile in 1938. See also István Székely, "A magyar filmgyártás eddigi müvészi és erkölcsi mérlege [The Present Artistic and Moral Balance Sheet for Hungarian Film Production]," *Filmkultura* VI, no. 11 (1 November 1933): 1–2. In this article, Székely stresses that it was just as important that films integrate the "Pest and Hungarian milieu" as it was that films be made in Hungary.

9. Interior Minister József Széll to Joseph Goebbels, coded Nr.157 789/1933 (undated, ca. 30 November 1933), Hungarian National Archives-Óbuda, Hunnia Filmgyár Rt., Z 1124, Raktári sz. 1, Dosszié sz. 20, 218–219, Német-magyar filmcsere: megállapodások, levelezés a Német Birodalmi Filmkamarával, 1933–1942 [German-Hungarian Film Exchange: Agreements, Correspondence with the Film Chamber of the Third Reich, 1933–1942].

10. Béla Kempelen, "A filmgyártás jövő feladatai [The Future Tasks of Film Production]," *Film Élet* (19–26 December 1933): 4–5.

11. Sándor Jeszenszky, "A magyar film—A magyar kultura egyik létkérdése [The Hungarian Film—One of the Life and Death Questions for Hungary's Culture]," *Filmkultura* VII, no. 4 (1 April 1934): 1–2. Italics in original.

12. Henrik Castiglione, "Magyarország film-világpiaci jelentősége [The Significance of Hungary in the World Film Market]," *Filmkultura* VII, no. 7–8 (July–August 1934): 1–4.

13. Miklós Lackó, *Korszellem és Tudomány 1910–1945 [Zeitgeist and Scholarship 1910–1945]* (Budapest, 1988), 181–210.

14. Member of Parliament Ernő Brody, quoted in an excerpted reprint of the 18–19 June 1935 Lower House hearings in *Filmkultura* VIII, no. 7–8 (1 July 1935): 10.

15. János Füki, "Hatósági jóindulat és kedvezmények szükségesek az uj vidéki mozik üzembehelyezésénél [Official Good Will and Discounts Necessary for Bringing New Countryside Theaters into Operation]," *Filmkultura* VIII, no. 3 (1 March 1935): 4–5.

16. András Komor, "Egy mozijáró naplójából [From the Diary of a Moviegoer]," *Magyar Filmkurir* X, no. 49–52 (24 December 1936): n.p.

17. Károly Nemes, in his well-known text on post–World War II Hungarian film, suggests that "inspired by the populist ('village explorer') writers, the 1940s witnessed the ascent of peasant heroes in Hungarian films." He is wrong. This change began in the mid-1930s. See Károly Nemes, *Films of Commitment. Socialist Cinema in Eastern Europe* (Budapest, 1985), 55.

18. Theodor W. Adorno, "Culture Industry Reconsidered," in J.M. Bernstein, ed., *The Culture Industry. Selected Essays on Mass Culture* (London, 1991), 89.

19. Sándor Eckhardt, "A Magyarság Külföldi Arcképe [The Portrait of Hungarianness Abroad]" in *Mi a magyar? [What is Hungarian?]*, ed. Gyula Szekfű (Budapest, 1939), 127–130.

20. This was in line with what was occurring in other world cinemas. Hollywood, for example, began making more social problem films, hero films, and historical dramas in the 1930s, even continuing with these genres during the war.

21. Antal Güttler, "Legyen 'új' az új filmgyártás! [Let the New Film Production be 'New'!]" *Magyar Film* I, no. 5 (18 March 1939): 2.

22. "Magyar film, vagy zsidó film? [Hungarian Film or Jewish Film?]," *Magyar Filmkurir* XI, no. 23–26 (26 August 1937): 4–5.

23. In May 1938, Hungary adopted Law XV/1938, known as the First Jewish Law or First Anti-Jewish Law. This legislation required that the number of Jews employed in professions or enrolled in universities and institutions of higher education be lowered to a maximum of twenty percent of that profession, faculty, or school by 30 June 1943. Hungary's Second Jewish Law, Law IV/1939, adopted in May 1939, defined Jews by blood and further low-

ered the maximum percentage to six percent. This legislation had a devastating effect on large numbers of Jews in the film industry. While scores continued to work, some overtly and others secretly, the large majority of Hungarian Jewish film experts were expelled from their jobs. A series of arrests of prominent Jewish film professionals in 1941 dissuaded all but a few Hungarian film companies and theaters from employing Hungarians of Jewish descent.

24. This suggestion appeared occasionally in the Andor Lajta edited *Filmkultura* and then regularly in the Géza Ágotai edited *Magyar Film*, the two main voices of the film community, as well as in numerous other trade journals. Wlassics, as head of the National Film Committee, was also a big proponent of this approach.

25. Ádám Szücs, "Van-e magyar filmstílus? [Is There a Hungarian Film Style?]," *Magyar Film* II, no. 29 (20 July 1940): 4–5. Szücs and many other conservative right and fascist cultural figures made similar recommendations. See Tibor Sándor, *Őrségváltás után: zsidókérdés és filmpolitika, 1938–44 [After the Changing of the Guard: the Jewish Question and Film Politics, 1938–44]* (Budapest, 1997), 165.

26. Mihály Fetter, "Egységes magyar filmgyártást! [We Must Unify Hungarian Film Production!]," *Magyar Film* I, no. 26 (12 August 1939): 16.

27. "Szabó Dezső előadása a filmről [Dezső Szabó's Speech about Film]," *Magyar Film* III, no. 23 (7 June 1941): 6.

28. János Dáloky, *Igy készül a magyar film. A magyar film multja és jelene, kulisszatitkai és problémái [This Is How Hungarian Film Is Made. The Past and Present of Hungarian Film, Its Inside Story and Its Problems]* (Budapest, 1942), 184–185.

29. Nemeskürty, *Word and Image,* 118.

30. Ibid., 118. Nemeskürty concludes that the genres of films made between 1939 and 1944 were, in general, quite similar to those made in the 1930s; it was only the casts, characters, and themes that changed.

31. The quotation, written far more concisely and eloquently than I ever could, is borrowed from the introduction to this volume, p. 13.

32. For a more detailed explanation of this phenomenon, see the chapter "The National Spirit Doesn't Stick to Celluloid," in David Frey, "National Cinema, World Stage: A History of Hungary's Sound Film Industry, 1929–44" (Ph.D. diss., Columbia University, 2003).

33. "Magyar mozi—magyar név [Hungarian Theater—Hungarian Name]," *A Filmszinházak Közlönye* I, no. 1 (4 August 1942): 3.

34. "A magyar filmgyártás ügye a képviselőház előtt [The Matter of Hungarian Film Production before the House of Representatives]," *Magyar Film* IV, no. 47 (23 November 1942): 2.

35. Pál Kolozs, "Film és magyarság [Film and Hungarianness]," *Magyar Músza* 1943, no. 2 (1 March 1943): 123–124.

36. István Balogh, quoted in Jegyzőkönyv felvétetett az Országos Nemzeti Filmbizottság 1943. december 10-iki üléséről [Minutes recorded from the National Film Committee's 10 December 1943 meeting]," Budapest Municipal Archives-Heinrich István ut., People's Court documents related to the trial of László Balogh, coded Nb. 1699/1945, 5 (file p. 663).

37. The Hungarian film historian Tibor Sándor cites the example of Hunnia studio head János Bingert repeatedly turning down proposals by the director Arzen Cserépy to film "the Hungarian *Jud Süß.*" The censorship board, meanwhile, rejected the more radical populist and anti-Semitic scripts it reviewed. Sándor, *Őrségváltás után,* 177–179.

38. Homi K. Bhabha, "The Commitment to Theory," in Jim Pines and Paul Willemen, eds., *Questions of Third Cinema* (London, 1989), 127–128.

39. "9 June 1943 Jegyzőkönyv—Hunnia Igazgatósági ülésről [Minutes—Hunnia Directorate meeting]," 5 (file p. 57), Hungarian National Archives-Óbuda, Hunnia Filmgyár Rt., Z 1123, Raktári sz. 1, Dosszié sz. 3. Igazgatósági jegyzőkönyvek, 1943–1945.

40. "16 February 1944 Jegyzőkönyv—Hunnia Igazgatósági ülésről [Minutes—Hunnia Directorate meeting]," 9, (file p. 41). Hungarian National Archives-Óbuda, Hunnia Filmgyár

Rt., Z 1123, Raktári sz. 1, Dosszié sz.3. Igazgatósági jegyzökönyvek, 1943–1945. The total cost estimate of 714,000 pengő comes from István Langer, "Fejezetek a filmgyár történetéből, I–II.rész, 1919–1945 [Chapters From the History of Film Production, 1919–1945]," 2 vols., 1980, MFI kézirat [Hungarian Film Institute, unpublished manuscript], Budapest, 316.

41. Géza Matolay, "Filmkritika és szakértelem [Film Criticism and Expertise]," *Magyar Film* V, no. 26 (30 June 1943): 1–2; and Géza Matolay, "Miért nem gyártunk történelmi filmet? [Why Don't They Produce Historical Film?]," *Magyar Film* V, no. 31 (4 August 1943): 1–2.

42. "Vaszary János komoly nyilatkozata a vidám filmről [János Vaszary's Serious Pronouncement about Happy Film],"*Mozi Ujság* III, no. 30 (28 July–3 August 1943): 2.

43. Nemeskürty, *Word and Image*, 124.

44. "Happy-end?" *Mozi Ujság* II, no. 43 (28 October–3 November 1942): n.p. This sentiment became more widespread after the debacle at Stalingrad.

45. "Jelentés a Jenes Nándor olaszországi utjáról [Nándor Jenes' Report about His Trip to Italy]," dated 3 November 1942, Hungarian National Archives, Magyar Filmiroda Rt, K 675, 3 csomó, 16 tétel, 1942–1943.

46. "Nagyváradi moziélet [Theater Life in Nagyvárad]," *Magyar Film* V, no. 49 (8 December 1943): 6–7.

47. Károly Molnár, "Film és közvélemény [Film and Public Opinion]," *Magyar Film* VI, no. 18–19 (1 October 1944): 2–3. That comedies were preferred is quite surprising, especially given the fact that very few of the respondents were from Budapest and its surroundings (16 of 525). The official results of the survey were: nearly 39 percent (203 of 525 respondents) wanted more films dealing with the Hungarian spirit and life-or-death questions; about 24 percent (125/525) wanted higher quality films; 18 percent (93/525) were satisfied with present situation; 11 percent (59/525) wanted more comedies; 4 percent (20/525) wanted more populist/everyday life type movies; 2.5 percent (13/525) wanted historical films; 0.76 percent (4/525) wanted more war films; 0.57 percent (3/525) wanted films dealing with agriculture/land matters; 0.38 percent (2/525) wanted erotic films. The survey was skewed by the vagueness of the first category, "films dealing with the Hungarian spirit and life-or-death questions," which was essentially code for everything not in pre-1939 films.

48. Károly Molnár, "Körjárat a fővárosi és pestkörnyéki mozikban [A Stroll through the Cinemas of the Capital and the Peripheries of Pest]," *Magyar Film* VI, no. 18–19 (1 October 1944): 4.

49. "Vaszary János komoly nyilatkozata a vidám filmről," *Mozi Ujság* III, no. 30 (28 July–3 August 1943): 2. Italics in original.

50. Imre Bencsik, "A nemzeti filmstilus kialakitása [The Creation of a National Film Style]," *Filmszolgálat. Az "Oroszlánkölyök" magyar filmmüvészeti mozgalom tájékoztató levele [Film Server. The Informative Letter of the "Lion Cubs" Hungarian Art Film Movement]* no. 2 (1 December 1943): 5.

Chapter 13

THE HUNGARIAN INSTITUTE FOR RESEARCH INTO THE JEWISH QUESTION AND ITS PARTICIPATION IN THE EXPROPRIATION AND EXPULSION OF HUNGARIAN JEWRY

Patricia von Papen-Bodek

Most scholars maintain that during the Third Reich, no historiographical revolution took place. However, a new discipline, *Judenforschung* (research on the Jews), emerged that thrived predominantly, but not exclusively, outside the universities. *Judenforschung* established categories of exclusion, provided tools for persecutory measures, and, most importantly, identified and targeted those to be excluded from German society. Thus *Judenforschung* publicly promoted social segregation and legitimized the expulsion of Jews from Germany and the confiscation of their property. Using scholarly journals, the daily press, the publications of the NSDAP, and even the educational brochures (*Schulungshefte*) edited by the High Command of the *Wehrmacht*, those who practiced *Judenforschung* disseminated their views in Germany and, after 1939, all over Nazi-occupied Europe.

The novelty of *Judenforschung* was its systematic approach: specific institutional centers for anti-Jewish research proliferated throughout Germany.[1] Alongside their regular legal acquisitions or holdings, the bulk of their libraries and archives consisted of looted Jewish materials through systematic state-directed plunder, since National Socialist legislation, and later, and on a much larger scale, the war itself opened up ample opportunities for ruthless confiscation of private and institutional Jewish property. The first institution to target the Jews was the *Institut zum Studium der Judenfrage,* established in 1934 by the Ministry of Propaganda in Berlin. One year later, the Ministry of Education nominated historian Walter Frank president of the *Reichsinstitut für Geschichte des neuen Deutschland.* In April 1936 Frank opened up a branch of this Institute in Munich that was exclusively devoted to the so-called "Jewish Question," the *Forschungsabteilung Judenfrage.*[2] In early 1939, two additional institutes were founded: the *Institut zur Erforschung und Beseitigung des jüdischen Einflusses auf das deutsche kirchliche Leben* in Eisenach, set up by a number of *Landeskirchen,*[3] and the *Außenstelle der Hohen Schule der NSDAP,* or *Institut zur Erforschung der Judenfrage,* established by party ideologue Alfred Rosenberg in Frankfurt am Main.[4] Until the *Außenstelle's* belated inauguration in March 1941, the Berlin *Reichsinstitut* claimed to be the center of anti-Jewish historical "research" in Germany. While Rosenberg's *Außenstelle* was financed by the party, as its name indicates, the *Reichsinstitut* and its *Forschungsabteilung Judenfrage,* were sponsored by the state.[5] Moreover, the *Reichssicherheitshauptamt* (RSHA) established its own anti-Jewish research division as part of its research on opponents of the regime (*Gegnerforschung*).[6] Despite immense rivalries amongst these various institutes—the worst of which was probably between the *Außenstelle* and the RSHA—the documents reveal their frighteningly effective collaboration with the *Reichsstelle für Sippenforschung* (Office for Genealogical Research), the Ministry of the Interior, the Ministry of Justice, the Foreign Office, the *Rassenpolitisches Amt,* and the *Gestapo* in persecuting Jews.

Recent scholarship has provided some insight into the work of these German anti-Jewish propaganda institutions, yet even less is known about similar institutions established during the war in Nazi-occupied Europe. Anti-Jewish research institutions were also set up in Cracow, Paris, Rome,[7] and Budapest, all of which had contacts with Alfred Rosenberg's *Außenstelle.* These institutes, with the exception of the one in Cracow, built on existing local anti-Semitic networks, employed local "know-how," and recruited badly needed additional local personnel. They facilitated local collaboration with the occupiers by extolling the advantages of persecuting the Jews and the benefits of the subsequent Aryanization of their belongings. The *Judenreferat* of the *Institut für deutsche Ostarbeit* in Cracow,[8] established by General Governor Hans Frank,[9] differed from the anti-Jewish institutes in France, Italy, and Hungary in that it had a German (as opposed to a local) director, Josef Sommerfeldt, and because the *Judenreferat* formed just one division of a larger prolific institute. Although the *Außenstelle* closely collaborated with Sommerfeldt's *Judenreferat* from autumn 1940 on, it also established its own short-lived branch in Lodz in 1942.[10] In his highly accomplished study of Nazi occupational policy in Northern Italy between 1943 and 1945, Michael Wedekind has recently demonstrated that the *Centro per lo studio del problema ebraico* in Trieste provided the SS with the data on local Jewry necessary for Nazi persecution policy. He has also meticulously examined the perfidious chain of Germans, Austrians, and Italians (of German descent) who profited from the enforced expropriation of the Jews.[11]

In their recent study on the Holocaust in Hungary, Christian Gerlach and Götz Aly maintain that the Hungarian Institute for Research into the Jewish Question "played no important role from the German point of view"[12] in the persecution and deportation of the Jews of Hungary. This conclusion is based on their interpretation of the May 1944 report by the *Außenstelle*'s deputy director about his trip to Southeast-Europe for the Foreign Office.[13] Gerlach and Aly weaken their own argument by adding that after the German occupation of Hungary in 1944, *SS-Hauptsturmführer* Heinz Ballensiefen "advised" the Institute, and thus by definition paid attention to it. This essay will examine the ways in which the Hungarian Institute for Research into the Jewish Question not only constructed and propagated a viciously anti-Semitic ideology, but also supported and thereby accelerated the persecution process in a practical way, thereby clearly facilitating German anti-Jewish measures. This essay is a preliminary attempt[14] to focus more attention on the Hungarian Institute, which was far more important than Aly and Gerlach suggest, if only because the Hungarian Institute belonged to a whole set of like-minded institutes all over Europe (see Figure 1).[15] A thorough study of the Hungarian Institute will also contribute to a better understanding of the activities of the anti-Jewish research division of the RSHA.[16]

What is most important, however, is that the Nazis worked closely with the Hungarian Institute for Research into the Jewish Question, which had already been established in 1942. After the German occupation of Hungary in March 1944, two founding members of the Institute, László Endre and Vitéz Mihály Kolosváry-Borcsa, were appointed as undersecretaries of state at the Hungarian Ministry of the Interior. The Institute's nominal director, Zoltán Bosnyák, assisted in the planning and implementation of the subsequent anti-Jewish decrees. According to the historian Randolph Braham, Ernst Kaltenbrunner, chief of the security police and the SD, and head of the RSHA, had been instrumental in arranging for László Endre to be appointed to the Ministry.[17] Thus the Institute was closely connected to the RSHA and Alfred Rosenberg's *Außenstelle*, which, along with the Foreign Office, used it to expedite the persecution of Hungarian Jews.

Connections between the Hungarian Institute and the German *Judenforscher* had long been close. In 1943, Vitéz Mihály Kolosváry-Borcsa (1896–1946), editor-in-chief of the racist journal *Függetlenség*, and one of the founding members of the Hungarian Institute, published a *Bibliography of the Literature on the Jewish Question in Hungary*.[18] It contained more than three thousand entries, including a work, *Die Judenfrage in Ungarn. Jüdische Assimilation und antisemitische Bewegung im 19. und 20. Jahrhundert,* by Klaus Schickert,[19] the deputy director of the Frankfurt *Institut zur Erforschung der Judenfrage,* and from mid-February 1944 a member of the *Antijüdische Auslandsaktion* of the German Foreign Office.[20] At the *Außenstelle*'s inauguration (26–28 March 1941), Schickert had lectured on "Jewish Emancipation in Southeast-Europe and its End."[21] In addition to providing official statistics on Jews in Hungary, Schickert identified at least 150,000 "bastards" (according to the statistician Kovács) and 400,000 converts. Pleading

City	Name of Institute	Year	Sponsor	Director
GERMAN REICH				
Berlin	Institut zum Studium der Judenfrage, since 1939 Antisemitische Aktion	1935	Ministry of Propaganda	Wilhelm Ziegler
Berlin	Reichsinstitut für Geschichte des neuen Deutschland	1935	Ministry of Education	Walter Frank (–1941)
Munich	Forschungsabteilung Judenfrage (Branch of RGND)	1936	Ministry of Education	Wilhelm Grau (–1938), Karl R. Ganzer
Eisenach	Institut zur Erforschung und Beseitigung des jüdischen Einflusses auf das deutsche kirchliche Leben	1939	Evangelische Landeskirchen	Walter Grundmann
Nürnberg	Antijüdische Liga		Der Stürmer	Paul Wurm
Bad Schwalbach	Welt-Dienst. Internationales Institut zur Aufklärung über die Judenfrage	1939	Alfred Rosenberg, NSDAP	August Schirmer
Frankfurt	Außenstelle der Hohen Schule der NSDAP or Institut zur Erforschung der Judenfrage	1939	Alfred Rosenberg, NSDAP	Wilhelm Grau (–1942), Klaus Schickert (1943–1945)
GAU WARTHELAND				
Lódz (GG)	Branch of the Außenstelle	1942	Alfred Rosenberg	Adolf Wendel
GENERAL GOVERNMENT				
Cracow (GG)	Institut für deutsche Ostarbeit—Judenreferat	1940	General Governor Hans Frank	Dr. Josef Sommerfeldt
ITALY				
Ancona	Institute for the Study of the Jewish Question	1941	Fascist Party's Racial Office Dr. Giovanni Preziosi	Guido Podaliri
Milan, Florence		1942	Ministry of Popular Culture	Alfredo Acito, Ugo Puccioni
Triest	Fascist Centro per lo Studio Problema Ebraico Centro Triestino per la Difesa della Razza	1942	Racial Office of the Ministry of Education	Ettore Martinoli
Bologna	Institute for the Study of Jewish Question	1943	Dr. Giovanni Preziosi	Dr. Mario Tirollo
FRANCE				
Paris	Institut d'Études des Questions Juives (until 1943)	1941	RSHA, German Embassy	Paul Sézille
Paris	Institut d'Études des Questions Juives et Ethno-Raciales	1943		George Montandon
Bordeaux	Institute for the Study of the Jewish Question	1941		Henri Labroue
HUNGARY				
Budapest	Hungarian Institute for Research into the Jewish Question	1944	RSHA, Heinz Ballensiefen	Zoltán Bosnyák

Table 13.1. Anti-Jewish Research Institutes in Europe 1935–1945

for the total "liberation" of Southeast-Europe of its estimated 1.35 to 2.3 million Jews, he argued:

> The revolution of National Socialism gave Southeast Europe a new direction, in fact inaugurated for it a new era. The solution which Germany has found for its Jewish Question works as an example and has had repercussions in all those countries ... All governments hope for the great emigration to come, and some explicitly declared their willingness to further it. Translating the thought into deeds transcends the power of any single state. For this purpose a master plan is needed, and so our discussion terminates in the idea that the Jewish Question in Southeastern Europe can be solved finally along uniform lines and in cooperation with the German Reich.[22]

It was on the basis of Kolosváry-Borcsa's *Bibliography on the Literature on the Jewish Question in Hungary* that the Hungarian Institute acquired its collection of antisemitica.[23] Along with László Endre (1895–1945), founder of the "Race-protecting Socialist Party" and Deputy Prefect of Pest County, in 1942 Kolosváry-Borcsa helped found the Hungarian Institute, which was led by the rabidly anti-Semitic teacher and prolific journalist Zoltán Bosnyák.[24] Initially, this private institute worked covertly,[25] and Bosnyák published under a pseudonym.[26] However, it quickly sought public affirmation, as an interview with Bosnyák in the *Deutsche Zeitung* of 24 March 1943 illustrates. Bosnyák unself-consciously included his institute alongside other institutions engaged in *Judenforschung* in Frankfurt, Rome, Florence,[27] and Paris. He claimed that his collaborators worked for free, were recruited from all strata of the population, and came from all over the country. According to him, collaboration between the Institute and the Hungarian population was most successful in Kaschau/ Kassa/Košice (Eastern Slovakia),[28] Debrecen, and Szeged. Inviting the population to denounce Jews, Bosnyák proclaimed that complaints regarding Jews addressed to the Institute would be directly forwarded to the Hungarian government. He emphasized his special connection to the Frankfurt Institute (Rosenberg's *Außenstelle*) and declared that his goal would be for Hungary to "evacuate" its 800,000 Jews.

German *Judenforscher* warmly applauded the Hungarian Institute. Bosnyák's work featured prominently in Schickert's *Die Judenfrage in Ungarn,* which appeared in a second edition in 1943, supported by the *Antisemitische Aktion* of the German Ministry of Propaganda.[29] On Easter 1944, the *Donauzeitung* in Belgrade hailed Schickert's "excellent" book as strong support for the newly established Hungarian Institute.[30] In an essay on "Hungary's Jewish Question" for the May 1943 issue of *Volk im Osten,* edited by the *Deutsche Volksgruppe* in Hermannstadt (Sibiu), Rumania,[31] Schickert not only mentioned the Hungarian Institute but also criticized the Hungarian parliament for not having confiscated Jewish private property thus far. In an article for the Frankfurt institute's journal *Weltkampf* on the "Exploration of the Jewish Question in Southeastern Europe,"[32] Schickert summarized the activities of local anti-Semites and emphasized the necessity for them to collaborate with the German Reich. Constantly updated by the Foreign Office about anti-Jewish legislation in Southeastern Europe,[33] Schickert travelled to the area on its behalf between mid-March and the end of April 1944 in order to meet anti-Semites and those who worked on the "Jewish Question" (*Judensachbearbeiter*) in the German legations.[34] At least one legation, Preßburg/ Bratislava, ordered his book, *Die Judenfrage in Ungarn,* because they regarded it as providing them with guidelines for their own work.[35]

On 22 March 1944, three days after the Germans occupied Hungary and installed Reich Plenipotentiary Dr. Edmund Veesenmayer, Döme Sztójay, the former Hungarian envoy in Berlin, formed a new Hungarian government.[36] Veesenmayer appointed *SS-Hauptsturmführer* and *"Judenreferent"* of *Amt VII* of the RSHA, Dr. Heinz Ballensiefen[37]—like Schickert also a member of the *Antijüdischer Aktionsausschuß* of the Foreign Office—as his propaganda-expert for Jewish matters. Before joining the RSHA, Ballensiefen had worked for Wilhelm Ziegler's *Institut zum Studium der Judenfrage,* which was associated with the Ministry of Propaganda. In 1939 he had published *Juden in Frankreich. Die französische Judenfrage in Geschichte und Gegenwart,* a work the RSHA wanted to expand and republish in 1943.[38] Ballensiefen edited the secret *Informationsberichte* of the RSHA for the ideological training of the staff of Nazi agencies. At a symposium in Silesia in April 1944, he lectured together with *Legationsrat* Eberhard von Thadden—the "expert" on Jewish affairs of the Foreign Office between 1943 and 1945—to the consultants on Aryanization at the German embassies about "current anti-Jewish executive measures."[39] In October 1944, he prevented the Spanish embassy in Budapest from rescuing Jewish children.[40]

Since Ballensiefen needed to promote the anti-Jewish measures quickly and thus needed to use an existing local, that is Hungarian, network, Zoltán Bosnyák, the head of the Hungarian Institute for Research on the Jewish Question, was the appropriate man for the job. Bosnyák's appeal to the Hungarian population in September 1943 to send publications regarding the Jewish question in Hungary to his institute[41] apparently had met with an unexpectedly positive response, according to the *Deutsche Zeitung* of 2 December 1943. In November 1943, he had presented his Institute in the *Europäischer Wissenschafts-Dienst,*[42] a manuscript-form, typed journal, edited, while it existed from 1941–1944, by Wilhelm Ziegler of the Berlin *Institut zum Studium der Judenfrage.* According to Bosnyák, the Hungarian Institute had six different divisions, each performing a distinct function: Historians elaborated the history of Jewry in Hungarian political life with special emphasis on the "Jewish-Marxist revolution of 1918." Social scientists scrutinized "Jewish plutocracy." Racial biologists analyzed questions of Jewish descent. Economists evaluated official statistics to examine the percentage of Jews engaged in the national economy, trade, industry, and the banking sector. Cultural historians described the "Judaization" of Hungarian intellectual life. The division for racial protection systematically collected antisemitica and press-clippings. Bosnyák planned a book series to include works by important foreign as well as Hungarian anti-Semites. Corresponding members across the country collected data and propagated the Institute's goals. Bosnyák anticipated that the total "evacuation" of European Jewry was close to being realized. Just a few weeks before the German invasion, Bosnyák used 8 March 1944, the 50th anniversary of Louis Kossuth's death, to repudiate liberal criticism of the anti-Jewish legislation. In *Függetlenség*[43] Bosnyák claimed that even the great liberal had pointed out that the Jews represented a serious danger for Hungary's farmers, that their immigration had to be controlled, and that anti-Semitism was deeply rooted in the country. Two weeks later, Bosnyák was able to draw upon income and capital tax reports in a tirade on "National Income and Jewry"[44] to show that Hungarian Jews earned six times as much as Christian Hungarians. "Their ... unjustified part of the national income" had to be reduced, he concluded.

The close relationship between the German occupiers and the Hungarian Institute can be seen in the publicity the Institute received in both Germany and Hungary: Kolosváry-Borcsa's and Bosnyák's writings were supposed to appear in a German translation[45] according to Schickert's report to Rosenberg, and both were also mentioned in *Weltkampf*, the journal of the Frankfurt *Aussenstelle*. In an interview on April 13, 1944, the newly appointed secretary of state in charge of Jewish affairs in the Hungarian Ministry of the Interior, László Endre,[46] declared in the *Deutsche Zeitung* that his Ministry had provided the Institute with adequate space (Bosnyák had an office in the department for Jewish affairs in the Ministry of the Interior) and consulted with it in order to identify Jews.[47] Thus a week after the Ministry of Economics had required Jews to close their businesses, official pronouncements *openly* stated that the Hungarian Institute assisted in identifying Jews.

The Hungarian Institute for Research on the Jewish Question prepared an elaborate propaganda campaign to accompany the ongoing anti-Jewish persecution. After the Nazi occupation, the Hungarian Institute called for the elimination of Jewish authors from the public sphere. On 29 March 1944, the day the yellow star was introduced,[48] *Függetlenség* legitimized the ongoing public anti-Jewish book campaign, and praised Kolosváry-Borcsa's *Bibliography*, which demanded the establishment of an anti-Jewish institute, the teaching of the "Jewish Question" in Hungarian schools, the removal of Jewish publications from public libraries, the public shredding of Jewish books, and the discussion of the "Jewish Question" in Hungarian universities and at the Academy of Sciences. On 23 April 1944, the day that special shopping-hours for Jews were introduced, Bosnyák published an infamous article, "The Past and Present of the Budapest Ghetto," in *Függetlenség*.[49] Here he revealed that between 1931 and 1940, 16,825 Jews had converted to Christianity. Preparing his readers for the planned concentration of Budapest's Jews, he insinuated that the capital's Jewry had always chosen and continued to choose ghettoization, that is, preferring to live near each other in Jewish neighborhoods. Of 53,505 Budapest Jewish landlords (60 percent of all Budapest landlords), Bosnyák located 32,893 in three districts of the city.

On 28 April 1944, the day Jewish bank accounts were blocked and more than 8,000 Jews arrested, Bosnyák informed Hungarian journalists as well as Dr. Ballensiefen about the reorganization of the Institute. He presented it as an "independent scholarly establishment" consisting of active members and friends, and acknowledged that it had a separate propaganda division of committed anti-Semitic Hungarian journalists. Its library, archive, and scholarly division were located at Bogar Street 43.[50] A wire from *Legationsrat* von Thadden to the German delegation in Budapest regarding Bosnyák's announcement is indicative of the temporary confusion of the Foreign Office with regard to the Frankfurt Institute: von Thadden inquired which of the German anti-Jewish institutes Bosnyák had mentioned, since he was still waiting for Schickert's report.[51]

This report, which, as a result of his participation in the *Antijüdische Auslandsaktion*, Schickert forwarded to the Foreign Office on 5 May, attests to his presence in Budapest from 24 April to 29 April. It warrants careful examination not only because it discloses Schickert's entire agenda as well as his contacts in Southeast-Europe, but also, and most important here, because of his evaluation of Bosnyák and the Institute. According to the report, Bosnyák, who hardly spoke any German, welcomed German support, and his Institute was closely linked to the German police. The press department of the Institute under Kolosváry-Borcsa was supposed to be greatly expanded. According to Schickert, it had never occurred to Bosnyák to collaborate with university professors—who criticized his dilettantism—or with the *Deutsches Wissenschaftliches Institut*. Since Bosnyák was more a propagandist than a serious scholar, parallel action was required: Schickert planned a *Weltkampf* issue devoted to the "Jewish Problem" in Hungary as Magyar writers perceived it. Dékány, a sociologist at Budapest University, had agreed to portray the "Influence of the Jewish Social Sciences 1905–1918" as the breeding-ground for the Bolshevik Revolution, and the internationally renowned Professor Orsós of the department of forensic medicine at Budapest University had offered to produce a "Reexamination of the Medical Opinion of the Ritual Murder Trial Tisza-Eszlár." Schickert was optimistic about Hungarian scholarly collaboration. He intended to have Hungarian contributions for the *Weltkampf* translated into German for distribution in the Reich, while the original Hungarian texts were to be published by Bosnyák.[52]

On 7 May, Bosnyák, who according to the contemporary observer Eugene Lévai "was constantly at the Ministry of the Interior and played an ... important part in the planning and execution of the anti-Jewish decrees,"[53] justified the new decrees concerning Jewish apartments in an article "Budapest Jewry Owned Most of the Better Apartments. Why is the Confiscation of Jewish Apartments Necessary?"[54] Apartments were needed, he argued, to compensate families who had become homeless due to bombing as well as to counter the general shortage of apartments. He concluded by reminding his readers that while his data covered only members of the Jewish community, many converts also owned large apartments.

The Hungarian Institute for Research on the Jewish Question, which before the Nazi occupation operated covertly, became a public institution in mid-May 1944, simultaneously with the start of the first deportations.[55] Located on the first floor at 4 Vörösmarty Square,[56] in the former Jewish Union-Club, it displayed confiscated ritual objects as well as Judaica from various Jewish institutions. Hungarian and German anti-Semites worked together in the Institute. Dr. Ballensiefen, who collaborated closely with Adolf Eichmann,[57] was now its supervisor,[58] and *SS-Obersturmführer* Döscher, who prior to his Hungarian mission had run a similar institution in Paris, was its practical manager. In the eyes of the Hungarian public, however, Bosnyák remained its head. Three Hungarian undersecretaries of state, László Endre[59] (simultaneously a member of the Institute), László Baky (of the Ministry of Interior charged with police matters),[60] and Dr. Miklós Mester (of the Ministry of Culture), participated in the Institute's inauguration. Budapest's mayor donated 5,000 *pengő* at the express order of Endre.[61] Here it is important to recall that it was Baky's and Endre's Ministry of the Interior and Eichmann's *Sondereinsatzkommando* that devised the scheme for the concentration of Hungarian Jewry.[62]

The close working relationship between Hungarian and German officials was made clear in the speeches they made at the ceremony marking the inauguration of the Institute. In his address, Endre, alluding to the already planned deportations, declared that the government had decided to "bring about a final solution to the Jewish Question within the shortest possible time."[63] He announced the expropriation of the Jews, and equated their "evacuation" with the end of the war. Ninety percent of the "spiritual cleansing," he maintained, had been completed by the action taken by the commissioner in charge of the press, radio, and publishing, Vitéz Kolosváry-Borcsa. Given the fact that even certain popes and canonized Hungarian kings had fought the "Jewish parasites" with drastic laws,[64] the present anti-Jewish legislation was not un-Christian either.[65] He emphasized Hungary's appreciation of German support in the anti-Jewish struggle, but stressed that it acted out of its *own* interests.[66] In his inaugural speech, Bosnyák pointed out that there were almost a million Jews in Hungary, and that 80–90 percent of banking, 70 percent of industry, and 55–60 percent of trade *had been* in Jewish hands.[67] More governmental statistics about Jewish property would follow. The Institute's library would shortly house 48,000 volumes as well as files on Jews, anti-Semites, and friends of the Jews.[68] A travelling exhibition was planned.

In his speech, the Nazi supervisor of the Institute, Dr. Ballensiefen, who also contributed to the Institute's journal, *Harc,*[69] targeted the alleged Jewish world conspiracy and its warmongering role. "The 5,000 year old hatred, which motivates Jewry against Gentiles, bombards now our cathedrals, workhouses and destroys the values of Christian culture."[70] Jewry's "ruthlessness" demanded action without any compromises.[71] *Harc*, a weekly of eight pages that appeared in 50,000 copies,[72] was financed by the SD and printed in the same building as the Hungarian National Socialist newspaper.[73] Its first issue was sold out within an hour, according to a report by von Thadden of 25 May 1944, the copies literally snatched from the sales personnel.[74] The Information Division of the Foreign Office furnished material, but also requested that the delegation's *Judenreferent* send the semimonthly *Mitteilungen* for the missions to the editors.[75] Camouflaging his real function as driving force behind the Institute, the *Völkischer Beobachter* misleadingly reported that Ballensiefen had especially arrived from Germany for the Institute's opening.[76] It is noteworthy, that he had *not* invited any members of the German delegation to the opening, nor even informed them.[77] Meanwhile the German Ministry of Propaganda wanted Schickert to write a second book with a more updated title that would take into consideration the "purification of Hungary," as the persecution of the Jews was euphemistically called, then under way.[78] Schickert himself intended to publish an updated third edition of his *Judenfrage in Ungarn.*

The Hungarians themselves often took the lead in announcing anti-Jewish measures. On 23 May, Secretary of State for Press Matters, Kolosváry-Borcsa, announced on the radio, that he had shut down several Budapest daily newspapers, 146 journals, and many Jewish bookstores and publishing houses. Public libraries were now handling "Jewish works" separately, reserving them for scholarly purposes only. He listed 120 Hungarian and 35 foreign Jewish authors whose books were destined for shredding, and asked his audience either to destroy their works or to donate them to the Institute. It is noteworthy, that a month earlier, on 22 April, SS *Sturmbannführer* Wilhelm Höttl, head of the Hungarian Department of Amt VI-E of the RSHA, had obtained László Baky's approval to go through the inventory of Jewish bookshops in Budapest in order to confiscate whatever seemed worthwhile for the RSHA to preserve.[79] On June 3, Bosnyák, too, appealed to Hungarian society for active collaboration in the work of the Institute.[80] Individuals as well as corporate bodies could become sponsoring members of the Institute.[81] The annual membership fee was only 120 *pengő*, and founding members could pay one flat fee of 1,000 *pengő*. Like Kolosváry-Borcsa, Bosnyák asked for "Jewish books" for the Institute's library and offered to send out lists of Jewish authors.[82] Whether this indicates that the Institute received little support from the population, as Elisabeth Eppler has suggested, deserves further exploration.

On 16 June 1944, half a million books (22 wagons) were destroyed on the grounds of the First Hungarian Cardboard Factory,[83] a measure initiated by Kolosváry-Borcsa, who was accompanied by the German press attaché.[84] While works of Hungarian and foreign Jews were shredded,[85] the commissioner suggested that book shredding was as much a patriotic duty as fighting at the front. In fact, the newly recycled paper supported the efforts at the front, so the population should collaborate eagerly.

One week later, on 23 June 1944, Ballensiefen and Dr. Johannes Pohl, a former member of Rosenberg's *Außenstelle* who had been transferred to Rosenberg's *Welt-Dienst*,[86] met with Hungarian anti-Semites in the guesthouse Eppenhain/Taunus outside Frankfurt. There they discussed how the anti-Jewish struggle in Hungary could be intensified. Among the Hungarians present were the longtime informer of the *Welt-Dienst*, Lits, as well as Andreka, Gosztonyi, Hubay, and Marschalko. In addition to Ballensiefen and Pohl, *Oberstarbeitsführer* Richter (of the *Welt-Dienst*), Fischer, Herrigel, Schwarzburg, and Seifert represented the German side. According to Lits, the Institute's library had grown to 80,000 volumes, and the Hungarian government had requisitioned several secondary school teachers to work at the Institute. Hubay requested that the *Welt-Dienst* be distributed in Budapest, estimating that up to 150,000 copies could be sold easily. According to the protocol, Richter replied that the *Welt-Dienst* depended upon Hungarian collaborators since only *they* (emphasis mine) were able to address Hungarian issues adequately. Ballensiefen was satisfied that the Institute's public image was that of an entirely Hungarian institution. He claimed that 80 percent of all Hungarian press or radio news regarding the Jewish Question in Hungary built upon propaganda material provided by the Institute.[87] He agreed to the Hungarian proposition that the *Welt-Dienst* be distributed to interested Hungarians who were registered in a special file at the Institute, as well as to Kolosváry-Borcsa and the press division of the German delegation. Ballensiefen maintained that the information service of the Institute needed an additional collaborator, someone however, who was *not* a party-member. As had been agreed upon, Bosnyák himself broadcasted propaganda pieces. While Lits pushed for a stronger recruitment of Hungarian anti-Semites via the universities and even pleaded for the establishment of a university chair for Bosnyák, Ballensiefen reminded him that, while it seemed paradoxical that the Germans were promoting a more "cautious" treatment of the Jewish Question than the Hungarians, *Realpolitik* (as opposed to *Wissenschaft*) was the order of the day.

On 2 July, and probably as a result of this meeting, Kolosváry-Borcsa's paper *Függetlenség*, published an interview with Johannes Pohl,[88] the so-called Talmud expert of Rosenberg's *Welt-Dienst*,[89] entitled "Kill the best of the Christians. Professor Pohl, the world's most distinguished Talmud expert, talks about Jewry's war goals."[90] Pohl was presented as being especially knowledgeable about different editions of the Talmud, and therefore well qualified to argue that Talmudic Jews considered Gentiles animals, excluded from humanity, beasts whom one could legally kill. Pohl established a connection between the Talmud and the terror bombings, and referred to a 1941 book, *Germany Must Be Destroyed*, by the Jewish president of the American Peace League, Kaufmann, according to which mass extermination of 80 million Germans was "impractical." Pohl's Kaufmann therefore suggested the sterilization of the Germans.

Although several of Bosnyák's collaborators (Lajos Méhely and László Levatich) had been longtime informers for Rosenberg,[91] and Rosenberg's employees Schickert and Pohl propagated Bosnyák's ideas in German-language publications[92] and were referred to in the Hungarian press, it was Dr. Ballensiefen of the RSHA who exercised the most visible influence on the Hungarian Institute and on the Hungarian anti-Jewish campaign. This SS-man emerges more as a man of action rather than of pure pseudo-scholarship. Although Hungarian newspapers often associated him with the Frankfurt Institute, most probably to further the Institute's "scholarly" image, the sources presently available do not indicate his direct allegiance to Frankfurt.[93] A thorough analysis of his "mission" is urgently needed. Furthermore, the story of SS *Sturmbannführer* Wilhelm Höttl in Budapest has yet to be written,[94] just as the role of SS *Obersturmführer* Döscher should be further examined. How did they relate to Bosnyák and what was their respective relationship to the staff of the German embassy?

Even at this early stage of our still rather limited knowledge of the Hungarian Institute as well as the activities of the RSHA staff involved in its activities, it is safe to say that Hungarians and Germans worked together to persecute the Jews. Both Bosnyák and Schickert were involved in preparing the anti-Jewish congress planned by Alfred Rosenberg in collaboration with the Foreign and Propaganda Ministries, the RSHA, and General Governor Hans Frank, which was scheduled to take place in Cracow in the summer of 1944, but cancelled due to the Allied invasion. A first reading of the available documents reveals that the Hungarian Institute collaborated with the *Amt Rosenberg*, Rosenberg's *Außenstelle* (the Frankfurt *Institut zur Erforschung der Judenfrage*), the Foreign Office, and the RSHA. Both *Hauptsturmführer* Ballensiefen (*Judenreferent* of the Amt VII of the RSHA as well as Veesenmayer's propaganda-expert) and Schickert (in his double function as member of the *Antijüdische Auslandsaktion/* Foreign Office as well as head of the *Außenstelle*) met with Bosnyák repeatedly. *Legationsrat* von Thadden (*Judenreferent* of the Foreign Office) inspected the Hungarian Institute in person. In addition, the Institute was well informed about foreign anti-Semitic institutions, and frequently launched reports about their activities in the Hungarian press.[95] The Hungarian Institute functioned as part of a set of like-minded institutions.

While Elisabeth Eppler believed in 1955 that the "Institute was unable to do more than publish a very unsubstantial bibliography and a short-lived illustrated paper ... produced with German money,"[96] and Götz Aly and Christian Gerlach in 2002 attributed little importance to it from the German point of view, in fact, the Hungarian Institute did play an important role in the persecution of the Jews of Hungary. Its systematic attempt to portray Hungarian Jews as mortal enemies who had to be killed as an act of self-defense was not only an effort to minimize human compassion for the Jews among Hungarians, it was nothing less than instigation to murder.[97] Its vicious propaganda-campaign not only sought to justify expropriation, it legitimized the "evacuation" of the country's Jews. Eichmann's friend Endre[98] and Bosnyák's men assisted the administration in legitimizing and implementing the Final Solution, a process facilitated by the very fact that Endre, Kolosváry-Borcsa, and Ballensiefen were simultaneously members of the Institute and of the authority structure in occupied Hungary. Thus the Institute, which publicly appeared as a Hungarian institution, was—like its Parisian counterpart, *L'Institut d'études des questions juives*—closely supervised by the RSHA.[99]

A future study of the Hungarian Institute for Research into the Jewish Question, which would have to be based on currently still unavailable Hungarian documents, will have to examine precisely how, where, when exactly, and to what extent Germans and Hungarians, in the face of an immense language barrier, actually communicated. Where did their interests overlap, where did they differ, and how did they profit from one another? Furthermore, such a study will have to differentiate between different stages in the development of the Institute. How was the Institute perceived by the Hungarian population? Did the population respond at all to the Institute's appeals, as Bosnyák claimed it did? Questions of local infrastructure could be resolved only by locals, so Bosnyák's network of informers and statisticians appears to have been a necessary and crucial precondition for an effective eliminatory administration. This network deserves much more attention than it has thus far received, since a case study of this Institute would reveal how ideology was translated into *Realpolitik* and how *Realpolitik* allowed an allegedly scholarly institution to legitimize the deportation of Hungarian Jews.

Notes

1. Max Weinreich, *Hitler's Professors: The Part of Scholarship in Germany's Crimes Against the Jewish People,* 2nd ed. (New Haven, 1999; orig. New York, 1946).
2. See Helmut Heiber, *Walter Frank und sein Reichsinstitut für Geschichte des neuen Deutschland* (Stuttgart, 1966); and more recently Patricia von Papen, "'Scholarly' Antisemitism During the Third Reich. The Reichsinstitut's Research on the 'Jewish Question,' 1935–1945 (Ph.D. diss., Columbia University, 1999); idem, "Schützenhilfe nationalsozialistischer Judenpolitik. Die 'Judenforschung' des 'Reichsinstituts für Geschichte des neuen Deutschland' 1935–1945," in Fritz Bauer Institut, ed., *"Beseitigung des jüdischen Einflusses...." Antisemitische Forschung, Eliten und Karrieren im Nationalsozialismus, Jahrbuch 1998/1999 zur Geschichte und Wirkung des Holocaust* (Frankfurt/New York, 1999), 17–42; and idem, "Vom engagierten Katholiken zum Rassenantisemiten. Die Karriere des Historikers der 'Judenfrage' Wilhelm Grau 1935–1945," in *Theologische Wissenschaft im Dritten Reich. Ein ökumenisches Projekt,* Georg Denzler, Leonore Siegele-Wenschkewitz, eds. (Frankfurt am Main, 2000), 68–113.
3. Susannah Heschel, "Theologen für Hitler. Walter Grundmann und das Institut zur Erforschung und Beseitigung des jüdischen Einflusses auf das deutsche kirchliche Leben," in Leonore Siegele-Wenschkewitz, ed., *Christlicher Antijudaismus und Antisemitismus* (Frankfurt am Main, 1994), 125–170.
4. See Reinhard Bollmus, "Zum Projekt einer nationalsozialistischen Alternativuniversität: Alfred Rosenbergs 'Hohe Schule,'" in Manfred Heinemann, ed., *Erziehung und Schulung im Dritten Reich* (Stuttgart, 1980), vol. 2, 125–152; and Dieter Schiefelbein, *"Das 'Institut zur Erforschung der Judenfrage Frankfurt am Main.' Vorgeschichte und Gründung 1935–1939,"* Materialien Nr.9 der Arbeitsstelle zur Vorbereitung des Frankfurter Lern- und Dokumentationszentrums des Holocaust, Fritz Bauer Institut in Gründung hrsg. in Zusammenhang mit dem Institut für Stadtgeschichte (Frankfurt am Main, 1994); and idem, "Das 'Institut zur Erforschung der Judenfrage Frankfurt am Main.' Antisemitismus als Karrieresprungbrett im NS Staat," in Fritz Bauer Institut, ed., "Beseitigung des jüdischen Einflusses...', " 43–71. See also my forthcoming essay "Anti-Jewish Research of the Institut zur Erforschung der Judenfrage or Außenstelle der Hohen Schule der NSDAP in Frankfurt am Main during World War II," in *Lessons and Legacies* VI, New Currents in Holocaust Research, ed. by the Holocaust Foundation Education (forthcoming, 2004).
5. Apart from reports which the anti-Semites themselves—Walter Frank, Wilhelm Grau, Günter Schlichting, Volkmar Eichstädt, and Johannes Pohl—published in the daily press or scholarly journals at the time, Jewish contemporaries, many of them scholars, including Cecil Roth, Bernhard Weinryb, Philip Friedman, Yitzhak Arad, Joshua Starr, and Joseph Billig, provided important background on these Institutes. More recently, on the *Einsatzstab Rosenberg's* looting of libraries and archives, see works by Donald Collins and Herbert Rothfeder, Frits Hoogewoud, Jacqueline Borin, Ernst Loewy, Peter Manasse, Alexander Smoltczyk, and Maurice Weiss, as well as Patricia Grimsted, David Shavit, and Evelyn

Adunka. The work of the Institutes, however, emerges only from a careful study of archives all over the world, since the bulk of their criminal activities was of course clandestinely performed. In addition, librarians and musicologists have generated interesting details. See especially Dov Schidorsky, "Das Schicksal jüdischer Bibliotheken im Dritten Reich," in Peter Vodosek and Manfred Komoroswki, eds., *Bibliotheken während des Nationalsozislismus* (Wiesbaden, 1992), vol. 2, 189–222; and idem, "Confiscation of Libraries and Assignments to Forced Labor. Two Documents of the Holocaust," *Libraries and Culture,* vol. 33, No. 4 (Fall 1998), 347–388; Antje Rapmund, "Die deutsche Bibliothekspolitik in der Tschechoslowakei und in Polen während des zweiten Weltkrieges" (Ph.D. diss., Humboldt University Berlin, 1993); Maria Kühn-Ludewig, *Johannes Pohl (1904–1960) Judaist und Bibliothekar im Dienste Rosenbergs. Eine biographische Dokumentation* (Hannover, 2000); as well as the musicologist studies by Willem de Vries, *Sonderstab Musik. Music Confiscations by the Einsatzstab Reichsleiter Rosenberg under the Nazi Occupation of Western Europe* (Amsterdam, 1997); and Eva Weissweiler, *Ausgemerzt. Das Lexikon der Juden in der Musik und seine mörderischen Folgen* (Cologne, 1999).

6. Traces of its work are revealed in the excellent analyses by Lutz Hachmeister, *Der Gegnerforscher. Die Karriere des SS-Führers Franz Alfred Six* (Munich, 1998) and in Joachim Lerchenmueller's documentary account *Die Geschichtswissenschaft in den Planungen des Sicherheitsdienstes des SS* (Bonn, 2001). Additional information can be pieced together from articles by Jürgen Matthäus, "Weltanschauliche Forschung und Auswertung," "Aus den Akten des Amtes VII im Reichssicherheitshauptamt," *Jahrbuch für Antisemitismusforschung* 5 (1996): 287–330; Klaus Drobisch, "Die Judenreferate des Geheimen Staatspolizeiamtes und des Sicherheitsdienstes," *Jahrbuch für Antisemitismusforschung* 2 (1993): 230–254; Wolfgang Behringer, "Von Krieg zu Krieg. Neue Perspektiven auf das Buch von Günther Franz 'Der Dreißigjährige Krieg und das deutsche Volk' 1940," in Hans Medick, Benigna von Krusenstjern, eds., *Zwischen Alltag und Katastrophe: Der Dreißigjährige Krieg aus der Nähe* (Göttingen, 1998), 541–591; idem, "Der Abwickler der Hexenforschung im Reichssicherheitshauptamt (RSHA): Günther Franz," in Sönke Lorenz, Dieter Bauer, Wolfgang Behringer, und Jürgen Michael Schmidt, eds., *Himmlers Hexenkartothek. Das Interesse des Nationalsozislismus an der Hexenverfolgung* (Bielefeld, 1999), 109–134; idem, "Bauern-Franz und Rassen-Günther. Die politische Geschichte des Agrarhistorikers Günther Franz (1902–1992)," in *Deutsche Historiker im Nationalsozialismus,* Winfried Schulze und Otto Gerhard Oexle, eds. (Frankfurt, 1999), 114–141; Gerhard Paul, "'Von Judenangelegenheiten hatte er bis dahin keine Ahnung.' Herbert Hagen, der Judenreferent aus Neumünster," *Informationen zur Schleswig-Holsteinischen Zeitgeschichte* 33/34 (September 1998): 63–78; and Jörg Rudolph, "'Sämtliche Sendungen sind zu richten an:...' Das RSHA-Amt VII 'Weltanschauliche Forschung und Auswertung'als Sammelstelle erbeuteter Archive und Bibliotheken," in Michael Wildt, ed., *Nachrichtendienst, politische Elite und Mordeinheit. Der Sicherheitsdienst des Reichsführers SS* (Hamburg, 2003), 204–240.

7. See Maria Theresa Picchetto, *Alle radici dell'odio. Preziosi et Benigni antisemiti* (Milan, 1983); Guiseppe Mayda, *Ebrei sotto Salò. La persecuzione antisemita 1943–1945* (Milan, 1978), 45–50; as well as von Papen, "Scholarly Antisemitism," 246–250.

8. On the Institut für deutsche Ostarbeit see Anetta Rybicka, *Instytut Niemieckiej Pracy Wschodniej: Institut für deutsche Ostarbeit: Kraków 1940–1945* (Warsaw, 2002).

9. See Gerhard Volkmer, "Die deutsche Forschung zum osteuropäischen Judentum in den Jahren 1933–1945," *Forschungen zur osteuropäischen Geschichte,* vol. 42 (Wiesbaden, 1989), 109–214; Michael Esch, "Das Krakauer 'Institut für Deutsche Ostarbeit.' Aufgaben, Struktur, Arbeitsweise 1940–1944" (M.A. Thesis, Düsseldorf University, 1990); and Basil Spiru et al., *September 1939* (Berlin, 1959).

10. The Breslau theologian Adolf Wendel had been chosen by Peter Heinz Seraphim for this task. Due to his former membership at the *Verein zur Abwehr des Antisemitismus,* however, Wendel was dismissed at the end of October 1942.

11. Michael Wedekind, *Nationalsozialistische Besatzungs- und Annexionspolitik in Norditalien 1943 bis 1945* (Munich, 2003), 365, 366. Based on the work of Italian historian Bon Gherardi (see note 27 below), Wedekind documents the way Italian Jewish books travelled to Vienna's National Library and how *Gaukonservator* Frodl tried to transfer books to the Klagenfurt *Gaumuseum* (370). The majority of Jewish assets went to *Gau* Carinthia.

12. See Christian Gerlach and Götz Aly, *Das letzte Kapitel. Realpolitik, Ideologie und der Mord an den ungarischen Juden 1944/1945* (Stuttgart/Munich, 2002), 212, fn. 297. See also the review by Arpád von Klimó, "Der ungarische Judenmord—eine deutsche Geschichte?" *Frankfurter Rundschau*, 20 March 2002, 10.

13. See "Bericht Dr. Klaus Schickerts vom 5.5.1944 über eine Reise, die im Auftrage des Auswärtigen Amtes, Inf.XIV (Antijüdische Auslandaktion) nach Südosteuropa durchgeführt wurde," BA, DC PA Klaus Schickert.

14. I would like to thank Adél and Mónika Kusztor, Budapest/Saarbrücken, very much for locating, finding, as well as translating all Hungarian articles for me, and for their time-consuming yet fruitless efforts to gain access to Budapest archives. I am also indebted to Prof. László Karsai for advice concerning the Bosnyák file in the Bureau of Contemporary History in Budapest.

15. Gerlach and Aly, *Das letzte Kapitel*, 37, 42, 49, 55, 81 where they use Klaus Schickert's work in particular without commenting on his political background. On 28 October 1943, Schickert was appointed deputy director of Rosenberg's *Außenstelle* and as of 1 September 1944 confirmed as director. See Rosenberg's letter to *Gauleiter* Sprenger on 6 September 1944 in Centre de Documentation Juive Contemporaine, Paris, CXLV-55. Also Patricia von Papen, "Antisemitic Research and its Political Applications: The Work of Klaus Schickert 1935–1945," Paper given at the Association for Jewish Studies Convention, Chicago, 1999. It would therefore also be worthwhile exploring whether the infamous Horst Seemann to whose diatribes in the *Siebenbürgische Deutsche Zeitung* Aly and Gerlach refer (*Das letzte Kapitel*, 189) is identical with the editor of *Die Judenfrage in Politik, Recht, Kultur und Wirtschaft*, organ of the Ministry of Propaganda's *Institut zum Studium der Judenfrage*. Since Johannes Pohl and Klaus Schickert also campaigned in German-speaking organs abroad, it seems plausible that Seemann too would incite Jew-hatred and propagate segregation and expropriation of the Jews. For a more complete survey of Seemann's campaign, see Hans Holzträger, "Judenverfolgung in Ungarn 1941–1944. Gewaltmaßnahmen gegen Juden im Spiegel der ungarndeutschen Presse," *Tribüne 70* (1979): 94–108. For Schickert's article on "Hungary's Jewish Question as Economic and Spiritual Problem," see the May/ June 1943 issue of *Volk im Osten* edited by the *Deutsche Volksgruppe* in Romania. Coauthors of this issue were Heinz Peter Seraphim, Dr. Otto Paul of Rosenberg's *Außenstelle*, as well as Alexandru Cuza. Aly and Gerlach occasionally mention National Socialist authors and journals without identifying them, assuming their readers' complete familiarity with these texts.

16. The anti-Jewish research division of the RSHA is missing in the chart in Figure 1 (which in itself is to be considered a work in progress), since it still needs to be much better analyzed, just as the French (especially the Bordeaux Institute), and the Italian institutes have to be examined. The purpose of the chart is to clarify the context. For the time being, the best and most comprehensive account on the looting of Jewish books by the RSHA is forthcoming from Werner Schroeder. See his fine abstract "Bestandsaufbau durch Plünderung Jüdischer Bibliotheken im RSHA 1936–1945" for the symposium "Raub und Restitution in Bibliotheken" held at Vienna's City Hall on April 23–24, 2003.

17. Randolph Braham, *The Destruction of Hungarian Jewry: A Documentary Account* (New York, 1963), vol. 1, xvi–xvii. Moreover, László Baky was a protégé of SS-*Sturmbannführer* Wilhelm Höttl, since March 1944 Himmler's representative in Budapest. See Ronald Zweig, *The Gold Train* (London, 2003), 40–41.

18. Mihály Kolosváry-Borcsa, *A zsidókérdés magyarországi irodalma. A zsidóság szerepe a magyar szellemi életben* (Budapest, 1943). Denis Silagi maintains that the list of "originally Jewish"

names is unreliable. See idem, "Die Juden in Ungarn in der Zwischenkriegszeit 1919–1939," *Ungarn-Jahrbuch,* vol. 5 (1973): 198–214.

19. *Die Judenfrage in Ungarn* was Schickert's thesis which he had published under the auspices of the *Institut zum Studium der Judenfrage* run by the Ministry of Propaganda. The Institute's director Ziegler introduced *Die Judenfrage in Ungarn* as the first volume of a series planned by the Institute entitled "The Jews in the Lives of the Peoples. Writings on the Jewish Question of the Present." Accordingly, Schickert published numerous extracts from the book in the Institute's journal, *Mitteilungen über die Judenfrage.* Since Hungary had the highest assimilation rate of Jews in Europe, it made for a case study par excellence. Schickert argued that anti-Semitism was no German import, but originated in Hungary itself.

20. The Foreign Minister had charged the envoy Rudolf Schleier to organize the *Informationsstelle* XIV, namely the *Antijüdische Auslandsaktion.* See Léon Poliakov and Josef Wulf, *Das Dritte Reich und seine Diener* (Wiesbaden, 1989); and Nachlaß Schleiers, especially 4 and 10, PA, AA Bonn.

21. See Klaus Schickert, "Die Judenemanzipation in Südosteuropa und ihr Ende," *Weltkampf,* April–September 1941: 30–42.

22. This is Max Weinreich's translation. See Weinreich, *Hitler's Professors* (1999), 118. Responding to an invitation of the German Foreign Office, the representatives of the Hungarian government, State Secretray Director General Alajos Kovács, and Section Chief Kultsár participated in the *Außenstelle*'s inauguration.

23. It should alarm—above all European—contemporaries today, that this bibliography unfortunately was reprinted in Budapest in 1999. See Mihály Vitéz Kolosváry-Borcsa, *A zsidókérdés magyarországi irodalma* (Budapest, 1999). In the epilogue, the editor calls Kolosváry-Borcsa a classic of Hungarian culture and recommends the reading of his work as an urgent duty in the service of national education!

24. "Zoltán Bosnyák über die Aufgaben des Instituts für Judenforschung," *Deutsche Zeitung* (Budapest), 12 January 1943; and "Wir sprachen mit Zoltán Bosnyák. Besuch im Institut zur Erforschung der Judenfrage," *Deutsche Zeitung,* 24 March 1943, 5. See also Elisabeth Eppler, "The Budapest Institute for the Study of the Jewish Problem," *Wiener Library Bulletin,* vol. 9, no. 1–2 (January–April 1955): 11; Weinreich, *Hitler's Professors,* 139. For a bibliography of Bosnyák's writings, see Margit Szőllősi-Janze, *Die Pfeilkreuzlerbewegung in Ungarn. Historischer Kontext, Entwicklung und Herrschaft* (Munich, 1989), 453. Among the founding members were Lajos Zimmermann, Géza Lator, and Ferenc Réthy-Haszlinger.

25. "Megnyílt a Zsidókérdést Kutató Magyar Intézet," *Függetlenség,* 14 May 1944, 7.

26. Eugene Lévai, *Black Book on the Martyrdom of Hungarian Jewry* (Zurich/Vienna, 1948), 169.

27. On Italian anti-Jewish research centers, see Silva Bon Gherardi, *La Persecuzione Antiebraica A Trieste (1938–1945)* (Udine, 1972), especially 167–174.

28. By the Treaty of Trianon, the city was ceded by Hungary to Czechoslovakia, but reverted to Hungary in 1939 at the beginning of World War II.

29. See Klaus Schickert, *Die Judenfrage in Ungarn. Jüdische Assimilation und antisemitische Bewegung im 19. und 20. Jahrhundert* (Essen, 1937).

30. Franz Riedl, "Die Judenfrage in Ungarn. Jüdische Assimilation und antisemitische Bewegung im 19. und 20.Jahrhundert," *Donauzeitung* (Belgrade), Easter, 9/10 April 1944, 7.

31. Klaus Schickert, "Ungarn's Judenfrage als wirtschaftliches und geistiges Problem," *Volk im Osten* (Hermannstadt), May–June 1943, 41–52. Since Schickert had represented the German News Agency in Bucharest between 1937 and 1941, he had multiple local contacts.

32. Klaus Schickert, "Die Erforschung der Judenfrage im Südostraum," *Weltkampf. Die Judenfrage in Geschichte und Gegenwart,* vol. 1 (January–April 1944): 1–8.

33. Generalbevollmächtigter für Ungarn, Veesenmayer to Auswärtiges Amt, 18 April 1944, Inhalt: Entjudung der Apotheken in Ungarn, NA, TM 120 4465, for instance, was forwarded by von Thadden to the Ministry of the Interior, the Ministry of Economics, the *Oberkom-*

mando der Wehrmacht, the Ministry of Propaganda, the RSHA, the *Antijüdische Weltliga,* the *Weltdienst,* the *Institut zur Erforschung der Judenfrage,* and to the *Reichsinstitut.*

34. Bericht vom 5.5.1944, BA, DC, PA Klaus Schickert.

35. Deutsche Gesandtschaft/ Preßburg to Auswärtiges Amt, 25 February 1944, NA, TM 120 4465.

36. The Sztójay government was in place until 25 August 1944, when, after the Romanians had changed sides, General Géza Lakatos formed a new government.

37. On Ballensiefen, see Behringer, "Bauern-Franz und Rassen-Günther," 123–124; Hachmeister, *Der Gegenerforscher,* 225–227; and Björn Potthast, *Das jüdische Zentralmuseum der SS in Prag. Gegnerforschung und Völkermord im Nationalsozialismmus,* (Frankfurt/Main, 2000), 318–319.

38. Heinz Ballensiefen, *Juden in Frankreich. Die französische Judenfrage in Geschichte und Gegenwart* (Berlin, 1939); and Behringer, "Bauern-Franz und Rassen-Günther," 124.

39. Hachmeister, *Der Gegnerforscher,* 226; Gerlach and Aly, *Das letzte Kapitel,* 187.

40. Matthäus, "*Weltanschauliche Forschung und Auswertung*," 291; Note of 24 October 1944 from Ballensiefen to Günther and von Thadden concerning the pro-Jewish activities of the Spanish Embassy in Budapest, reprinted in Randolph L. Braham, *The Destruction of Hungarian Jewry. A Documentary Account,* Part II (New York, 1963), 756, 757–758.

41. "Jüdische Bücher," *Deutsche Zeitung* (Budapest), 2 December 1943, 3.

42. Zoltán Bosnyák, "'Das Ungarische Institut zur Erforschung der Judenfrage.' Wissenschaftliche Forschungsarbeit auf dem Gebiete der Judenfrage in Ungarn," *Europäischer Wissenschaftsdienst,* vol. 3, no. 11 (1943): 10–14.

43. Zoltán Bosnyák, "Kossuth Lajos és a zsidókérdés. Három nyilatkozat az erkölcsromboló zsidó terjeszkedésről, az emancipáció ellen és az antiszemitizmusról," *Függetlenség,* 8 March 1944.

44. "Das nationale Einkommen und das Judentum. Vom Leiter des Institutes zur Erforschung der Judenfrage, Zoltán Bosnyák," *Deutsche Zeitung* (Budapest), 22 March 1944.

45. Klaus Schickert über die in Vorbereitung befindlichen Schriften des Instituts am 23.Februar 1944, BA, NS 8/ 266.

46. On Endre, see *Encyclopedia of the Holocaust,* Israel Gutman, ed. (New York, 1990). Endre was undersecretary of state between 9 April and 5 September 1944. While not included in the Lakatos Government formed in August 1944, Endre was reappointed to a high governmental position after the Szálasi coup of 15 October 1944. He fled with the retreating Nazis but was captured by the Americans and extradited. Found guilty of war crimes, he was executed on 29 March 1946.

47. "Nichtjuden erhalten Personalausweise. Staatssekretär Endre über das innenpolitische Leben," *Deutsche Zeitung,* 13 April 1944, 4. Eugene Lévai therefore called Bosnyák a "functionary of the government." See his *Black Book,* 130, 168.

48. Raul Hilberg, *Die Vernichtung der europäischen Juden. Die Gesamtgeschichte des Holocaust* (Berlin, 1982), 564.

49. Zoltán Bosnyák, "A budapesti gettó múltja és jelene," *Függetlenség,* 23 April 1944, 7; and "A zsidóság budapesti térfoglalása," *Függetlenség,* 9 April 1944, 5.

50. "A Zsidókérdést Kutató Magyar Intézet újra megkezdi működését," *Függetlenség,* 28 April 1944, 5.

51. von Thadden am 28.4. an Dt.Gesandtschaft in Budapest, NA, TM 120 4652. A month later, von Thadden visited the new institute. See his letter to Wagner enclosing a report on his mission to Budapest of 25 May 1944 in Braham, *The Destruction of Hungarian Jewry,* vol. 1, 384; and Report from Veesenmayer to the Foreign Office on the Inauguration of the Hungarian Institute for Research into the Jewish Question in ibid., 376–377.

52. Dr. Klaus Schickert's Bericht vom 5.5.1944 über eine Reise, die im Auftrage des Auswärtigen Amtes, Inf.XIV (Antijüdische Auslandaktion) nach Südosteuropa durchgeführt wurde, BA, DC PA Klaus Schickert.

53. Lévai, *Black Book*, 168. See also Report by the Generalbevollmächtigter für Ungarn Veesenmayer to the Auswärtige Amt, 22 May 1944. Inhalt: Eröffnung des ungarischen Instituts zur Erforschung der Judenfrage, NA, TM 120 4465.

54. Zoltán Bosnyák, "A budapesti zsidóság foglalta el a jobb lakosság nagyrészét," *Függetlenség*, 7 May 1944, 5.

55. Ibid., 566.

56. "A Zsidókérdést Kutató Magyar Intézet Ünnepi Megnyitása," *Harc*, 10 June 1944, 6.

57. See Note from von Thadden to Veesenmayer Regarding the Transfer of Grell to Budapest to Replace Hezinger of 2 June 1944 in Braham, *The Destruction of Hungarian Jewry*, vol. 1, 394. On Grell, see Gerlach and Aly, *Das letzte Kapitel*, 280.

58. See Letter from Thadden to Wagner Enclosing a Report on His Mission to Budapest of 25 May 1944 in Braham, *The Destruction of Hungarian Jewry*, vol. 1, 384.

59. According to Raul Hilberg, the RSHA watched even Endre closely. See Hilberg, *Die Vernichtung der europäischen Juden*, 561: "Um allerdings sicherzustellen, daß die ungarischen Gesetze nicht allzu eigenständig ausfielen, setzte Veesenmayer einen RSHA Mann in Endres Dienststelle der dem Ungarn" in dauernder persönlicher Fühlungnahme "bei der Ausarbeitung und Durchführung von Verordnungen zur Hand zu gehen hatte."

60. According to Randolph Braham, it was Ernst Kaltenbrunner, chief of the Security Police and SD, who had been instrumental in having László Endre and László Baky included in the Ministry. They became Eichmann's closest collaborators, and worked out the scheme leading to the "Final Solution." See Braham, *The Destruction of Hungarian Jewry*, vol. 1, xvi–xvii.

61. Lévai, *Black Book*, 169; Eppler, "The Budapest Institute," 11.

62. Hilberg, *Die Vernichtung der europäischen Juden*, 566.

63. Compare "Ungarisches Institut zur Erforschung der Judenfrage," *Völkischer Beobachter* (Vienna edition), 14 May 1944, 2; and "Pest vármegyében kijeltölték a zsidók lakhelyét," *Pesti Hírlap*, 16 May 1944, 5.

64. "Ungarisches Institut für Judenfragen," *Völkischer Beobachter* (Berlin edition), 16 May 1944, 2.

65. "Megnyílt a Zsidókérdést Kutató Magyar Intézet," *Függetlenség*, 14 May 1944, 7.

66. "A Zsidókérdést Kutató Magyar Intézet Ünnepi Megnyitása," *Harc*, 10 June 1944, 6.

67. "Ungarn's Wirtschaft im Aufbruch. Einheitliche Erzeugung auf der ganzen Linie—was Imrédy's Ernennung bedeutet," *Donauzeitung* (Belgrade), 27–28 May 1944, 5, where these data were reproduced to justify the expulsion of Jews from the economy.

68. Most books came from Sub-Carpathian Rus, from the libraries of the Hungarian Jewish Museum, the Jewish Theological Seminary of Budapest, and the Jewish community of Pest, or from the personal library of Prof. Michael Gutmann, late director of the Jewish Theological Seminary. See *Genizah Publications in Memory of Prof. Dr. David Kaufmann*, Samuel Löwinger and Alexander Schreiber, eds. (Budapest, 1949), vi. The Jewish Research Institute was hit by bombs, and its collection of books destroyed, with the exception of part of the library of M. Guttmann, installed on the ground floor of the building. The Jewish community library's Varro Collection, some 500 anti-Semitic brochures that the community had acquired at a sale in 1941, was also incorporated. When the Union Club became too crowded, the Institute moved to the hills on the right bank of the Danube, where it almost at once fell victim to an incendiary bomb. See Philip Friedman, "The Fate of the Jewish Book during the Nazi Era," *Jewish Book Annual*, vol. 15 (1957–1958): 3–13, esp. 11, where Friedman mentions the confiscated library of the late Rabbi Emmanuel Löw in Szeged.

69. Letter from von Thadden to Wagner Enclosing a Report on His Mission to Budapest of 25 May 1944, in Braham, *The Destruction of Hungarian Jewry*, vol. 1, 381.

70. "Megnyílt a Zsidókérdést Kutató Magyar Intézet," *Függetlenség*, 14 May 1944, 7.

71. "A Zsidókérdést Kutató Magyar Intézet Ünnepi Megnyitása," *Harc*, 10 June 1944, 6.

72. See Aufzeichnung Schleiers am 28.Juni 1944 für den Reichsaußenminister mit Durchdrucken für LR von Thadden und Herrn Botschafter Rintelen, PA-AA Bonn, 5425. Bal-

lensiefen, on the other hand, reported 80,000 copies of the first issue of *Harc,* which had to be reprinted in a second edition. See Protokoll über die Arbeitsbesprechung im Gästehaus Eppenhain am 23.Juni 1944 betreffs Behandlung der Judenfrage in Ungarn und Zusammenarbeit zwischen dem "Welt-Dienst" und den ungarischen Gästen, Centre de Documentation Juive Contemporaine, Paris, CXLIV-407, 2.

73. Ibid.

74. See von Thadden's letter to Wagner enclosing a Report on His Mission to Budapest of 25 May 1944 in Braham, *The Destruction of Hungarian Jewry,* vol. 1, 384. "Besonders wurde beobachtet, daß Juden bis zu 30 Exemplaren kauften. Es steht aber zu hoffen, daß das Blatt auch arische Abnehmer gefunden hat ... Leiter des Instituts ist Prof. Bosnyák, der sich in seiner Rolle offensichtlich nicht sehr wohl fühlt, da er nicht propagandistisch, sondern wissenschaftlich arbeiten möchte, dazu aber zur Zeit naturgemäß nicht kommt."

75. See Schleier an die dt.Gesandtschaft Budapest z.Hd. des Judenreferenten Herrn Konsul Dr.Grell/ Budapest am 12.Juli 1944, PA AA Bonn, 5425. On Grell, see Hilberg, *Die Vernichtung der europäischen Juden* (Frankfurt, 1990), vol. 2, 886.

76. "Ungarisches Institut für Judenfragen," *Völkischer Beobachter* (Berlin edition), 16 May 1944, 2.

77. Randolph L. Braham, *The Politics of Genocide. The Holocaust in Hungary,* revised and enlarged edition (New York, 1994), vol. 1, 534.

78. See Essener Verlagsanstalt to Schickert, 24 May 1944, NA, TM 120 4658. On 24 May 1944, that is after the deportations of Jews from zones one and two, namely from the Carpathians and Transylvania, had started, Schickert's publisher informed him that the third edition had been expanded to 15,000 copies. In his report to von Thadden of 30 December 1943, Schickert had argued that one of the reasons for travelling to Hungary was the updating of his book for a third edition. See NA, TM 120 4651. See also von Thadden an Polizeipräsident Berlin am 27. Juni 1944, NA, TM 120 4658. The Ministry offered Schickert the money for a new trip. The documents reveal that he planned to travel to Preßburg and Budapest again at the end of June to meet local anti-Semitic "scholars."

79. See Zweig, *The Gold Train,* 248. The document that Zweig refers to and which I have not yet seen in the original and in its entirety raises a number of questions: Did the RSHA confiscate the contents of bookshops, archives, seminaries, and apartments *before* members of the Hungarian Institute and their helpers could lay their hands on the loot? Or, less likely, was there simply a division of labor? Where and what did Höttl plunder, and how big was his task force, and where did the loot disappear to subsequently? Were the most precious pieces sent to Berlin? What was stored in the Hungarian Institute, and how much of the loot was sold or even destroyed?

80. *Harc,* 3 June 1944.

81. *Harc,* 1 July 1944, 8, in which Bosnyák, as an example of how ordinary people fought "Judaization," reprinted a letter by the director of the savings-bank of Szeged-Csongrád who had transferred 1,000 pengő to the Institute.

82. Zoltán Bosnyák, "A zsidókérdést kutató..." *Harc,* 3 June 1944, 8.

83. *Pesti Hírlap,* 17 June 1944, 4, as well as *Függetlenség,* 17 June 1944. See also István Eörsi, "'Staatliche Schlachtfelder.' Ungarns Weg nach Europa ist krumm," *Frankfurter Allgemeine Zeitung,* 2 January 2001, 46.

84. Brunhoff, like Ballensiefen, was part of the propaganda staff of the German delegation. See Hilberg, *Die Vernichtung der europäischen Juden* (1982), 559.

85. See also *Genizah Publications in memory of Prof. Dr. David Kaufmann.*

86. Originally the *Welt-Dienst* had been founded by a retired colonel, *Oberstleutnant a.D.*Ulrich Fleischhauer from Erfurt. In March 1939 Rosenberg's Office took it over, moved its archive to Frankfurt, and put August Schirmer in charge of it. By 1944, the *Welt-Dienst. Internationale Korrespondenz zur Aufklärung über die Judenfrage* was published in more than twenty languages. On Schirmer, see Weinreich, *Hitler's Professors* (1999), 118–119. In

autumn 1941, the Hungarian Society for Race Protection had invited Schirmer to Hungary. See Viktor Lorenz, "Gespräch der 'Deutschen Zeitung' mit zwei Kennern der Judenfrage: Vor einer Gesamteuropäischen Lösung der Judenfrage," *Deutsche Zeitung* (Budapest), 9 November 1941, 3–4, where Schirmer and Bosnyák are interviewed at great length.

87. This is hardly surprising, since Vitéz Mihály Kolosváry-Borcsa was both secretary of state for press, radio, and publishing as well as head of the Institute's press department.

88. On Pohl, see Kühn-Ludewig, *Johannes Pohl*. On Ballensiefen's and Pohl's meeting with Hungarian anti-Semites and other German members of the *Welt-Dienst* on 23 June 1944, see "Protokoll über die Arbeitsbesprechung im Gästehaus Eppenhain am 23. Juni 1944 betreffs Behandlung der Judenfrage in Ungarn und Zusammenarbeit zwischen dem 'Welt-Dienst' und den ungarischen Gästen," Centre de Documentation Juive Contemporaine, Paris, CXLIV-407, 1.

89. Johann Pohl, *Jüdische Selbstzeugnisse* (Munich, 1943).

90. "Gyilkold meg a keresztények legjobbját," *Függetlenség*, 2 July 1944, 5.

91. Lévai, *Black Book,* 108, 169.

92. Klaus Schickert, "Ungarn's Judenfrage als wirtschaftliches und geistiges Problem," *Volk im Osten* (Hermannstadt), May–June 1943, 52; and "Die Erforschung der Judenfrage im Südostraum," *Weltkampf. Die Judenfrage in Geschichte und Gegenwart*, vol. 1 (January–April 1944), 1–8.

93. Behringer, "Bauern-Franz und Rassen-Günther," 123–124; Hachmeister, *Der Gegnerforscher,* 225, 267; and Matthäus, "'Weltanschauliche Forschung und Auswertung,'" 291.

94. For an introductory text on Höttl, see Thorsten Querg, "Wilhelm Hoettl—vom Informanten zum Sturmbannführer im Sicherheitsdienst der SS," in Barbara Danckwortt, Thorsten Querg, Claudia Schöningh, eds., *Historische Rassismusforschung. Ideologen—Täter—Opfer* (Hamburg, 1995), 208–230. See also Katrin Paehler's forthcoming dissertation (American University).

95. "Juden und Freimaurer. Die Drahtzieher des Badoglio-Verrates," *Deutsche Zeitung* (Budapest), 9 March 1944, 3 (on Giovanni Preziosi); "Kriegsschuld der Juden," *Deutsche Zeitung* (Budapest), 24 March 1944 (on Henri Labroue); "A zsidóság bosszúja," *Harc*, 26 August 1944, 1–2 (on the assassination attempt on George Montandon).

96. Eppler, "The Budapest Institute," 11.

97. Zsuzsanna Osváth, "Can words kill? Anti-Semitic Texts and Their Impact on the Hungarian Jewish Catastrophe," in Randolph Braham and Attila Pók, *The Holocaust in Hungary Fifty Years Later* (New York, 1997), 79–116.

98. Lévai, *Black Book,* 109.

99. Braham, *The Destruction of Hungarian Jewry,* vol. 1, 384.

Chapter 14

Indigenous Collaboration in the Government General

The Case of the *Sonderdienst**

Peter Black

An auxiliary executive force deployed in Nazi-occupied Poland, the *Sonderdienst* (Special Service) never numbered more than about 3,500 men. Between 1940 and 1944, it was deployed at the lowest level of German occupation administration in Poland and was engaged in so-called routine occupation tasks: street and road patrol, securing the harvest, ensuring the collection of taxes and fines, and enforcing the regulations issued by the local authorities. As an organization, the *Sonderdienst* received little contemporaneous attention outside of occupied Poland, and even less from postwar scholars.[1]

Why then subject this organization to a study? Four factors warrant a closer look. First, the *Sonderdienst* highlights the dependence of German administration in the Government General on locally recruited auxiliaries, particularly in the countryside.[2] Second, the *Sonderdienst* was conceived, developed, expanded, and deployed within the context of a bitter battle between German civilian authorities and the SS/police apparatus over control of local executive police power. This is hardly new; yet the Government General is unusual in that the civilian authorities were able to fight the SS to a draw on this issue. Third, since its formation followed the recruitment of the "ethnic" and ideological "cream" of the ethnic German population of Poland into predecessor agencies, the *Sonderdienst* represents an early effort of the National Socialist authorities to fashion an ethnically conscious and ideologically committed corps from young men of questionable, even dubious, German ancestry and heritage. Finally, a study of the

Sonderdienst reveals not only the complicity of the civilian authorities in Nazi crimes, but the link between "routine" duties in Nazi-occupied Europe and the brutal persecution of groups targeted as enemies of the German Reich. Such issues make the *Sonderdienst* well worth exploring.

After the speedy conquest of Poland, the Germans annexed Danzig, West Prussia, Poznań, and Upper Silesia directly to the Reich and designated the remainder of the territory they occupied as the Government General. Immediate goals involved deporting hundreds of thousands of Poles and Jews from the annexed territories to the Government General in order to make room for the settlement of ethnic Germans from Soviet-occupied or Soviet-coveted territory.[3] The German invaders aimed to eliminate Poland's political and cultural elite by either shooting them or deporting them to concentration camps.[4] They concentrated the Jewish population into enclosures under the "self-administration" of Jewish Councils, whose members were responsible for the implementation of German orders.[5] Moreover, they sought to mobilize and exploit the vast potential for manual labor in the Government General by instituting compulsory labor requirements for both Poles and Jews.[6]

Implementation of such policies required manpower: reliable and armed auxiliaries, prepared to employ lethal force against unarmed civilians. In both the annexed territories and in the Government General, the SS recruited or reorganized local ethnic German *Selbstschutz* (self-defense) units and deployed them in support of the German Order Police (*Ordnungspolizei*) at a variety of police duties ranging from street patrol to shooting civilians. In 1940, the *Selbstschutz,* particularly in District Lublin, drew criticism from the civilian authorities for being unavailable and corrupt, and, ironically, for the use of excessive force. The recruitment of ethnic Germans by the SS served two purposes: (1) it provided a structure for "recapturing" German blood and for binding the scattered ethnic Germans of central and eastern Poland to the fortunes of the Nazi rulers; and (2) it served the SS as a tool to implement German police policy in occupied Poland.[7]

The *Sonderdienst* evolved in response to the demand of the German civilian occupation authorities for operational control over local police personnel. Local police power was essential to maintain security from the first days of the occupation. Established formally on 26 October 1939, the Government General was ruled by a civilian Governor General with his seat in Cracow; this position was held by the Nazi lawyer Hans Frank for the duration of the German occupation. Below Frank, State Secretary Josef Bühler managed administrative "main departments" (*Hauptabteilungen*): among them internal administration (which included an office for population policy and welfare), food and agriculture, and labor. The Government General was divided administratively into four districts (*Distrikte*) with seats in Warsaw, Cracow, Lublin, and Radom. To these was added a District "Galicia" (seat Lemberg/Lwów/L'viv) after the Germans conquered it from the Soviet Union in 1941. Each district was managed by a civilian district governor, who presided over a series of "departments" (*Abteilungen*) analogous to those at the center. Each District was divided into municipalities, directed by *Stadthauptmänner,* and *Kreise* (rural districts), ruled by *Kreishaupt-männer.*[8] In theory, the *Kreishauptmann* was absolute lord over his territory and was expected to "carry out measures and orders on his own initiative corresponding to the political guidelines set by the Government General." He was required to feed his *Kreis,* and to maintain basic services and transportation routes. He had to mobilize the local population for work, secure imposed agricultural quotas, and monitor trade and pricing. He was expected, on the local level, to reestablish order and security with the assistance of German gendarmes and Polish police. He investigated and stewarded the adjudication of crimes perpetrated in his *Kreis* and ensured that "individual political agitators were rendered harmless." He was to enforce "administrative penalties" for those who refused to obey German decrees, and to incarcerate "absolutely malevolent elements" in labor camps where a regimen of hard manual labor would induce "naturally indolent Poles" to obey their German masters. He was to "energetically fight Jewish profiteering and usury," confiscating Jewish-owned concerns and businesses, and interdicting Jewish-managed trade and commerce. Until the summer of 1942, he was responsible for monitoring the movements of Jews residing in or being deported to his *Kreis.*[9]

The civilian authorities in occupied Poland in fact lacked sufficient manpower to guard ammunition dumps, let alone to carry out the tasks assigned to them.[10] Less than one week after the Government General was established, its Higher SS and Police Leader (*Höhere SS- und Polizeiführer*—HSSPF), *SS-Obergruppenführer* Friedrich Wilhelm Krüger, confessed to Governor General Frank that "available police forces" were "in no way sufficient to secure the countryside."[11] Worse still, German municipal police (*Schutzpolizei*) and gendarmerie units were billeted in the cities and deployed in closed units. When the Order Police finally established thirteen gendarmerie companies in the Government General and deployed a platoon of gendarmes to each *Kreis* in June 1940, their functions were explicitly limited to supervising the Polish police and carrying out police duties only in "special cases in which Reich or ethnic German interests are affected."[12] By the spring of 1940, reports of the *Kreishauptmänner* reflected a nearly unanimous lament that they lacked the enforcement personnel to guarantee basic security in their regions, let alone to exploit them.[13] The inability of the civilian authorities to gain operational control of the few German police personnel deployed in their *Kreise* prompted, as Main Department for Internal Administration chief Friedrich Wilhelm Siebert noted in 1943, the creation of the *Sonderdienst.*[14]

Months before the dissolution of the *Selbstschutz,* Frank sought to respond to the demands of the regional civilian administrators. When in March 1940, despite continuing poor relations between police and administration, Krüger offered to select twenty "qualified people" from the *Selbstschutz* to assign to each *Kreishaupt-mann,* Frank enthusiastically designated these promised units to be a *Sonderdienst* (Special Service).[15] To develop a plan for coordinating the selection and training of these new units, Siebert assigned Hermann Hammerle from the Main Department of Internal Administration. On 10 April, Hammerle reported to Frank that he conceived of the *Sonderdienst* as a "type of police unit made up of ethnic Germans," deployed in units of 20–30 and subordinated to the *Kreis-* and *Stadthauptmänner*. As a regional force, the *Sonderdienst* must be subordinated to the Governor General, that is, to the civilian authority.[16]

By 6 May 1940, Hammerle and Siebert had a decree ready for Frank to sign. Published on 10 May 1940, it placed the *Sonderdienst* at the disposal of the *Kreishauptmänner* in order to "carry out administrative measures," and subordinated all *Sonderdienst* personnel exclusively to the civilian authorities. To forestall SS objections and to distinguish the *Sonderdienst* from the police forces, the decree stipulated that the *Sonderdienst* was to be deployed "in principle only for administrative-technical tasks." It could be assigned to "carry out police duties, whenever police units are not available" with the requirement that the "appropriate police authorities" were informed beforehand, but only "insofar as this [was] … possible." If the *Sonderdienst* were deployed as reinforcement of a police-directed operation, however, the police commander would assume operational control for the duration of the operation.[17]

To administer and supply the new force, an Inspectorate of the *Sonderdienst* (*Inspektion des Sonderdienstes*) was established under Hammerle's leadership within the Main Department for Internal Administration.[18] As Frank exulted to his department heads on 10 May, the new *Sonderdienst* units provided the *Kreis-* and *Stadthauptmänner* "in every district and every city" with "a well-armed, well-organized, and disciplined unit of approximately 20–30 men, subordinated directly and exclusively to them." The civilian administrators could deploy these units "in cases of dire emergency for extraordinary circumstances or for the normal implementation of tasks which are not carried out by the police, but which are nevertheless important."[19]

To announce the establishment of the *Sonderdienst* was not actually to deploy the units. On 31 May, Siebert reported that only 14 out of 45 *Kreise* actually had units in place and that none of these had service regulations or personnel files.[20] In June, "almost all" of the *Kreis-* and *Stadthauptleute* reported that "the available police forces" were "too small to enforce official measures," and complained that threats of enforcement without follow-up "only weaken German authority."[21] *Kreis* Jaroslau (District Cracow) reported that the *Sonderdienst* had served well so far, but that the promised second detachment had not yet arrived and was urgently needed; *Kreis* Siedlce (District Warsaw) referred to the "urgent necessity to deploy ethnic German police forces."[22] On 18 July 1940, Hammerle reported that only sixteen *Kreise* had units of one officer and 24 men; to deploy in all of the other *Kreise*, the strength of the units would have to be halved.[23]

Though grateful for the assistance,[24] several *Kreishauptmänner* were appalled at the skills level of the first *Sonderdienst* units. The *Kreishauptmann* in Opatów (District Radom) complained that his men were "incapable of composing a simple written report," since they spoke poor German or no German at all. In Neu-Sandez/Nowy Sącz (District Cracow), the *Kreishauptmann* noted that the men in his *Sonderdienst* unit lacked sufficient command of the German language to answer the telephones. The *Kreishauptmann* in Ostrów-Mazowiecki (District Warsaw) opined that the *Sonderdienst* was "merely a financial burden" and was "scarcely suited for deployment." The *Kreishauptmann* in Miechów returned his detachment to Lublin after determining that, out of fear of the dark, they had fired on German gendarmes in the streets of Miechów.[25]

Part of the problem in securing "qualified personnel" and appropriate equipment lay with the SS and police. After weeks of bickering, Frank, Krüger, and District Lublin SS and Police Leader Odilo Globocnik reached a compromise in July 1940 that called for the transfer of the most able *Selbstschutz* recruits into the *Waffen SS* or the *Sonderdienst*. Globocnik would continue to supply the recruits and supervise their training in a *Sonderdienst* Replacement Battalion based in Lublin.[26] At a conference in Lublin on 18 July, however, Hammerle heard several of the *Kreishauptmänner* complain about the poor equipment and inadequate uniforms supplied to the *Sonderdienst* men.[27] In October, Hammerle reported to Frank that he had had to conscript directly among ethnic Germans to get the last 650 men needed to meet the requirements of the *Kreishauptmänner*.[28] In November, the District Governor in Warsaw reported that 218 men serving in the district *Sonderdienst* were now properly equipped and performing satisfactorily, but that the *Kreishauptmänner* had complained about the work and attitude of the SS noncommissioned officers who acted as detachment commanders.[29] The *Kreishauptmann* in Siedlce requested that his detachment commander be replaced since he did "not respond to the demands [of the position] and does not exhibit the personality to hold the ethnic German young people together."[30]

Confronted with this criticism, Globocnik requested in a huff that Frank relieve him of any responsibility for the *Sonderdienst*. During the first two months of 1941, Hammerle moved the *Sonderdienst* administrative and supply offices as well as the training school from Lublin to Cracow; by March, he could report a reduction of tension between the *Sonderdienst* and the SS/police.[31] The real reason for the tension with the police lay in the efforts of the civilian authorities to establish an executive force independent of the Higher SS and Police Leader. As Frank told Hammerle on 14 December 1940, the significance of the *Sonderdienst* as an agency with executive power was so great that the civilian authorities "must consciously minimize its importance ... to distract the attention of other circles."[32]

Freed from the tutelage of the SS and police, Hammerle sought to expand the *Sonderdienst* units. In September 1940, Frank had authorized him to recruit ethnic Ukrainians in order to increase personnel available to 50 per *Kreis*.[33] By mid-July 1941, 2,500 men were serving in the *Sonderdienst;* Hammerle hoped to recruit another 2,000 from young ethnic Germans recently resettled in *Gau Wartheland*.[34] Four months later, however, only 2,600 men were serving in the *Sonderdienst,* with further recruitment deemed difficult due to lack of German language skills among the potential recruits.[35] In the autumn of 1942, the Commander of Order Police estimated that nearly 75 percent of the new *Sonderdienst* recruits did not speak German.[36]

During its first year, the *Sonderdienst* trained 4,000 men. The civilian authorities had intended the *Sonderdienst* to consist of ethnic Germans who would eventually serve in the German administration. Training included not only physical conditioning, weapons use and care, military drill, and field maneuvers, but also German language instruction. Though the genealogical pedigree of many of the *Sonderdienst* men did not conform to the strictest Nazi standards, the civilian authorities aimed to create a consciousness of being German sufficient to inspire active commitment to Hitler's war against Jews and Bolsheviks, Poles and Russians. *Sonderdienst* recruits endured lectures on German history, Nazi ideology, and "geography in alignment with German principles." Although no training manuals are known to have survived the war, articles in the Inspectorate's periodical seem to reflect themes that the German trainers hoped to reinforce. One theme was "race consciousness." *Sonderdienst* men were instructed, often condescendingly, that the blood of all the Germanic "races" (even if that of the "Nordic race" was represented only to "a limited percent") flowed in their veins. They were praised for having been able to sustain their Germanness against the "influence of alien blood."[37] As one purpose of their basic training, the *Sonderdienst* men were to be brought to the "educational-cultural level of their German racial compatriots [*Volksgenossen*] from the Old Reich." Through their auxiliary police work the *Sonderdienst* men had "energetically assisted in anchoring ever more firmly the essence [*Wesen*] of the German administrative work in the population of the Government General."[38]

Sonderdienst men were urged to identify completely with the fate of the German Reich. The goal was not to create "ethnic German fellow human beings (*Mitmenschen*), but [engaged] members of the German *Volk;*" the men must "feel … and act at every moment as loyal followers of the Führer in any situation or danger." They had to be educated to be "battle conscious (*kampfbewußt*) and ready for sacrifice and to suppress and extirpate … former aspirations anchored in the Polish state." The *Sonderdienst* man must understand that he is "not to vegetate without resolution, but at all times to be a fighter for the light against the darkness, that is, a fighter for National Socialism against Bolshevism and world Jewry.…"[39] Hitler's struggle was his struggle and would "determine the fate and future of the German nation for millennia."[40]

Despite the propaganda, the Inspectorate was aware that Reich Germans did not always treat the ethnic Germans in the *Sonderdienst* as equals. The first issue of the *Sonderdienst* official gazette referred to these inferiority feelings, and admonished Reich Germans that it was false to "view the ethnic Germans in the *Sonderdienst* as second-rank members of the nation."[41] At a review of the *Sonderdienst* Replacement Battalion on 10 August 1943, Frank told the new trainees that they had the right to call themselves soldiers of the German ideal and that it was his wish to "develop the *Sonderdienst* … into a proud instrument of the German leadership in this region."[42]

The periodical also lectured on the National Socialist value that struggle, battle, and violence were positive ends in themselves. The "meaning of life" was "identical with the struggle for life." Whosoever wished to live, had to fight; life had "never yet been granted as a gift to the cowardly and the lazy." *Sonderdienst* men were exhorted to sacrifice their lives in the assurance that those who did were "not dead;" their "heroic spirit" would live on in the "community" [*Gemeinschaft*]. In such "death, life is fulfilled." The present time of "our great struggle … signified nothing other than the realization of that natural law that gives to the stronger the right to take possession of land and empty space, to cultivate it, and to make it useful for the *Volk*."[43]

The Jewish archenemy of National Socialist mythology was clearly defined for the *Sonderdienst* men. An article entitled "The Struggle for Europe" opined that "the Jewish spirit [*Geist*] that crept into Europe from the Orient" had throughout history "maliciously and destructively sought to annihilate the races, nations, politics, and the economy." Having already saved Germany from the Jewish threat, the National Socialists were obligated to "do everything possible to deflect this danger from Europe."[44] A "brainteaser" in the November 1942 issue challenged readers to consider in which city Hitler first came "to know the faces of Marxism, Jewry, and parliamentarianism."[45] An article from 1943 attributed the Second World War to the "infamous" work of those "Jewish agitators and exploiters who see in German achievement and German toil a constant threat to their parasitical lifestyle.…"[46] Bolshevism that had developed in Russia as the "Jewish-subversive doctrine of Karl Marx" migrated east, where it could find "most of its supporters among the Jews, whom the doctrine, since it was racially determined, suited extraordinarily well."[47] Examples of Jewish "perfidy" in the Vistula basin, which they had "viewed entirely as their own domain," were cited in yet another article, which, appearing in mid-1943, concluded ominously: "They have now finally received the bill."[48]

Lacking both sufficient personnel records to determine the relative strength of German ethnicity among the *Sonderdienst* men and information as to whether they absorbed or even read these newspaper articles, we cannot measure the success of the German occupiers in molding these men into good Germans and committed Nazis. Not only the hints of second-class treatment referred to above, but also the fact that the Institute for German Work in the East (*Institut für deutsche Ostarbeit*—IdO) based in Cracow chose 110 members of the *Sonderdienst* for a racial-anthropological study[49] (along with Jews of Tarnów, Goralians of Nowy Targ, and Polish laborers working in the German Construction Service) would indicate that Reich Germans considered the *Sonderdienst* men as less than fully German. Practical need for enforcers of German occupation policy proved more important, however, than purity of German ancestry.

After completing training, *Sonderdienst* recruits received the rank of *Sonderdienstmann*. Platoon commanders were subordinate to the detachment commander, who was operationally responsible to the *Kreishauptmann* and administratively subordinate to the Commissioner for the *Sonderdienst* at the District level.[50] By summer 1941, the *Sonderdienst* had groomed an indigenous noncommissioned officer corps and had begun to train officers. In order to weed out incompetents, the Inspectorate instituted an examination and established an evaluation board. Especially qualified *Sonderdienst* men could hope for career advancement in the civilian administrative apparatus.[51]

During training in the fiscal year 1941, for which figures are available, the *Sonderdienst* men were paid 60 złotys a month. Once in the field, the *Sonderdienstmann* received 90 złotys per month with a supplement of 11 złotys per month when on active duty outside the normal duty station.[52] By the summer of 1941, *Sonderdienst* men were receiving benefits, including free housing and uniforms as well as an untaxed food allowance of 2.70 złotys per day. Each *Sonderdienst* man was eligible to receive ten days of leave per year. Those whose families owned or worked farms could apply for an additional harvest leave for up to two weeks. As of 1 August 1941, a dependent support benefits package equivalent to that paid to families of ethnic Germans working for Reich agencies in Poland was introduced.[53] By March 1942, a personnel budget of just over two million złotys put 2,700 *Sonderdienst* men into the field, wearing field gray uniforms with armbands bearing the inscription *"Sonderdienst des Generalgouvernements."*[54]

Sonderdienst units were engaged in five main areas of enforcement activity: securing agricultural produce quota deliveries, collection of taxes and administrative fines, interdicting illicit trade, monitoring prices, and "guard and security service." Between October 1940 and the end of June 1941, the *Sonderdienst* had robbed the peasant populace of at least 4,766,334 kg of grain, 12,900,171 kg of potatoes, and 3,017 head of cattle. During the same period, *Sonderdienst* units collected 2,998,560 złotys in taxes and 670,644 more złotys in fines, and seized over a million złotys worth of goods traded on the black market (mostly livestock, grain, and potatoes).[55]

Wherever the *Sonderdienst* men were assigned to guard and security service, civilian officials in the *Kreise* "appreciated" their services. Three months after he received his detachment in May 1940, the *Kreishauptmann* in Puławy (District Lublin) reported that the *Sonderdienst* men had recovered 45 percent of "back taxes," largely due to the incentive that "the mere presence of the *Sonderdienst* in a community" provided for tax delinquents to "fulfill their obligations." Once reinforced, the unit rounded up Jewish labor for snow removal in the winter of 1941 and, acting "with all severity," achieved "satisfactory results" in seizing hidden stocks of livestock and grain.[56] In July 1940, the Chełm *Sonderdienst* guarded a detention camp for Gypsies deported from the Reich to the small village of Krychów.[57] One month later, the *Sonderdienst* supported Police Battalion 104 in *Kreis* Krasnystaw and *Kreis* Hrubieszów (District Lublin) in rounding up healthy male Jews for transport to the SS labor camp at Belzec.[58] On 24 August 1940, the *Sonderdienst* Replacement Battalion delivered 300 Jews from Lublin to the forced labor camp in Terespol on the Bug River (*Kreis* Biała-Podlaska) sponsored by the Water Economy Inspectorate.[59] In September 1940, *Sonderdienst* men interpreted for the Security Police and SD personnel conducting search-and-seizure operations for weapons and other war supplies.[60] The following year, *Sonderdienst* units guarded camps in *Kreise* Biłgoraj and Janów-Lubelski for "work-shy Jews" and

Polish prisoners who had violated the regulations of the German authorities and who were engaged in manual labor on Bug River water regulation.[61]

The *Kreishauptmänner* in District Radom deployed the *Sonderdienst* men at a variety of auxiliary police duties. *Kreis* Opatów reported that the *Sonderdienst* men had "proved themselves" supporting police operations to conscript forced labor and to provide Jewish labor for German contractors on local road construction sites. Though police and *Sonderdienst* could not "prevent the flight of the Polish population from the labor office recruiters," the *Sonderdienst* had been deployed successfully in "securing the [Jewish] labor forces." The *Kreishauptmann* in Końskie deployed his *Sonderdienst* unit "successfully in two Jewish communities to combat smugglers and hoarders." In Busko, the *Kreishauptmann* requested a reinforcement of the *Sonderdienst* in order to "break ... immediately with police force" resistance of the local population to perform compulsory labor and to pay taxes.[62]

The Warsaw *Kreise* were less enthusiastic. The *Kreishauptmann* in Minsk-Mazowiecki reported for September that "the present skimpy selection" of *Sonderdienst* men was insufficient to implement "the cleansing of ... remote areas." *Kreis* Siedlce, located on the Nazi-Soviet demarcation line, reported in September 1940 that his *Sonderdienst* was too small to be effective in halting black marketeering; but indicated five months later that the unit was deployed "with success" at this activity. Skierniewice reported, however, that, with the assistance of German municipal police and *Sonderdienst* from Warsaw, *Kreis* authorities had seized 197,900 kg of rye, 2,100 kg of wheat, 34,900 kg of oats, and 8,700 kg of barley in January 1941 alone.[63]

Even relatively "innocuous" activities such as "securing the harvest" were not innocuous to the targets of such operations. The *Kreishauptmann* in Radomsko (District Radom) decreed in November 1942 that he would hold the entire population of the *Kreis* responsible on pain of death for securing any movable or immovable assets related to the harvest.[64] In the summer of 1943, Governor General Frank decreed that violations punishable by swift execution included failure "with malicious intent" to deliver required quotas of agricultural product, deliberate damage or destruction of livestock or agricultural produce, and incitement to any such offense.[65] Frustrated by the resistance of the Polish peasantry to providing required deliveries of agricultural goods or to performing compulsory labor, and doubting the continued usefulness of fines as a deterrent, officials in the Radom Department for Food and Agriculture proposed the establishment of labor camps to incarcerate "delinquents" for one to two months and to deploy them in "intensified" labor on road construction and river regulation projects. The civilian authorities would define and round up the suspects "through [use of] the *Sonderdienst*." Besides punishing so-called offenders, the camps would make available inexpensive, useful labor for public works projects, ease the burden of enforcement activities and reduce regular court dockets, and induce capital investments in construction projects by guaranteeing cheap labor. One month later, permission for the establishment of four camps was granted: Solec (*Kreis*

Starachowice), Słupia (*Kreis* Busko), Modrzejowice (*Kreis* Radom-Land), and Zameczek (*Kreis* Tomaszów-Mazowiecki).[66]

While *Sonderdienst* success was widely publicized,[67] there were disciplinary problems. In January 1941, the *Kreishauptmann* in Neu-Sandez (District Cracow) reported that *Sonderdienst* men were dismissed and imprisoned because they had broken into apartments, requisitioned goods for personal gain, and injured Polish civilians without "justifiable reason," acts which the "disappointed" *Kreishauptmann* deemed "unworthy of the reputation of the German administration."[68] In Kielce (District Radom), a *Sonderdienst* man received two years' imprisonment in February 1941 for, in addition to being frequently intoxicated, perpetrating robberies, muggings, and assaults with the help of "Jews whom he was supposed to supervise in a labor camp." The *Kreishauptmann* in Ostrów-Mazowiecki (District Warsaw) reported in February 1941 the arrest of two *Sonderdienst* men for unauthorized breaking and entering, for assault, and for impersonating Gestapo officials.[69]

Suppression of "illicit trade" and "monitoring prices" were responsibilities of the *Kreishauptmänner,* the enforcement of which belonged to the more "routine" duties of the *Sonderdienst.* The German authorities understood that black marketeering meant survival for the Polish Jews. Determining that "such a large number of Jewish inhabitants was insufferable for a government city," Frank ordered the expulsion of some 70,000 Jews from Cracow between June 1940 and January 1941. As most of the Jews had little recourse other than to settle on the outskirts of the city, the *Kreishauptmann* for *Kreis* Krakau-Land complained that the operation only exacerbated his problem with illicit trade, since the Jews were now closer to agricultural producers. With perceptive if not humane insight, he noted in September that because the Jews "scarcely have an opportunity to make a living legally.... They are ... driven by necessity to illicit trade."[70] During the forcible displacement of 20,000 Cracow city Jews in December 1940 and January 1941, the *Kreishauptmann* deployed night patrols of gendarmes, Polish police, and *Sonderdienst* to look for Jews not wearing their armbands or moving about outside their restricted residences. He noted 221 arrests during December 1940; one month later, he reported that the *Sonderdienst* had been deployed to "supervise the influx of Jews."[71]

Up to and into the beginnings of the deportations of the Polish Jews to the killing centers in eastern Poland, *Sonderdienst* units were deployed in small-scale resettlements of Jewish populations. In mid-January 1941, *Sonderdienst* units moved some 2,000 Jews from the town of Sochaczew (*Kreis* Sochaczew) to Żyradów (*Kreis* Warsaw-Land), a distance of roughly fifteen miles. On 14 November 1941, 584 Jewish residents of Cracow arrived in Zaklików (*Kreis* Janów-Lubelski) accompanied by *Sonderdienst* guards. Two hundred of them had to march on foot to the Zaklików ghetto; the other 384 were transported to the neighboring town Radomysl.[72] Prior to the March 1942 deportations from Lublin, the *Kreishauptmann* for Biłgoraj (District Lublin) deployed the *Sonderdienst* in the deportation of 57 Jewish families (221 persons) from Biłgoraj to Tarnogrod.[73]

The *Sonderdienst* was also deployed whenever its manpower was needed in the deportation of Polish Jews to the killing centers of "Operation Reinhard." The deportation of the Jews of Wieliczka and environs to Belzec was carried out on 18 August 1942 by local Polish police, German policemen from Cracow City, and the *Sonderdienst* unit assigned to the *Kreishauptmann* in Krakau-Land.[74] On 8 November 1942, the last 351 Jews of Proszowice were removed to Miechów on horse carts, accompanied by Polish police and *Sonderdienst* men. A survivor of the Bochnia ghetto recalled that *Sonderdienst* personnel participated in a shooting operation of Bochnia Jews in a field outside town on 25 August 1942.[75]

A Security Police official who participated in the deportation of the Jews from the Warsaw ghetto in the summer of 1942 recalled the deployment of a "*Sonderdienst* unit, subordinate to the civilian governor ... which consisted exclusively of ethnic Germans."[76] The *Kreishauptmann* in Radom-Land reported in August 1942 that a *Sonderdienst* detachment had transported sixty-nine Jews from the village of Ryczywol to Sobibor.[77] In preparation for the liquidation of the Warsaw ghetto in spring 1943, the SSPF Warsaw, *SS-Oberführer* Ferdinand von Sammern-Frankenegg, gave orders to all *Kreishauptmänner* in *Kreise* near Warsaw to "seize" "immediately with the utmost energy" all local Jews they could identify and to deliver them to the German gendarmerie "for liquidation." For this operation they were to deploy "all *Sonderdienst*, Polish police, and any available agents."[78] Recently Bogdan Musial has identified *Sonderdienst* units deployed in deportations from Hrubieszów, Biłgoraj, and Puławy in District Lublin.[79]

In District Galicia, *Sonderdienst* personnel were deployed at every major stage of the deportation and murder process. *Sonderdienst* men participated in the initial deportations from the Lwów ghetto in March 1942.[80] In his concluding report on the murder of the Galician Jews, *SS-Gruppenführer* Fritz Katzmann, the SSPF in Lwów, reported that 434,329 Jews had been "resettled," and that "in view of the large number of Jews and the geographical expanse of the area to be covered, the operations were carried out in numerous individual actions, including forces of the Security Police, the Order Police, the Gendarmerie, the *Sonderdienst*, and the Ukrainian police...."[81]

Committed to brutal terror and wasteful economic exploitation in the Government General, the Germans never had enough police officials to maintain basic security in the countryside, let alone enforce the regulations of the civilian administration. During 1942, the German Order Police had stationed just over 15,000 police personnel in the region (including administrative personnel). Added to this force were between 15,000 and 16,500 "indigenous police," including locally stationed Polish and ethnic Ukrainian policemen and 2,000 former Soviet prisoners of war serving out of the base training camp at Trawniki in support of "Operation Reinhard."[82] During 1942, much of this police manpower was diverted from routine security to mass murder and population resettlement operations. At this time, partisan resistance did not take a serious toll on the policemen: the German Order Police reported a total of 70 dead and 121 wounded; non-German police suffered 211 casualties (including eleven *Sonderdienst* men).[83]

Beginning in late 1942, as partisan resistance increased, the police began to take more serious casualties: between January 1942 and the end of May 1943, the Order Police in District Lublin alone reported the loss of 85 dead and 345 wounded.[84] In this context the German police officials became increasingly dependent on *Sonderdienst* auxiliary support. In a speech to Government General officials on 25 January 1943, HSSPF Krüger reported that no more German police officials could be expected from the Reich. Since non-German police could not be trusted in the event of real internal unrest, Krüger warned that the Germans would have to depend on the Order Police, Security Police, and ethnic German *Sonderdienst*.[85]

Its development into an effective force and the need for manpower again rendered the *Sonderdienst* a pawn in efforts of the police to usurp civilian authority over security matters. As early as April 1941, Krüger had advocated that the police be anchored in a State Secretariat for Security. Led by Frank and Bühler, civilian officials sought to tie locally and regionally stationed police forces to the Departments for Internal Administration and to devolve local authority to the *Kreishauptmänner*.[86] Among the new weapons in Krüger's arsenal in 1941 was the conscription of ethnic Germans into the *Waffen* SS to deplete the pool of manpower available to the civilian authorities. In February, the Governor for District Warsaw reported that mustering of *Sonderdienst* men for the Waffen SS had caused "a certain degree of disquietude" among the men; those inducted would have to be replaced, "since otherwise the activity of the *Sonderdienst* is endangered."[87] On 29 March 1941, Hammerle suggested to Frank that *Sonderdienst* men be barred from registering for conscription; Himmler's threat to withdraw all police forces from the Government General put an end to this initiative.[88]

The real issue was apparent from Krüger's complaint to Himmler in January 1942 that the civilian authorities in the Government General were seeking to "give the *Sonderdienst* the character of a unit, that, though subordinate to the *Kreishauptleute,* carries out tasks of a police-administrative nature as an executive along side of the German police."[89] Krüger was not the only SS official concerned: the Gestapo in Berlin passed on to the Chief of Security Police and SD an advertisement in the *Berliner Lokal-Anzeiger* of 15 December 1941, soliciting military personnel for the training of an "administrative troop" subordinated to the *Kreishauptleute* in the Government General.[90] Himmler himself was concerned enough to admonish SS and police officials, in dealings with civilian officials, to "object most sharply to all measures which undermine our autonomous organization [*Selbstorganization*] of police in the Government General."[91]

Frank and the civilian authorities held their own into the last weeks of winter 1942, when the SS unearthed a corruption scandal that embroiled the District Governor in Radom, Karl Lasch, and reached to Frank himself.[92] On 5 March 1942, during a "comradely interrogation" conducted at Hitler's headquarters in Berlin, Himmler demanded that Frank establish a State Secretariat for Security under Krüger that would handle all police matters, and to which the *Sonderdienst* would be subordinated.[93] Nine days later, Frank surrendered: Krüger would become a State Secretary and receive orders directly from Himmler. In return, the SS promised to subordinate locally stationed gendarmes to the *Kreishauptmänner*.[94]

The Hitler decree mandating the establishment of the State Secretary for Security in the Government General was signed on 7 May 1942: its provisions directed Frank and Himmler to reach an accommodation on the powers of the position.[95] The stubbornness with which Frank fought to keep the *Sonderdienst* under civilian control is reflected in Himmler's frustration over Krüger's inability to force the issue: "I must say to you in all seriousness that you must, for once, fight for yourself in the matter. The Führer decree has been signed. You are the State Secretary. You are now sitting on the horse, so ride it already."[96] The SS victory was finally sealed with Krüger's formal appointment as State Secretary for Security Matters [*Sicherheitswesen*] on 3 June 1942.[97] The decree provided that all security matters, even those for which the civilian authorities had had jurisdiction and explicitly including all matters relating to the Jews, fell under Krüger's domain as State Secretary. Part of the booty was the Inspectorate of the *Sonderdienst* with all subordinate units. On 10 June 1942, State Secretary Bühler issued a circular confirming the transfer of the Inspectorate (including the Replacement Battalion, the *Sonderdienst* Training School, and the Supply Office) from the Main Branch Internal Administration to the State Secretary for Security Matters.[98] A 20 June Krüger decree placed the district *Sonderdienst* commanders under the authority of the regional SS and Police Leaders.[99] Krüger dutifully permitted the *Kreis-* and *Stadthauptmänner* to remain responsible for the "police executive" for their domains and allowed them to give instructions to local municipal police or gendarmerie commanders. "General measures" related to the police would be issued by the State Secretary for Security Matters via the regional Commanders of the Order Police and the District Governors.[100]

Now awake to the threat to their police prerogatives, Himmler and the SS clearly did not wish the *Sonderdienst* to survive. In mid-August 1942, SS Main Office chief Gottlob Berger informed Krüger that Himmler expected the *Sonderdienst* to be dissolved within the next two weeks.[101] Despite his "personal reluctance to relinquish an agency that he had created himself and that had proved itself," Frank acquiesced in Krüger's decree of 1 October 1942 transferring the *Sonderdienst* to the jurisdiction of the Commander of the Order Police (BdO). Krüger reported to Himmler on 20 October that the "incorporation of the *Sonderdienst* into the Order Police was proceeding," and that a recruitment office had been established in Poznań to screen *Sonderdienst* men for induction into the *Waffen* SS.[102]

Nevertheless, the civilian authorities were able to maintain operational control over the *Sonderdienst* units in the field until they ceased to exist in the summer of 1944. This circumstance related to the desperate need for manpower that even the police authorities acknowledged. In 1943, much of the daily routine of the *Sonderdienst* detachments consisted of guarding buildings, official offices, and installations such as sawmills and agricultural produce storage depots.[103] With the Jews murdered, the reserve of young Polish laborers depleted, and the Red Army threatening to overrun Poland before the next harvest, the *Sonderdienst* units settled into these more routine, but increasingly dangerous security duties.[104] By spring 1943, *Sonderdienst* men, both as individuals and, occasionally, entire units with weapons, began to desert. The available reserve of ethnic Germans to replace them was virtually nonexistent.[105] Towards the end of 1943, *SS-Obergruppenführer* Wilhelm Koppe, who had replaced Krüger as HSSPF in November 1943, ordered all *Sonderdienst* guard units that guarded urban facilities reincorporated into companies "at the disposal of the SS and Police Leaders for guard duties and short-term police missions."[106] As Koppe reported in May 1944, some 220 *Sonderdienst* men were serving in Lublin City and the ten *Kreise* in District Lublin. Nevertheless, only units of virtual company strength (100 men) could be deployed: one day earlier, a unit of 32 *Sonderdienst* men had taken serious casualties during an attack by more than 200 partisans.[107] Those *Sonderdienst* men cited for awards and cash bonuses were usually cited for uncovering and eliminating "nests of bandits" and guarding supplies against "bandit attacks." The citation for *Sonderdienst* man Stefan Ney noted that one of the "bandits" he had shot to death had been a Jew.[108]

Neither Koppe nor Himmler had the energy to fight the civilian authorities over the *Sonderdienst* during the summer of 1944, as the Red Army swept through eastern Poland to the Vistula. When the SS informed him in late May 1944 that no new police trainers were available, Hammerle turned to the *Wehrmacht* to recruit detachment commanders; the High Command of the Army (*Oberkommando des Heeres*-OKH) supplied fifteen officers and thirty-seven noncommissioned officers.[109] After speedy negotiations, Hammerle presented for Frank's signature on 3 June a decree that essentially turned the *Sonderdienst* units over to military command, supply, and deployment. For deployment at civilian tasks the *Sonderdienst* still took instructions from the civilian authorities—that is, from the Governor General through the Inspectorate of the *Sonderdienst*.[110]

In July 1944, the central sector of the German Eastern Front collapsed: Lublin fell on 24 July; Lwów on 27 July. Frantic demand to deploy *Sonderdienst* men as cannon fodder on the disintegrating front and a Hitler decree requiring military service for all ethnic Germans forced Frank, Bühler, and Hammerle to transfer operational control over the *Sonderdienst* to the *Wehrmacht* on 16 September 1944. As the individual *Kreise* were overrun, the field units would merge into the retreating *Wehrmacht* units. By 29 September, Bühler reported that the *Sonderdienst* was now a part of the *Wehrmacht*.[111] The Inspectorate continued a shadow existence, recommending individual *Sonderdienst* men for awards, until it dissolved itself on 27 February 1945, nearly six weeks after the Government General ceased to exist.[112] The *Sonderdienst* thus passed into history.

Though few in numbers and dispersed in the localities, the *Sonderdienst* men represented the only reliable force available to local civilian officials. German police agencies were available to "manage" the Jews—at least once the Jews were concentrated in the cities and towns; but the *Kreishauptmänner* lacked the authority to dispatch police units in small groups to deal with Jews or Poles in the countryside. No doubt, too, they came to depend on the *Sonderdienst* because the latter were ethnic Germans, who could speak enough of the language to make the administrators feel comfortable in a stressful and increasingly dangerous environment. As the *Kreishauptmann* in Siedłce (District Warsaw) noted in the summer of 1940, while awaiting the arrival of his *Sonderdienst* unit: "how urgently necessary is the deployment of ethnic German police forces, who both with their eager German hands and with their Polish language ability form an indispensable support for the Reich German police officials."[113]

The *Sonderdienst* also represented a potential tool for the civilian authorities to actively participate in creating the new Reich. With the *Sonderdienst* at their disposal, the civilian authorities did not need to sit idle while the SS and police determined (and received the credit for) security policy and practice. Though they miscalculated the ability of the civilian authorities to fashion a police executive, Himmler and Krüger understood by 1941 that the *Sonderdienst* threatened SS and police interests in the Government General.[114] They sought to destroy it in the summer of 1942, but, absent an equivalent service to the *Kreishauptmänner*, they failed to pry the local detachments loose from the civilian authorities.

Too much should not be made of this jurisdictional struggle when examining the implementation of ideologically driven policy. Both civilian administrators and police authorities shared the "National Socialist consensus"[115] in occupied Poland. They wanted to exterminate the Jews and the Polish intelligentsia, to exploit the labor potential of the Polish masses, and to turn the Government General into a region of German settlement. As a part of this vision, the *Sonderdienst* was to serve not only as a police executive, but as a political and cultural stepping-stone to full acceptance into the German "racial community." When it came to such core issues, SS and police and civilian authorities cooperated more often than they fought, with disastrous results for their victims. The effectiveness of the *Sonderdienst* in implementing such policies is difficult to gauge, but the reports of the local authorities indicate that it played an essential role. Moreover, there is no question that, even in "routine" duties, the *Sonderdienst* participated, more or less willingly, in the implementation of the most evil racist policies of the National Socialist regime.

Notes

* The opinions expressed herein are exclusively those of the author and are not to be viewed as official statements of the United States Holocaust Memorial Museum.

1. The literature so far has been minimal. See Martin Broszat, "Der 'Sonderdienst' im Generalgouvernement," in *Gutachten des Instituts für Zeitgeschichte*, I (Munich, 1958), 408–410. The *Sonderdienst* has received little more than passing mention in the standard works on German occupation policy in Poland. See Martin Broszat, *Nationalsozialistische Polenpolitik, 1939–1945* (Frankfurt/Main, 1965), 64; Czesław Madajczyk, *Die Okkupationspolitik Nazideutschlands in Polen, 1939–1945* (Berlin [East], 1987), 201–202; Dieter Pohl, *Nationalsozialistische Judenverfolgung in Ostgalizien, 1941–1944; Organisation und Durch-*

führung eines staatlichen Massenverbrechens (Munich, 1997), 83, 290. Dieter Pohl, *Von der "Judenpolitik" zum Judenmord: Der Distrikt Lublin des Generalgouvernements, 1939–1944* (Frankfurt/Main, 1993) and Thomas Sandkühler, *Endlösung in Galizien: Der Judenmord in Ostpolen und die Rettungsinitiativen von Berthold Beitz, 1941–1944* (Bonn, 1996) do not mention the *Sonderdienst* at all. Recently, Bogdan Musial has identified the *Sonderdienst's* role as an auxiliary force in the operations to murder the Polish Jews. See Musial, *Deutsche Zivilverwaltung und Judenverfolgung im Generalgouvernement: Eine Fallstudie zum Distrikt Lublin, 1939–1944* (Wiesbaden, 1999), 248–266, 290–312.

2. This has been stressed for areas of the occupied Soviet Union by Martin Dean, *Collaboration in the Holocaust: Crimes of the Local Police in Belorussia and Ukraine, 1941–1944* (New York, 2000), viii, 161–167; Michael MacQueen "Nazi Policy towards the Jews in the *Reichskommissariat Ostland,* June–December 1941: From White Terror to Holocaust in Lithuania," in Zvi Gitelman, ed., *Bitter Legacy: Confronting the Holocaust in the USSR* (Bloomington, IN, 1997), 100–101; Christian Gerlach, *Kalkulierte Mord: Die deutsche Wirtschafts- und Vernichtungspolitik in Weißrußland, 1941–1944* (Hamburg, 1999); and Jonathan Steinberg, "The Third Reich Reflected: German Civil Administration in the Occupied Soviet Union, 1941–1944," *The English Historical Review,* vol. 110, no. 437 (June 1995): 636–637. Dieter Pohl and Bogdan Musial have stressed the importance of the responsibilities of the civilian administration in the Government General for implementing all aspects of Nazi policy, including the persecution and murder of the Jews. See Dieter Pohl, "Die Ermordung der Juden im Generalgouvernement," in Ulrich Herbert, ed., *Nationalsozialistische Vernichtungspolitik, 1939–1945: Neue Forschungen und Kontroversen* (Frankfurt/Main, 1998), 108–110; Musial, *Zivilverwaltung, passim.*

3. Broszat, *Polenpolitik,* 84–98. Between 1939 and the spring of 1941, between 325,000 and 365,000 non-Jewish Poles and approximately 100,000 Polish Jews were deported from the annexed territories into the Government General. See also Götz Aly, *"Endlösung": Völkerverschiebung und der Mord an den europäischen Juden* (Frankfurt/Main, 1995), 59–135.

4. See Broszat, *Polenpolitik,* 41–51; Madajczyk, *Okkupationspolitik,* 356–364.

5. "Decree on the Appointment of Jewish Councils," November 28, 1939, *Verordnungsblatt des Generalgouverneurs für die besetzten polnische Gebiete* (after January 1941, *Verordnungsblatt für das Generalgouvernement*—hereafter VOBl. GG), No. 9, 6 December 1939, 72–73, Library of Congress (hereafter: LC).

6. "Decree on the Introduction of Obligatory Labor for the Polish Population of the Government General," 26 October 1939, VOBl. GG, No. 1, 26 October 1939, 5–6; "Decree on the Introduction of Compulsory Labor for the Jewish Population of the Government General," 26 October 1939, ibid., 6.

7. On the *Selbstschutz,* see Christian Jansen and Arno Weckbecker, *"Der Volksdeutsche Selbstschutz" in Polen 1939/40* (Munich, 1992), especially 55–79, 94–159, 193–197. For *Selbstschutz* in the Government General, particularly in Lublin District, see Peter R. Black, "Rehearsal for Reinhard?: Odilo Globocnik and the Lublin Selbstschutz," *Central European History* 25, no. 2 (1992): 194–226; Pohl, *Judenmord,* 68.

8. *Die Ostgebiete des Deutschen Reiches und das Generalgouvernement der besetzten polnischen Gebiete in statistischen Angaben* (Berlin, 1940), 77–120; Max Freiherr du Prel, *Das Generalgouvernement* (Würzburg, 1942), 381–386; Office of the Governor General, "Report on the Organization of the Government General to July 1, 1940," July 1940, Trial of Josef Bühler (hereafter: Bühler Trial), NTN 277, 4-228, Archiwum Głównej Komisji Badania Zbrodni Przeciwko Narodowi Polskiemu (hereafter: AGK). In order to avoid confusion in the English between the German terms *Distrikt* and *Kreis,* I will use henceforth the German term *Kreis,* and the English term "District" for *Distrikt.* Given the awkwardness of the English terms "municipal district captaincy" (*Stadthauptmannschaft*) and "rural district captaincy" (*Kreishauptmannschaft*) and the potential confusion of "Captain" (*Stadt- und Kreishauptmann*) with the military rank, I will use the German terms for both administrators and administrations.

9. Friedrich Gollert, *Warschau unter deutscher Herrschaft: Deutsche Aufbauarbeit im Distrikt Warschau* (Cracow, 1942), 87–103.

10. As late as May 1943, for example, the District administrative seat in Radom employed 420 Germans (of whom 67 were *Beamte* [officials] and 134 were female employees) and 252 Poles. Distributed between ten *Kreishauptmannschaften* and three *Stadthauptmannschaften* were 477 German *Beamte* (officials) and *Angestellte* (employees), an average of just over 35 German personnel for each *Kreis*. See remarks of Governor Kundt at a conference in Radom, "Service Diary of Governor General Hans Frank," 38 volumes, RG-238, 2233-PS (hereafter: Frank Diary), National Archives and Records Administration (hereafter: NARA), here entry for 26 May 1943, XXVI, 339. See also the discussion and data in Musial, *Zivilverwaltung*, 86–91.

11. Frank Diary, entry for 31 October 1939, I, 25–26.

12. Order of Reichsführer SS and Chief of German Police [signed Bomhard] to the HSSPF/BdO, Cracow, 5 June 1940, Bühler Trial, NTN 258, 71–72, AGK; circular of Krüger, 17 June 1940, ibid., 70. For the strength levels of Municipal Police for the Government General projected for fiscal year 1941, see "Organization of the Reich Municipal Police in the Government General," no date [internal evidence indicates May or June 1940], R 19/270, 212–227, Bundesarchiv, Berlin (hereafter: BAB). Strength levels for Polish police personnel available in District Lublin are in the report of the Commander of Gendarmerie (KdG) Lublin [signed Hahnzog] to the Commander of Order Police (BdO), 9 June 1940, R 70 Polen/178, 45–46, BAB.

13. See Main Department for Internal Administration, "Situation Reports of the *Kreis* and *Stadthauptleute* for May 1940," n.d. [June 17, 1940], Bühler Trial, NTN 269, 139–148, AGK, and, in particular, *Kreishauptmann* Siedlce to Office of Governor General, 9 July 1940, Bühler Trial, NTN 273, 157, AGK.

14. Ministerialrat Friedrich Wilhelm Siebert, "The Administration in the Government General with Particular Regard for the Activity of the Main Department for Internal Administration," in Josef Bühler, ed., *Das Generalgouvernement: Seine Verwaltung und seine Wirtschaft* (Cracow, 1943), 75–88.

15. Frank Diary, 16 March 1940, III, 213–214.

16. Ibid., 10 April 1940, IV, 286–287.

17. Decree of Frank, "Decree on the Establishment of a *Sonderdienst*," 6 May 1940, VOBl. GG, 10 May 1940, no. 38 (1940), Part 1, 186, LC. On Krüger's objections and Frank's concern about using the "police" label, see Frank Diary, 6 May 1940, IV, 377. After the war, Hammerle stated explicitly that the *Sonderdienst* was intended to enable Frank to extricate himself from dependence on the SS and police for enforcement of administrative regulations. Interrogation of Hermann Hammerle, 8 March 1967, Proceedings against Ansbach et al., file 208 AR-7 76/61, 4707-4716, Bundesarchiv/Zentrale Stelle der Landesverwaltungen zur Verfolgung nationalsozialistischer Verbrechen, Ludwigsburg (hereafter: BA-ZdL).

18. Du Prel, *Generalgouvernement*, 376–377. The Inspectorate became section IV of the Main Department Internal Administration.

19. Speech of Hans Frank at the Bergakademie, Cracow, 10 May 1940, Frank Diary, II, 145.

20. Frank Diary, 31 May 1940, IV, 552.

21. Main Department Internal Administration, "Situation Reports of the *Kreis* and *Stadthauptleute*," 17 June 1940, Bühler Trial, NTN 269, 141, AGK.

22. Main Department Internal Administration, "Situation Reports of the *Kreis* and *Stadthauptleute*," 16 July 1940, ibid., 184.

23. Undated Memorandum of Hans Damrau [District Lublin], related to an 18 July 1940 conference of civilian officials in Lublin, file Gouverneur, Distrikt Lublin, sygn. 63, 28, Wojewódzkie Archiwum Państwowe, Lublin (hereafter: WAPL).

24. In only one known case did local officials oppose the *Sonderdienst*. When the *Stadthauptmann* in Częstochowa learned that his budget would have to cover salaries and equipment

for his *Sonderdienst* unit, he reported that his unit of 60 German municipal police and 200 Polish police were sufficient to secure the city. See Stadthauptmann Częstochowa to the Office of the Governor General, "Situation Report for February 1941," 8 March 1941, Dok. I.-151, vol. 28, 45, Instytut Zachodni, Poznań (hereafter: IZP).

25. *Kreishauptmann* Opatów to Main Department Internal Administration, "Situation Report for June 1940," 10 July 1940, Bühler Trial, NTN 273, 131–136, AGK; *Kreishauptmann* Opatów, "Situation Report for May 1940," 8 June 1940, ibid., NTN 272, 166; *Kreishauptmann* Neu-Sandez to Office of the Governor General, "Situation Report for August 1940," 9 September 1940, Dok. I.-151, vol. 5, 19–26, IZP; *Kreishauptmann* Ostrów-Mazowiecki to the office of the Governor General, "Situation Report for August 1940," 2 September 1940, ibid., vol. 6, 13–17; *Kreishauptmann* Ostrów-Mazowiecki to the office of the Governor General, "Situation Report for September 1940," 30 September 1940, Bühler Trial, NTN 275, 218, AGK; *Kreishauptmann* Miechów to Governor General, "Situation Report for August 1940," 1 September 1940, Dok. I.-151, vol. 5, 53–58, IZP.

26. Frank Diary, 10 July 1940, published in *Das Diensttagebuch des deutschen Generalgouverneurs in Polen, 1939–1945*, Werner Präg and Wolfgang Jacobmeyer, eds. (Stuttgart, 1975), 248; Black, "Rehearsal for Reinhard," 222.

27. Undated Memorandum of Hans Damrau [District Lublin], related to an 18 July 1940 conference of civilian officials in Lublin, file Gouverneur, Distrikt Lublin, sygn. 63, 28, WAPL.

28. Frank Diary, 18 October 1940, VI, 998. One month later, the word went out to the *Kreishauptmänner* that they were to supply lists of male ethnic German residents of arms-bearing age. Department Internal Administration/Inspectorate of the *Sonderdienst* [signed Hammerle] to *Kreishauptmann* Radom-Land, 4 November 1940, file Kreishauptmann Radom-Land, vol. 14, p. 27, Wojewódzkie Archiwum Państwowe, Radom (hereafter: WAPR); *Kreishauptmann* Radom-Land to Inspectorate of the *Sonderdienst*, 12 November 1940, ibid., 28–36.

29. Office, District Governor in Warsaw to Office, Governor General, "Report of District Warsaw for October 1940," 15 November 1940, Dok. I.-151, vol. 13, 1–16, IZP; report of Chief of the Office, District Governor in Warsaw, "Monthly Report of the Department Internal Administration for October 1940," 7 November 1940, ibid., vol. 14, 1–8.

30. *Kreishauptmann* Siedlce to Chief, Office of Governor General, 5 March 1941, ibid., vol. 27, 33, IZP.

31. Frank Diary, 13 and 14 December, 1940, VI, 1127, 1128; interrogation of Hermann Hammerle, 29 March 1963, Proceedings against Friedrich Paulus, file 4 Ks 1/74 (hereafter: Paulus Trial), vol. 2, 225, Staatsanwaltschaft Frankfurt/Main; statement of J.O., 26 February 1964, ibid., 339; on reduction of tension, see report of the Inspectorate of the *Sonderdienst* [signed Hammerle], 24 September 1941, Bühler Trial, NTN 283, 14–26, AGK; Frank Diary, 29 March 1941 and 8 April 1941, X, 172, 255.

32. Frank Diary, 14 December 1940, VI, 1128.

33. Frank Diary, 19 September 1940, V, 880–881.

34. Frank Diary, 21 July 1941, XII, 661.

35. Frank Diary, 6 September, 21 September 1941, and 21 November 1941, XII, 809, 884 and XIII, 1081–1082.

36. Author unknown, "The Branch Section Population Policy and Welfare: Implementer of Ethnic-Political Work in the Government General," n.d. [probably autumn 1941], Bühler Trial, NTN 282, 66, AGK; Frank Diary, 21 November 1942, XXI, 1221–1222.

37. "The *Sonderdienst:* The University of Ethnic German Consciousness in the Government General," in *Sonderdienst GG,* 1943, no. 6, 4, National Library in Warsaw (hereafter NLW). Copies of the newsletter of the Inspectorate of the Sonderdienst have survived in part for the years 1942 through 1943. During 1942, its title was *Sonderdienst GG;* in 1943, the title was changed to *Mitteilungsblatt für den Sonderdienst, Hilfspolizei im Generalgouvernement.* For convenience's sake, I have used *Sonderdienst GG* in the notes for all issues of the newsletter.

38. "The *Sonderdienst* as the Primary School of Ethnic German Men," *Sonderdienst GG*, 1943, no. 7, 4, NLW.

39. "Education in the *Sonderdienst*," *Sonderdienst GG*, 1942, no. 1 (May), 5–6, NLW.

40. "Adolf Hitler: Life, Work, and Struggle," *Sonderdienst GG*, 1942, no. 2 (June), 16, NLW.

41. "Education in the *Sonderdienst*," *Sonderdienst GG*, 1942, no. 1 (May), 5–6, NLW.

42. Frank Diary, 10 August 1943, XXVIII, 854.

43. "Physical Education: On Military Education in the *Sonderdienst*," *Sonderdienst GG*, 1942, no. 4, (August) 61, NLW; "Germany's Right to Lebensraum," ibid., no. 3 (July), 36.

44. "The Battle for Europe," pt. 1, *Sonderdienst GG*, 1942, no. 4 (August), 56–57, NLW.

45. *Sonderdienst GG*, 1942, no. 7 (November 1942), Bühler Trial, NTN 303, 398–407, AGK.

46. "Our Honor is Loyalty," *Sonderdienst GG*, 1943, no. 7, 2, NLW.

47. "The Struggle against Bolshevism," ibid., no. 4, 8.

48. "Sie haben nun endlich die Quitting dafür erhalten," ibid., no. 6, 6.

49. Deutsche *Sonderdienst*, Records of the Institut für Deutsche Ostarbeit, Box 30, folder 2, National Anthropological Archives and Human Studies Film Archives, Suitland, Maryland; Gretchen E. Schafft and Gerhard Zeidler, "Register to the Materials of the Institut für Deutsche Ostarbeit," unpublished manuscript, National Anthropological Archives, 1998, 19–20. I am very grateful to Dr. Margit Berner of Vienna for alerting me to this collection of materials.

50. Circular No. 23 of the Inspectorate of the *Sonderdienst* [signed Hammerle], 5 August 1941, file Regierung GG/Inspektion des Sonderdienstes, II/380, 32–33, AGK.

51. Report of the Inspectorate of the *Sonderdienst* [signed Hammerle], 24 September 1941, Bühler Trial, NTN 283, 14–26, AGK.

52. "Budget of the Government General for the Fiscal Year 1941," ibid., NTN 344, 114. See also Office of the Government General, "Report on the Organization of the Government General to 1 July 1940," July 1940, ibid., NTN 277, 87–88. On pay scales for upper ranks, see Circular no. 23 of the Inspectorate of the *Sonderdienst* [signed Hammerle], 5 August 1941, Regierung GG/Inspektion des Sonderdienstes, II/380, 32–33, AGK.

53. Circular No. 9 of the Inspectorate of the *Sonderdienst*, 5 August 1940, file Regierung GG/Inspektion des Sonderdienstes, II/380, 8–9, AGK; circular No. 23 of the Inspectorate of the *Sonderdienst* [signed Hammerle], 5 August 1941, ibid., 32–33. In 1942, Frank introduced a dependent's benefits package equivalent to that received by members of the German armed forces, the Reich Labor Service, and the *Waffen SS*. See "Decree on the Provision of Family Subsistence to the Relatives of German Nationality of the Men Inducted into the *Sonderdienst*," 22 April 1942, VOBl. GG, no. 34, 30 April 1942, 220–221, LC.

54. "Budget of the Government General for Fiscal Year 1941," Bühler Trial, NTN 344, vol. 98, 114, AGK. The total budget for 1941 was projected at just under eleven million złotys. On uniforms, see circular signed Hammerle, 5 November 1940, file Regierung GG/Inspektion des Sonderdienstes, II/381, 23, AGK.

55. Report of the Inspectorate of the *Sonderdienst* [signed Hammerle], 24 September 1941, Bühler Trial, NTN 283, 20–21, AGK.

56. *Kreishauptmann* Puławy to Main Department Internal Administration, 8 June 1940, ibid., NTN 272, 129; same to same, "Situation Report for August 1940," Dok. I.-151, vol. 4, 19–25, IZP; *Kreishauptmann* Puławy to Office of Governor General, 5 February 1941, Bühler Trial, NTN 280, 174–175, 178, AGK; *Kreishauptmann* Puławy to Office of Governor General, 27 February 1941, Dok. I.-151, vol. 29, 29, IZP.

57. Main Department Internal Administration, "Excerpt from the Situation Reports of the *Kreis-* and *Stadthauptleute* for July 1940," 30 August 1940, Bühler Trial, NTN 269, v. 23, 195, AGK.

58. Police Battalion 104, "Supplementary Order to the Operations Order (Secret) of the SS and Police Leader in District Lublin 23/40(g) of 9 August 1940," 12 August 1940, file Polizei-Batallion 104, 314, sygn. 30, 29–31, WAPL; memorandum to the Director of the German

Labor Office in Lublin, 28 August 1940, File Gouverneur/Distrikt Lublin, sygn. 746, 119–120, WAPL. From May until November 1940 there was a labor camp on the outskirts of Belzec in the vicinity of the site later used for the construction of the killing center in 1941. The Jews and Gypsies deported there were forced to work on fortification trenches along the Nazi-Soviet demarcation line.

59. Memorandum from District Lublin/Labor Department to the *Sonderdienst* Replacement Battalion, 18 September 1940, file Gouverneur/Distrikt Lublin, sygn. 746, 139; memorandum from District Lublin/Department Labor to the director of the Labor Office in Biała-Podlaska, ibid., 140.

60. Strictly confidential order of the Police Battalion 104, 27 September 1940, file Polizei-Batallion 104, 314, sygn. 30, 53–55, WAPL.

61. *Kreishauptmann* Biłgoraj to Department Internal Administration/Office for Population and Welfare, 29 September 1941, file Gouverneur, District Lublin, sygn. 148, 17, WAPL; *Kreishauptmann* Janów-Lubelski to Department Internal Administration/Office for Population Policy and Welfare, 1 September 1941, ibid., 25.

62. *Kreishauptmann* Opatów to Main Department Internal Administration, "Situation Report for June 1940," 10 July 1940, Bühler Trial, NTN 273, 131–136, AGK; *Kreishauptmann* Opatów, "Situation Report for May 1940," 8 June 1940, ibid., NTN 272, 166; Main Department Internal Administration, "Situation Reports of the *Kreis-* and *Stadthauptleute* for May 1940," 17 June 1940, ibid., NTN 269, 145; *Kreishauptmann* in Busko to Office of Government General, 6 June 1940, ibid., NTN 272, 137–138.

63. *Kreishauptmann* Minsk Mazowiecki to Main Department Internal Administration, 11 October 1940, Bühler Trial, NTN 275, 208, AGK; *Kreishauptmann* Siedlce to Office of Governor General, 4 September 1940, ibid., NTN 274, 180–181; *Kreishauptmann* Siedlce to Office of Governor General, 23 February 1941, ibid., NTN 280, 278; *Kreishauptmann* Skierniewice to Office of Governor General, 7 February 1940, ibid., NTN 280, 281.

64. Order of the *Kreishauptmann* Radomsko [signed Driessen], 11 November 1942, R 102 II/9, 172, BAB.

65. "Decree for the Protection of Harvesting the Crop and for Securing Food Supplies in Fiscal Year 1943/1944," signed Frank, 14 July 1943, VOBl. GG, no. 56, 26 July 1943, 320–321, LC.

66. Memorandum from Department of Food and Agriculture [signed Hess] to SSPF Radom, "Establishment of Forced Labor Camps in District Radom," 21 January 1942, file Gouverneur, Distrikt Radom/Abteilung Ernährung und Landwirtschaft, sygn. 227, 1–4, WAPR; Department Internal Administration in District Radom, "Establishment of Administrative Penal Camps in District Radom," 21 February 1942, ibid., 6–8; "Decree on the Establishment of Administrative Penal Camps in District Radom," [signed Kundt], 3 February 1942, ibid., 9–10; Department Internal Administration in District Radom, "Implementation Regulation for the Decree of 3 February 1942 on the Establishment of Administrative Penal Camps in District Radom," 21 February 1942, ibid., 13–14. In July 1942, the civilian authorities assigned the Commander of the *Sonderdienst* for District Radom the task of staffing the guard units and ensuring their discipline. See Department Internal Administration, District Radom, "2nd Implementation Regulation for the Decree on 3 February 1942 on Establishment of Administrative Penal Camps in District Radom," 11 July 1942, file Gouverneur Distrikt Radom/Abteilung Innere Verwaltung, sygn. 82, 1–3, WAPR.

67. "The *Sonderdienst:* The University of Ethnic German Consciousness in the Government General," *Sonderdienst GG*, 1943, no. 6, 4, NLW.

68. *Kreishauptmann* in Neu-Sandez to Office of Governor General, 31 January 1941, Bühler Trial, NTN 280, 75–76, AGK.

69. *Kreishauptmann* Kielce to Office of Governor General, "Situation Report for January 1941," 8 February 1941, NTN 280, 199, AGK; *Kreishauptmann* Ostrów-Mazowiecki to Office of

Governor General, "Situation Report for February 1941," 3 March 1941, Dok. I.-151, vol. 27, 26, IZP.

70. *Kreishauptmann* Krakau-Land to Office of Governor General, "Situation Report, September 1940," 8 October 1940, Bühler Trial, NTN 275, 56, AGK. On the 1940 expulsions, see Peter Longerich, *Politik der Vernichtung: Ein Gesamtdarstellung der nationalsozialistischen Judenverfolgung* (Munich, 1998), 272; Frank Golczewski, "Polen," in Wolfgang Benz, ed., *Dimension des Völkermords,* 433–435.

71. *Kreishauptmann* Krakau-Land to Office of Governor General, "Situation Report, December 1940," 10 January 1941, Bühler Trial, NTN 275, 34, AGK; *Kreishauptmann* Krakau-Land to Office of Governor General, "Situation Report, January 1941," February 10, 1941, ibid., NTN 280, p. 61; Governor of District Cracow [Wächter] to Chief of Office of Governor General [Bühler], "Situation Report for December 1940," 27 January 1941, Dok. I.-151, vol. 21, 24–25, IZP.

72. Report from Operations Staff [1a] of the Supreme Military Commander, Government General to Operations Staff [1a], Army Group B, 19 January 1941, RG-242, T-501/213/1514, NARA; Main Department Internal Administration/Office for Population Matters and Welfare to Department of Internal Administration, District Lublin, Office for Population Matters and Welfare, 10 November 1941, R 102 II/31, BAB; Gendarmerie Post Zaklików to *Kreishauptmann* Janów-Lubelski, 15 November 1941, ibid.; *Kreishauptmann* Janów-Lubelski to Main Department Internal Administration, Office for Population Matters and Welfare, 18 November 1941, ibid.

73. *Kreishauptmann* in Biłgoraj to Office of District Governor/Department Internal Administration/Population Policy and Welfare, 27 April 1942, R 102 II/27, BAB; partially reproduced, but incorrectly dated at 7 April 1942 in Berenstein et al., *Massenmord,* 271.

74. As related to a Polish Jewish survivor by a member of the unit. See interrogation of E.K., 17 March 1967, file 206 AR-Z 610/67, vol. 1, 164–169, ZdL. See also Musial, *Zivilverwaltung,* 303. On the date, see Golczewski, "Polen," 466. Yitzhak Arad maintains that these deportations occurred on August 25–30. See Arad, *Belzec, Sobibor, Treblinka: The Operation Reinhard Death Camps* (Bloomington, IN, 1987), 387.

75. Interrogation of A.K., a participant, 20 March 1967, file 206 AR-Z 610/67, vol. 6, 1035–1039, BA-ZdL; interrogation of N.R., 28 March 1967, ibid., vol. 1, 170–177. The witness could no longer recall whether the *Sonderdienst* participated in another Bochnia action in November 1942, but did recall them hunting for hidden Jews after the small ghetto was finally liquidated in early September 1943.

76. Interrogation of A.H., 21 October 1960, Proceedings against Ludwig Hahn, file 141 Js 192/60, vol. 6, 1008–1009, StA Hamburg. The witness recalled that the *Sonderdienst* unit had "behaved brutally."

77. *Kreishauptmann* Radom-Land to Department Internal Administration, Office for Population Matters and Welfare in District Lublin, 4 August 1942, file Gouverneur/Distrikt Lublin, sygn. 893, 252, WAPL.

78. Circular of SSPF Warsaw [signed von Sammern-Frankenegg] to *Kreishauptmänner* in Warsaw District, 13 March 1943, Document No. 275 in Berenstein et al., *Massenmord, 352.* See also Musial, *Zivilverwaltung,* 310–311.

79. Musial, *Zivilverwaltung,* 250–251, 253, 259–260, 291, 309, 335.

80. Ukrainian Police Commissariat in Lwów/L'viv to commander of Ukrainian Police in Lwów/L'viv, 30 March 1942, RG Ukrainian Police Commissariats in Lwów/L'viv, R-16, Deržavnyj Archiv L'vivs'koi Oblasti [State Oblast Archive, L'viv].

81. Report of SSPF Galizien [signed Katzmann] to HSSPF Ost [Krüger], "Solution of the Jewish Question in District Galicia," 30 June 1943, Nuremberg Document, L-18, International Military Tribunal, *Trial of the Major War Criminals,* XXXVII, 401, 404.

82. In February 1943, the Main Office Order Police in Berlin reported the deployment of 15,186 German police personnel (*Schutzpolizei* and Gendarmerie) and 14,297 indigenous

police in the Government General. See "Report of the Chief of the Order Police ... on the Strength and Military Deployment of the Order Police in 1942," 1 February 1942, RG-242, T-175/3/2503393-2503394, NARA. The Commander of Security Police and SD (BdS) Cracow reported on 25 January 1943 that 10,190 active Order Police personnel were serving in the Government General, supported by 16,337 "foreign police." "Conference in Belvedere Castle in Warsaw on 25 January 1943," Frank Diary, XXXIII, no page numbers.

83. "Conference ... on January 25, 1943," pp. 25–26, Frank Diary, XXXIII, no page numbers.
84. Report of Kintrup, "Conference in the Conference Hall of the District Building (Lublin)," Frank Diary, 29 May 1943, XXVI, 428–429; "Conference, Security in the Government General," p. 2, 31 May 1943, Frank Diary, XXXIII, no page numbers.
85. "Conference ... on 25 January 1943," pp. 21–22, 23, Frank Diary, XXXIII, no page numbers.
86. "Discussion on Police Matters," Frank Diary, 30 April 1941, XI, 384–391.
87. Governor, District Warsaw to State Secretary, Government General [Bühler], "Report of the Chief of Warsaw District of 10 March 1941 to the Government of the Government General for February 1941," 10 March 1941, Dok. I.-151, vol. 27, 76, IZP. For individual *Kreis* concerns, see *Kreishauptmann* Neumarkt to Office, Governor General, 3 March 1941, Bühler Trial, NTN 281, 12, AGK; *Kreishauptmann* Siedłce to Office, Governor General, 5 March 1941, Dok. I.-151, vol. 27, 33, IZP.
88. Frank Diary, 29 March 1941, X, 172–173. Eventually, Hammerle agreed to permit *Sonderdienst* men to volunteer for service in the *Waffen SS*. See director of *Waffen SS* Recruitment Station XXI (Warthe) to *Kreishauptmann* Radom-Land, 26 July 1941, file Kreishauptmann Radom-Land, vol. 38, 16, WAPR; "Detailed Conditions of Recruitment for the *Waffen SS*," ibid., 19.
89. Krüger to Himmler, 8 January 1942, RG-242, T-175/67/2583926-2583927, NARA.
90. Memorandum from *Gruppe* IV D, RSHA to Chief of Amt IV and Chief of Security Police and SD, 15 January 1942, R 43 II/1341b, 13-14, BAB.
91. Chief of Order Police [signed Daluege] to Office for Administration and Law in the Order Police Main Office, 2 February [1942], R 19/405, 16–17, BAB.
92. Under pressure, Lasch stated that Frank and Bühler were using the *Sonderdienst* to develop an armed counterweight to the SS ambitions in the Government General. See BdS Government General [signed Schöngarth] to HSSPF Government General [Krüger], 25 April 1942, RG-238, Nuremberg Document 3815-PS, NARA.
93. Memorandum of Himmler, 5 March 1942, in "Die Verwaltung des Generalgouvernements," Part 21, 22a–22c, BA-ZdL; entry for 5 March 1942, in *Der Dienstkalender Heinrich Himmlers 1941/42*, Peter Witte et al., editors (Hamburg, 1999), 369.
94. Handwritten agreement signed Himmler and Frank, 14 March 1942, in "Die Verwaltung des Generalgouvernements," 1967, part 21, 23–24, ZdL. Text of the agreement reproduced in Frank Diary, 21 April 1942, XVIII, 390–391.
95. "Decree of the Führer on the Establishment of a State Secretary for Security Matters in the Government General," signed Hitler, 7 May 1942, VOBl. GG, No. 41, 27 May 1942, 263–264, LC.
96. Telegram, Himmler to Krüger, 15 May 1942, F.W. Krüger SS officer file, NARA.
97. "Decree on the Transfer of Official Duties to the State Secretary for Security Matters," signed Frank, 3 June 1942, VOBl. GG, No. 50, 23 June 1942, 321–324, LC.
98. Circular of State Secretary of the Governor General [signed Bühler], "Inspectorate of the *Sonderdienst*," 13 June 1942, file Gouverneur, Distrikt Radom/Abteilung Innere Verwaltung, vol. 23, 373, WAPR.
99. The decree was referenced in a published circular of Hammerle on 23 June 1942. See *Sonderdienst GG*, 1942, no. 3 (July), 35, NLW.
100. Circular of the HSSPF, State Secretary for Security Matters [signed Krüger], 26 June 1942, Bühler Trial, NTN 258, 85–89, AGK.

101. Berger to Krüger, 14 August 1942, RG-242, T-175/122/2647603, NARA.

102. Cable from Krüger to Detachment Staff RFSS, 20 October 1942, RG-242, T-175/67/2583925, NARA; Siebert to Reich Finance Ministry, 25 September 1942, R 2/5049, BAB.

103. Many of the *Sonderdienst* men who were interrogated after the war claimed as their exclusive duties the guarding of buildings, offices, and persons of the German civilian administration. One of their trainers, however, knew better, and testified after the war that the *Sonderdienst* men were deployed "partly on guard duty, partly as interpreters, and partly as support for the German police." Interrogation of K.S., 15 March 1962, Paulus Trial, vol. I, 35.

104. For individual examples of partisan attacks on facilities guarded by the *Sonderdienst,* see KdO Lublin to BdO Cracow, 16 September 1943, file Ortskommandantur I/524, sygn. 13, 21–24, WAPL; cable from KdO Lublin to BdO Krakau, 13 January 1944, ibid., sygn. 21, 55; daily situation report of the KdO Lublin District, 11 May 1944, ibid., sygn. 25, 74.

105. After the German occupation of Hungary in March 1944, Hammerle, desperate to find recruits with a trace of German "blood," proposed to recruit among the ethnic Germans of Hungary. Frank Diary, 6 May, and 24 May 1944, XXXV, 387, 581–582. On desertions, see report of *Oberfeldkommandantur* 372 [Lublin] to Military Commander, Government General, "Monthly Report for the Period from April 16 to May 15, 1943," 19 May 1943, RG-242, T-501/217/163, NARA.

106. Office of District Governor, Lublin, to State Secretary in the Government General, 3 February 1944, file Gouverneur, District Lublin, sygn. 3, 14, WAPL; Frank Diary, 26 January 1944, XXXIV, 131.

107. Frank Diary, 10 May 1944, XXXV, 458.

108. For a collection of these citations and justifications, see Record Group Zbior wniosków na odznaczenia/file Inspektion des Sonderdienstes, 1944, VI/1, 3–5, 7–21, 25–36, 38–43, 45–50, AGK, and file Kommandeur des Schutzgebietes West und Ost im Distrikt Krakau, 1943–1944, VI/10, 86, 104, 107–108, 117, 119–121, AGK.

109. These soldiers remained subordinate to the Military Commander in the Government General. See telegram of the OKW, Armed Forces Operations Staff, Organization (II) to Central Office, Army Personnel Office, 24 May 1944, RG-242, T-501/229/62, NARA; OKH, Chief of Army Armaments Office, Branch Troops to Military District Detachment Government General, 26 May 1944, ibid., 63.

110. Order of the Chief of General Staff for the Military District Headquarters in the Government General, 5 June 1944, RG-242, T-501/229/68-69, NARA. By consigning *Sonderdienst* discipline to the *Wehrmacht* officers on 24 June, Hammerle in effect surrendered civilian control over the discipline of the *Sonderdienst.* Decree of Inspector of the *Sonderdienst,* 24 June 1944, RG-242, T-501/229/76, NARA; decree of Chief of General Staff, Military District Detachment, Government General, 23 June 1944, ibid., 74–75.

111. Frank Diary, 15 September and 29 September 1944, 2–3 and 3, XXXVII, no page numbers; memorandum signed Hammerle, "The Agreement with the High Command of the *Wehrmacht* on the *Sonderdienst,*" 16 September 1944, Regierung GG/Inspektion des Sonderdienstes, II/378, 6–7, AGK. Hammerle was able, in this Pyrrhic victory, to prevent the *Sonderdienst* from absorption into the *Waffen SS.*

112. Recommendations for 4 November and 10 December 1944, R 52 II/137, 17–19, 21–23, 33–40, BA Berlin. On dissolution, see interrogation of K.R., 15 February 1966, Paulus Trial, vol. IV, 662.

113. *Kreishauptmann* Siedłce to Office, Governor General, 9 July 1940, Bühler Trial, NTN 273, 157, AGK.

114. In October 1941, Reich Minister for the Occupied Eastern Territories Alfred Rosenberg expressed interest in the *Sonderdienst* as an institution with potential for the occupied Soviet territories. See memorandum of 14 October 1941, appendix to Frank Diary, 13 October 1941, XIII, 932. Apparently there was an unconfirmed flicker of interest from the civilian

Reich Commissar in Ukraine, Erich Koch, to have a civilian-administrative executive unit at his disposal. Memorandum of RSHA IV D to chief, Amt IV, RSHA, and Chief of Security Police and SD, 15 January 1942, R 43 II/1341b, BAB.

115. First identified by Gerhard Weinberg, *The Foreign Policy of Hitler's Germany: Starting World War II* (Chicago, 1980), 664.

Chapter 15

GETTING THE SMALL DECREE
Czech National Honor in the Aftermath of the Nazi Occupation*

Benjamin Frommer

Near the end of Bohumil Hrabal's hilariously irreverent novel, *I Served the King of England,* the impish narrator informs the reader, "I got the Small Decree."[1] In the language of the so-called "small" Czechoslovak Decree of 27 October 1945, the diminutive Czech waiter had committed an "offense against national honor," for which he was sentenced to six months in prison. He had offended by baring his private parts for a Nazi race examination to obtain permission to marry a German woman. Hrabal's offhand reference to the Small Decree unsurprisingly baffles most foreign readers of this modern classic. But it probably confuses many Czechs too. Thanks to the absence of relevant historical literature,[2] few now remember the country's postwar investigation of nearly 180,000 persons for "offenses against national honor."[3] In its time, however, the Small Decree played a critical role in the delineation of the thitherto-imaginary boundary between the Czech and German nations. By punishing individuals like Hrabal's narrator, who had fraternized with Germans during the occupation, honor tribunals dissuaded Czechs from hindering the post-war expulsion of Sudeten Germans from the country. But the Small Decree was more than a means to support the so-called Transfer; the concept of "national honor" represented the apotheosis of the nationalist ideal, which mandated that a person owed allegiance not only to his state, but to his nation as well.

The Small Decree was an afterthought, added to the Czech retribution system nearly six months after the end of the war. (Retribution in Slovakia was governed by a different set of laws and administered by a separate system of courts, and is therefore not examined here.[4]) In July 1945 the government had promulgated the so-called Great Decree, which established regional People's Courts throughout the provinces of Bohemia, Moravia, and Silesia to try "Nazis, traitors, and their accomplices." At the same time, the regime created a National Court located in Prague to judge the most prominent collaborators among Czech politicians, industrialists, and journalists. Although the Great Decree retroactively criminalized a wide range of collaborationist activities, prosecutors soon confronted thousands of detainees who could not be tried by the People's Courts. Rather than release alleged collaborators, who had clearly not transgressed according to the Great Decree, proponents of punishment argued that a new decree was necessary "to close a loophole in the legal system of retribution."[5] In particular, the Communist Party leadership pushed to expand retribution, while other members of the country's multiparty government unsuccessfully resisted the attempt to undermine legal certainty through yet another punitive, ex post facto law. In the end, as a contemporary article explained, the Small Decree was written to match the criminal: "The Decree for the protection of national honor punishes ... the considerable number of those who were detained and cannot be tried before a people's court according to the [Great] decree."[6]

Czech journalists immediately and vociferously criticized the Small Decree. Columnists rightly feared that this expansion of retribution would become a weapon in the political struggle for mastery of the country.[7] Critics were especially outraged that the government had promulgated the decree on the eve of the first meeting of the postwar parliament, thereby circumventing public debate.[8] But amidst this unprecedented wave of dissent, few stopped to note the revolutionary nature of the very concept "national honor." Almost alone, Helena Koželuhová, one of the most outspoken critics of the country's leadership, remarked that "national honor" had no basis in Czechoslovak law.[9] Perhaps it is unsurprising that most Czechs did not seem to notice. After all, the postwar regime had attached the modifier "national" to all sorts of events and institutions: the Nationally Democratic Revolution of May 1945, the National Front, national committees, national administrators, and, of course, the National Court.

The punishment of "offenses against national honor" was itself part of the Czechs' postwar "national cleansing" [*národní očista*]. As Norman Naimark explains, "In both Slavic and German usages, 'cleansing' has a dual meaning; one purges the native community of foreign bodies, and one purges one's own people of alien elements."[10] In the Czech case, the "foreign bodies" were the so-called Sudeten Germans, nearly three million of whom were expelled from the country in the aftermath of the war. But the "national cleansing" also aimed to punish "alien elements" within the Czech nation who had associated with the German "foreign bodies." If treason under traditional law necessitated conspiracy with a foreign power or subject, treachery now could occur even within the citizenry, via contacts with non-Czech inhabitants of the state. This radical redefinition of a citizen's basic obligations had practical consequences. In the midst of the expulsion of several million native Germans, the national honor tribunals played a critical role in defining, demarcating, and solidifying the boundaries of the Czech nation. The punishment of "offenses against national honor" thus represented another element of postwar Czechoslovakia's "ethnic unmixing," a process whose effect on mixed-marriage families I have described elsewhere.[11]

Rogers Brubaker has called on scholars to investigate "how ... nationhood as a political and cultural form [is] institutionalized."[12] The Small Decree, this article argues, was one of the ways in which Czech nationhood was institutionalized after the Second World War. The codification of national honor was in part a culmination of the long process by which, according to Jeremy King, politics and law were "nationalized."[13] In the decades before the First World War, Bohemians, Moravians, and Silesians increasingly came to view themselves as members of either the Czech or the German nation. No longer just loyal subjects of the Habsburgs, they also acquired obligations to their respective nations. The creation of Czechoslovakia in 1918 had represented only a partial victory for the nationalist ideal, which Ernest Gellner defines succinctly as the belief that "the political and the national unit should be congruent."[14] After all, in addition to Czechs and Slovaks, interwar Czechoslovakia contained substantial national minorities, first and foremost, the Sudeten Germans. Thus, the Czechoslovak regime adopted the policies of a "nationalizing state" and promoted primarily the interests of Czechs and (to a lesser extent) Slovaks.[15] Only in the aftermath of the Nazis' defeat did Czech leaders have the opportunity to fulfill the ideal posited by Gellner. With the forced removal of the German minority, Czechs theoretically achieved congruence between the boundaries of their state and the limits of their nation. In reality, the continued existence of Slovak inhabitants, not to mention Magyars and other minorities, made Czechoslovakia anything but a nation-state. Nonetheless, the Small Decree represented a further step in the alignment of nation and state within Bohemia, Moravia, and Silesia at the least. "Offenses against national honor" conflated the nation and state by making loyalty to one contingent upon loyalty to the other. The codification of national allegiance thus arguably represented the logical conclusion of a century in which the provinces of Bohemia, Moravia, and Silesia truly became the *Czech* Lands.

The Small Decree and the Codification of National Allegiance

The text of the "Small" Decree lived up to its moniker. Only four paragraphs long, it defined an "offense against national honor" as "behavior insulting to the national sentiments of the Czech or Slovak people."[16] But, as Koželuhová acerbically remarked, "If someone can figure out from this decree what national sentiment is, then he's a magician."[17] The crime may have been unspecified, but the punishment at least was clear: convicted offenders faced up to a year's imprisonment, a maximum fine of one million Czechoslovak crowns,[18] and/or public censure. The decree's vagueness was qualified by the statement that subsequent "directives concerning this matter issued by the Interior Ministry are binding on national committees." On 26 November 1945, the Interior Ministry issued formal instructions to govern the punishment of "offenses against national honor." Where the Small Decree was brief and vague, the Interior Ministry's national honor directive was extensive and particular. Even so, confusion and inconsistencies prompted the publishing of two official guidebooks to provide more detail and answer commonly posed questions.[19]

The Interior Ministry directive confirmed critics' fears. The power to judge "offenses against national honor" had already been granted by the Small Decree to District National Committees, revolutionary administrative bodies that had regularly trampled on the rights of Czechoslovak citizens. Now the directive empowered each national committee to create another revolutionary institution, a four-person penal commission to investigate and rule on individual cases. The directive recommended that one commission member have some legal training, but none had to be a judge.[20] If honor commission members agreed, the accused could bring counsel to the proceedings, but once there, a defense lawyer had to remain silent. The defendant could not call character witnesses and could not even view the evidence—it was the commission's responsibility to assemble the case both for and against the accused. In short, commission members acted as investigators, prosecutors, defense lawyers, and, ultimately, judges. And they did so in closed chambers from which the public was excluded.[21]

Like the Small Decree, the Interior Ministry's directive did not define "national honor;" it only specified nine types of "behavior" that allegedly offended Czech "national sentiments." The nine types fell roughly into two categories. Most of the offenses consisted of forms of political collaboration with the Nazis and their domestic enablers. For example, the directive targeted individuals who had participated in fascist groups, praised the Nazis, or defended the occupation. Similarly, the directive declared attempts to gain rewards from or offer bribes to the occupiers worthy of punishment. These offenses were similar to those outlined in the Great Decree, but of a less serious nature and therefore not likely to be punished by the People's Courts. In some instances, for example, "tyrannizing, defaming, or terrorizing Czechs," the directive merely restated crimes already spelled out in the Great Decree. Here the national honor directive simply followed through on the Small Decree's promise to establish a lower threshold for punishment. Nonetheless, these were still crimes against the state—acts of political collaboration with an occupying power and its minions.

But the Interior Ministry directive went far beyond the Great Decree when it outlined two offenses that defined collaboration *nationally,* not politically. The directive instructed penal commissions to punish:

> i. The declaration of German ... nationality, if it did not result in the loss of Czechoslovak citizenship, ... or the conscious support of the denationalization efforts of the Germans.

> ii. Social relations with Germans ... to a greater extent than necessary.[22]

The first offense transformed what had thitherto been a legal personal decision into a criminal act with collective connotations. Until then, bilingual and inter-married individuals had chosen their nationality according to the circumstances, if they chose it at all. Now these "amphibians" faced up to a year in prison for their latest national transmogrification.[23] The second offense penalized Czechs who had fraternized with Germans during the war. It criminalized collaboration with Germans, *qua* Germans, irrespective of their wartime conduct or even po-litical beliefs. Together, these two offenses singled out Czechs who had flirted with the imaginary boundary between the two nations. Although the Small De-cree introduced the concept of "national honor," it was actually the Interior Min-istry that thus created an entirely new form of treason—against the nation, not the state.

Unlike conventional allegiance to the state, "national honor" was not an ob-ligation shared equally by all of Czechoslovakia's denizens. It would have been absurd to punish Germans for fraternization with other Germans. Aside from two specifically political offenses, the Interior Ministry directive instructed that the Small Decree could be applied "only against Czechoslovak citizens of Czech, Slovak or another Slavic nationality."[24] Germans, after all, were expected to have maintained their own national honor, not that of the Czechs. Moreover, Ger-mans who remained true to Germany earned their own special retribution. On 2 August 1945 the government issued Decree no. 33, which aimed, in the words of a high-ranking Interior Ministry official, "to strip Germans ... of Czechoslo-vak citizenship in order to prepare their transfer from Czechoslovak territory."[25] Only Germans who had fought actively against the occupation or had suffered Nazi or fascist persecution could request reinstatement as Czechoslovak citizens. Even these "anti-fascists" needed to demonstrate that they had remained loyal to the Czechoslovak Republic and had never wronged the Czech or Slovak people. Prewar "Czechs," who during the occupation had officially declared themselves to be "German," could only regain Czechoslovak citizenship if they proved that they had converted under threat or extreme duress.

The national honor directive confusingly criminalized the "declaration of German ... nationality, if it did not result in the loss of Czechoslovak citizen-ship." But Decree no. 33 had already denaturalized individuals who voluntarily declared themselves German, so, as noncitizens, such former Czechs could not be tried by national honor commissions. Individuals who had regained their cit-izenship because they had been forced to adopt German nationality could not be punished either. The national honor directive specified that anyone who had committed an offense under duress was exempt from the Small Decree.[26] But if Czechs who became German were exempt from the Small Decree, then whom did the directive aim to punish? By process of elimination, only those Czechs who declared German nationality but did not legally become German were liable. An official guidebook gives the example of a Czech man who tried to intimidate his neighbors by claiming he was actually a German. Because he had not officially applied for German citizenship, he had not been denaturalized after the war.[27] Most cases, however, likely concerned Czechs who had applied for German citizenship, but rejected by the Nazis as unfit. Emil Holub, a middle-aged painter, was one of those two-time losers who were first turned down by the Germans only to be later punished by the Czechs. On 11 November 1946 a Prague penal commission sentenced him to six months, twenty-two days in prison, plus a sentence of "public censure"—the verdict was to be posted in public for two weeks.[28]

Prewar Czechs who had become German were not supposed to escape punishment altogether. According to an Interior Ministry pamphlet, "Such a person is already punished by the fact that he is now treated as a German."[29] Originally, it was assumed that such "former" Czechs would be deported along with their new German countrymen and thus face a severe penalty for their betrayal—banishment. Events did not, however, proceed as planned. In an internal memorandum, an Interior Ministry official revealed: "When the [national honor] directive was issued it was expected that these individuals would be included in the transfer—which in and of itself would have been sufficient punishment—but this prediction was not realized."[30] Czechoslovakia's plans to expel Germans "of Czech origin" foundered on opposition from the Allied occupation authorities in Germany, which proved reluctant to accept yet more refugees.[31] While they awaited resolution of their claims for renaturalization, these "former Czechs" existed in a legal limbo fraught with dangers, but they were beyond the reach of the national honor commissions.

National committees repeatedly complained to the Interior Ministry that Czechs who had become German during the occupation, and had not been deported after liberation, were evading punishment. Local authorities feared that the Small Decree would lapse before these individuals regained their citizenship and became eligible for prosecution. The discovery of a wartime archive containing more than one hundred thousand requests for German citizenship only added to these concerns.[32] An Interior Ministry official admitted, "It was not known, and only now is it becoming clear, that the number of such individuals is so considerable." The Moravian Provincial National Committee had received 500 requests, and in Prague 10,000 cases were expected. Afraid of the public's reaction, the official suggested a change in the national honor directive. From the beginning of 1947, commissions gained the power to prosecute successful declarations of German nationality; from then on they could, in fact, punish any Slav regardless of his or her citizenship.[33]

Seeking German nationality was one of the more frequently prosecuted offenses, but it does not appear to have been punished harshly. The Litoměřice penal commission, for example, convicted Josef Swatuschka applying for German citizenship and sentenced him on 3 May 1947 to pay a 2,000-crown fine and face public censure. Jan Svatuška, Josef's next-door neighbor (and likely his relative), received a one-week jail sentence and a 500-crown fine for the same offense.[34] In Kutná Hora, Antonín Jahoda was fined 3,000 crowns for having written in a letter, "I'm unhappy that I'm a Czech, and if I knew German, I'd never call myself a Czech."[35] Another Czech who applied for German citizenship and joined the *Deutsche Arbeitsfront* had to pay only a 1,000-crown fine because of his ill health and two minor children.[36] Božena Dürschmiedová was also fined 1,000 crowns for having declared herself German. The penal commission ruled that her claim to unbearable pressure could not be substantiated, but that she was a good person nonetheless and did not deserve harsh punishment.[37]

Doubly-rejected Emil Holub's incongruously harsh six-month sentence likely stemmed from the fact that he had also "consciously support[ed] the denationalization efforts of the Germans." Holub had encouraged his neighbor to apply for German citizenship, and had even declared his daughter to be German.[38] The Germanization of Czech children was one of the most feared aspects of the occupation. Thus, it is hardly surprising that a penal commission also harshly punished Růžena Matauška with six months in prison, a 5,000-crown fine, and public censure for having enrolled her daughter in a local German school.[39] In a similar case, a mother claimed in defense that she had only wanted her child to learn German. The defendant further argued that a mere year in a German school was not enough time for her daughter to lose her national identity, especially since the child had immediately thereafter taken the entrance examination for a Czech vocational school. Even though the penal commission accepted the validity of this excuse, it nonetheless decided that sending one's child to a German school ipso facto offended national honor because everyone knew that such institutions were hotbeds of pro-Nazi and anti-Czech propaganda.[40]

The national honor directive aimed to punish not only those who permanently crossed over the imaginary boundary between the Czech and German nations, but even those who merely flirted with it. The directive criminalized "social relations with Germans … to an extent exceeding unavoidable necessity." Since native Germans did not technically lose their Czechoslovak citizenship until 2 August 1945, this clause effectively punished Czechs for their fraternization with a domestic, not a foreign enemy. In the words of an official pamphlet, social relations "included not only attendance at German theaters, concerts, amusements, [and] hunting and drinking with Germans, but also frequent or regular visits to German families or inviting Germans into one's home."[41] Penal commissions tried Czechs for sending congratulatory notes to Germans, for attending Germans' birthday parties, and for playing cards with them.[42]

One of the instructional pamphlets urged, "Amorous relations are particularly meant to be apprehended."[43] Unsurprisingly, Czech women bore the brunt of this stipulation. Penalties in Kutná Hora ranged from one month of public censure to a 20,000-crown fine or four months' imprisonment. The commission gave harsher penalties to defendants who, in addition to amorous relations, committed other offenses, for example, hanging pictures of Hitler in their homes or businesses, or in one case, attending a party to celebrate Franklin D. Roosevelt's death.[44] In one of the longer sentences, Růžena Pokorná received six months for having "cultivated social relations with Germans." On appeal, a review commission refused to reduce her term because it concluded: "Your objection—that you had to interact socially with Germans in order to conceal the fact that you knew that your fiancé ... had deserted the German army to the Russians—is in and of itself illogical." In the eyes of the commission, she had violated both her obligation to her nation and her vow to her betrothed.[45] In an example of how indefinite nationality could mix with dishonorable amorous relations, Marie Jouzová of Roudnice nad Labem received a 10,000-crown fine and public censure for her ties to František Novotný. Novotný had begun the war as a Czech fascist and finished as a German Gestapo confidant.[46] In a more notorious case, a Prague honor commission punished the glamorous Czech film star Adina Mandlová for "social relations" with a German man. Ironically, he himself regained Czechoslovak citizenship the very next week thanks to his wartime service to the Czech nation.[47]

Czech women who had consorted with German soldiers faced especially harsh punishment. In Kutná Hora, Marie Bartůňková received an eight-month sentence and public censure for relations with Germans, threatening Czechs, and testifying against them.[48] Marie Moziková was issued a sentence of eight weeks in jail and a sizeable 25,000-crown fine. She had attended Wehrmacht concerts, had told Czechs that Germans had priority at her store, and had "provocatively Germanized" herself.[49] The commission ordered six months' imprisonment for Františka Radikovská, a Czech midwife who had "intimate relations" with a German soldier for almost the entire war, sent her daughter to a German school, and hung a picture of Hitler in her apartment.[50]

Certificates of National Reliability

For defendants convicted by penal commissions, their sentences often turned out to be just part of their tribulations. For, along with jail time, a fine, and/or public censure, another onerous "national" penalty loomed—a person guilty of an "offense against national honor" could not acquire a "certificate of national reliability." A citizen without a certificate essentially functioned as if he or she had been sentenced to a loss of civic rights: he or she was unable to exercise any position of authority in society or to work in any occupation considered vital to the country's health. To be without a certificate was to be an outcast and face destitution. In a letter to the Czechoslovak president, a woman pleaded:

> We are now fighting for our very existence.... My husband can't even get a job. *Because he doesn't have national reliability.* We are in a situation where we stand like beggars at the crossroads....[51]

The case of Zikmund Hess, a Polish railway worker from Těšín, demonstrates how the withholding of "certificates of national reliability" functioned as a supplementary penalty. He had been accused of working for the *Deutsche Reichsbahn* during the war and of having adopted German nationality. A penal commission convicted him of an offense against national honor, but handed down a moderate penalty, a fine of 2,000 crowns. In retrospect, Hess lamented:

> [I] accepted the punishment assuming that when I paid the fine the matter would be settled, that I would finally have peace. Only now am I feeling the consequences.... As a result of my punishment I have been released from the service of Č.S.D. [Czechoslovak railways] ... [am] without pension [and] for three months I have been without work.

Hess pleaded for help and asked for a presidential pardon, in his words, "So that I can get back civic rights and a pension for working a full 32 years."[52]

"Certificates of national reliability" were actually an unanticipated by-product of Czechoslovakia's expropriation of its German population. When background checks for "national administrators"—the caretakers appointed to run confiscated businesses—proved too laborious, the onus to demonstrate reliability was shifted onto the shoulders of applicants, who were thenceforth required to acquire "certificates of national reliability." According to an official handbook, "Very soon that institution became commonplace and took hold universally."[53] But as representatives of the Interior Ministry admitted: "Certificates of national reliability ... have no legal basis!"[54] Not only were there no guidelines for issuing the certificates, it was also unclear when and where such documentation was even necessary.[55] Unsurprisingly, national committees—not known for their judicious and consistent execution of laws or directives—failed to enforce an extralegal, uncodified sanction to anyone's satisfaction. In October 1945 the Moravian Provincial National Committee commented: "The issuance of a certificate is often refused for reasons that do not pass legal muster.... Certificates are refused due to personal grudges, animus, prejudice, or for various petty personal interests." Though many individuals were unfairly determined to be "nationally unreliable," other applicants were unjustly approved: "By contrast, there are ... cases where such certificates have been issued very benevolently to individuals to whom they could not have and should not have been issued."[56]

Originally, the threshold for acquiring a certificate was even higher than that employed by penal commissions to judge "offenses against national honor." Not only could convicted collaborators be denied, but ordinary rank-and-file members of fascist groups, whom the commissions could not punish, were also deemed "nationally unreliable." Former members of the banned Agrarians, Czechoslovakia's largest prewar political party, who could not prove their wartime patriotism, were also ineligible for certificates.[57] Moreover, until cleared by a penal commission, anyone under suspicion of having committed an "offense against national honor" was considered "unreliable." Although the parliament never passed a law governing "certificates of national reliability," the Interior Ministry eventually issued a pamphlet so that citizens would no longer face "legal uncertainty."[58] The handbook established a generous standard: "We have (in fact, we must have) trust in anyone who has not yet disappointed us; that is, ... anyone who ... did not waver either as a citizen of the republic, or as a Czech, Slovak, or Slav."[59] By the beginning of 1947, passions had cooled considerably and the Prague Provincial National Committee issued more lenient guidelines for certificates: unless already convicted or under indictment by a retribution tribunal, every Slav deserved certification. Moreover, anyone who was acquitted or had his or her case dismissed had to be issued a certificate.[60]

Enforcing the Transfer

In a vicious circle of postwar sanctions, "certificates of national reliability" themselves soon became the subject of prosecution for "offenses against national honor." In March 1946, Gustav Czaban, the secretary of the Communist Party parliamentary club, urged national committee members to punish anyone who falsely testified or carelessly signed a "certificate of national reliability" in favor of a collaborator.[61] On 7 May 1946, the Interior Ministry heeded Czaban's call, seconded by various communist organs, and issued an amendment to its earlier Small Decree directive. A new paragraph punished anyone who deceptively vouched for the reliability of someone else.[62]

This revision to the national honor directive was possible only because the Small Decree actually authorized commissions to prosecute Czechs for offenses committed *after the war was over.* The Decree's jurisdiction covered acts committed during "the period of heightened danger to the republic," defined as the span from 21 May 1938 "until the date determined by government edict."[63] The government considered several possible dates for the end of this period and finally settled upon 31 December 1946.[64] In other words, the commissions could still punish "behavior insulting to the national sentiment of the Czech ... people" committed more than eighteen months after the end of the war. In January 1946 the communist weekly for national committee members, *Lidová správa* [People's Administration], exhorted party cadres to police their fellow citizens' conduct:

> Don't forget that "social relations" with Germans are also punishable; don't forget that there are still people who not only interact with Germans far more than is necessary, but who even want to marry German women.... Apprehend these cases and, as necessary, make an example of them.[65]

In February 1946 the national committee in Ústí nad Labem informed the Interior Ministry that it could not estimate the number of expected cases because "in this district criminal transgressions against the decree on national honor, particularly cases of unapproved contact with Germans, *are still being committed.*"[66] Coming from the town that in July 1945 had been the site of a murderous anti-German pogrom, the threat undoubtedly resonated.[67] In the midst of the expulsion of several million Germans, the honor commissions were granted the power to punish Czechs who continued to fraternize with the declared enemies of the nation.

The ability to punish postwar "offenses against national honor" was not an empty threat. On 3 May 1947 a Litoměřice tribunal separately tried and punished two men for having "maintained amorous relations" with their German female partners after the war was over. The commission issued a two-week jail sentence to Michal Stojko, a veteran of the Czech forces that fought with the Allies on the Western Front. In July 1946 his German partner had been expelled from the country, but afterwards she returned and took up residence with him. Stojko's offense had apparently been exacerbated by the birth of a newborn. On the same day, Otto Francl, a former chairman of a postwar national committee, was sentenced to two weeks and a 1,000-crown fine. Francl's partner had also been deported, but he, unlike Stojko, traveled illegally to join her in occupied Germany.[68] In a third case, a "national administrator" was convicted for a night he spent with two German women a year after the war had ended. His crime apparently consisted of the fact that alcohol had been imbibed and, above all, that he had kissed them.[69] It is probably no coincidence that the three men—a veteran, a national administrator, and a national committee chairman—all had held positions of respect within postwar Czech society. The authorities clearly wanted to send a message that even prominent individuals (and even men) were not permitted to challenge the gelling boundary between the Czech and German nations. In Stojko's case the commission made this point explicit: "A prison sentence has been assessed because the accused, as a member of the Czechoslovak foreign army, should have in every respect paid attention to national honor."[70]

In a contemporary polemic, evocatively titled, "The Devil Speaks German," a leading noncommunist politician pronounced, "We must rap the knuckles of anyone who for any reason would want to favor the Germans in our borderlands."[71] The Small Decree, thanks to its ability to punish postwar acts, was a powerful means to "rap the knuckles" of Czechs who maintained relationships with Germans that they had built in the preceding years, including the peaceful decades before 1938. The punishment of "offenses against national honor" thus stigmatized precisely those Czechs, who—thanks to professional contacts, personal friendships, or intimate relations—might otherwise have intervened to help or defend individual Germans. Instead, these Czechs also became potential targets of punishment. It is unknown how many Czechs were prosecuted for maintaining relations with Germans after the war, but we can assume that the threat of retribution dissuaded many from violating the ethnic segregation that ensured the thoroughness of the Transfer. In deterring Czechs from violating newly drawn national boundaries, the Small Decree thus isolated the Germans and thereby facilitated their deportation. As such, the honor commissions illustrate how auxiliary laws and institutions can provide the conditions necessary for "ethnic cleansing" to succeed.

Conclusion

The Czech quest to codify and enforce fidelity to the nation cannot be summarily dismissed as the product of some atavistic Eastern European nationalism. More than a year before the Small Decree was enacted, the French National Assembly passed its own "Ordinance Instituting National Indignity."[72] The Ordinance created "Honor Juries" to punish any French citizen who had collaborated with the enemy. Like the Czech Small Decree, the French statute was meant to cover cases that fell beyond the scope of the regular courts. In the words of the law's gloss: "The criminal conduct of those who collaborated with the enemy did not always take the form of a specific act for which there could be provided a specific penalty … under a strict interpretation of the law." The Honor Juries could not punish a defendant with imprisonment, but they could abrogate civic rights, confiscate property, and ban residence in a particular area.[73] As in Czechoslovakia, the new concept was controversial, but Albert Camus stepped forward in its defense: "It is just that a man who showed no concern for his country be excluded from the debates which are deciding the future of this country. It is not less just that his property … returns to the nation he abandoned."[74]

But while a state of "national indignity" was in many ways similar to the loss of "national honor," the French did not actually punish national treachery, in the sense that contacts with individuals from another nation were not prohibited. In the French case the proscribed offenses consisted of political collaboration with a foreign occupier and its agents, not with an internal national enemy. According to the French Ordinance, national misconduct included rank-and-file membership in one of some fourteen collaborationist groups, and any public activity in favor of collaboration, or in support of racism or the tenets of totalitarianism.[75] The difference between the two countries may be more a question of circumstance than philosophy. Outside perhaps of Alsace-Lorraine, the French faced Germans only as foreign occupiers, not as treacherous fellow citizens. Unlike Czechoslovakia, France did not have an enormous national minority that was widely blamed for contributing to the occupation. Therefore, the question of national treachery distinct from civic treachery did not arise.

Consequently, the concept of "national indignity" did not necessarily represent a radically new stage in the conflation of the French nation and state. For a century and a half the French nation and state had been considered congruent, even if the reality, as Eugen Weber has shown, was long otherwise.[76] In the Czech case, by contrast, the codification of national loyalty coincided with the near-achievement of a nation-state. In less than a century, the obligations of Bohemians, Moravians, and Silesians had developed from a subject's loyalty to his sovereign and a believer's to his church, to a citizen's allegiance to his state and an individual's to his nation. Just as religious and dynastic fealty were once considered inseparable, now national and state allegiance became one and the same. Ultimately, however, the codification of national allegiance proved an ephemeral phenomenon, not a permanent achievement of nationalism. Certificates of national reliability soon lapsed, and the Small Decree expired in May 1947. Although the new communist regime reestablished national honor tribunals after the February 1948 coup d'état, by the end of that year even it had abandoned the concept. Instead, in its place the country's rulers offered another novel form of allegiance: loyalty to the Communist Party and to the "people's democratic" order.

Notes

* The research for and writing of this article was partially supported by grants from the International Research and Exchanges Board (IREX), the American Council of Learned Societies (ACLS), and the Harvard University Center for European Studies.

1. Bohumil Hrabal, *Obsluhoval jsem anglického krále* (Prague, 1989), 152.

2. From the communist coup of February 1948 until the Velvet Revolution of 1989, not a single scholarly piece, not to mention a monograph, was written on the punishment of "offenses against national honor" either in Czechoslovakia or in the West. Over the past decade several authors have briefly commented on the Small Decree, but only recently have the first articles on the topic emerged, and these consider only the prosecution of anti-Semitic acts. See the articles by Marie Crhová, Miroslav Kružík, Andrea Lněníčková, and Jan Ryba in Mečislav Borák, ed., *Retribuce v ČSR a národní podoby antisemitismu: Židovská problematika a antisemitismus ve spisech mimořádných lidových soudů a trestních komisí ONV v letech 1945–1948* (Prague and Opava, 2002). For more on the punishment of "offenses against national honor," see Benjamin Frommer, *National Cleansing: Retribution Against Nazi Collaborators in Postwar Czechoslovakia* (New York, forthcoming).

3. The Interior Ministry never published final results for the Small Decree, but an internal report from August 1947 demonstrates how massive the process was. In total, honor commissions considered 179,896 cases and settled three-quarters of them. The commissions convicted 46,422 defendants and dismissed charges against 88,845 persons. Overall, commissions handed out penalties of 3,115 years and fines of 182,524,140 Czechoslovak crowns. MV č. B-2220-12/8-47-I/2, "Informace pro pana ministra vnitra: Výsledek činnosti národních výborů podle dekretu č. 138/45 sb." (18 August 1947), Státní ústřední archiv (SÚA) Prague, f. MV-NR (B2220), k. 2017, sv. 2.

4. Thanks to the massive 1944 Uprising against the Tiso regime and the Nazis, the Slovak resistance emerged from the war in a strong enough position to claim the right to punish Slovak collaborators themselves. As a result, postwar Czechoslovakia came to have a dualistic system of retribution: one set of laws and courts for Slovakia, another for the Czech provinces. The Slovak system did not include the punishment of "offenses against national honor."

5. "Honour and Justice," *The Weekly Bulletin*, 3 February 1946, 65.

6. "Ochrana národní cti," *Svobodné noviny*, 4 November 1945, 1.

7. The significance of the Small Decree extended to politics and the 1946 elections, but that remains beyond the scope of this article. Thanks to the disenfranchisement of suspected collaborators, false accusations for "offenses against national honor" proved an effective way to remove supporters of political opponents from voter lists. See, for example, Hubert Ripka, *Le Coup de Prague: Une Révolution préfabriquée* (Paris, 1949), 38–39.

8. Ladislav Gut, "Ať' promluví sněmovna," *Svobodné slovo*, 21 November 1945, 1; H. Pánková, "O cti a bezecti," *Lidová demokracie*, 24 November 1945, 1–2; Ferdinand Peroutka, "A přece…," *Svobodné noviny*, 11 November 1945, 1; Peroutka, "Parlamentní úvahy," *Svobodné noviny*, 8 December 1945, 1.

9. Helena Koželuhová, "Naše národní čest," *Obzory* I:15, 15 December 1945, 229.

10. Norman Naimark, *Fires of Hatred: Ethnic Cleansing in Twentieth Century Europe* (Cambridge, MA, 2001), 4–5.

11. Benjamin Frommer, "Expulsion or Integration: Unmixing Interethnic Marriage in Postwar Czechoslovakia," *East European Politics and Societies* 14:2 (2000): 381–410.

12. Rogers Brubaker, *Nationalism Reframed: Nationhood and the National Question in the New Europe* (Cambridge, 1996), 16.

13. Jeremy King, *Budweisers into Czechs and Germans: A Local History of Bohemian Politics, 1848–1948* (Princeton, 2002), 210.

14. Ernest Gellner, *Nations and Nationalism* (Ithaca, 1983), 1.

15. Brubaker, *Nationalism Reframed*, 83–84.

16. Although it speaks of the "Czech and Slovak people," the Small Decree was applied only in the provinces of Bohemia and Moravia-Silesia. *Sbírka dekretů,* Decree no. 138/45, 236.

17. Koželuhová, "Naše národní čest," 229.

18. This was an astronomical sum at the time. In 1948 the average worker earned 834 crowns per month. According to Jan Michal, Czech wages increased only slightly between 1947 and 1948, while inflation remained relatively low. Milan Kučera, *Populace České republiky 1918–1991* (Prague, 1994), 57; Jan M. Michal, "Postwar Economic Development," in *A History of the Czechoslovak Republic, 1918–1948,* ed. by Victor S. Mamatey and Radomír Luža (Princeton, 1973), 436, 446–447.

19. Jaroslav Fusek, *Provinění proti národní cti* (Prague, 1946); Jindřich Stach, *Provinění proti národní cti* (Brno, 1946).

20. Although the directive stated that at least one of the four commission members had "to have acquired a doctorate in law or completed all the mandated state exams," Fusek categorically dismissed this requirement in his pamphlet: "It is not a procedural error if one of the commission members is not legally trained." Fusek, *Provinění,* 23.

21. Stach, *Provinění,* 19–20.

22. The second offense also included "economic relations with Germans" if these contacts aimed for "above-average enrichment," but this economic offense was qualified by the statement that the defendant also had to aim for the "intentional support of the occupiers." In other words, it too concerned political collaboration to the extent that it was dependant on the occupiers.

23. For more on "amphibianism" in the Nazi Protectorate and after, see Chad Bryant, "Either Czech or German: Fixing Nationality in Bohemia and Moravia, 1939–1946," *Slavic Review* 61:4 (2002): 683–706.

24. According to the Small Decree, any Slav, not just a Czech, could be punished for an "offense against national honor." Since the Small Decree was applied only in the provinces of Bohemia, Moravia, and Silesia, the inclusion of the Slovaks did not play a major role. As for other Slavs, in most regions this point was largely immaterial, but in the northeast corner of the Czech provinces, around Těšín, Poles formed a significant minority (for example, see the Zikmund Hess case below). Several villages of Croats in southern Moravia were also potentially affected.

25. Vladimír Verner, "Státní občanství podle ústavního dekretu Presidenta republiky ze dne 2. srpna 1945, č. 33 Sb." *Právní prakse* IX:1 (1946): 161.

26. For example, in cases where individuals related to Jews or people of Jewish origin sought refuge in preemptive and obfuscative declarations of German nationality, the Olomouc district commissions usually acquitted defendants. In one of the few exceptions, a commission convicted a Jewish woman who had apparently become an ardent supporter of Nazism. She even displayed pictures of Hitler in her windows, but her application to join the Nazi Party was rejected, and in spring 1945 she was deported to the Theresienstadt concentration camp. Although the postwar Czech honor commission convicted her, it assessed only one month of public censure (with the verdict to be displayed on the Olomouc city hall) in recognition of the fact that she had acted out of fear of persecution for being a Jew. Marie Crhová, "Židovská problematika a antisemitismus ve spisech podle tzv. Malého dekretu v oblasti Krajského soudu Olomouc 1945–1948," in Borák, ed., *Retribuce v ČSR,* 123–124.

27. Stach, *Provinění,* 9.

28. Archiv Ministerstva vnitra (AMV), Prague, no. 305-583-4, KS-Stb-Praha.

29. Stach, *Provinění,* 8–9.

30. MV no. B2220-28/11-1946-I/2 (23 Dec. 1946), SÚA, f. MV-NR (B2220), k. 2016.

31. In late November 1946 a high-ranking government official noted, "Soviet and American authorities are already now requesting that our offices permit the return of those Germans who were transferred and are of Czech origin." ÚPV no. 44535-II-8701/46 (25 November 1946), SÚA, f. ÚPV-běž., k. 1032, sign. 1364/2.

32. "Sto tisíc dokumentů národní zrady nalezeno," *Rudé právo,* 17 March 1946, 1.
33. MV no. B2220-28/11-1946-I/2 (23 Dec. 1946), SÚA, f. MV-NR (B2220), k. 2016; MV no. VIII/C-3426, Státní okresní archiv (SOkA) Kutná Hora, f. ONV-KH, k. 89, sign. III/21c; VK-ONV Kolín (10 Oct. 1946) to MV, SÚA, f. MV-NR (B2220), k. 2016.
34. TNK no. 32864/46 (3 May 1947), SOkA Lovosice, f. ONV Litoměřice, k. 141.
35. No. 19 (12 March 1946), SOkA Kutná Hora, f. ONV-KH, kniha č. 31, "Protokoly o schůzích TNK (1945–46)."
36. TNK no. 14, case no. M17, SOkA Kutná Hora, f. ONV-KH, k. 89, sign. III/21b/c (TNK 1947).
37. ÚNV Prague TNK no. 53, case no. 256/47, SOkA Kutná Hora, f. ONV-KH, k. 89, sign. III/21b/c (TNK 1947).
38. AMV, 305-583-4, KS-Stb-Praha.
39. TOK 16/46 (20 March 1946), SÚA, f. ZNV-Pr, sign. TOK, k. 373.
40. On appeal, the Supreme Administrative Court upheld both the ruling and the sentence. Josef Plzák, "Malý retribuční dekret (Dekret pres. rep. č. 138/1945 Sb.) ve světle judikatury Nejvyššího správního soudu," *Právní prakse* XI (1947–48): 123.
41. Stach, *Provinění,* 11.
42. Verdict of OS Kutná Hora no. St 66/47 (16 Jan. 1948), SOkA Kutná Hora, f. ONV-KH, k. 90, sign. III/21c; Plzák, "Malý retribuční dekret," 120–121, 129.
43. Fusek, *Provinění,* 30.
44. Trestní nález no. R14/421/46 (31 May 1946), SOkA Kutná Hora, f. ONV-KH, k. 88, sign. III/21b.
45. TOK 12/46 (10 April 1946), SÚA, f. ZNV-Pr, sign. TOK, k. 373.
46. TOK 2044/46 (22 October 1947), SÚA, f. ZNV-Pr, sign. TOK, k. 392.
47. Mandlová was given time-served. Adina Mandlová, *Dneska už se tomu směju* (Toronto, 1976), 183–184.
48. "Protokoly o schůzích TNK" (1945–46), SOkA Kutná Hora, f. ONV-KH, kniha no. 31, 16.
49. Trestní nález, ÚNV Prague no. M/6, TNK no. 32 (18 Sept. 1946), SOkA Kutná Hora, f. ONV-KH, k. 89, sign. III 21b/c (TNK 1947).
50. Trestní nález, TNK Kutná Hora no. R14/130/46 (4 January 1946) SOkA Kutná Hora, f. ONV-KH, k. 88, sign. III 21b.
51. Emphasis in original. B. Kozáková to KPR no. P902/46, Archiv Kanceláře prezidenta republiky (AKPR), s. D-11377/47, k. 262(b).
52. KPR no. R05464/47 (17 April 1947), no. R13728/47 (3 Oct. 1947), AKPR, f. D-11377/47, k. 262(b).
53. Stanislav Šulc, *Národní výbory: Vývoj, právní základy, poslání, práce* (Brno, 1946), 308–309.
54. "Provádění dekretu o národní cti," *Lidová správa,* I:8, 1 February 1946, 11.
55. J. Dubský, ed., *Slovník lidové správy* (Prague, 1947), 296; "Potřeba zákona o národní spolehlivosti," *Lidová správa* I:27, 1 November 1946, 6–7.
56. Šulc, *Národní výbory,* 309.
57. Šulc, *Národní výbory,* 313; Jaroslav Fusek, *Osvědčení o státní a národní spolehlivosti* (Brno, 1946), 8–15, 19–20.
58. Fusek, *Osvědčení,* 3.
59. Fusek, *Osvědčení,* 8.
60. Vyhláška ZNV Prague no. 183/2-1946 (17 January 1947), SOkA Kutná Hora, f. ONV-KH, k. 89, sign. III/21c.
61. G. C., "Do rázného útoku proti zrádcům a kolaborantům," *Lidová správa* I:9–10 (1 March 1946), 7–8.
62. MV č. B-2220-12/4-46-I/2 (7 May 1946), "Dodatek ke směrnicím ministra vnitra … k provedení dekretu presidenta republiky č. 138/1945 Sb., o trestání některých provinění proti národní cti," SÚA, f. MV-NR (B2220), k. 2018.

63. 21 May 1938 was the date of the first Czechoslovak military mobilization against the Nazi threat.

64. Vládní nařízení č. 217/1946 Sb., Kaplan and Jech, *Dekrety,* I:179, n. 2.

65. V. Adámek, "Ještě k dekretu o národní cti," *Lidová správa* I:6, 1 January 1946, 8.

66. Italics added. ONV Ústí nad Labem (11 Feb. 46) to MV, SÚA, f. MV-NR (B2220), k. 2017.

67. At the end of July 1945 Ústí nad Labem experienced one of the most vicious postwar massacres of Sudeten Germans. In a period of hours, Czech mobs killed at least two hundred Germans in the town. Some sources claim thousands were murdered. Tomáš Staněk, "Co se stalo v Ústí nad Labem 31. července 1945?" *Dějiny a současnost* 2 (1990): 48–51; Karel Kaplan, *Poválečné Československo 1945–1948: Národy a hranice* (Munich, 1985), 139–140; Eagle Glassheim, "National Mythologies and Ethnic Cleansing: The Expulsion of Czechoslovak Germans in 1945," *Central European History* 33:4 (2000): 479–482.

68. TNK no. 18718/47 (3 May 1947) and no. 19789/47 (3 May 1947), SOkA Lovosice, f. ONV Litoměřice, k. 141.

69. Plzák, "Malý retribuční dekret," 129.

70. TNK no. 18718/47 (3 May 1947), SOkA Lovosice, f. ONV Litoměřice, k. 141.

71. Ivan Herben, "Ďábel mluví německy," in *My a Němci: Dějinný úkol strany národně socialistické při vystěhování Němců z Československa* (Prague, 1945), 8.

72. P.H. Doublet, *La Collaboration: L'épuration, la confiscation, les réparations aux victimes de l'occupation* (Paris, 1945), 28–30.

73. Peter Novick, *The Resistance versus Vichy: The Purge of Collaborators in Liberated France* (New York, 1968), 146–149.

74. Herbert Lottman, *The Purge* (New York, 1986), 135.

75. Doublet, *La Collaboration,* 30.

76. Eugen Weber, *Peasants into Frenchmen: The Modernization of Rural France, 1870–1914* (Stanford, 1976).

INDEX

Lightning Source UK Ltd.
Milton Keynes UK
UKHW020636240722
406281UK00005B/513